HUMANISM AND
MARX'S THOUGHT

Publication Number 803
AMERICAN LECTURE SERIES®

A Monograph in
The BANNERSTONE DIVISION *of*
AMERICAN LECTURES IN PHILOSOPHY

Edited by
MARVIN FARBER
State University of New York at Buffalo
Buffalo, New York

It is the purpose of this Series to give representation to all important tendencies and points of view in philosophy, without any implied concurrence on the part of the Editor and Publisher.

HUMANISM AND MARX'S THOUGHT

By

HOWARD L. PARSONS

Professor and Chairman
Philosophy Department
University of Bridgeport
Bridgeport, Connecticut

CHARLES C THOMAS · PUBLISHER
Springfield • Illinois • U.S.A.

Published and Distributed Throughout the World by
CHARLES C THOMAS · PUBLISHER
BANNERSTONE HOUSE
301-327 East Lawrence Avenue, Springfield, Illinois, U.S.A.
NATCHEZ PLANTATION HOUSE
735 North Atlantic Boulevard, Fort Lauderdale, Florida, U.S.A.

© *1971, by* CHARLES C THOMAS · PUBLISHER
Library of Congress Catalog Card Number: 76-135940

With **THOMAS BOOKS** *careful attention is given to all details of
manufacturing and design. It is the Publisher's desire to present books
that are satisfactory as to their physical qualities and artistic possibilities
and appropriate for their particular use.* THOMAS BOOKS *will be true
to those laws of quality that assure a good name and good will.*

Printed in the United States of America
H-2

PREFACE

THIS WORK, in three parts, is (1) an exposition of my own concept of humanism, (2) an exposition of humanism as it appears in the writings of Karl Marx, and (3) an application of Marxist humanism to certain social questions.

In Part One, The Meaning of Humanism, my own concept of humanism is one which is continuous with the general tradition of Marx's humanism, while at the same time, I trust, it contributes something new to that tradition. In turn, in Part Two, The Humanism of Marx, my exposition of Marx's humanism has no doubt been influenced by my own particular concerns. Part Three, Marxist Humanism and Social Questions, is an effort, from a Marxist-humanist perspective, to analyze and evaluate critically and constructively some of the major social questions in the United States and the world today. By "Marxist" here I mean what is explicit in, implicit in, or consistent with the general spirit of Marx's work, particularly his humanism.

Humanism I take to be a theory, an attitude, and a practice which regards man's needs and powers to be central and necessary in the determination of what is real, knowable, and valuable. In Part One, The Meaning of Humanism, I have concentrated on questions pertaining to man's needs, possibilities, values, and fulfillment, more than on questions of reality and knowledge. In Part Two, The Humanism of Marx, I have similarly directed my attention to Marx's theory of man and of human values. In Part Three, I have applied these Marxist-humanist views on man and human values to concrete social issues.

As an exposition of humanism, this work aims to facilitate and guide the survival and fulfillment of man on our planet. All true and useful theory has its ultimate source and test in man's sensuous, social *practice*. And as important as it is for philosophers and others to interpret the world—and Marx devoted much of his life to this task—"the point, however, is to *change* it."

But this is not a book about specific tactics. It develops certain general principles about man and his values and relates these to certain social problems. Tactics are indispensable; but to be effective they must be based on a sound general understanding of man and his values.

HOWARD L. PARSONS

ACKNOWLEDGMENTS

I would like to thank the following editors and publishers for their kind permission to reprint in revised form certain papers of mine that have appeared in their publications:

Professor Marvin Farber, editor of *Philosophy and Phenomenological Research,* for permission to reprint from Vol. XXIV, No. 3 (March, 1964) of that journal "Value and Mental Health in the Thought of Marx."

Dr. Franco Ferri, Secretary-General of the Gramsci Institute, and the Gramsci Institute, for permission to reprint "The Human Roots of Human Morality," a paper originally delivered at "Morale e società," a convention in Rome organized by the Gramsci Institute, May 22-25, 1964, and subsequently printed in the volume, *Morale e società* (Roma: Editori Riuniti-Instituto Gramsci, 1966).

Mark Frank and Progress Books, for permission to reprint from *Horizons, 25* (Spring, 1968) "Philosophy and the New Left in the U. S. A. Today" and from *Horizons 26* (Summer, 1968) "The Young Marx and the Young Generation."

M. Mamardashvili and the other editors of *Voprosy Filosofii,* for permission to reprint from that journal, 1968, No. 6, "Zhiznennaia filosofiia amerikantsa i 'novye levye'."

Rafael Moreno, Director of Dirección General de Publicaciones, Universidad Nacional Autónoma de México, publishers of *El Problema del Hombre. Memorias del XIII Congreso Internacional de Filosofía,* Vol. II (México, D. F. 1963), for permission to reprint from that volume my essay, "Philosophy and the Problem of Man's Mental Health"; and Dr. José Luis Curiel, Secretario General of the XIII Congreso Internacional de Filosofía.

Gajo Petrović and the other editors of *Praxis* for permission to reprint from their journal "Socialism and Democracy: How Each Demands the Other," from the 1st year, 2/3 (1965), and "Technology and Humanism," from the 5th year, 1/2 (1969).

The papers which formed the original nucleus of this work were first presented to and discussed by professional and public audiences in the United States, Mexico, Canada, Italy, Yugoslavia, the German Democratic Republic, and the Soviet Union. I want to thank the many persons, too numerous to mention here, who arranged and participated in these discussions and who helped to broaden, deepen, and humanize my outlook.

In addition, I would like to thank Mrs. Elsie Havanich, who has faithfully and competently typed the manuscript. An award from the Faculty Research and Experimental Fund of the University of Bridgeport has helped to defray the costs of preparing the manuscript for publication. I would like to acknowledge with thanks this support.

Professor Marvin Farber, Editor of the American Lectures in Philosophy, has helped to see this volume through the press, and I wish to express my special indebtedness to him. Final responsibility for the work rests, of course, with the author.

I would like to acknowledge the permission of the following authors and publishers to quote copyrighted material:

George Allen and Unwin Ltd. for selections from *The Condition of the Working-Class in 1844* by Frederick Engels, copyright 1968; and selections from *Karl Marx: The Story of His Life* by Franz Mehring, translated by Edward Fitzgerald, copyright 1936.

The American Academy of Arts and Sciences for passages from "Full Citizenship for the Negro American? A Sociological Problem" by Talcott Parsons, in *Daedalus*, Vol. 94, No. 4, copyright 1965.

Basil Blackwell, Publisher for a passage from *Philosophical Investigations* by Ludwig Wittgenstein, copyright 1958.

Cambridge University Press for passages from *Philosophy and Myth in Karl Marx* by Robert Tucker, copyright 1961.

Sir George E. Gordon Catlin for selections from *The Story of Political Philosophers* by George Catlin, copyright 1947 by George Catlin.

Crown Publishers for selections from *Karl Marx: The Story of His Life* by Franz Mehring, translated by Edward Fitzgerald, copyright 1935 by Covici, Friede, Incorporated.

Doubleday and Company, Inc., Loyd D. Easton, and Kurt H. Guddat for passages from the book, *Writings of the Young Marx on*

Philosophy and Society, copyright © 1967 by Loyd D. Easton and Kurt H. Guddat.

Doubleday and Company, Inc. for selections from *Marxism and Existentialism* by Walter Odajnik, copyright 1965 by Walter Odajnik; from *The Marxism of Jean-Paul Sartre* by Wilfrid Desan, copyright 1965 by Wilfrid Desan; and from *Socialist Humanism* edited by Erich Fromm, copyright 1965.

Harper and Row, Publishers for a passage from *The Authoritarian Personality* by T. W. Adorno, E. Frenkel-Brunswik, D. J. Levinson, and R. N. Sanford, copyright 1950; and for a passage from *Being and Time* by Martin Heidegger, translated by John Macquarrie and Edward Robinson, copyright 1962.

Hogarth Press Ltd. for passages from *The Political and Social Doctrine of Fascism* by Benito Mussolini, translated by Jane Soames, copyright 1933.

Holt, Rinehart and Winston, Inc. for a passage from *Man for Himself* by Erich Fromm, copyright 1947 by Erich Fromm.

Houghton Mifflin Company, Boston, Mass., for passages from *Mein Kampf* by Adolph Hitler, copyright 1932.

International Publishers Co., Inc. for passages from *The German Ideology, Parts I and III* by Karl Marx and Friedrich Engels, edited by R. Pascal, copyright 1947; *Manifesto of the Communist Party* by Karl Marx and Friedrich Engels, authorized English translation, copyright 1948; *Letters to Americans 1848-1895* by Karl Marx and Friedrich Engels, copyright 1953; and *Pre-Capitalist Economic Formations* by Karl Marx, edited by E. J. Hobsbawm and translated by Jack Cohen, copyright 1965. And Jack Cohen for passages from *Pre-Capitalist Economic Formations*.

Journal of Humanistic Psychology for passages from "A Theory of Metamotivation: the Biological Rooting of the Value-Life" by A. H. Maslow, in *Journal of Humanistic Psychology*, vol. 7, pp. 93-127, copyright 1967.

Alfred A. Knopf, Inc. for passages from *Search for a Method (The Problem of Method)* by Jean-Paul Sartre, translated by Hazel E. Barnes, copyright 1963.

The Macmillan Company for a passage from *Science and the Modern World* by A. N. Whitehead, copyright 1926.

McGraw-Hill Book Company and Marshall McLuhan for a passage from *Understanding Media* by Marshall McLuhan, copyright 1964 by Marshall McLuhan.

David McKay Company for a passage from *Mao Tse-Tung. Ruler of Red China* by Robert Payne, copyright 1969.

G. and C. Merriam Company for a passage from *Webster's New International Dictionary,* 2nd edition, copyright © 1959 by G. & C. Merriam Co., Publishers of the Merriam-Webster Dictionaries.

W. W. Norton and Company, Inc. for a passage from *Childhood and Society* by Erik H. Erikson, copyright 1950, © 1963.

Oxford University Press for passages from *Karl Marx. His Life and Environment* by Isaiah Berlin, copyright 1963, and for a passage from *The Pursuit of the Millennium* by Norman Cohn, copyright 1957.

Philosophical Library, Inc. for a passage from *An Encyclopedia of Religion* edited by Vergilius Ferm, copyright 1945; and for a passage from *Being and Nothingness* by Jean-Paul Sartre, translated by Hazel E. Barnes, copyright 1956.

Ramdom House, Inc. for a passage from *Ten Days That Shook the World* by John Reed, copyright 1960.

Simon and Schuster, Inc. for passages from *What is Science?* edited by James R. Newman, copyright 1955 by James R. Newman.

B. F. Skinner and the Macmillan Company for passages from *Walden Two,* copyright 1948 by B. F. Skinner.

St. Martin's Press, Inc., Macmillan and Co., Ltd. for a passage from *The First and Second Discourses* by Jean-Jacques Rousseau, translated by Roger D. and Judith R. Masters, copyright 1964.

The University of Chicago Press for a passage from *Varieties of Human Value* by Charles Morris, copyright © 1956 by the University of Chicago; and a passage from *The Philosophy of the Act* edited by Charles Morris, copyright 1938 by the University of Chicago.

The Viking Press Inc. for a passage from *The American Democracy* by Harold Laski, copyright 1948; for passages from *The Drugstore Liberal: Hubert H. Humphrey in Politics* by Robert Sherrill and Harry W. Ernst, Grossman Publishers, Inc., copyright 1968; and for a passage from *The Portable Nietzsche* edited and translated by Walter Kaufman, copyright 1954.

C. A. Watts Ltd. for passages from *Economic and Philosophical*

Manuscripts by Karl Marx, translated by T. B. Bottomore, copyright 1963 by T. B. Bottomore.

Care has been taken to determine the ownership of rights to passages quoted, to secure permission to reprint them, and to acknowledge such permission. Errors or omissions in regard to these matters will be corrected in any future editions if notification is sent to the publisher.

Finally, for her careful editorial work, I would like to thank Mrs. C. E. Hildreth, Associate Editor of Charles C Thomas, the publisher of this volume.

H.L.P.

CONTENTS

HUMANISM AND
MARX'S THOUGHT

PART ONE
THE MEANING OF HUMANISM

I

THE HUMAN ROOTS OF HUMAN MORALITY

Man must eat, drink, clothe and shelter himself, and otherwise maintain his bodily life before he can do anything else. If he does not eat, drink, etc., he will die. Normally man prefers to live. He thus prefers (values) eating, drinking, etc. before he engages in activities which distinguish man as a species, e.g., religion, politics, the arts, and the sciences.

Man's body, evolved in nature over billions of years on this planet, has developed need-drives like hunger and thirst which sensitize and orient his body toward the external world of nature and fulfillment there. In short, man is a material creature satisfying his needs in a material environment by being acted on by it, perceiving it, thinking about it, and acting on it, i.e., by dialectical action. (Here we use "material" to mean the irreducible, self-creating, spatiotemporal, objective, concrete, diversified basis for all activities and relations in the universe. "Dialectical" means an interaction of material beings involving dynamic opposition and unity, quantitative and qualitative changes, recurrent negations, etc.) Thus man in his effort to live has naturally a materialist point of view toward himself and the world, though he may not explicitly formulate that point of view. Furthermore, in this effort he is naturally, though not explicitly, a humanist, impelled predominantly to fulfill his own and others' needs.

For humanism is a theory and an attitude, exemplified in practice, which holds that man's interests, preferences, and fulfillment should be taken as primary in man's decisions and actions. Throughout human history a variety of humanisms have appeared—the humanisms of some of the Indian philosophers; of the Chinese Taoists and Confucianists; of many Greek philosophers; of some thinkers in the great religions like Buddhism, Judaism, Christianity, and Islam; of the European Renaissance and the eighteenth century Enlightenment;

and of nineteenth century liberals like Comte and Mill. However, these humanisms have often been partial and truncated. For example, most thinkers in Judaism, Christianity, and Islam have regarded service to God as more important than the welfare of man. Moreover, none of these humanisms fully grasped the material basis of man's life. Most of them, abstract and idealistic, called for the fulfillment of man without taking into account the material needs and environment of man as the causes, conditions, and means necessary for the achievement of the good life. Some of these humanists were materialistic or semimaterialistic—e.g., some of the Taoists; the Charvaka school; Heraclitus; Empedocles; the Greek atomists; the middle age nominalists; pantheists like Bruno and Spinoza; the seventeenth and eighteenth century materialists like Bacon, Hobbes, and Locke; and the French materialists of the eighteenth century, such as Diderot and Holbach.

None of these materialistic humanists, however, understood the *social, historical,* and *dialectical* character of man's material needs. Not until Marx and Engels arrived was the fuller picture of the material basis of man's life provided, and with it a powerful tool for understanding and changing human society and history. Beginning with French materialism as mediated to them through the humanism of Feuerbach, Marx and Engels used the comprehensive dialectical method of Hegel to show that humanism to be effective must be grounded in an understanding and control of the material forces and conflicts in man's present and past societies. Marx later reinforced this dialectical materialism by an empirical and dialectical study of capitalism, absorbing and transcending the work of the British bourgeois humanistic economists like Adam Smith.

In the present work we begin where all men naturally begin— at the point where men are driven to live in a material world and to fulfill their needs. A materialist, dialectical understanding of man leads naturally to a full humanism without restriction as to class, nation, race, sex, age, and the like. And such a humanism in turn must lead us back to try to understand more effectively the material conditions of man and his environment. Thus, for the humanism proposed here, values for man are to be found and created in man's dialectical interaction with things and persons. They are functions of man's needs, his environment, and his exchanges with the environment. Values, conceived and symbolized, in process of creation in practice, and finally materialized, are facts in the material, natural world. They are not supernatural mysteries, known only to God, nor merely subjective whims or satisfactions beyond inquiry. Values can be known and controlled; and it is only through such knowledge and control that man as individual personality and as species can be fulfilled.

To know what man's fulfillment might be, we must begin with an inquiry into the potentialities of man's nature. To know what his morality ought to be, we must study those material powers in his body, in his activities and relations, which form the bases and means for the development of morality. To understand the full process of the development of man and his morality, we must understand its origins in man's roots.

The task of understanding is not simple, however. It itself requires decisions as to human values and generates its own problem—the definition of the field of morality, the meaning of "roots," where moral analysis should begin, the definition of normative value for man, and the meaning of the distinction between a humanistic and nonhumanistic theory of morality. We shall therefore consider these problems of method before directly dealing with questions of the roots of man's morality.

The idea of the "roots" of morality signifies a foundation or stable ground for morality. It implies also the ideas of derivation from something basic, of growth and maturing, and of fruits. Moralists have recurrently used this metaphor. The *Tao Te Ching* speaks of "returning to the Root" (the *Tao*); Plato describes man as a being whose "roots are in heaven"; and the author of Ephesians says that Christians must be "rooted and grounded in love." In so speaking, man observes an analogy between his own moral life and development and that natural, orderly growth which he perceives in plants. And his search for roots in his life is especially intense in times of social change and moral uncertainty.

"Morality," in its ancient Latin roots, has the connotation of something heavy, almost immovable, and peasant-like: the "mores" are the customs and folkways of a people imbued with habits that lie at the base of their characters and bind them into one solid bundle. Break those mores and you break men, you break a society. But traditional morality today does not satisfy most men. Societies and mores with them are in upheaval as never before. Hence our search must reach not so much toward a new morality (as fruits), nor toward old moralities (hollow trunks), as toward the ever living and generic *roots* of a universal, human morality.

How shall we initially define this field of morality with its own ecology? We are not passive observers; we ourselves define and investigate morality. It is we, human beings, who are the subjects, the roots, and the cultivators of the roots. Hence what we have to say about the roots and their cultivation will reveal what we are, actually and potentially, as well as what we choose to be. And that can strike true for other men only as it strikes them at the roots, only as it penetrates to the depths of their generic human situation, becomes known, and is chosen. Moreover, the human plant does not grow necessarily and smoothly, like a healthy and symmetrical Alpine fir or a noble savage in a perfect state of nature. Man's potentialities are fragile and contingent. They do not tend toward preordained, harmonious unfoldment. They must be protected and nurtured if they are to yield the fruits or values that we cherish and idealize in our imaginations. The point of analysis, therefore, is not merely to describe man's roots and moral ecology, but to find conditions and methods of nourishing those roots. The point is to help man to grow into his full human and moral stature.

Hence, let us begin with a definition that determines the scope of our problem. The domain of "morality" has to do with voluntary human conduct aiming at some value. The aim may be poor and the value bad; it is the freedom of choice, with its consequent accountability, which makes the action moral. Such action imports guiding ideas or standards in virtue of which such concrete conduct is judged to be good and which exercise some kind of obligation upon the actor. These two aspects of morality—"good" and "virtue" on the one side, "ought" and "duty" on the other—indicate that the moral act is one of creation. An actor, a human being, is confronted with alternatives of action with regard to value (or disvalue); chooses one; organizes certain conditions (materials, ideas) according to certain implicit or explicit rules or standards which he takes as obligatory; acts on the basis of certain motives; and, if successful, creates some form of value or avoids some form of disvalue. "Value" in its elemental sense is here taken to mean any satisfaction or fulfillment of any human interest. The task of moral analysis that is of preeminent importance is to make explicit and criticize standards for choosing and creating values. It is to find out which "values" are objectively, generically, and universally good for human beings, i.e., which interests ought to be satisfied if man as a human being is to be fulfilled.

Thus, to say that an act falls within the domain of morality does not necessarily mean that it is good. This domain embraces both morally good and morally bad acts. Morality involves choice concerning value-alternatives with a discernible difference, whereas nonmoral actions—like sneezing or a Southern Negro's choice as to whether to vote for segregationist A or segregationist B—do not. Unless moral analysis makes possible and facilitates our discovery of a method for distinguishing better and worse, of what use can it be for man?

I take it that the term "roots of morality" here refers to two fundamental aspects of the moral situation: (1) those conditions necessary to any moral act whatsoever, i.e., to any act that creates human value (be the value positive or negative); and (2) that direction of human behavior, or goal, or state which defines the objective standard of value by which all moral acts can be realistically guided and judged. The roots of morality, in short, lie in what man *is* as a choosing, creating, *moral* being productive of values, and also in what man *might* be and *ought* to be. These roots are in reality one. Man must be capable of both good and bad conduct, and capable of choice before he can be called moral and accountable to an ought. In this sense the nature of man is the root of his morality. Without that rootage in man all appeals to the "ought" are like trying to get figs from thistles. On the other side, the mere capacity in man to choose and create values is too broad a root to yield automatically the plant that satisfies us. Left alone this root gives rise to wild growths, rigid structures, and flowers of evil. Man's very nature and power to choose values requires a direction of choosing and a criterion of choice, lest he choose what will drive him into any one of various forms of degradation and destruction—exploitation, physical and mental impoverishment, individual and social psychosis, suicide, and genocide. As man's being gives rise to the ought as a possibility, so the ought sets a limit to what man's being can become.

Where ought man to begin his moral analysis? This is in itself a moral question, for the answer to the question must always rise from a real, concrete man whose decision has concrete and moral roots and consequences of one kind or another, whether his decision takes him farther away from the moral situation or more fully into it. The general drift of western philosophy, and of philosophy throughout the world, is that moral analysis should direct itself to man's concrete moral situation. But moral philosophers differ on just which features of this moral situation characterize morality and its roots, on which method of study to use, and on which features to emphasize in analysis.

Some concentrate on the analysis of ordinary language and its usages; some, on phenomenological analysis of the "essential structures of transcendental subjectivity"; some, on an exhibition of existential decision and ambiguity; some, on an explicaton of the view that man lives in two realms and by two moralities, that of the body, and that of the soul; some, on an empirical description of the relations and contexts of events defining the moral situation; and some, on a dialectical analysis of "practice." Most of these schools of moral analysis would agree on the premise that the concrete is as important as the abstract in the moral experience or moral situation. Some even conceive the concrete as prior to the abstract, which is derived from it. But they differ in defining morality and its generic characteristics.

Since differences in such definitions are partially moral differences, we are driven back to the question of how to deal with such differences. Here the only philosophical method that offers any prospect of success is to appeal to the common moral experiences, situations, and activities of men, with their common roots. Failing in that effort to achieve a concrete consensus on man and his morality, philosophers have no recourse but to fight out their differences, with weapons of propaganda or of physical force. In this problem of moral analysis and its possible solutions, philosophers reflect and epitomize the problem facing the political leaders and peoples of different nations, namely, the problem of how to discover, formulate, confirm, and extend those common human values which can unite men and nations and form a framework for the constructive exchange of their differences. An important task of moral philosophers today is to describe and analyze the common, generic values of men. As they succeed in this humanistic task, they will reveal to men their own *human* natures, with their needs and values, shaped, to be sure, by their own particular situations and societies. In becoming the voices of an otherwise inarticulate or misled humanity, philosophers can help lead men to an understanding of themselves and others, and hence to that practice that will eventually produce their mutual and common—though individually and culturally different—fulfillment.

To define morality as man's concrete, creative activity throws the primary responsibility on *man,* both as thinker and actor. If moral analysis initially assumes the contrary—that man, lacking in power to change his life, is unfree—then such analysis is by definition vain and contradicts a common meaning of the term "morality." In addition, this definition throws the responsibility on us as thinkers to discover a criterion for distinguishing between better and worse creativity. Such a definition, furthermore, does not exclude the traditional meaning of the term "mores" as stable customs and folkways. Indeed, it opens the way for a search for that method of creation in human affairs which, because it has the deepest roots possible, can alone stabilize man's moral life and his free decisions.

Since man is here the creator of his values, for good or ill, he must be a central root in the moral situation. This is not self-evident, for many locate the roots of morality in what lies outside and beyond man as an individual or species—in an authoritative Personality, Nature, God, the Absolute, a Transcendental realm of ideas or values, the Society, the State, etc. If, as here, we think of morality as involving an actor, a process of acting, and something acted on, then at least one of the sources of morality is man. As Marx said, "for man the root is man himself." [1]

Thus, the primary fact of man's moral life is man's creation of values. Hence, the primary premise of moral analysis must reflect this fact. How is this connection of reflection established? Ultimately, from the demand that analysis must facilitate and improve most practice. Suppose one begins by seeking the roots of man's moral life in sacred texts, a supernatural God, etc. Later, one may discover and

---

[1]Marx, Karl: Contribution to the critique of Hegel's philosophy of right. Introduction. In Marx, K., and Engels, F.: *On Religion.* Moscow, Foreign Languages Publishing House, ND., p. 50.

demonstrate that the decision to be faithful to the facts in moral analysis can be established in a justifiable or reasonable way on pragmatic grounds. That is, one discovers that the method of humanistic, rational empiricism enables us more effectively to understand, predict, and control our moral life. But such a justification assumes, of course, what is assumed here initially, that man is the center of the moral life and the creator of values. To say that moral analysis begins with man's creation of his values is a humanistic judgment, both descriptive and prescriptive. It presupposes that man *is* a value creator and that he *ought to* be the best kind of value creator possible.

Let us notice the dialectic of movement in which this judgment is involved. As human beings we are initially engaged in many activities: we are hungry, we labor, we eat, we communicate, we exploit or are exploited by others, we cooperate with others, etc. Reflection shows that in some sense we create ourselves. Then, from among the great range of our traits and activities, we select for our purposes (1) those human traits and activities which indicate man's creativity and—to take the second, implied step—(2) a generic, normative direction of that creativity. Out of a welter of human facts, in short, we select and organize those which seem to us to define man as a *generic, normative* creature. Such a definition then functions as a kind of hypothesis which we take back to the concrete behavior of men: we ask ourselves whether in conjunction with certain postulates or known laws about man it can explain the behavior of men, and whether, practically speaking, it can facilitate man's quest for values. Thus, to corroborate the definition of man as creative, we must make sure that man is in fact generically creative—even if some of the facts of his situation seem to indicate that he is destructive. And in order to do this it becomes necessary to engage in action to remove the conditions that obstruct his creativity and provide the conditions that release his creativity. Thus, the definition of man as creative grows out of an existing impulse of creativity and a preanalytical conviction of its importance. And the definition aims to facilitate that impulse in practice. Other definitions of man and his moral life may also be humanistic to some degree in origin and intention; but the ultimate test of their value is the extent to which they facilitate in practice the moral action and creativity of man. For such creative action is presupposed by all men driven to live and fulfill themselves. This facilitation is ordinarily more effective if it has a normative theory of value to guide it.

What is the standard or normative value for man? Such value as an ideal requires a base in the potentialities of man's real nature, while such value as realized must enter into that real nature and become a part of it. Man has reality to the extent that he realizes value; he has value to the extent that he valuizes his nature. (We shall discuss this relation of value and fact in man more fully in the next chapter.) Man's genus is his real potentiality for value. Hence, his generic fulfillment as a man is his fulfillment of value. The norm of his value, then, is the direction of his essentially human dispositions. Loss and destruction of values may be involved in this process, but in the long run this is a constructive, cumulative process whose products accelerate the process, whose creations make possible further creation.

A definition of morality that does not give man the power of creation in his moral life must be to that extent alienated from man and his situation. In turn, in its human effects, it must impair the power of man to create and improve his morality and himself. A slave morality takes the power of moral creation and discovery from man, a master or class morality gives it to a few, and a superhuman, religious morality robs man of it altogether (though in practice conferring it on a ruling economic class and priesthood). A fundamental dividing line between moralists is thus drawn by the distinction between humanism and antihumanism. A humanistic theory of morality stimulates among the masses of men a cooperative enterprize in discovering and achieving the normative course of their human fulfillment. A nonhumanistic theory of morality calls for arresting inquiry and experiment, for reinforcing the *status quo* in economic, political, and social relations, and for extending the rule of the few over the many. This is why theories of morality ultimately sort out into two class moralities, the morality of the oppressing and dying class and the morality of the oppressed and rising class. The morality of the first class is only partially and abstractly human; it is elitist, reactionary, exploitive, and destructive. The morality of the second class, so far as it reflects the deepest needs of that class, must be fully and concretely human, democratic, revolutionary, cooperative, and creative. Of course individual exceptions may be found in each class. A Pope John XXIII may in certain respects be more humanistic in his outlook and human relations than a self-styled "socialist" whose personality is thoroughly authoritarian and antihuman.

The morality of the small ruling group in any class society is in the long run doomed because it reflects not the generically human values, i.e., the values of all the men in the society, but instead those specific values that define the life of the ruling class. Thus, it cannot appeal to all men and lead them because it does not originate in the root of the human, moral situation, namely, man. On the contrary such morality must by its very class loyalty distort in theory, and oppose in practice, the creative development and highest good of all men— including the men who belong to the ruling class. This opposition assumes many forms—exploitation of men in a system of private property, racism, male supremacy, disregard of the needs of children, persecution of minorities, dehumanizing propaganda and thought-control, ban on critical and progressive persons and associations, exclusion of the masses from political decisions, imperialism, and war.

Let me illustrate by citing an example from my own country, the United States, with which I am most familiar. Two-fifths of our people are "poor," [2] in one of the richest, most productive nations in the world. Our unemployment consistently numbers in the millions. Many millions of Blacks are deprived of their rights to eat, to be housed adequately, to receive medical care, to work, to vote, to be educated, etc. Millions of workers are limited in their right to strike and to share in the increasing productivity of labor and technology. Most of the mass media echo and support the viewpoint of the ruling groups, being owned and controlled for the most part by those same groups. A great mass of legislation has in effect outlawed "subversive" organizations and barred political radicals from employment. The undeclared, illegal, and inhuman war in Vietnam grinds on, with $100 billion spent, a million Vietnamese dead, and 40,000 Americans dead. The CIA arm of American foreign policy has intervened to establish or support oppressive governments in Iran, Guatemala, Indonesia, Cuba, and elsewhere.[3] And the United States military-industrial com-

---

[2] Conference on Economic Progress: *Poverty and Deprivation in the United States. The Plight of Two-fifths of a Nation.* Washington, D. C., 1964.

[3] Wise, David, and Ross, Thomas B: *The Invisible Government.* New York, Random, 1964.

plex has developed now a colonial foreign market whose size for domestic and United States-owned foreign firms is equal to two-fifths the domestic output of farms, factories, and mines.[4]

All these actions are "moral" actions, but they represent a decadent and antihuman morality initiated by a group who represent their own "vital interests"—which they identify with those of the nation. They deny and destroy the generic values of men, whether taken as individuals, as a nation, or as mankind as a whole.

It follows that those who are least apt to discern the roots of human morality are those who are alienated from their generic human needs, human nature, and human fulfillment by reason of their dominant identification with a narrow interest and point of view. Such an interest excludes their own generic fulfillment and hinders the fulfillment of all men. In feudal and capitalistic societies, this alienation may be clearly observed in ruling groups identified with their class interests. But it is possible also to observe alienation among many peasants, who are identified with traditional habits and customs; in urban workers and the urban poor who are so deprived of the necessities of life and of vital energy that they passively accept the established social order; and in the masses of white-collar and industrial workers in a highly developed technological society like the United States who, for various reasons, emotionally desire and adopt the values of the ruling group.

By the same token those who are most apt to discern the roots of human morality are those who for one reason or another, material or intellectual or both, are separated from the protective interests of an exclusive kind—e.g., the interests of the ruling class, the interests of a special occupation or career—and who are thrown back upon, and willingly accept, the generically *human* interests and values for themselves, and hence, implicitly, for all men, as their dominant interests. Such a group can include men from all walks of life. But those most likely to be humanistic in this sense are those who have suffered oppression and alienation and who, through an inherited body of humanistic ideas or their own reflection, have formulated for themselves that oppression and a solution for overcoming it. Separated from the

---

[4]U. S. Department of Commerce. Cited by Magdoff, Harry: Economic aspects of U. S. imperialism. *Monthly Review, 18*:15, 1966.

powers and values of the ruling class, but also alienated from their own human fulfillment, oppressed people sometimes have the choice of pursuing the values determined by the modes of life of the ruling class, or of affirming their own creative essence. In the United States, where an unprecedentedly large middle stratum of white-collar workers exist, such a choice is available to increasing numbers. Many, of course, choose to aim at identification with the ruling ideas and values; but some have gone over to the cause of the oppressed. By contrast, where there is little or no prospect of participating in the wealth and the ruling class values which it makes possible, people are then forced either to abandon themselves in resignation to their oppression, or to seek to recover the root of their alienated humanity in acts of affirmative revolutionary defiance. Accepting the fact that they are *nothing* in their society, as Marx observed,[5] they can then freely accept their necessity and aim to become *everything* in a new society. This is one reason why the socialist revolutions in the twentieth century have occurred in those countries where class lines were sharply polarized. There the ruling class could not (as it has done in England, America, and other advanced capitalist countries) lure and lull the ruled classes with the promise of material betterment for themselves or their children.

Men struggle to live. And since their livelihoods and the necessities for living are geared into systems of social production, this struggle becomes social. A few own and rule, while most are owned and are ruled. The result is class struggle. There is a clash of real material interests. The dominant interest of the few members of the ruling class under capitalism appears to be profit and expanded power. The dominant interest of the many members of the ruled class appears to be better wages. Are we to take these apparent interests to be the real and final interests of men?

To ask which interests ought to be satisfied if man as a human being is to be fulfilled is to ask which interests are generic to man. "Fulfillment" is both a value-concept and a fact-concept, and in man's existence fact and value are dialectically related. Man as a natural being is a set of processes and tendencies with implicit goals which are at

---

[5] Marx, Karl: Contribution to the critique of Hegel's philosophy of right. Introduction, p. 58.

first conceived values and then, when achieved, actual values. Factual man is in this sense the source of man's value and fulfillment. But in the process of valuation, of selecting, organizing, and directing certain existing tendencies and rejecting others, man creates for himself a new kind of factuality. Value in this sense, both as conceived and as finally actualized, is the source of man's factuality. The question of "What is human nature?" is in part a value question, for our definition must choose from among the great number and diversity of human qualities and activities. The question of "What is human value?" is in part a factual question, for in order for an act or state to have human value it must be a fulfillment of some existing human capacity or tendency.

The first factuality of man is his body with its needs and capacities, given to him by the materials and processes of biophysical nature. But these needs (some vital and others distinctively human)—to breathe, to eat, to drink, to act, to rest, to sleep, to eliminate, to avoid pain and injury, to be stimulated, to express oneself, to communicate, to explore, to play, to create, etc.[6]—must be satisfied in interchange with a social and natural environment. The social environment consists of persons, man-made objects, and sign-processes which form and guide the behavior of the individual person and the social group and generate roles and institutions. The social environment in turn is set within the larger context of nonhuman nature, where members of the society are engaged in exchange as they satisfy their needs. Thus the newborn baby moves toward the fulfillment of its biological nature in and by means of the persons, things, and processes of its social and ecological contexts. It is a bio-social-ecological being in process of creation. Let us look in some detail at this threefold root of man.

The newborn baby is impelled by the imperative drive to live. Expelled from the womb, where he lived in an easy parasitic relation to his mother, he enters into a new symbiotic relation with her in which each stimulates and reinforces certain actions in the other with mutually beneficial results. His "drive to live" takes the form of specific drives or needs: the needs for oxygen, water, food, protection against

---

[6]Those who study man are not entirely agreed on human needs, but most would agree on those needs necessary to man's life, and many are agreed on those needs which must be satisfied (including the vital needs) if man is to develop as a distinctively human kind of being.

injurious environment, activity, rest, etc. Continuing deprivation of these needs produces death. Because the baby is born helpless and dependent and remains so for a long period, he must satisfy these survival needs through the attention and care of others. On their side, developed dispositions of empathy and habits of nurture passed from one generation to another lead these others to respond to the baby's needs. The baby, in turn, otherwise weak and impuissant, has one sole resource, his cry: the cry for air, the cry for food, the cry for comfort. Such a cry is a commandment, a categorical imperative, of the human individual and the human species. It is an unconditional command on the part of the infant that life be fulfilled. Those human beings who hear it commonly hear it with sympathy, discomfort, and the constraint of obligation. For them that cry is a communicative sign: it indicates a human life in need, out there; it indicates also a kindred need in the hearer, elicited by empathic identification with the crier in distress; and it indicates some kind of required action to relieve the need in the infant by appropriate action on the part of the hearer. In short, this cry of the infant initiates a complex sign situation, leading from the infant's life-need to others and back through them and their action to the fulfillment of that need and the sustaining of infant life. This sign situation is a paradigm situation for the life of man, and forms the matrix out of which human life and morality develop.

For any morality whatsoever to exist and develop, human life must be sustained and contribute to new life. Morality involves the creation of human values, and consequently the foundational moral act is the preservation and care of human life. This is the first and great commandment. And the second is like unto it: Thou shalt not commit genocide. As individual human beings do not maintain and create themselves alone, but do so only in interaction with others and the world, the essential unit of human life is the human group. In the case of the newborn or young infant, this need of the individual person for the aid of others is normally satisfied directly through the family. Here, no sharp distinction can be observed between biological and psychological needs, for both kinds originate in the body and are satisfied in exchange with the environment. Moreover, as bodily needs they are intimately related in a total system of needs. Margaret Ribble in her studies of infants demonstrated, for example, that in taking milk at his mother's breast the infant's needs for food, oxygen, and love are satisfied simultaneously and he grows as a healthy psychosomatic unity. But if he is not so nurtured—if he is not held, fondled, stroked, talked to, sung to—but is given the physical essentials alone, he suffers in both dimensions of his personality, the psychic and somatic.[7]

I need the other for my fulfilled being, both as individual and as human, because only in and through him and my productive relation to him can I be awakened, sensitized, and activated to my full possibilities. Only through him and our relation can I be realized in the whole range of my human capacities—for sense and feeling, for symbolic thought, for skill in action, for empathy and communication, for cooperative labor, and for trust in myself, others, and the process of human development. Such a relation is a creative one, a bond of mutual affirmation that empowers and enhances. In it I express myself, I criticize myself, I differentiate and integrate myself, I explore myself, I discover myself, I extend myself. This occurs only as I express and am expressed to, criticize and am criticized, etc. By these acts of mine—my expression and unfoldment—I fulfill and elaborate my powers, and such an act of fulfillment includes in its very origins my concern for the fulfillment of the other. His human identity draws out, deepens, and confirms my own. Thus my need includes his need, and my fulfillment can be complete only to the extent that his is also. In this way we become mutual sustainers and creators. As I need the other I need myself, for I need myself-in-creative-relation-to-the-other. Thus the need for the other is a generic and indispensable need of man. Apart from it and its fulfillmnt man declines and dies. In his *Economic and Philosophical Manuscripts,* Marx grasped this fact with the insight of a young genius, long before modern social psychologists caught glimpses of it. Had Marx remained at the stage of psychological analysis he would have become in all likelihood the giant of the science. But his adventurous and thoroughly humanistic spirit carried him onward from an analysis of human interpersonal relations and productive activity and their pathology, to their ultimate origins in society and history, and to a program of social action. He went, in

---

[7]Ribble, Margaret: *The Rights of Infants.* New York, Columbia University, 1943. See also Bowlby, John: *Attachment.* New York, Basic, 1969.

short, to the roots of man's situation, and was content, not with the cultivation of a few individual flowers, but only with radical therapy for *all mankind*.

Man's living relations of creative mutuality with others, in the context of their productive relations to the world, are the source of his developed moral feelings and dispositions. Man is amoral and nonhuman to the extent that he is lacking in such relations, feelings, and dispositions. Only in such relations can he learn to care about himself and others and humanity, and to feel and to obey the categorical imperative of creative fulfillment.

The developed capacity for his communication and cooperative mutuality among adults has its roots in the very young infant and his relation to others. Dependent, empathic, sensitive, responsive, social, vocal, innovative, integrative, educable, driven by the dynamics of biological maturation—the infant soon learns to remember and anticipate events, qualities, and relations by means of meaningful signs, to produce his own signs, to respond to signs (his own or those of others) as others do—i.e., to communicate.[8] Only in the disciplines of that communicative matrix does he become the recipient of that security that frees him for autonomy in the creation of his actions, his meanings, and his evolving life-style. Only in love is individuality nourished. Thus he progressively enters into the opportunities and responsibilities of the full human community. Caught up in that living dialogue and drama of human interaction which ever weaves the textures of culture and history, the infant grows into his roles and plays his parts as he moves, changes, and adjusts to his family, his peers, his neighbors, the diverse representatives of occupations and generations, and the demands of his own constitution, temperament, and ontogeny.

How do the infant and child, the preadolescent and the adolescent, know which roles to take? How do they know indeed what the *human* role is? What disposes them to be sociable, communicative, moral? Individual man, like many other individual animals studied by ethologists, has an instinctive sense, recognition, and outreach for his own kind. Recent experiments show that the young baby is disposed to respond preferentially to certain colors, shapes and rudimentary facial

---

[8]Mead, George Herbert: *Mind, Self, and Society*. Charles W. Morris (Ed.). Chicago, University of Chicago, 1934.

Gestalten.[9] But deeper than the instinctive recognition of forms and signs is the disposition of relatedness, of trust, and of expectant hope towards others. This emerges in the infant's very early experience of a reliable caretaker, before language.[10] Beyond that, the nine months in the womb confer a sense of stability: the infant is securely rooted by umbilicus to the body of the mother much as a plant is rooted in the body of Mother Nature. He absorbs the nutrients of his environing world, which cradles him in liquid comfort. Back still farther, our animal ancestry has for millions upon millions of years generated a hardy vitality and a preservative social instinct—a strength, a virtue —that turns into the forms of trust and hope in the newborn human mammal.

This vigorous, curious, grasping, sensitive, exploratory, playful, cognitive movement outward, toward mother first, then toward others and objects generally, carries with it an empathic identification with persons and objects which George Herbert Mead called "role-taking." [11] The root of role-taking lies precisely in infantile weakness, namely, the passive capability of absorbing, taking on, and then reenacting the qualities and forms of what is perceived. This first appears in lalling and imitation. The infant then observes a single gesture and what follows it: his mother presents him with milk, and he drinks it. Here, to recur to Mead's analysis, the first part of the gesture becomes a sign of what follows, preparing him to respond to the consequent; and this connection is remembered and anticipated by the infant. He rehearses it when he is hungry, or when he observes the sequence beginning. Moreover, the mother says "milk" to the infant who hears the sound, follows her lips, and imitates her. Eventually the infant is able to form the word himself, and through social learning (rooted again in imitation), to interpret it as a sign of the seen and tasted milk. When he can produce the word, overtly or subvocally, anticipate the response of another to it, and regulate his behavior accordingly—then the otherwise individual sign has become a "significant symbol," the individual has become socialized, and the infant body

---

[9]Fantz, Robert L.: The origin of form perception. *Scientific American, 204*: 66-72, 1961.

[10]Erikson, E. H.: The roots of virtue. In Huxley, Julian (Ed.): *The Humanist Frame.* New York, Harper, 1961, p. 154.

[11]*Op. cit.*

has become a fully "minded" body and is truly human. Social symbols, in short, greatly release and advance the original mammalian empathic power and infantile role-taking.

Society, then, with its rich tradition of symbolic meanings and its meaningful technologies, is the nurturing ground in which the individual body, with its social roots, grows, emerges into minded personality, and becomes moral. Society provides these stable patterns of interwoven customary activities, as a network of paths by which the newborn and the young may get about. These patterns are mediated to them by the stable presence, activity, and linguistic usage of the mother and others who care for them. Behind these accumulated meanings and mores lie the long development of social instincts and ecological patterns of anthropoidal, mammalian, and vertebrate evolution. A full treatment of the roots of morality would go back to these origins[12] and would eventually concern itself with the ontology of morality, i.e., the general conditions and laws of our biosphere and the universe which are relevant to morality.

The minded, personalized body of the infant is the creation of an interaction between infant and members of society formed and guided by social signs (symbols). Mind in turn, as the individual creation and use of symbols, is thus social in its origins and consequences. Rooted in empathic identification and the need for creative relatedness, the infant's mind develops into the means or meanings by which these roots flower into personality and society. Personal minding is the individualizing of a social process. It is the means by which the individual becomes fully socialized and moralized. It is the means by which he directs and controls his actions through the signified consequences of possible actions. It is the means by which he makes himself an object to himself from the perspectives of others and from his unique perspective, and is able to criticize, correct, and create himself. It is the means by which he can take the role of unseen contemporary and future men and act for their welfare. It is the means by which he can put himself in the place of natural objects, plants, and animals, relate them meaningfully to his personal and social world of meanings and values, and

---

[12]See, for example, Berrill, N. J.: *Man's Emerging Mind*. New York, Dodd, 1955; and Hockett, Charles F., and Ascher, Robert: The human revolution. *Current Anthropology*, 5: 135-168, 1964.

act morally toward them. As Marx observed, when man is truly human, freed from the alienation, exclusive role, and possessiveness of a social system of private property, then he freely enters into a relation with nature in which man, as a humanized and socialized body with nature, assimilates and humanizes nature. "The eye has become a *human* eye, just as its *object* has become a social, *human* object—an object emanating from man for man." [13] In sum, man's mind, when free, is a means for the creation of values that support and enhance man's fulfillment individually and collectively.

The infant passes from his rudimentary empathic relations with his mother and others to role-taking by means of self-produced symbols. Through the use of symbols, anticipatory and integrative, he learns to control his own manipulative and locomotive behavior with respect to the future. He develops will and initiative. He participates in play and in games. He experiments in trying one course of activity after another, exploring their consequences in the free sphere of play. In his play with peers, and in his games, he learns the meaning of rules, and through taking the role of a "generalized other" [14] he develops that conscience first acquired in the family—an internalized social perspective upon himself and his activity. Meanwhile his own ego-identity has emerged, guided by mind and driven by autonomous purpose, and mediating between impressions from the outside, impulses from below, and the demands of a social conscience from above. Soon he is a mature child, ready to master essential human skills and industrious habits under more or less formal instruction—reading, writing, numbers, manual training, etc. Such mastery prepares the ground for his participation in a mature morality; for it gives him the tools to create, with and for others, the values that sustain life at a civilized level. Adolescence comes, with its demand for unitary purpose, for adult identity, for a career to be aspired to, and for a significant life-commitment. Here, the moral energies of our species reach their peak. Young men and women make crucial decisions that decide not only their individual destinies, but the destinies of societies and civilizations. They become delinquents, criminals, drifters, con-

---

[13]Marx, Karl: *Economic and Philosophic Manuscripts of 1844,* trans. by Martin Milligan. Moscow, Foreign Languages Publishing House, p. 107.
[14]Mead, George Herbert: *Op. cit.*

formists—or critical and creative citizens, heroes in action, thinkers, moralists. That society will best succeed which can convert such adolescent energies into great human and moral loyalties.

As these energies achieve balance and personal and social purpose through some ideology, adolescents enter upon mature adulthood. This means intimate interpersonal relations, the sharing of deep identities, the emergence of mutual care. It means perhaps sexual love, and, with or without such love, the recapturing, at a higher level, of those tender affections of nurture felt as infants and children. It means the infusing of those feelings with adult intelligence, integrity, concern, and responsibility. The roots now have been realized in the high branches and blossoms of love. What then? Now man is ready to have children, not alone in a biological sense, but in a psychological one—he commands the power of care, the sense of responsibility, the long yearning for human flowering, the need to nurture the tender roots of the human species. What was once only roots and in need of being nurtured, is now mature and in need of nurturing. He who loves others as his human peers, who cares for them as for children, as for fellow human beings of the same family, will not stop with a mere familial, Confucian morality. For he has already arrived at a generic and hence universal human sympathy. His morality is rooted in, and must flower through, the most thorough humanism possible: nothing human can be alien to him. This means the greatest passion and commitment toward the liberation and fulfillment of mankind. "Do you charge us," cried Marx and Engels, "with wanting to stop the exploitation of children by their parents? To this crime we plead guilty." [15] When the roots of morality have grown to fruition in a man, that must mean that he feels united with his own life and its development, that he loves and respects it, and that he therefore desires for man "the absolute elaboration of his creative dispositions" and "the evolution of all human powers as such." [16]

We have said that the matrix of human morality is human communication and mutual aid, and that the paradigm situation for this is

---

[15]Marx, Karl, and Engels, Friedrich: *Manifesto of the Communist Party.* Authorized English translation, Friedrich Engels (Ed.). New York, International, 1948, p. 27.

[16]Marx, Karl: *Pre-Capitalist Economic Formations,* trans. by Jack. Cohen, E. J. Hobsbawm (Ed.). New York, International, 1965, pp. 84-85.

the relation between the human infant and those who care for him. We have traced this relation briefly through its evolution into interpersonal relations between mature adults.

To make more complete this account of human morality and its matrix—its roots—we must turn to that wider matrix which makes possible the care of the infant. That is human labor. To live, men, women, and children must eat, drink, clothe themselves, and fulfill other functions vital to survival and to a realized existence. To secure these use values men must engage in productive transactions with nature and do so in cooperative fashion. Such values do not fall like manna from heaven, but must be formed and created by man's collective operations. Such creation is a fundamental moral act. As the nurturance of human life and development is man's categorical imperative, man's productive labor is likewise an imperative, both as a way of life, intrinsically good in itself, and as an instrument for sustaining and improving life. The fact that man comes out of, depends on, and is in part created by nature—as well as by a long historical process—means that man does not make or command all that he is or values. Many of his human and moral roots lie below, around, and behind him. Recognition of these sustaining sources of value— as Marx recognized them[17]—means not fatalism, but instead a lively inquiry to discover how man can cooperate with and guide such sources to secure their most creative issue.

A man's productive life in nature requires other men. Conversely, in his relations to other human beings man experiences his most immediate and natural relation to nature.[18] Man in nature making a living is man socialized, and natural man communicating with his fellow man in nature is nature humanized. The sounds, facial expressions, gestures, and postures of the mother's body, of which the baby has direct empathic feeling, become signs of absent and future events rele-

---

[17]"Labor is *not the source* of all wealth. *Nature* is just as much the source of use values (and it is surely of such that material wealth consists) as labor, which itself is only a manisfestation of a force of nature, human labor power." Marx, Karl: *Critique of the Gotha Programme.* Moscow, Foreign Languages Publishing House, 1954, p. 15. In *Pre-Capitalist Economic Formations* Marx refers to man's "appropriation of the natural conditions of labour, of the *earth* as the original instrument of labour, both laboratory and repository of its raw materials." *Op. cit.,* p. 81.

[18]*Economic and Philosophic Manuscripts of 1884,* p. 104.

vant to the baby's vital needs. A smile signifies food; a cry is a warning of danger among men or in nature. Similarly, for adult man such natural signs, whose vehicles are the natural motions of the body, direct attention to what lies in the social, natural environment. Gibbons and other primates emit vocal signals which signify the discovery of food, the detection of danger, an interest in company, the location of the caller, etc.[19] Probably human language derived from similar primitive and vital signals in the first hominid groups wherein man's collective needs for food, safety, association, etc. drove him into cooperation in dealing with one another and the natural world.

In such activity the hand played a necessary role. The hand is a natural tool for the human body in establishing an adjustive relation to other human bodies and to the things of nonhuman nature. By means of the hand man handles, moves, changes, and makes things. Furthermore, the hand has the power to extend itself; it is man's tool for making tools. A tool, like the gesturing or pointing hand, indicates something beyond, absent and future; and what is indicated, moreover, is controlled by present action and thought, for man has the present in hand as his hand grasps his tool. To grasp a tool is to grasp a world and to grasp a future. Man thus has a means of ordering nature and society by his prediction and control. He has a means for changing the materials and processes of nature. Shaped from nature's materials, a tool links man to nature, drawing external nature into the domain of man's own material bodily minding and humanizing it. A spear signifies an animal and the act of killing it; a stone signifies the wood hewn or to be hewn. We know that man's speech and his thought processes must have been greatly accelerated as the human group using tools grappled with the problems of survival in nature. Evidence indicates that in the developing hominid of the Pleistocene period the making of crude stone tools was accompanied by bipedal posture, the consequent release of man's hands for carrying, the throwing of stone as weapons, the elaboration of language, and the growth of the brain.[20]

---

[19]Hockett, Charles F., and Ascher, Robert: *Op. cit.*

[20]*Ibid.* Frederick Engels, in his essay, "The Part Played by Labour in the Transition from Ape to Man," anticipated some of the notions of modern anthropologists, though he had many less data available to him than they have.

All productive labor presupposes a social and communicative life as its origin, content, and end. A tool or weapon is a *social* product and instrument. (Though probably the first stone with which primitive man killed an animal was fortuitously found and thrown, *thereafter* it was shaped and intended by him.) The meaning, the intended consequence of a spear, just as cries, must be internalized in the individual hunters if their tribal hunt is to be successful; the use value of the axe lies in its usability by different members of the group over a period of time. The tool is a moralizing agent—it gives rise to shared meanings, and it serves common values. As it is passed down from one generation to another and its form and function are improved, it becomes the focus for enriched meanings. As an instrument for man's productive labor in securing the necessities of life, a tool itself becomes necessary; it defines and gives direction to man's social life. Consider, for example, the effects on the mode of life of men who depended on the water mill in medieval Europe, the spinning machines in nineteenth century England, and the assembly line of the modern factory.

In primitive social labor, the natural attitude of the men directly engaged in making their own living, in creating what they need and joining themselves to what they make in both production and consumption, is one of identification with their products. For them, labor is the natural, right, and moral thing to do. It is an integral part of the imperative of human life. Wealth and accumulation of products are not isolated as ends which man must serve; rather, man's basic needs stand at the center of life and dictate the processes and products of labor. Thus labor has as much dignity as human life itself. To be a man, to develop one's powers, to create—all of that means to engage in productive labor with other men and in transaction with nature. Such living labor generates its own intrinsic morality: the morality of necessary means (skills, procedures) disciplined to serve necessary human ends; the morality of the effective fashioning and use of tools and of their service to human values; the morality of collective, cooperative, and diversified work; the morality of humanistic production and consumption of values; the morality of creating human institutions designed to liberate human powers; the morality of conserving the essential resources of the natural environment for present and future use and enjoyment by man; the morality of human fulfillment through creative and cooperative activity.

But in many societies today the morality of living labor does not prevail. Under capitalism classes divide men into the owners and the owned, the deciders and the decided-for, the determiners and the determined, the few and the many. Most men must sell their labor to others as a commodity. They are thus estranged from their work, their tools, their creations, their fellow man, and themselves. The morality of collective labor is dominated by the morality of egoistic competition. The morality of laboring in order to live is superseded by the morality of living in order to labor. Things become the great alluring pot of gold, the idol, the fetish of men. Accumulation becomes men's driving obsession. Morality sinks to the level of exploitive self-interest; men are forced either to be used by others or to use them. Even in an "affluent" capitalistic society like the United States, hunger, disease, and illiteracy prevail among more than ten million people. Neuroses and psychoses are widespread. All manner of crimes and destructive behavior proliferate: fraud, theft, crimes against property, and crimes of violence against persons. Such crimes on the part of the ruling groups become institutionalized or lie beyond the law: monopoly of resources and productive power, pollution, wastage of natural resources and human talents, impoverishment of the masses, imperialism, war, genocide. Government, whose policies are a direct reflection of the demands of a military-industrial complex, wields an unexampled power. Lenin spoke of the state as "an organ of oppression of one class by another" and referred to bureaucracy and the standing army as institutions characterizing the state machinery of bourgeois society.[21] Since 1917, however, the military apparatus in capitalist societies like Nazi Germany and, later the United States has developed a power and autonomy of its own. In the United States today, the military establishment,[22] the largest corporation in the society, takes two-thirds of the national budget, maintains 3.5 million troops at home and abroad and 1.2 million civilian employees, controls 31 million acres, in one year

---

[21]Lenin, V. I.: *State and Revolution*. Revised translation. New York, International, 1932, pp. 9, 26.

[22]For documentation on the subject, see Swomley, John M., Jr.: *The Military Establishment*. Boston, Beacon, 1964.

provides business with $39 billion in defense contracts [23] and unprecedented profits, furnishes hundreds of generals, admirals, and officers as employees of armaments manufacturers,[24] and commands the resources of major American universities in war research, including that on biological and chemical warfare. One of a thousand and one symptoms of the endemic disease of inhumanism of such a system is that it spends more on chemical and biological warfare than it spends on cancer research. National security is determined through the algebra of overkill by "experts" like Herman Kahn and Edward Teller. The mathematics of death rather than the love of life decide foreign policy. The morals that conserve and develop human life have been replaced by "the morals of extermination." [25] And in its heedless acceleration of nuclear missile systems the American government irresponsibly approaches the ultimate immorality, the destruction of life on this planet.

At the same time, however, there is a humanistic movement opposing this descent into barbarism and death. That movement is rooted in the disposition of men to affirm their creative and cooperative powers, in their common work and play, in their trust and hope for the future, in their care for human life. It shows itself in the national liberation movements of peasants and colored peoples against imperialism and colonialism, in the struggle of industrial workers for justice, in the demand of wide sectors of the population for peace and peaceful coexistence, in the insistence on democracy within authoritarian institutions like government and religion, in the alarm of scientists over a despoiled environment, in the indignation of youth and women against inequalities, and in many other ways. These are the true forces of human morality. They are struggling not only for man's present life, but for his future. And if man is to have any future whatsoever, it will be because their morality of life prevails over the morality of death.

For man to be fulfilled—to feel deeply and finely; to yearn passionately; to aspire highly; to think imaginatively, clearly, and comprehensively; to control himself and his world effectively; to care lovingly; to

---

[23]Friends Committee on National Legislation, *Washington Newsletter,* 289, 1968.
[24]Wells, Donald A.: *The War Myth.* New York, Western, 1967, pp. 211.
[25]Mumford, Lewis: The morals of extermination. *The Atlantic, 204*: 38-44, 1959.

struggle and fight courageously; to communicate freely; to work with others faithfully; to nurture and encourage all that is humanly creative and needful; and to commit himself in faith to the human adventure—men must together undertake to guard and nourish the roots of human morality. These roots lie deep in man's body, the social mutuality of the human situation, and man's relation to nature. Productive communication, and communicative production, are the two interdependent forms of this situation. The roots are there, waiting for realization. They are the roots out of which man in his genus is created and grows toward fulfillment. They are the roots which at once stabilize man at the base, and, energizing him, free him to unfold with zest and morale.

Socialism, as a social and economic form of man's life, is, correctly conceived and carried into practice, the only means by which men can produce a natural, human morality that fosters such creation, growth and fulfillment. The morality of socialism is the most humanistic and the most necessary of moralities, so far as it is and remains a morality that places man as the root. The morality of socialism promises humanism at its highest because it relies on man at his deepest. Its radical task, in the hands of socialists, is to rescue radical man from his bondage and to release him into the air and sunlight of his free and fraternal development.

We are told by an anthropologist that "no culture tolerates indiscriminate lying, stealing, or violence with the group." [26] These prohibitions are indicators of some minimal moral conditions for human life in society. A society built on the principle of the systematic exploitation of man, at home and abroad, is therefore built on a self-defeating morality. As man at the root of his nature is not, in such a society and morality, grounded in what he needs for his healthy growth, but instead starves and suffers the deformity of his humanity, what is to be done? The solution is the righting of wrongs; the overturning of a situation already overturned; the rectification of man's uprootedness; the renaturalizing of a denaturalized condition; the return of alienated man to himself; the humanizing of humanity. Concretely, oppressed men must unite to remove from power that class which oppressess

---

[26]Kluckhohn, Clyde: Anthropology. In Newman, James R. (Ed.): *What is Science?* New York, Simon and Schuster, 1955, p. 344.

them, transforming private property in production to collective ownership and control and establishing the rule of the vast majority of working men in the new state—a genuine government of the people, by
the people, and for the people.

II

THE FULFILLMENT OF MAN

In the previous chapter we have been concerned with the sources of man's moral life and his fulfillment. We now turn to a fuller consideration of the nature of human fulfillment itself and the way in which the concept of fulfillment can be validated.

The dictionary meaning of "fulfill" is as follows: to carry into effect, as an intention; bring to pass, as a design; also, reflexively, to realize or manifest completely. (Webster) All of these suggest, but do not completely pinpoint, the meaning we have in mind when we use the term. The dictionary meaning suggests that in every case of fulfillment there is an Aristotelian final cause at work and that fulfillment occurs when this is fully realized. Thus, in the case of "the fulfillment of man" man is fulfilled to the extent that his activity realizes this final cause. If this were true, then we should need to discover (in the manner of Aristotle) the activity that is unique to man, show that he aims at it, and then demonstrate that his fulfillment occurs as he fulfills or completes it. Much modern thought is skeptical of discovering any single conscious purpose which dominates and distinguishes man; and were it to discover such, it would question whether man, in his fragmentariness, can complete this particular purpose and in this sense fulfill himself. Nevertheless, "fulfillment" as we define it must have something in common with this traditional usage; otherwise we would more rightly use another word. What is this? It is that fulfillment is the *realization,* the making real, of man. It is his coming into being, his becoming, the process of his becoming himself, his human growth, his being-made-human.

There is another common connotation of the term "fulfillment" that must be looked at. That is that man is fulfilled when he is filled full, in a similar way that a cistern has fulfilled its function when it is filled full of water. Man has a certain capacity, an emptiness, a set of definite deprivations to be filled and satisfied. His fulfillment consists in such filling up and satisfying—and finishing. His repletion is his completion. This concept of fulfillment with its emphasis on consumption is apt to attract people who are very poor and hence deprived of food, drink, clothes, and other necessities for human existence. Or it may be popular among people whose economy disposes them to the pursuit of material goods. But this concept defines only one aspect of human fulfillment. Certainly man's fulfillment must include the satisfaction of man's biologically vital need-dispositions. But fulfillment is more than mere satisfaction, or satisfaction of this kind. People do not genuinely feel fulfilled, though they may deceive themselves, when they are fulfilled in this sense. They feel drawn on to somthing more. And it is this something more that distinguishes human fulfillment, as John Stuart Mill observed, from the fulfillment of a pig.

What does "man" mean in the expression, "the fulfillment of man"? Throughout the greater part of human history the concept "man" has been highly exclusive, depending on the particular class structure and the prevailing forms of exploitation. Slaves and plebeians, vassals and serfs, the unpropertied and landless, wage laborers and peasants, colonials and colored peoples, criminals and paupers, the insane and handicapped, aliens and enemies, captives and pagans, women and children—all, in both theory and the actual institutional practices of men, have for the most part been regarded as semihuman, subhuman, or nonhuman. And here we are speaking not only of the specialized theorists and professional groups surrounding them whose task it is in every class society to create and organize the symbols, ideas, and ideologies that will facilitate the position of the dominant class—the priests, the philosophers, the scribes, the propagandists, the chroniclers, etc. We are speaking also of the great mass of men who accepted the view already created for them that only a few males, economically and militarily and politically powerful, are, or could be, human, while the rest of the population are not essentially human, and, if they are to become human, can become so only in an afterlife. This highly exclusive concept of man has been, of course, a reflection of the real situation in human affairs: in societies in which economic scarcity and class oppression prevailed, only the ruling few might be, or realistically aspire to be, human. The lives of most men were crippled or crushed by hunger, inadequate clothing and housing, disease, suffering, ignorance, superstition, hard labor, fatigue, indignity, and hopelessness.

But within recent centuries the concept of man has been greatly transformed. As long ago as the Iron Age lay prophets, seers, and philosophers in China, India, and the Mediterranean area and Near East, challenged the traditional limits of the concept. They had the vision of a much more universal concept of man. While their humanism has inspired many since, their vision as well as their concept of the means of achieving it were limited by their class situations. The emergence of capitalism and the development of applied science in Europe produced a rennaissance of this older humanism as well as new forms of humanism. The Industrial Revolution, the French Revolution, and the Socialist Revolution were both effect and cause of the new humanism and democracy. The chief historical change here was the application and promise of scientific technology for improving the lives of large masses of men, and for achieving the fulfillment that the prophets, seers, and philosophers had only vaguely and restrictedly dreamed of.

Nevertheless, many thinkers today still propagate an exclusive concept of man, neglecting or degrading the colored races, the Asians, the Africans, the Latin Americans, radicals, the Negroes, women, children, peasants, farmers, manual workers, etc. The exclusive concept of man is based an exclusive, class society, with exclusive social, political, and educational systems.[1] It thus makes an appeal to established

---

[1] People who possess power and advantage tend to believe that they possess these things in virtue of some inherent superiority over the mass of persons who do not possess such power and advantage. This belief is one of the premises that lies at the base of the apparatus of ideology—economic, political, legal, religious, social, etc.—which surrounds and supports a given class system. In slave society and in feudal society it was customary to proclaim openly and exploit fully such a premise: the king was god or at least was divine; the king possessed certain divine rights. Capitalistic society at one time flaunted the Calvinistic theory of the elect; in late nineteenth century America Social Darwinism was used to justify it. Now, however, the ideology of the American capitalistic elite remains in the background, though still at work: it has no major powerful spokesman (Russell Kirk, Clinton Rossiter, and Peter Viereck are not Burkes); it is disguised in the liberal rhetoric of public relations. There are a number of reasons for this: the pragmatic attitude of Americans, including business men, the populist distrust of government, the absence of social groups (landed aristocracy, peasants, etc.) that would support a conservative tradition, the lack of development of social theory, including conservative theory, and the fact that the ideology of liberalism is widespread and hence usable as the convenient cloak for elitist policies. In

fact, both past and present. But the fact of exclusiveness is changing, challenged by economic and political forces which open new opportunities for many in the economic, political, and educational order. The conditions of an industrial, expansive capitalism have concentrated workers in cities and evoked in them demands and united actions for equality of opportunity for development. Peasants have developed their powers of thought and action in collective resistance to colonialism. Women have been increasingly released from their restricted roles. Socialist states have greatly widened the opportunities for all people within their boundaries. Under public, universal, compulsory education, the capacities of each child may begin to show themselves. Special schools for the mentally ill, the handicapped, and the retarded likewise reveal hitherto undetected capacities. Thus a changed experience for many kinds of persons shows that, with the exception of those rare babies congenitally deficient and incapable of developing beyond the vegetative state, every person has capacities that are distinctively human. Such capacities are nothing more than what appears in practice under certain circumstances; and it has been the new circumstances that have disclosed the capacities. Hence when we speak here of "the fulfillment of man," we mean the fulfillment, throughout life, of each and every baby born of human parentage.

"The fulfillment of man" is both a factual concept and a value concept. Many people experience fulfillment every day. At the same time, to speak of the fulfillment of man ordinarily connotes approval, i.e., an ethical judgment that it is better than, preferable to, the absence of fulfillment. Certain philosophers have chosen to magnify and even sanctify this distinction between the factual and the ethical. Certainly the distinction exists, and it is painfully accentuated by the existing distinction and indeed contradiction between the ethical ideals of western society, inherited from the Jewish prophets and Greek humanists, and the actual practices of human impoverishment and exploitation in western society. But in man the factual and the ethical, the real and the ideal, are organically and dialectically related.

---

short, in America today the economic system reinforced by a "democratic" ideology gears men into a certain unity and conformity; but as economic and social problems deepen, many men increasingly recognize the contradiction between this ideology and the facts of their existence. Economic crises can thus be expected to produce an explicit polarization between elitist and democratic ideologies.

The existing human being is the ground and material for the possible and ideal man. His actual tendencies indicate the structure and direction of what he might become, i.e., his fulfillment. *What* is fulfilled is precisely those tendencies, chosen as something worth cultivating, developing, and guiding. Apart from those tendencies, what might the ideal form of man be derived from, with what materials might it be supplied, how might it be sanctioned? From Augustine to Kant we have been offered various transcendental forms to serve this function; but it has never been explained why man must turn away from his nature in order to fulfill it. Likewise, some modern existentialisms offer us the mysterious *creatio ex nihilo* as the principle of man's nature and fulfillment; but it is equally strange how man can create himself out of nothing.

The most recent version of this split between the *is* and the *ought* is that which, following G. E. Moore, holds that the term "good" must refer to a non-natural quality.[2] Moore was correct in holding that the term "good" does not signify some observable sensory property of an object at a certain place and time. But he failed to see its signification in the whole span of the human evaluative activity. Suppose I say, as most men say or indicate when they are hungry and want to live, "Food is good and I ought to seek it." This utterance functions as an appraisive sign[3] that disposes me to act toward certain objects or kinds of objects in the environment in a positively preferential way, expecting that they will have such properties as will satisfy my hunger. It also functions as a prescriptive sign disposing me to employ a certain preferential way of acting as a means of obtaining food. If the prescriptive language, "I ought to seek it," directs my response in such a way that it is successful, so that I obtain the food, and if the appraisive language, "Food is good," turns out to correspond to an objective state of affairs, such that some food does satisfy, then the sharp division of subject and object, of "nonnatural" and natural, does not hold. "Satisfying" is a term that in this context signifies the capacity of the object to satisfy a disposition in the whole

---

[2] Moore, George E.: *Principia Ethica*. Cambridge, England, Cambridge University, 1903.

[3] I am here following the terminology of Morris, Charles: *Signs, Language, and Behavior*. New York, Prentice-Hall, 1946.

context of the continuum of the initiating subject preference, expectation, action of subject toward object, object preference, and the consummatory satisfaction. A need disposition leads to an idealized state of affairs; there is a transaction with a real object; and there is an integration of the ideal and real to form a new reality.

Thus an appraisive sign like "good" in its most elemental sense signifies, if reliable, the property of an object or context of objects, events, and relations capable of satisfying or fulfilling a preferential disposition. A prescriptive sign like "ought" signifies, if reliable, the action to be taken toward the object or context if satisfaction is to be realized. Also, certain actions can be called "good" while certain properties of objects or objects themselves can be signified as that which "ought" to be.[4] Normally, when something is appraised as good the appraisal is accompanied by a prescription to act preferentially toward it; but this is not always the case. One might signify food as good, but refrain from signifying the effort to get it in order for someone else more needful of it to have it. In spite of these complications, however, the problems of determining what is good and what ought to be done are both in principle decidable by empirical investigation into man and his interactions with objects.

"Ought" can signify also a kind of action that aims not at the fulfillment of a specific disposition, but at the fulfillment of man as man. Thus, from the humanistic position set forth in the last chapter we can affirm that man ought to fulfill himself *as man* and ought to avoid a dehumanized or nonhuman life. This is a categorical "ought"— prescribing "the good" in general for man, "the good life"—that presupposes a certain form of "good" to be realized as well as an appeal to a certain "is" or nature of man and his world. Such an ought is not entirely reducible to what actually is; for if man had already realized fulfillment as man there would be no point in prescribing that he realize that.

Yet as we saw in the previous chapter, the prescriptive *ought* of man's fulfillment must be grounded in the actuality of man and his world if it is to have any relevance to him whatsoever. This *is* is actual tendency toward realization. It is elicited, revealed, and developed

---

[4]Morris, Charles: *Signification and Significance.* Cambridge, Mass., M. I. T., 1964. I have slightly modified Morris' usage of these terms.

as it moves toward the form signified by the *ought*. If the *ought* is defined as *any* development of human tendencies, it becomes assimilated to the *is*, the distinction disappears, and so does the dialectic between the two. To act without choosing among possible alternatives perpetuates actuality indiscriminately without distinction of better and worse. The *ought* prescribes a selection and rejection among possibilities or tendencies already existing. In turn these tendencies of the *is* set the limits of the *ought*, so that the *ought* to be effective must always be a projection of what *is*, of what is in process, of what is possible. At the same time by selecting which tendencies are to be developed and in which order, the *ought* defines and determines the emergent *is*, eliciting and supplementing what already *is* by nature with the new *is* of creative decision. Thus, man's nature as a fulfilling nature is a growing creative synthesis of the *is* and of the *ought*, i.e., of (1) tendencies inherent in the body at birth plus these tendencies as modified and supplemented by future develpoment, and (2) the symbolic forms from which the creative person selects to emphasize, organize, guide, and progressively supplement those tendencies. In short, judgments derived from social life, values as ideals, work back upon the natural body and transform its activities while the body and these activities in turn set the limits and form the materials for such social values. Hence, it is impossible to separate, except for purposes of analysis, the biology of man from his sociology, the body of man from his mind, or the factuality of man from his ideality.

Yet precisely because of this duality and tension in man's condition, those who would present an authentic and integrated picture of man are sometimes caught in an unsolvable dilemma. On the one hand, to describe man just as he is, in all the variety of detail manifested by myriad individuals in diverse cultures, would be impossible. No anthropologist would attempt that. But even a selective definition of man, such as, "Man is a cultural species," which endeavors to differentiate man as a species, implies a norm and hence a distinction between man-as-a-better-man and man-as-a-worse-man. On this definition, other things being equal, a baby one month old is less human than an infant one year old, for it is more acculturated.

It has been fashionable in recent years among some, e.g., many scientists and positivists, to maintain a sharp distinction between informative and emotive language, between "objective" description and "value judgment." Such a distinction, however, does not stand up under investigation. In the case of determining what man is, for example, scientists or positivistic philosophers begin with the value judgment that it is better to take evidence rather than subjective wish or cultural tradition as the validating basis for statements about man. Moreover, what is taken as "evidence" is subject to decisions which may shift in the course of time. Why then is evidence defined, for example, by the standards of coherence, logic, and empirical test? Because the application of these standards appears in practice to produce what the investigators are interested in, namely, consistency among ideas and ideas that guide them in predicting and controlling the objects of the world. In the broad sense of the term, these standards facilitate "satisfaction" on the theoretical and practical levels. Man has needs to understand the world and to solve the problems that he encounters in it; and he has discovered through history that the most effective way to fulfill these needs is to apply to his ideas and statements criteria that take into account the character of the external world and his method of dealing with it. But why does he need to understand and adjust to the world? Ultimately, to survive and to fulfill his basic needs. Hence a "value-free" description or a "neutral" science is a fiction. Description of something in the external world always is a function of some man or group of men who have certain needs and interests toward that thing and world, and who therefore appraise things and prescribe actions toward them in preferential ways. As they discover features of things these in turn react back upon appraisal and prescription. The result is that inquiry is a dialectical process between man and the world, and the standards for determining value and truth develop in this process.

Similarly, as we determine what it means to *be* human, we also determine the *value* of being human. To describe man is implicitly to choose a certain kind of human life; to signify an ideal for man is to presuppose something about his existing being. Historically men have displayed two extremes in dealing with the relation between the really human and the ideally human. Some have sharply separated the two, asserting that the "higher" value for man is some supernatural principle or being radically different from man's natural body and the domain of society and nature. Such supernaturalism or transcendentalism has been the common ideology of those religions serving as the major ideological tool by which ruling groups maintained power and suppressed the masses. Such dualism of value and fact, spirit and nature, and divine and human, reflected and secured the existing dualism of social classes. When some critics, as in Hinduism and Christianity, dared to assert that there is a real, though not immediately apparent, identity between the divine and man, then the ruling theology answered—either (as in Hinduism) by acknowledging the identity, but holding that men occupy different positions in an ascending hierarchy of levels of spirituality; or (as in Christianity) by holding the claim of identity to be heretical. The Christian mystics, communalists, and others who made this idealistic claim were, unlike the conservative ruling classes whom they opposed, humanistic in thought. But because they tended to affirm the spirituality of man primarily in thought, independently of clearly developed plans of action for changing existing society, the net effect of their utopian position was ineffectual and conservative.

At the other extreme from supernaturalism and idealism we see the various kinds of philosophical naturalism and materialism, certain forms of Taoism, the Charvaka school, the Greek atomists, the mechanical materialists of the seventeenth and eighteenth centuries in Europe, and others. Such views tended to assimilate the ideal to the present state of things. But the emphasis on the materiality of man's nature has throughout history been used with two quite different motives. Some materialists, influenced by developments in the sciences, have assaulted the claims of supernaturalism. To this extent their ideas represented or were used by an insurgent class against a ruling class, e.g., by the French industrialists, technicians, and other bourgeois against the feudalists of the late eighteenth century. They wished to change the present state of things, and saw materialism as a tool for doing that.

However, materialism of various kinds has been used by ruling classes to achieve or maintain their power, and we can find spokesmen for this elitist position in China (the Legalists), in India, and in the West (Machiavelli). Thus, their interest in the existing bodies and powers of man and of nature came not from the desire to change things, but from the desire to maintain and increase the control of a ruling group over the masses. For this kind of elitist the knowledge of power and power politics became necessary for the exploitive manipulation of people and social forces. As with the conservative who appealed to some "higher" value to reinforce his own position of superiority, this conservative looked with cynical contempt on the material realities and values of the masses.

The impasse between radicals and conservatives, between humanists and antihumanists, was first broken when humanists began to understand the origin and function of ideas in relation to material forces in history. But such understanding was not purely theoretical; it was the reflex of a real movement of workers against the oppression of capitalism, just as the impasse in theory was a reflex of a real material opposition of classes. Reflecting this movement, Marx was the first systematically to point out how ideas arise in response to the material and class structure of society, and how in turn they can be used by man to guide material and social change. If one looks to social *practice,* to the demands of men to live and to liberate themselves from the contradictions between their needs (and idealized values projected from those needs) and their real existences, one sees that both ideal and material, subjective and objective factors must be taken into consideration. Circumstances change men, and men, through rational, social activity, change circumstances. The theory of such dialectic is neither idealism nor materialism in the traditional senses. For such activity is *"revolutionizing practice,"* as Marx said in *Theses on Feuerbach.* The concept of dialectical materialism is the ideational form of a practice that overcomes the traditional division between man's thought and the real world, between the mind and "spirit" of the ruling classes and the bodily labor of the masses. This new concept negates and transforms the opposites of traditional idealism and materialism, just as the social humanism of revolutionizing practice transforms traditional practices—the limited humanistic practices of both religious, idealistic utopianism and "scientific" mechanical materialism, and the inhumanism of religious, idealistic conservatism and of "realistic" conservatism.

Bourgeois science and philosophy, which defined their position *vis à vis* the dualism of religious supernaturalism, have tended to assert that all descriptions of man must be free of considerations of value. If, further, it is said, as said here, that the process of evaluation is inherent in all description, they ask how it is possible to arrive at any universally valid and "objective" definition of man. A large number of ideal values have throughout history been proposed for the human species. At least some, perhaps most, of these have been false and destructive values, the most recent example being the Nazi ideal of the superior Aryan race. But the bourgeois question about the possibility of an "objective" and value-free definition of man is a "pseudo-question" based on a false, class-bound assumption of the separability of fact and value. The question is: Can we objectively discover man's generic value-tendencies and fulfillments?

When some philosophers became concerned about man and his fulfillment, notably during the classical periods of Greek, Indian, and Chinese philosophy, and then during the European Renaissance, the problem assumed to them a rather simple form. In contrast to religious views, they sought to locate the good of man not in the supernatural gods or the gods' decrees, but in nature, and consequently in man as a part of nature. They took seriously man's experiences of values, success in achieving his practical purposes, knowledge, love, friendship, beauty, joy, etc. If man, then, can be, or become, or possess good, what is it that prevents or limits him from doing so? It must be that man is *potentially* good in *himself,* otherwise how could he *become* good? Therefore, the obstructions must lie outside the real nature of man. The way to secure the realization of the good of man is to clear away the obstacles, much as a farmer might clear away the obstacles to his naturally growing and developing crops, or as a physician might clear away the obstacles to the naturally health-giving processes of the body. Let man do what comes naturally in order to become a man; let the inherent "nature" of man be "natured" itself into full realization. (The Latin *natura* is from *natus,* the participle of *nasci,* to be born.) Hence the idea of fulfillment as recorded in the dictionary—"to realize or manifest completely."

Consequently, emphasis in these philosophies fell on the nature of man as given prior to society, i.e., the inborn, antecedently determined, fixed nature of man, whether this was conceived as a spiritual principle (as in Confucianism, Vedanta, Platonism, etc.), as a semibiological principle (as in Aristotle), or as a physical principle (as in the materialists). This means, then, that the social relations of the individual man, the society in which he lives, cannot positively affect what he is; at best they can merely release an antecedent nature.

Similarly, among the humanists of the Renaissance the great cry was for liberation from conditions which oppressed and crippled a prior, and inherently good, human nature. What this meant among the more advanced thinkers was liberation from oppressive conditions imposed by church or state. Once man was thus liberated, so the theory ran, then his individual and social life would develop naturally and automatically into a harmonious order—a common ideal pictured differently by Thomas More, Montaigne, and Bacon, anticipated by the medieval Brethren of the Free Spirit, and carried into the modern period by men like Rousseau and Adam Smith. Modern humanists located the principles of man's fulfillment in the "laws of nature," either divinely given (Leibniz, Locke), or autonomous (Diderot, La Mettrie, Holbach).

The evolution of social relations in the life of the individual and society, the interdependence of man and man, and the social nature of man, had not fully dawned on them. The fiction of a "social contract" had to be added to the fiction of preexisting individuals in order to explain and justify society and its government. A deep understanding of the true social nature of man, anticipated by thinkers like Eckhart, Spinoza, Rousseau and Owen, had not yet developed. The common appeal of humanists up to the nineteenth century was to a divine indwelling Spirit, innate "rights," "reason," "passions" (Fourier), "the law of righteousness . . . established in [man's] heart" (Winstanley), or some other innate quality which only needed to be elicited. This view reflected the rising bourgeois order wherein individual men might, by their own enterprizing efforts, achieve economic success and thus become "self-made" men.

On the other side, absolutely idealism (Hegel) was an attempt to shows the organic interrelatedness of all things, though at the price of wiping away the particular individual. It represented the *illusory* and *idealized* side of individualism. For the Absolute is a supreme individual, modeled on the subjective experience of the isolated human ego. In the case of atomic individualism, the causes of the individual's character lie in his nature prior to birth, in his "reason" or in his "will." In the case of idealism, these causes lie in the Absolute, or God. (Calvin brought these two nations together.) In both cases education, social relations, and society are derivative. History is thought to be made by individuals or by God, and not by his social relations and social forces. In the one, the stress was all on activity and appropriation; in the other, on passivity and being appropriated.

Marx was among the first to grasp the profoundly social nature of man and the significance of this fact. That he was able to do so was due to his inheritance of the dialectical method from Hegel, and his application of this to historical and contemporary economic conditions. Thus, the *sociality* of man was evident to him in the productive process of the nineteenth century factory system. But even before his economic analyses Marx had in his early writings explored the relation of man to man and produced penetrating insights into its social character. "*Just* as society itself produces *man* as *man,* so is society *produced* by him. Activity and consumption, both in their content and in their *mode of existence,* are *social*: *social* activity and *social* consumption." [5] Marx illuminated this concept by its opposite, that of *alienation,* and his later work was concerned with the dynamics of the causes of this opposition. Hence, he did not work out the direct implications of this early social psychology. But his view represented both a negation and a supersession of the individualistic and absolute idealistic views; it gave due emphasis to both individual and social poles in a dialectical relation.

Marx's view should be contrasted with the existentialist view which denies that man has a distinctive structure either prior to society or in his social relations—a view that is itself an antithesis to the traditional deterministic views of individualism and idealism, and that, like Kierkegaard's and Nietzsche's, opposes the dehumanizing trends of mass society. Sartre, for instance, while he holds that "the for-itself causes a human-reality to exist as a species," [6] at the same time says "freedom has no essence." [7] For Marx, man is his self-activity, his

[5]Marx, Karl: *Economic and Philosophic Manuscripts of 1844,* pp. 103-104.

[6]Sartre, Jean-Paul: *Being and Nothingness. An Essay in Phenomenological Ontology,* trans. by Hazel E. Barnes. New York, Philosophical Library, 1956, p. 551.

[7]*Ibid.,* p. 428.

project, his self-realization; here he agrees so far with the existentialists who have given up seeking the Hegelian *Geist* in its cosmic setting and have found its habitat to be human history. At the same time man has, for Marx, a definite form of development determined by antecedent biological tendencies and social and natural forces. What does it mean to say that man is thus determined, except that his nature dialectically develops as a bio-social-ecological process? Man *always,* as man, has certain biological needs (hunger, thirst, etc.). He *always* is born into an environment which is biophysical and with which he, through exchanges, maintains himself. He is *always* born into a society and he *always* develops in it and becomes human in, and through, his social relations to others. He always learns certain patterns of behavior from others through symbolic processes, communicates with others, and participates, as patient and agent, in the transmission of cultural patterns to the new generation. These are the variables whose values are determined by the whole context, and whose interaction, unity, and evolution define the developing human being.

A biological need is never a mere animal need; it is always interpreted, expressed and modified, frustrated and satisfied in a social context. The measure of whether it *is* human is the degree and character of its socialization. The need is affected by the biophysical environment where the infant is born and reared. Climate, natural resources, terrain, etc., which are in turn affected by society, and its needs as determined in that particular ecological context, will shape the personality of the infant. Finally, infant and society create one another. For the infant has direct interaction with others in primary relations, and he adopts, through reciprocal adjustment, the folkways of those around him via the meanings, techniques, and tools that mediate his behavior in relation to persons and to things.

Hence man has an absolute or invariant human nature in that this nature always emerges and develops in the same way; but the particular form of that nature is relative and varies according to the nature of the various forces, including man's own creative activity, whose intersection produces the particular man. Man has a "species-life" that reveals itself under all social conditions, even those of degradation. The definition of man's species-life emerges in the biosocial actualization of "the capabilities of his species." [8] What are these capabilities? The inclusive or generic one is the disposition to productive relations with others and the natural world. "Productivity" here means the creation of the self, of others, of social relations and habits, of tools and machines, and of products fashioned out of natural resources like soil, minerals, plants, and animals. Thus the realization of man's species-capabilities is a social-natural complex, spread out in space, interpenetrating nature, and ongoing through time. This species-capability includes as subcapabilities the need-dispositions to live, struggle, think, sense and feel, elaborate one's powers, communicate, co-operate, imagine, achieve identity, discover others, transform nature, create values that will satisfy needs, exchange values, transform values, etc. Man's one dominant need and drive is the drive toward many-sided "all-round development." [9] And while in achieving this some of his acts may be destructive—e.g., the destruction of false ideas, of prejudice, of ignorance, and of disease and cruelty—such destruction must always be for the sake of creation of more fully developed human beings in a system of society and nature in which the elements are mutually supporting.

Marx observed that the social system of capitalism is inimical to man's development as man. The species-capabilities are there, but they are "crippled" and "dehumanized." Why is this? The relations of men determined by property relations—buying, selling, exploiting others, etc.—have become "fetters" binding and contradicting the productive and social process. Collectively, the producers revolt against such conditions. A struggle ensues and in society is fought out along class lines between rulers and ruled. Humanistically, what these fetters, contradictions, and struggle mean for the individual is that his productive capacities as a man, a real and a potential man, have been thwarted and that he rebels and struggles against them. He drives toward removing the contradiction and the fetters, but not alone, for he is a social being bound to the company of fellow-sufferers and fellow-rebels. That is to say, the species-capability of man drives

---

[8] Marx, Karl: *Capital. A Critical Analysis of Capitalist Production,* trans. from the third German edition by Samuel Moore and Edward Aveling, Frederick Engels (Ed.). Moscow, Foreign Languages Publishing House, ND., vol. I, p. 329.

[9] Marx, Karl: *Critique of the Gotha Programme,* p. 27.

toward preservation and fulfillment and asserts itself in the face of obstacles. It is aroused and wakened to new critical consciousness and practical activity by the fetters of its oppression. It is resolved to destroy the crippling and dehumanizing contradictions in its life precisely because it is driven by an instinctive and socially produced need to be itself by becoming itself. This is an affirmation toward increasing and strengthening integrity with oneself, with others, and with the natural world.

The bio-social-ecological view of man grows out of man's social practice. In contrast, traditional views have stressed the innate or external determination of man and have minimized the reconstruction of the environment. The environment was thought to receive its order from natural or divine forces, or from the conjunction of individual wills. The bio-social-ecological view does not deny the existence of antecedent factors in the production of man nor does it deny differences between men. It asserts that man always *evolves* in consequence of the interaction of biological, social, and ecological forces whose potentialities are realized in that interaction. Consequently, man can be realized in different ways, depending on the ingredient forces and the character of their interaction. The evidence for this changeability of man, Marx and Engels observed, may be found in an examination of different historical epochs, with their different social and ecological situations. The practical, scientific implication then leaps to mind: if man's realization has changed as his conditions of life have changed, cannot man himself, by deliberate experimental intervention, change those conditions and so change himself? This indeed is what the socialists, utopian and otherwise, had realized before Marx and Engels.

A common procedure in the natural sciences is to discover some entity in its natural state (say, an organic compound), to produce it by deliberate effort ("artificially"), and then to use it in the control and relief of man's estate (hormones, vitamins, antibiotics). The utopians, having made their discovery of the social nature of man, found it impossible to produce and synthesize their model communities within established society. And so, outside of it, their experiments often succeeded for a period, and then failed. They failed because, unlike a new synthesis in a chemical laboratory, they could not survive the circumambient social conditions, both internal and external.

Owen's son described the members of his father's colony in New Harmony as "a heterogeneous collection of radicals, enthusiastic devotees of principle, honest latitudinarians and lazy theorists, with a sprinkling of unprincipled sharpers thrown in." [10] All were products of an unsocial, dehumanized society. Also the larger American society was dominated by the god of money and the fetish of private property.

The advanced grasp of the concept of social change and its successful application awaited the advanced development of the reality of social change, i.e., the interaction of men in large factories, trade unions, urban neighborhoods, and other associations.

The concept of a truly humanized man is thus the reflex of observing what man *is* in a dehumanized economy, inferring what he is *not*, and then imagining what he might be in a humanized economy. The bourgeois revolution against the shackles of the feudal order called forth a deeper, but historically doomed, revolution of the lowest classes, the peasants and the plebians, whose vision of man's possibilities went beyond that of the new bourgeois. Similarly, in the twentieth century this consciousness of man's capabilities, generated under capitalism, has acted back upon the social system to produce revolutionary changes in it and to extend the view of that consciousness. The optimism about man's perfectibility that was proclaimed by the Renaissance humanists —contemporary with bourgeois optimism and consequently individualistic and limited—has now spread to millions. Their daily practice, the changes in themselves and their fellow man that they have witnessed in their own lifetimes, are testimony to the fact that man can change man by collectively changing the social and ecological conditions of his life. To find out what capabilities a thing has, one must act upon it. To find out *what* capabilities a man has, that man must act and react. Capabilities are then defined by that interaction.

But, it will objected, man has many capabilities, including capabilities for idleness, egoism, parasitism, greed, deception, distrust, hate, torture, exploitation, and so on. What makes us believe that the pattern of development described by socialist humanists is any more human than any other pattern? Is not the selection of the pattern purely arbitrary? Is not this particularly so if it is admitted that man has no

---

[10] Quoted in an article, Communistic settlements, secular. In Ferm, Vergilius (Ed.): *An Encyclopedia of Religion*. New York, Philosophical Library, 1945, p. 189.

antecedent and fixed nature? And if this is so, then are we not reduced to the conclusion of Sartre, that since man always seems to be pursuing some projected goal, striving to fulfill some capability, the only thing that matters in human life is not the goal of man but his "degree of consciousness" of his goal.[11]

The first point resolves itself into the meaning of "capability." As noted, we cannot understand what man *can* do except as we observe what he *does* do. But he cannot do *anything*, he cannot survive, apart from some social existence. Man is not born like a solitary wasp, nor does he live like a hermit crab, nor is he a bisexual organism who reproduces himself. This means that whatever capabilities he does develop are developed in a social-ecological context. But all such contexts exhibit certain constant characteristics. We have already cited the statement of one anthropologist, Clyde Kluckhohn, that "no culture tolerates indiscriminate lying, stealing, or violence within the group." Kluckhohn lists other cultural constants:

> The essential universality of the incest taboo is well known. No culture places a value upon suffering as an end in itself. . . . We know of no culture in either space or time . . . . that does not ceremonialize the fact of death . . . . all cultures define as abnormal individuals who are permanently inaccessible to communication or who consistently fail to maintain some degree of control over their impulse life. Social life is impossible without communication, without some measure of order: the behavior of any "normal" individual must be predictable—with a certain range— by his fellows and interpretable by them.[12]

Few, if any, anthropologists would take issue with this small set of cultural constants. Many, in fact, would extend the list. George Peter Murdock, for example, lists more than seventy items which to his knowledge occur "in every culture known to history or ethnography." They include—to select what seem some more significant items for the present analysis—community organization, cooperative labor, division of labor, education, ethics, family, folklore, government, language, law, medicine, property rights, toolmaking, and trade.[13] Aside from the corectness of such a list as an empirical description, it is necessary to

---

[11]Sartre, Jean-Paul: *Being and Nothingness,* p. 627.

[12]Kluckhohn, Clyde, *op. cit.,* 344-345.

[13]Murdock, George Peter: The common denominator of cultures. In Linton, Ralph (Ed.): *The Science of Man in the World Crisis.* New York, Columbia, 1945, p. 124.

ask philosophically whether certain items express, or are reducible to, certain generic components—whether the items as such are contingent in some respects, or whether they are recurrent and necessary. For example, it would seem that community organization and toolmaking are more probably necessary than hair styles. If hair styles represent the needs of human beings to express their common and individualized identities and to observe such identities in others, then conceivably these needs might without loss be expressed in other forms of bodily modification. Speaking generally, we can say that all cultures exhibit a self-identical pattern because they are defined by individuals with similar biosocially defined needs who face and solve similar problems in similar social and natural environments. The result is similar techniques emerging in this interaction, the techniques of social, cooperative, symbol-using communicative activity.

The second point is that the transformation process by which man (either as individual neonate or species) passes from the prehuman to the human is definitive of his human nature. Man's *natura* is something born, produced, a structured process that continues from birth to death. The choice for man, then, is whether he wishes to amplify and develop that humanizing process.

This question is an urgent practical one. In fact, it does not resolve into a question at all, except for those spirits who have been crippled by despair and debate seriously with themselves (and it is a *subjective* debate) the question of whether "to be or not to be." Man exists. He concentrates all his energies on surviving: he struggles against strangling, against physical confinement, against hunger and thirst. Now what does this brute, categorical fact mean? Analyze it in its causes, its setting, its implications, its consequences. Man as a species has evolved over millions of years, surviving because he developed adaptive mechanisms for dealing with dangers, adversities, and values. He is a social creature and a communicative one. He plans and executes plans. A pattern of human life, of human direction and fulfillment, is all there, if ever so seldom completed by any one person, let alone any society of persons. The patterns spells what it means to be human. We can choose to be human in many different ways (within limits) but it is unlikely that we can choose to be nonhuman altogether unless we give up living altogether.

But to choose to be human in any one of these many specific ways means to choose to be human in a generic way. What does that mean? We cannot know completely, either in the abstract or the concrete; though unless we know something of the outlines of what man is and therefore ought to become, we could take no action whatsoever. To choose genuinely and authentically to be human means to commit oneself to man's development. This means that one must search diligently for the conditions that conduce to that development. And this means to seek a description of man that can become a means of changing the world, and through it changing man. The description of man as expropriated and exploited is one such description. It implies a social program of expropriating the expropriators, i.e., of removing a source of man's dehumanization and of liberating more fully his human capabilities. Those who feel that man's capabilities are fully or sufficiently defined under the class system are not disposed to offer a definition of man or a social program that will change man. They do not believe that man needs to, or can, or ought to, discover and create himself. Indeed, he is already defined by his position in the social order. Consequently, the definition they offer of man is conservative: it is drawn from what man is in his present society, i.e., what he appears to be, and it is designed to conserve that society with its definition of "man." What man generally *is* includes what he *might* be, i.e., his capabilities. But the radical definition of man goes to the *root* of the human situation, and proclaims that man can *grow* into a fuller manhood if in thought and practice he will grasp the conditions of his life and control them as means to that growth. Thus, the radical man emphasizes the *developmental* capabilities of man; the generic and hence *common* character of these capabilities; the social or *cooperative* capabilities of man; and the fact that through *practical,* revolutionizing activity man changes and develops himself. By contrast, the conservative approach to the problem of man is static, elitist, individualistic, and hostile to great social change.

The radical approach to man cannot deny a certain kind of conserving activity, for such activity is generic to man and necessary to his fulfillment. In order to develop creatively, man must conserve the basic pattern of his individual and social life and his relations to nature, as well as the conditions necessary to maintaining and elaborating that pattern. Conservation here means the avoidance of wastage of natural resources and human energies and products. It means that whatever is destroyed—materials, human relations, achieved values like buildings and books—must be destroyed with a purpose that is productive of the optimum human value in the long run. Far from being concerned about the future generations of mankind and the advancement of values through a historical process, the egocentric political and economic conservative wishes to hold things and values as they are, to arrest them around the present, or to "return" to some fancied "golden age" of the past. For if he believed in conserving natural resources for future generations of mankind (and not just for the progeny of an élite) he would express a concern for others which is not evident. The word "conservation" in his mouth means: prevent broad social changes so that I and my élite may continue to enjoy the privileges conferred by our private wealth and power. The radical, by contrast, wishes to conserve so that all men might be more creative. This is the difference between conserving for the sake of conserving the imaginary human welfare of a few, and conserving for the sake of advancing the real human welfare of all.

The radical feels his kinship with other men acutely, he takes their role sympathetically, and he is able to sacrifice his own immediate interests and pleasures for the sake of a future and general good. Consequently, he sees himself as partial owner and trustee of the resources of nature and the cultural resources of the human race, so that these may be passed down to future generations in a way that will best serve them. In this sense the radical, and only the radical, is the truly human conservative. For only the love of man for man, the desire to conserve and develop the most precious thing that man knows—namely, man— can impel and justify this kind of conservation.

Someone may reply that a man is always free to commit suicide, that it is not compulsory for him to live, that he may, as Sartre says, always call himself and his career into question. That is true. But what does this prove? The method and direction of men's choices do not come out of thin air; they are the result of the convergence of specific physical, biological, and social conditions. Just as the disposition to commit suicide can be changed by changed circumstances, so it is generated by different circumstances. Statistically, relatively few persons do commit suicide even under the worst conditions, and relatively few persons are prepared to instigate genocide or widespread extermination of peoples through modern war. *Pari passu,* most people would dismiss as unduly imaginative or demented the suggestion that they adopt, as a whole, and as a positive philosophy, the path of suicide. What is the explanation for this? It is that the circumstances of human life are such that they produce an affirmation of life and a denial of death. In spite of the upsurge of destructive and morbid persons, classes, and conditions in human history, the predominant trend has been toward the preservation and development of human life. Philosophers at various times thoughout history have been opposed to this trend. But most of them have been in favor of *some* form of human life, if only for themselves or some élite such as the ruling class. And ascetics and life-deniers who took their own doctrines seriously have ordinarily not convinced large masses of people of their doctrine. To do so would end in a contradiction destructive of the pursuit of suicide itself.

Where, then, does the living philosopher begin? With his own life, and the lives of others, with whom he is inextricably bound up. Once this basic premise is accepted, then what? His task is to examine and elaborate the full meaning of the enterprize of life-affirmation. What is man? What is his relation to his fellow man, in virtue of which he becomes human and develops in a human way? What is his relation to the world? What ought he to do in relation to that world, to himself, and to his fellow man? How does he know what is and ought to be? Philosophers throughout history have diverged in many ways, in part because of differences in the conditions of their life, in part because of temperamental and constitutional differences. But insofar as the conditions of their life become more and more common—insofar as the people of the planet move toward a single society—and insofar as they collectively concentrate in practice on creating a more human world for all men—then insofar will their ideas converge and a worldwide, universally human philosophy will emerge.

Thus questions centering around the nature, causes, consequences, and obstacles of man's fulfillment are preeminently *practical* questions. How is it possible to *know* what it means to be human unless one and one's associates behave in a human way? Such human behavior is not merely instinctual and customary. It moves toward its completion and fulfillment when men themselves exert an effort to be human, when they struggle, labor, think, and cooperate with others to discover and produce the conditions of their common life that will release their full potential for human activity. At the same time man is *impelled* to live and develop by the deepest disposition that is in him. But to follow this disposition steadfastly is to bring thought into full play in all its powers, as an instrument to the fulfillment of that disposition. Thus in the interplay of thought and labor, of the individual and others, of social activity and the objects of nature, man moves into the form of a fulfilled humanity.

Man is, so far as he *is,* active and exploratory, securing control over the things and events of his world by means of productive action on them. He exacts a living from nature by means of action upon it, shaping tools to facilitate his power of perception, manipulation, insight, and foresight. But he cannot experience or know the full meaning of his power of control until he and indeed all men exert themselves with optimum energy to control their lives. Men, to be men, must collectively eliminate what threatens and undermines their existence (natural disasters, hunger, disease, poverty, etc.). They must bring to pass what will safeguard and develop them—an economy owned and controlled by all, eliciting from each his maximum ability and returning to each as he needs; educational opportunity for all, adapted to the distinctive needs, talents, and interests of all; etc.

Man is, so far as he is, a sensitive being, capable of reverberating to the qualities around him in the natural and human world as these appear in his tranactions with things and persons. He feels finely and profoundly a great variety and range of affects. These extend from the subtle qualities of color and sound, to the tidal human emotions of love, indignation, sorrow, hope, fervor, and the ecstasy of union with some transcendent project in art, science, politics, and religion, or in a significant human association. But man cannot experience or know the full meaning of his sensitivity until he and all men exert themselves collectively, in thought and action, to transform the conditions of their living. For it is man's exertion, the conditions around him, and the interaction of the two, which produce change and growth in man's sensitivity. Man is born sensitive, with an all-round sensitivity unmatched among creatures on the planet. But he cannot enter into the full development of his sensitive powers until he becomes sensitive enough to sense the need for nurturing and developing that sensitivity through his own critical and social action.

Man is, so far as he is, a thinking creature. He early acquires the use of symbols and through their production and combination he remembers, senses and analyzes problems, forms plans, deduces and predicts consequences, and prospectively and retrospectively relates himself to others and the world. As he becomes social he acquires the power of thought, which in turn facilitates his social powers. He thinks theoretically and practically. Indeed, he thinks in as many ways as there are modes of symbolic expression: scientifically, pictorially, philosophically, poetically, politically, etc. To think is to weave a network of meanings around the world of one's experiences, thus relating the self retrospectively and prospectively to that world. But man cannot experience or know the full meaning of his power of thought until he and all men exert themselves to think through and act out what must be done to transform their processes of thought into more comprehensive, precise, and effective forms.

Man is, so far as he is, social and communicative. The upsurge and elaboration of his life of action, of feeling, and of thought comes in and through his intimate relations with others, relations of common work, action, and interaction with them, relations arousing common and diversified feelings, relations stimulating, creating, destroying, and remaking thought. While man's relations with the world of natural objects and of artifacts made by man evoke and form his life and activity as human, the originating and most profound changes in him come from his communicative relations with others—not merely linguistic communications, but the whole complex of signs and symbols of the human community, including words, facial expressions, gestures, postures, sounds, tools, skills and techniques, etc.

But man's power to communicate is confined and hobbled by the forms of his economic, social, and individual life. The deepest communication of man with man occurs in a revolutionary situation, when together men are working towards goals that transcend their own immediate welfare, and that include the welfare of individuals and groups other than themselves. They communicate their common dangers, sacrifices, sufferings, hopes, and aspirations and break down the barriers of protective selves. In turn, their communication advances their common cause. But in an extremely impoverished society adversity may reduce communication to an almost animal level. And in an affluent society, in the absence of any transcendent goal, communication becomes a pathic way of expressing individualistic values, of controlling, manipulating, and exploiting others, or of learning to conform to the values of others. When men have no revolutionary purpose to impel, direct, or use them and draw them out of themselves, they turn inward and begin to use and feed on one another. Man cannot experience or know his full communicative power until all men exert themselves to provide the conditions to bring forth that power. Men must together act, think, feel, communicate—with the end in view of discovering and providing the conditions that will release new communication. Then man will begin to know the meaning of his fulfillment as a communicative creature.

Apart from a continuing, revolutionary transformation in man's communicative relations, what happens to man? He settles down into the dulling routine of customary, stereotyped, rigidly ceremonial forms of communication. He is consequently isolated from others in the sense that what he has in common with them is impoverished; hence he loses the meaning of what they are in their unique individuality as well as, in equal degree, a sense of his own active and productive individuality. He becomes an exploitive or "other-directed" personality seeing others as specific objects either to be used or to conform to. His resourcefulness and sense of responsibility are impaired because they are not elicited and practiced. The life of his feeling remains latent, inchoate, vague, and weak; his affect flattens out and becomes passive insofar as his relations with others are not intimate, vigorous, and active in drawing out and vivifying his powers to sense and feel. Similarly, his thought suffers; it becomes superficial, fragmentary, disorganized, subjective, illusory. It becomes uncertain, unpurposeful, and unclear, like his feeling and activity. Is it possible for a society that possesses an abundance of material goods and services for its people to produce this deterioration in man's communicative life and hence in man? Of course it is. The socializing of the means of production does not necessarily mean that men will carry forward indefinitely a revolution in their communicative relations, though certainly it disposes men in that direction. This is in part the problem that the recent "cultural revolution" in China has focussed on.

Man is, so far as he is, a cooperative being. He emerges into being as his biological impulses encounter the activity of others, and as a systematic and cooperative mode of adjustment ensues between those others and his own activity. He meets his needs and develops new needs and satisfactions as he successfully enters into cooperation with others. Cooperative activity calls forth new energies, new morale, new feelings and aspirations, new ideas and plans, new activities. It stimulates and reinforces man's exertions and creates in him a sense of security and solidarity. It meets his deep need to develop his individuality in a dialectical relation to others. Cooperative activity corrects, changes, and redirects the individual's activities, thoughts, and feelings. Apart from it, the individual tends to lose his sense of reality, to become subjective and autistic, to develop distorted perspectives about what is significant, to degrade or idolize others and himself. For human reality is defined precisely by the impact of others upon us, as well as by the impact of things that we experience through activity upon them. "Truth" in human affairs is reached through the funding and mutual correction and corroboration of perspectives, both through social exchange and through cooperative, active inquiry into a common world.

Man cannot experience or know the full meaning of the power of cooperation until all men exert themselves to make an environment that will bring forth that power. Cooperating to produce the economic basis of a socialistic society is the first step of many. Patterns of sensitivity and responsiveness, of initiative and responsibility, of criticism and self-criticism must be developed throughout the whole society, in all institutional life. Goals and methods must come under vigilant, continual, and widespread scrutiny, criticism, and evaluation on the part of the people. Only in this way can the revolutionizing activity moving men from individualism to collectivism, from egoism to cooperation, from exploitation to mutual aid and mutual improvement, be maintained and advanced.

Now we have arrived at the question of how it is possible to validate the conception of the value, the fulfillment, of man. In the sciences and common sense, we say that a proposed idea (proposition) is validated to the extent that a variety of investigators, using observation, reason and practice under specified conditions, find the idea to be true, i.e., correctly descriptive of a state of affairs. This validation process involves not only repetition of a certain specified activity by a single observer under specified conditions, but also mutual corroboration of an indefinite number of observers. Similarly, with respect to the problem of discovering and validating a pattern of good carpentry (as a pattern of thought or practice) we would accept the critical consensus of all who are capable of practicing the craft, who have engaged in the craft industriously, and whose analyzed, tested, reanalyzed, and retested observations, reasonings, and actions indicate better and worse ways of carpentering and hence an ideally "best" way.

How might we then discover the "best way" of being human, of developing the craft of humanization? In an analogous fashion: we would consult and accept the critical consensus of all those who are capable of practicing the craft, who have engaged in it industriously, and whose analyzed, tested, reanalyzed, and retested experiences indicate better and worse ways of being human and hence an ideally "best" way. Here the whole developmental, dialectical, and self-corrective method of the sciences is implied. The most reliable way of discovering the truth in any matter is to have some experience and knowledge in the field of observation in question: to coordinate it with relevant, expert, and established knowledge; to prepare a hypothesis, derived from a theoretical scheme; to deduce its consequences in the form of predicting for sensory observation and action; to devise experiments under particular conditions with specified tools; to analyze the observed results of such experiments; to note wherein those results conform to, or depart from, predictions and the body of established knowledge by checking these analyses with others and discussing them with others; to revise the hypothesis and repeat the procedure with all necessary changes; to repeat this procedure and have others do so from various perspectives so as to understand their corrections and to test and correct their corrections; and to do all this until the hypothesis is progressively freed of contradiction with perspectives established in these ways.[14]

_____

[14]The application of the principle of noncontradiction here means that a proposi-

The conditions necessary for the method to go forward are important: the investigator must be equipped with the observational sensitivity, manipulative skills, and symbolic techniques required to give him access to the relevant data; the range and variety of perspectives, including theory that coordinates these, already established in the field must be taken into account; the hypothesis brought forward must be by definition something *proposed,* something uncertain and yet to be tested and proved; the hypothesis must be based on previous observation and knowledge, i.e., a relevant tradition—but it must go beyond that, in the form of prediction and probing action; some program of practical observations and experimental actions must be thought of and pursued; the conditions, procedures, and usage of the tools of the experiment must be specified and limited, thus excluding as irrelevant the perspectives of those who do not conform to the limitations of those conditions, procedures, and usage of tools; within these limitations the conditions must be varied as much as possible to establish the invariance of the general pattern; the observations, analyses, and criticisms of others in the field are essential at every step in the production of a critical, growing consensus; the experiment with its observations must be repeated and the formulated results analyzed by a variety of persons and confirmed by them as their various perspectives converge on a common conclusion.

How then shall we validate any given idea of human fulfillment? We must do so by critical, social *practice,* i.e., by the kind of investigative activity just described. But the crucial question is, who shall do the investigating? In a given scientific field, such as biochemistry, we say that only those capable, trained, and experienced in the subject in a competent way can be reliable investigators. In matters of human fulfillment, who are the capable, competent investigators?

Two main answers have been given to this question. The first is that of the conservative elitist. He contends that only a few select persons

---

tion—e.g., "This is a chair in this room here and now"—cannot be both true and false. But the notion of truth here requires in our perspectives and formulations the reflection of the movement, change, and opposition in the real world. For example, the proposition, "This chair is both chair and nonchair: its identity is changing into its nonidentity," is a true proposition. As such, it cannot be false. See Somerville, John: *The Philosophy of Marxism. An Exposition.* New York, Random, 1967.

are capable and competent to define human fulfillment. Indeed, for him most people do not only not know what their own good is; they could not on their own achieve it if given the chance. In short, they are not as fully human and hence not as valuable as the élite.

The other answer is given by the democratic radical. For him all persons are capable of experiencing and understanding the meaning of human fulfillment, for the simple reason that all, as human, contain the possibilities for human development. One person may be more endowed with a genetic potential for observation and intelligence, another may be naturally stronger, another more sensitive esthetically, etc. One may constitutionally tend to be active, another dependent, another detached.[15] Again, because of arrangements in the social order, one may have more opportunity to develop his talents, and hence his human character. But the pattern of the dialectical human development is the same in all men; in principle all men can experience and understand and practice it.

The idea of human fulfillment is by definition an idea that applies to *all* men. To be true it must be exemplified *universally*. But the problem consists in precisely the fact that in the full concreteness of being, it is *not* exemplified universally. Therefore, in order for it to be exemplified universally, it must be *achieved* by all men. Human fulfillment is not something antecedently finished, like the laws of planetary motions, waiting there to be found and described in pictorial or mathematical fashion. It is, rather, like a species of wheat, which is discovered in a natural state but must also be cultivated and selectively nurtured. But if it must be achieved by all men, then all men must in some sense be investigators. For the *achievement* or *creation* of fulfillment is also the exploratory *discovery* of fulfillment. That is, whatever the achievement of human fulfillment consists in concretely, it must always involve the free investigative activity described. Neither psychological expert, philosopher, nor political ruler can achieve my fulfillment for me. I must engage myself in my own self-creation. This means that I become simultaneously investigator and investigated. My effort to live the good life, expressed in some particular program of activity, is a hypothesis proposed, tried out in practice, revised in the

---

[15]Sheldon, William S., with the collaboration of Stevens, S. S., and Tucker, W. B.: *The Varieties of Human Physique.* New York and London, Harper, 1940.

light of observation and criticism, and reproposed in the form of some new effort. Thus I am my own subject of investigation because in seeking my fulfillment I am learning the meaning of human fulfillment.

As I so learn, I acquire knowledge of the relevant data as well as the sensitivity, skills, and techniques needed to give me access to the relevant data. Accordingly, one of the conditions of the investigative method is fulfilled. Other persons do observe my behavior and draw their own conclusions about what is best for me. But no psychiatrist— or doting parent or dictator—can think entirely for *me,* can propose hypotheses for my actions which are *mine,* can choose and resolve for *me,* can engage and commit *me* in exploratory action, can feel and judge and communicate and criticize for *me.* I may repeat what others say about my fulfillment and I may copy or carry out faithfully the plans they have laid out for me. Furthermore, they may speak general truths about human fulfillment and hence fulfillment for me. But I can never be authentically convinced of the truth of what they say, and I can never exemplify human fulfillment, and hence the truth about human fulfillment can never (to that extent) be universal, until I become my own creator and investigator. In the case of human fulfillment, to have access to the data, and hence to the truth, means that those who strive to fulfill themselves do by that fact create experiences as data, and thus give themselves access to the data and hence to the eventual truth about human fulfillment.

Such a creative and investigative process in order to be objective as well as universally valid, must be social or intersubjective. Truth is not something static like a photograph that can be handed from one individual to another, but must be achieved in active give-and-take with the world of things and other persons. Truth about human fulfillment is not exclusively private and solitary. Human fulfillment must be sought, created, and discovered by all human beings if the maximum truth about it is to be evinced. The truth for humanity means the truth for each and every individual human being, for a generalization is no stronger than its particular cases. But the general truth, the generic truth, is arrived at by a *variety* of human efforts and experiments toward fulfillment, each communicating to others and criticizing, correcting, supplementing, and facilitating one another. Thus, the quest for and discovery of human fulfillment must be at all points social, developing a growing and critical consensus in both thought and practice. The truth about man's fulfillment progresses only as the process of social creation progresses among men.

Now what conditions are necessary for this social creation to take place? History shows us that the investigative process as it has gone forward heretofore in the sciences has operated under two limitations. The first is the limitation imposed by the economic, and hence political and social, order. The technical, industrial, commercial, and other economic demands of society helped to bring the various sciences into being, to support them, and to determine their content and development. The other limitation is imposed by the character of the investigative process itself. Only those who are equipped with appropriate sensitivity, skills, and techniques; who conform to the specified conditions and procedures; who take into account established and relevant perspectives; who propose hypotheses for themselves and test and revise them in a certain general way; who subject their observations and conclusions to analytical criticism; who consult the observations, criticisms, and variant perspectives of others; who seek to develop with others a critical and progressive consensus with other investigators; and who submit themselves to the disciplines of such mutual investigation—only such persons are eligible to participate in inquiry and are worthy to be listened to.

With regard to the problem of creating and discovering human fulfillment, these two limitations are interdependent. Heretofore relatively few persons have been free to develop in a creative way because of the limitations imposed by class societies exploiting the energies of the masses of men in the service of a few. Consequently, those who were equipped with the appropriate sensitivity, skills, and techniques, who were acquainted with the principles and tradition of humanism, who knew how to cooperate with other investigators, etc.—those who were relatively free to explore the meaning of human fulfillment— were limited in number. They were also limited in perspective, for they consulted only a like-minded élite. Their hypothesis that only a highly select group of human males was capable of human fulfillment found its confirmation in what they observed. For could not everyone see that the lives of the masses were "poor, solitary, nasty, brutish, and short"? The deficiency of this experiment, conducted under the conditions of a class society, is its narowness. It bars most of the potential investigators from the investigative process. Because the society frees only a few for development—and their development must be necessarily limited, for the same reason that the science of the Nazis was limited, namely, that it excluded fructifying diversity—it binds into bondage and unfulfillment the rest and prevents the emergence of the universal truth.

Thus, the necessary path by which man might achieve and understand human fulfillment is the elimination of class structure. The first step in this is public ownership and control of major resources, means of production and distribution, and services. No less important, and no less difficult, is the development, in all persons, of a driving interest in human fulfillment, an interest which is expressed in both unconscious habits and in thought and planning. The development of this interest depends in large part on the leaders of institutions, who must with their associates discover and provide those conditions which stimulate and reinforce this humanistic interest. It depends in particular upon educators, who more than any others have the power to influence the rising generations. At this point socialism as a system of thought and practice faces its severest challenge and test. The best devotees of socialism possess an understanding of the historical process, an insight into the material basis of change, techniques for producing changes, and revolutionary appeal to oppressed peoples. But their genius is their discovery of man as a being who is, might be, and ought to be continuously creative in cooperation with his fellow man—a being whose greatness is his power to grow, to realize his latent capacities for feeling, for thought, for love, for knowledge, for control, for cooperation, for communication, for faith in himself and his humankind. What now remains is to extend this vision still further into practice.

III

THE DIALECTICS OF MAN'S SOCIAL RELATIONS

In the two previous chapters we have been concerned with the nature of man and his fulfillment. We have emphasized the *social* origin and character of man, indicating that man becomes humanized and fulfilled as a certain kind of interaction occurs between the biological individual on the one side, and persons and the ecological environment on the other. In the present chapter we propose to examine further this social development of man.

At birth man has no fully *human* nature, no genus; lacking what distinguishes man as a genus—language, habits of culture, reason, etc. —he is only preman. Yet he is an organism with structures and functions that define his potentialities for action and interaction in a human way. (A baby chimpanzee never becomes human, never acquires the use of human, combinatorial language, no matter how much he is cared for and talked to by human beings.) These potential actions become real actions under certain conditions of interaction of organism and environment. For example, if touched on the palm of the hand, the newborn, biologically normal infant will grasp; as in the first weeks of life the eyes develop, he will pay attention to moving colored objects; if spoken to and cared for, he will learn to speak. Each action potential requires its appropriate environmental counterpart to call it out, and the action in turn affects the environment. The infant is not a fixed substance, nor on the other hand an "empty" organism, but a set of potentialities for action. The history of the species indicates why this is so. The species survived and developed in a world of processes and interactions; and those individuals survived and reproduced which developed the adaptive equipment for interacting successfully in such a world. The human individuals surviving today are distinguished by their capacities for interaction, for dialectical interchange, in a variety of ways in a variety of environments.

The action potentials of the infant are fairly specific; they drive him toward getting food, liquid, activity, rest, etc. Yet each allows for a range of activities and environments in which the actions might be carried out. For example, man has learned to eat many different things in many different habitats—Arctic and tropics, water and land, desert and river valley, plain and mountain. The bodily potentials, together with the conditions of the social and ecological environment, set the boundaries for the actualization of the potentials.

Based in organismic structures, moreover, the potentialities develop as the organism interacts and matures and as the range of possible behavior changes. For example, the newborn *Homo sapiens* has a small pharynx (the portion of the throat above the larynx or voice box). Like the lower primates which have a similarly small pharyngeal space, it lacks the physical equipment to make the range of distinctively human sounds.[1] As the infant's body develops, however, the pharyngeal space enlarges. In time, under appropriate conditions of stimulation, the infant begins to make human sounds and to form language, a possibility not present in the chimpanzee and other primates because of their limited physical vocal structure.

The distinguishing features of the infantile preman are ultimately determined by the form and function of the basic building blocks of the body, DNA molecules, RNA molecules, and protein, and by the environment in which these function. DNA molecules "know" how to replicate themselves and, working together in a favorable environment of raw materials, temperature, oxygen, etc., all three types of molecules "know" how to produce a highly differentiated and integrated body of cells, beginning with the tiny fertilized egg cell and proceeding to some one hundred million million cells.[2] It has been estimated that the nucleus of a single cell of a human being contains the equivalent of 340 million words of information, enough to fill one thousand printed volumes.[3] This informational system not only guides the con-

---

[1]Lieberman, P. M.; Klatt, D. H., and Wilson, W. H.: Vocal tract limitations on the vowel repertoires of rhesus monkey and other non-human primates. *Science*, *164*: 1185-1187, 1969.

[2]Huxley, Julian: *Man in the Modern World*. New York, New American Library of World Literature, 1948, p. 90.

[3]Beadle, George W.: The new genetics: the threads of life. In *Britannica Book of the Year 1964*. Chicago, Encyclopedia Britannica, Inc., 1964, p. 57.

struction of the individual body and its reproduction; it also takes account of the environment by experimentally developing, over evolutionary time, structures and dispositions that adapt the body for survival—eyes and ears for seeing and hearing food, a skeleto-muscular system for moving toward it, hands for grasping it, the color, sounds, and forms of species, and the instinctive recognition of these. Such information equipment provides a dialectical guidance system for an organism interacting in a wide variety of environments.

The building blocks with their coded information have in the case of man constructed a species with prolonged infantile dependency, acute sensitivity, absence of overspecialized organs and functions, upright posture, voice mechanism, brain, and hand. In response to the environment over millions of years of time they have also generated needs and instinctive behavior accompanying them (e.g., the need for food and the exploratory search for food when hungry), and reflexes (salivating and swallowing when food is taken in to the mouth). These developed needs carry an imperative quality; their fulfillment is necessary to the survival of the individual and the species. Instinctive and reflexive behavior are forms of "knowledge," inherited tendencies of responses. In hunger, for example, contractions in the walls of the stomach convey impulses along nerves and produce sensations of pangs, random muscular movements, and use of the distance receptors in search of appropriate objects in the environment. *How* this need will be satisfied, *what* food will be eaten, etc., are partial functions of the physical environment and cultural patterns. But the distinctively human dispositions to eat when hungry, to drink when thirsty, to breathe when lacking oxygen, to rest when fatigued, to be active when restless, to sleep when somnolent, to micturate when having bladder pressure, to defecate when having colon pressure, to escape when in danger, to avoid pain when feeling pain, to seek excitement when bored, to seek others when lonesome, to express oneself when feeling psychic tension[4] —these need-drives appear to be common to all men, varying in their manifest form and direction as individual bodies determine and are de-

---

[4]Montagu, A.: *On Being Human.* Revised edition. New York, Hawthorn, Inc., 1966. This list of needs is taken as illustrative and not definitive.

termined by physical and cultural environment. These begin to affect the infant even before he is born.[5]

From conception onward the embryonic body lives, metabolizes, and grows in dialectical exchange with the things and processes in its environment. Before birth the exchange is primarily physical, chemical and biological. At birth the infant undergoes a qualitative change from an aquatic to an aerific existence, from a parasitic to an autonomous life, from a narrow to a wide environment, from a biological to a biosocial life. At the same time when the infant's relations of exchange with its world are altered with regard to meeting its needs for food, oxygen, elimination, warmth, rest, etc., its relations of exchange with persons arises. An infant born into human society does not just explore his world for food, ingest it, and eventually eliminate it, as any animal might. Instead, he is given it—food of a certain kind, in specified amounts, at specified times, and places, under specified conditions, in the presence of others. The physical act of eating is invested with the symbols and social meanings of a culture. The same is true of urogenital and anal activity. Even breathing, as Margaret Ribble's studies demonstrated, is depressed or accelerated by the quality of the exchange that the sucking infant has with the one who feeds it.[6]

Thus, in this new biosocial context, survival needs are transformed into *social* and specifically human needs. At the level of animal impulse and interaction, things and events acquire *meaning*: a thing acts as a stimulus on an organism and disposes it to expect and respond to something not at the moment a stimulus.[7] Man is the kind of animal that makes sounds and marks and objects which he substitutes for those natural signs: he is a language-making animal. And man's society is a group of individuals who display common and cooperative behavior. Their behavior, expectations, motivations, and values are shared in virtue of a common language or social meanings. The biological infant born into such a society acquires mind, personality, and sociality, i.e., his *human* nature, in virtue of his learning of the lan-

---

[5]Bowlby, John, *et. al.*: *Maternal Care and Mental Health*. New York, Schocken, 1966, pp. 13-14.

[6]Ribble, Margaret A.: *Op. cit.*

[7]Morris, Charles: *Signs, Language, and Behavior.*

guage responses or social meanings of the society. ("Infant" is from the Latin *infans,* from *in-* not + *fari* to speak.) The process of interaction of the infantile biological body with language-using persons in the society and the consequent creation of mind and personality is a complicated, dialectical process.[8]

Among the interpretations of the relations of body to mind, we encounter two major views. The first argues that the processes described as "mind," "society," etc., are nothing more than physical or biological processes and that therefore they can be explained by the same laws that pertain to physical bodies and organisms generally. The second view is that mental and social processes are essentially different from physical and biological processes and constitute a domain independent of them. The first view is a form of reductive materialism; the second is idealism. Both views are mistaken. Man is neither an unminded body nor a disembodied mind; he is a minding body, a biosocial being whose bodily potentials for language, communication, and cooperation become actualized in a social system and function dialectically in relation to other human beings and the nonhuman world.

Much American empirical psychology, in reaction against the speculativeness of idealistic psychology, and in avoidance of the real social problems of American society, has taken the form of some kind of reductive materialism. In B. F. Skinner's physchology, for example, man is portrayed as an organism who lacks freedom and whose language is no different from animal signs.[9] It is not surprizing, therefore, that when he comes to indicating the social and political solutions to man's problems, Skinner describes a utopia in which the major problems are not economic, but psychological conflicts between individuals (not groups or classes) are the "original sin," and the leaders of the utopian society are engaged in "behavioral engineering." [10] To make his "objective" approach work, Skinner like Plato is forced to postulate a community outside of established society. Thus his "science" is successful only when it does not direct itself to the problems of existing society.

Caught in the implications of his own reductive materialism, Skinner

---

[8]Mead, George H.: *Mind, Self, and Society.*

[9]Skinner, B. F.: *Science and Human Behavior.* New York, Macmillan, 1953.

[10]Skinner, B. F.: *Walden Two.* New York, Macmillan, 1962, pp. 80, 104, 103.

sees no dynamic for change in existing society, no dialectical movement against it in order to transform it. Yet, like the nineteenth century utopians, he supposes that people wil be attracted to the ideal community because it is rational, true, and just.[11] Yet the material interests of most men bind them to their jobs in existing societies. (Here the empiricism of Skinner, built on the model of "reinforcement," turns out to be idealism.) And the domination of society by a class will remain until overturned.

Examples of an idealistic emphasis may be found in the work of psychologists like Karen Horney, Erich Fromm, and A. H. Maslow. All three acknowledge the activities and needs of the body as basic to the "higher" values, but tend to concentrate their research on these values, to forget their rootage in the body, and hence to intimate an implicit split between body and spirit. Horney and Fromm, in reaction against Freud, have stressed social influences in the formation of personality; and together with Maslow they have dealt with patients who were affluent members of the middle or upper classes, and have tended to concern themselves with problems that appear to arise *after* bodily needs are satisfied. Examining the members of an affluent class, they have thus *assumed as universal* the division between bodily need and satisfaction and spiritual need and fulfillment, a division that in American society is associated with the division of class.

Maslow has described a hierarchy of emerging human needs beginning with physiological needs for food, water, safety, etc. As these are satisfied a new level of needs emerges, called psychological—the needs for love, social belongingness, respect, and status. Finally, as these prior needs are satisfied, a third level emerges, the needs for self-actualization. These last include the needs to satisfy curiosity, to acquire knowledge, to produce meaning and order out of experience through symbolic manipulation, the need for self-expression through symbols, and the need to actualize more potentialities.[12]

This description correctly indicates the material and bodily basis of all human development. If men are not adequately fed, clothed, sheltered, and shielded from bodily harm and disease, they cannot become

[11]Cf. Frederick Engels' criticisms of utopians in *Socialism: Utopian and Scientific,* trans. by Edward Aveling. New York, International, 1935, p. 43.

[12]Maslow, A. H.: *Motivation and Personality.* New York, Harper, 1954.

wholly human; and unless they have an adequate psychosocial life, they cannot develop as creative individuals. But Maslow tends to separate too sharply the levels of the developing hierarchy. It is false to say that man is first a body, then a social creature, and at last an individual seeking self-realization. There is no body apart from social relations, and there are no social relations apart from some incipient individuality. From the moment of conception the infant's growing body interacts with the body of its mother and through the mediation of bodily process in the mother is subject to the influences of society. It is affected, for example, by the nutrition of the mother, her diseases, her drugs and cigarette-smoking, and her emotions[13]—all of them social factors. After birth the infant's bodily needs are directly shaped and satisfied in a social context in social ways. At the moment of fertilization, also, genetic materials form the individualized basis for the development of the embryonic body and personality. Man is always a body, his body is always social, his mind and personality are ways in which body acts, and his socialized, minded, personalized body is always engaged in the dialectical process of creation.

In his later work Maslow makes an effort to overcome what appears to be dualism. He speaks, for example, of "the metamotivations of self-actualizing people"—the drive toward truth, beauty, justice, etc. —as "biological necessities." [14] Nevertheless, the idealistic emphasis remains. Would it be unrealistic to suggest that one reason for this emphasis is that by his own admission "many" or "most" of Maslow's subjects are "paid for doing that which [they] passionately [love] to do"? [15] Maslow's concern with the affluent person in mid-twentieth century America also leads him to an individualism which minimizes the larger social forces which shape personality and which emphasizes "eupsychic" and utopian experiments separated from ongoing society.

The failure to understand that man from conception to death is a material body developing dialectically results in serious practical errors. Reductive and mechanical materialism, which views man as a body whose mental and social dimensions make no significant difference to

---

[13]Hutt, Max L.; Isaacson, Robert L.; and Blum, Milton, L.: *Psychology: The Science of Interpersonal Behavior.* New York, Harper and Row, 1966, pp. 56-57.

[14]Maslow, A. H.: A theory of metamotivation: the biological rooting of the value-life. *Journal of Humanistic Psychology, 7*: 93-127, 1967.

[15]Ibid., p. 97.

his behavior, stresses the construction of an economy which concentrates on the satisfaction of man's biological or consumer needs. Such materialism considers that the satisfactions of man's social and "spiritual" needs are secondary and will automatically find their own satisfaction. In social planning the creation and cultivation of institutions to develop social, creative persons as a whole is neglected. Some self-styled socialists view man as essentially an economic animal. They view the building of socialism as the building of factories, farms, mines, railroads, houses, schools, hospitals, etc. Such physical constructions of course satisfy important human needs and impress the empirically and statistically minded. But these same socialists pay insufficient attention to the development of creative, free, responsible persons who work in the factories and study in the schools. A similar error is committed by many people who make far-reaching social decisions under the capitalism of the United States. They believe, for example, that the solution to the problem of poverty, recently "discovered" by politicians, is a simple, mechanical, materialist one, that is, to provide money or material goods for the poor in what is called a "welfare" program dispensed by the government. But the real welfare of people, while it includes the conquest of poverty, is their own self-determining, creative, social development. This kind of welfare, of course, is impossible under capitalism, and is identical with genuine socialist democracy. Thus a simple, mechanical view of man (which reflects the capitalist aggressive and manipulative outlook on life) is inadequate as a political guide that will satisfy men.

On the other hand the idealist view of man, held, for example, by Marshall McLuhan, makes the opposite error of considering the vital needs of the body to occupy a secondary position and the spirit to be primary. He presumes that the problems of world poverty, imperialist wars, colonialism, and class oppression are of little consequence and speaks as if it were possible to proceed immediately into the world of the unfettered spirit, "the global village" of universal spiritual communication. McLuhan called the cold war "really an electric battle of information." [16] One has only to look at the world steadily and seriously to see that such proposals are the pipe dreams of utopians

---

[16] McLuhan, Marshall: *Understanding Media: The Extensions of Man.* New York, New American Library, 1964, p. 294.

who take their own lives or the lives of comfortable and affluent Americans as typical of the three billion people on earth, about one-half of whom are starving and sick and illiterate as a consequence of exploitive economic systems.

There can be no effective guide to improving the lives of men without an adequate theory of man and social change, coupled with an adequate approach for effecting social change. The adequate theory needed is indicated by the sciences. The theory is that man is a body developing its generic potentials by dialectical interaction with its environment, both human and nonhuman. To understand and change man, therefore, requires a method that accurately reflects and takes account of man and the ways in which he develops. That is to say, both the theory and the method must be dialectical.

Here, therefore, it is our task to set forth the meaning of dialectics, particularly as it pertains to an understanding of man in his social dimension and to the improvement of man in social practice.

In the established literature, dialectics has been defined by three basic laws pertaining both to reality and method for grasping reality: the Law of Strife, Interpenetration, and Unity of Opposites; the Law of Transformation from Quantity to Quality; and the Law of the Negation of the Negation.[17] In what follows we shall presuppose these three Laws, taking the dialectical process to be constituted by the subprocesses of individualizing, opposing, unifying, mutualizing, creating, and destroying. Let us first give a general description of this process and then look at its working in man's development in his social relations.

Unlike the common-sensical, bourgeois, or Aristotelian descriptions of reality, a dialectical description does not begin with the existence of preestablished "individuals" as primary and enduring entities which then acquire (by "free will" or imposed mechanical order) properties and relations. Rather, dialectics as a method of understanding the world takes *process,* action, change (or more broadly, interaction) to be the primary category. The individuals or identities which undergo such change and enter into such interaction are taken as secondary; an individual in fact is an interlocking and stabilizing of processes. In

---

[17]Engels, Frederick: *Dialectics of Nature.* Moscow, Foreign Languages Publishing House, 1954, pp. 83 ff.

some actions there is a simple linear process of one thing affecting another—e.g., light falling on the retina or sound waves impinging on the tympanum. But taken over a period of time an essential feature of individuals is their interaction with other individuals.

An "individual" is literally an entity that is not divided, that is partless. Here we shall use the term in a relative sense. An individual shall be roughly any actual entity, simple or composite, discriminable from other such entities, separate, independent in space-time. An animal body is an individual in this sense, with a relatively definite spatial boundary and temporal activity of its own.

Dialectical action is the action of an individual on what is other than itself (one or more individuals) and a reciprocal action from the environment of individuals. Each individual is internally determined and other-determined, constantly changing. Individuality is a function of the individual's changing relations, both those relations in its "body" and between its body and its "environment." ("Body" and "environment" are relative, polar terms; it is impossible to draw a sharp line between the two, because the two definite domains of processes are in continuous interaction.) Also, the relations into which individuals enter are functions of the individuals. Thus "individuality" must be taken in a relative and not an absolute sense. The only characteristic of reality that is continuous and nonrelative is dialectical process itself.

This view of individuality should be contrasted with the view which holds that individuals comprize the ultimate units of the world and are not affected by their relations. In a classical expression of this latter view, Bertrand Russell in *The Philosophy of Logical Atomism* asserts that the world consists of particular sensa and their relations. The particular appearances which I get of a chair form a part of my mental experiences at the present moment; they also form a part of that set of appearances had by myself and others and called physical. Russell's "propositions" are intended to reflect the structure of these particulars. While Russell admits that particulars are transient and succeeded by new particulars, like Hume he never deals with the movement and transformation of things. The world is a succession of kaleidoscopic arangements of particulars; and the structures of these particulars appear as independent of the particulars. Thus propositional knowledge of such structures is static and nondialectical.

Such a view, which is characteristic of modern positivism and phenomenalism, reflects an indigeneous individualism in bourgeois society. The view of autonomous individual particulars requires the imposition of "law and order" from the outside in order to hold them in place. Such a view suits those social leaders who are pleased to cultivate the belief in people that they possess their individuality independent of their relations to others and the world, and who at the same time control the social and economic structures that in fact determine individuality.

The particulars of which Russell speaks are abstractions. Things are internally self-determining in some degree; but they also arise and are sustained in their relations to other things, and in this interaction they are changed until they eventually pass out of existence. When Russell comes to "negative facts" like "Socrates is not alive," he equivocates; they would undermine the atomic neatness of his world view. In order to interpret such facts correctly, one must take note of the *dynamic relation* of particulars to one another. At one time the world existed and Socrates did not; then, as a result of the conjunction of certain materials and events, Socrates came into existence, inheriting and internalizing a part of the world, living in a mutually affirming and negating relation with the things of the world; in time, Socrates as a unique particular event was negated, leaving in the world his effects. The "positive fact" of Socrates cannot be accurately described without taking into account his absolute negation before he existed, his positive emergence into existence which negated that previous state of the world and continued in a positive-negative dialectical relation with the world, and finally his qualified negation by the world wherein he left the marks of his affirmative and negative actions on the world.

All that is not an individual represents its opposite, though observation reveals a limited number of things with which it interacts. Opposition, or reality posed over against other reality, is inherent in a world of process and interaction. (There are many different kinds of such opposition.)[18] Thus in opposition unity arises, changes, disintegrates, and passes away. It is in this way that the unity of individual atoms, molecules, cells, organisms, and societies are created. Since

---

[18]McGill, V. J.; and Parry, W. T.: The Unity of Opposites: A Dialectical Principle. *Science and Society, 12*: 418-444, 1948.

unity is the ongoing, defining form of an individual, concrete unity is continuously changing. Individuality and unity are temporary, change and opposition are permanent.

The interaction of individual opposites is more than mechanical action-reaction. Each opposing individual effects a change in the other. There is not only reciprocal change; there is exchange and mutual transformation. This mutualizing creates new individualities, new unities, and new relations. Such creation includes both creative and destructive processes.

How does man develop in a dialectical way?

The development of the human individual begins when the egg is fertilized, is implanted in the uterine wall, and begins to exchange materials with its environment. Quantitative and qualitative changes occur in the developing embryo, producing in turn new levels of interaction. Cells divide and mass; the whole invades the uterine lining and attaches itself there. *Villi,* or rootlike processes, are put out by the embryo into the uterus; within them embryonic blood vessels grow, brought into contact with the maternal blood seeping through the uterine lining among the *villi.* Thus oxygen and nutritive substances are received by the embryo, which in turn deposits its waste products for disposal into the maternal blood. The cells, tissues, and organs develop in interaction with their internal and external environments. One developing structure induces an adjacent structure to develop— e.g., an optic vesicle stimulates a lens to develop, provided that the context is favorable and in its own proper stage of development. The developing organism is differentiated into morphogenetic fields which are self-differentiating as a whole, but whose potentials are developed only over a period of time under specific conditions of interaction. For example, transplants from the heart (or other) region of an undeveloped salamander embryo to the corresponding region in another embryo will produce a heart.[19] Such transplants show the critical role of both genetic material and fields in the development of undifferentiated tissue.

At birth there is a great qualitative leap into a new environment where new interactions emerge—breathing, taking food through the

[19]Hamburger, V.: Experimental Embryology. In *Encyclopaedia Britannica.* Chicago, London, Toronto, Encyclopaedia Britannica, 1959, vol. VIII, p. 977.

mouth, visual perceiving and motor response, touching and being touched by human beings, etc. New biological interactions, such as feeding and being fed, implicate a new level of social interactions. But the socializing of the infant's responses are not discontinuous with his biological development. They are an extension and differentiation of it. The generic drive and need persisting through all such qualitative changes is the drive for dialectical development. All other needs and their corresponding fulfillments are expressive of that and properly instrumental to its fulfillment.

It is true that for most persons thus far in human history man's dialectical activity is governed by an order of demands, with the more imperative biological needs for survival ordinarily taking precedence. A very hungry man normally will seek food before he will compose a song. But biological satisfaction alone in this limited sense will not satisfy a being whose essence is creative, dialectical process. Man is bio-social-ecological. He needs others, and he needs to be needed by them. He needs the domain of nonhuman nature, as the continuous field with which he is always united and against which he must always differentiate and oppose himself. Only such a concept of man can explain why men will sometimes forego the satisfactions of their own specific biological or social needs in devotion to a society or mankind. Man has a need to exercise his dialectical power in a widening environment of space-time—to interpenetrate his living activity with the activities of other persons, nature, and human species; to unify his identity with opposite identities; and in these relations to transform the world and his experience of it in quantitative and qualitative ways.

This generic, dialectical drive is inherent in animal organisms, and thus in man, under the stimulus of social conditions, expresses itself in a special way. W. H. Thorpe[20] and others have discovered in animals a disposition to organize and perceptually constitute their worlds in a unitary way, a way that will satisfy a sense of order and at-home-ness, of identity and community, in a world of space and time. Such disposition appears to be semipurposive and providential, displaying a principle of expectancy and exploration in the neural and perceptual structure. Perception is a temporal ordering of elements, a striving

---

[20]Thorpe, W. H.: *Learning and Instinct in Animals*. Cambridge, Harvard, 1956.

toward a form that will unite otherwise disparate elements.[21] And insofar as the form does not appear spontaneously in sensations, but must be selectively received or "recognized" by the organism, there must be some predisposition in the organism to receive it. Perceptual activity, which is both receptive and active, i.e., interactional, is therefore creative activity: it is the mode in which the animal organism molds the materials of the world it encounters in response to its purposes. Social interaction on the part of the human infant elicits such inherent creativity and extends its scope.

Individual animals have a natural bodily integrity. Bounded by skin, balanced by homeostatic mechanisms, moving and guiding their bodies, they stand alone and autonomous among their species and in their natural niches. While the newborn infant of *Homo sapiens* does not yet have a *human* individuality, he is still marked by the distinctive unity of his genetic constitution. The uniqueness of his unfolding self begins to reveal itself in his transactions with things and persons. Such socially created individuality arises through opposition. From the time of conception the individual entity encounters resisting, opposing forces on all sides and survives only as he exerts a counter-resistance and achieves some adaptive equilibrium with them. As a bundle of needs the infant *demands* food, liquid, comfort, etc. from his environment; as a social creature subjected to the demands of others, he learns to accommodate his own demands to the demands of others through patterns of interaction that generate unity within opposition and mutuality within individuality. These patterns are the established habits of culture, the roles and institutions more or less imposed on the infant and guided by the symbols of culture, and the forms of symbolic interaction in which the infant exercises an increasingly innovative activity.

Human individuality, latent in the unique genetic makeup but undetermined in detail, is gradualy filled out and actualized as the organism with its peculiar capacities responds to the distinctive stimulus of symbol-using creatures. Ordinarily the first such contact is with the biological mother, with whom the infant has a natural symbiotic relation. Each releases in the other innate response mechanisms which facilitate the survival of the young.[22] Each "recognizes" the face of

---

[21]Cobb, Edith: The ecology of imagination in childhood. *Daedalus, 88*: 537-548, 1959.

[22]Lorenz, Konrad Z.: The role of gestalt perception in animal and human

the other, responding to it by expectant approach. The mother, cuddling the baby, disposes it to relax; touching the infant's lips with her breast, she releases the sucking reflex. Each is attracted to the other through the disposition of empathy, the capacity to sense and feel directly the qualities of the other. This empathic disposition is not only feeling; it is attentiveness to the other, readiness to respond, actual movement toward, imitativeness, identification. It is reciprocated by other persons generally. It is the other-regarding drive which expresses itself in various forms of infantile dependence, adult nurturance, kindness, a sense of kinship, curiosity, the desire to know, the esthetic drive to feel and reproduce and communicate to others what one has been affected by, and adult sexuality. Thus a basic biological unity antedates and underlies the unity of infant and mother developed in the language of gestures and vocal signs.

The essential quality of this paradigm of human relations is trust. This means a confidence in the reality and reliability of one's human and nonhuman world. It means a readiness to act toward other persons and things in a free, exploratory way, to pursue the line of action directed by one's needs. It means also a readiness to respond realistically and respectfully to the qualities, relations, and meanings of others and the world. It means a readiness to act, react, act, and undergo the consequent transformation and development. Trust is a perceptual openness to others and the world: the eyes and ears open, the whole body ready to respond expectantly to qualities and new meanings. Trust is the root disposition out of which all human development and fulfillment grow.[23] It is the foundational form and quality of the dialectical process exemplified in all the creative activities of man—art, science, love, social reconstruction, etc. Its original form is found in the exploratory "latent learning" of the animal.

It is no mere empty tautology to say that man has *human* needs. For that means not only a concept of man, but also a program of action designed to create an environment worthy of man and serviceable to his need to be human. "Human" means a nature that needs

behavior. In Whyte, L. L. (Ed.): *Aspects of Form*. London, Percy Lund Humphries, 1952.

[23]Bowlby, John, *et. al., op. cit.* Erikson, E. H.: *Childhood and Society*. New York, Norton, 1950.

to be developed, that demands to be attended to and nurtured, if all of its natural needs and potentials are to be realized. To be human is to be involved in mutual trust and care with others. Mutual caring marks the life of mammals, and in the human species it is powerfully reinforced and develop by the cultural life of linguistic communication and the collective activity of work, play, knowledge, ritual, art, etc. As the infant learns care in face-to-face relations with others, he also learns to care about the character of his work, the consequences of his actions, his own future and the future of others, knowledge, art, the values of culture and tradition, and the welfare of men and societies.

In the uterus the embryo lives as a *natural* being exchanging materials with another natural body. After birth the newborn enters into a new natural relation, a mammalian relation. But this new relation has implicit in it still another relation, a *human* relation; for the nursing mother is a *humanized* being whose human qualities immediately affect the nursing infant. As he interacts, the infant seeks trustingly to hit upon those relations with things that will bring new quality and order into his perceived world.[24] He moves toward things with expectancy, with a search for qualities and forms to come out of present experience. This looking forward, this need for constituting himself and his world of space and time, eventuates, as it does with the higher animals, in sign-relations: things present signify things to come, they prepare specific responses to the future. The face of the mother, associated with consequent pleasant sensations like the taste of the milk, the dryness of diapers, and the feeling of being held, becomes the sign of them. But this unfolding system of natural signs becomes soon linked to a system of already established social signs and transformed by it. The mother and others around the infant use signs to which they respond in common, a sharing made possible because they utter sounds which, being heard by more than one, serve as signs for all the hearers. In his first year the infant with his emphatic, imitative capacity learns to repeat some of these sounds ("holophrases") like "mummy," in the second year combining them in syntactical order. This order is one way in which he elaborates that world of temporal

---

[24]Cantril, Hadley: *The "Why" of Man's Experience.* New York, Macmillan, 1950.

and spatial order which the forms of perception had already begun to carve out. Moreover, the ordering of linguistic signs in this way links him to the order of the human community of sign-makers and sign-sharers. For in taking the role of others, in assuming their attitudes of expectancy, he becomes disposed to respond to things as they respond, i.e., in a socially significant way.

Thus, the otherwise merely physical things and happenings, with their qualities and forms, are drawn into the circle of human meaning, lifted out of the unsymbolized and meaningless domain, and transformed into objects socially perceived and dealt with. The infant's original bodily, mammalian relation to the other acquires then a new quality: this face, this body, becomes a source and recipient of meanings that can be reached and responded to at a new level. The symbolic meanings, learned by the infant in communication with others, place natural things in a human frame of reference, of purposes, memories, values, actions. They direct, shape, sharpen, and organize perceptions. They create and fix a world which is simultaneously a world of nature and a world of man, an individual world and a social world. In turn, the qualities and forms of human experience evoke and transform the symbolic world; symbols are modified, created, and organized anew by individuals who resist the established sign system even as they are created by it. The human world is formed at this point where symbolic meanings and nature touch, unite, diversify, and transform one another.

One idealist interpretation of symbols (Bergson's, Husserl's) makes a sharp distinction between the events of "nature" and the events of "mind." A study of the natural history of symbols in man and the minding activity of other organisms, however, shows the continuity between them. The things that serve as the original human signs or the vehicles for those signs are always physical things of nature: the face that signifies food, the hand that signifies the contact qualities of an object, the gestures of the hand that anticipate and point to things, the attitudes of the body preparatory to perceiving, moving toward, or handling things, the stick or stone in the hand of man that signifies the object toward which human intention moves it. In these cases what transforms natural things and events into signs is the action of an organism that is driven by a need to bring its body into contact with what in the environment will satisfy that need and that can guide present bodily response to future bodily response. The object of contact that the infant in his early years most needs is the other person, on whom he depends for the satisfaction of vital needs like hunger, thirst, comfort, safety, communication. Evolutionary processes have formed in the infant innate sign *Gestalten* providing recognition of the human face, i.e., unlearned anticipatory responses to it soon after birth.[25] They have also created the reciprocal, innate, maternal, and nurturance responses of adults toward infants. Infant and parent are being prepared for a dialectical relation of mutuality from the moment the infant begins to grow in the body of the mother. All social learning is conditioning built upon the foundation of these innate response mechanisms and their releasers.

Man belongs to the class of mammals. This means a primary and innate relation of mutuality between nursing mother and infant which lays down the theme to be developed in all subsequent sociality in the infant. To be human is to be cared for by others and to care for them —as adults care for infants and adults, and infants care for adults and infants. To be humanized is to grow in the power to care and to bring to bear upon the simple mammalian empathy of one person for another the resources of the cultural and symbolic world—intelligence, imagination, insight, foresight, problem-solving, informed cooperation. Care is watchful attention, caution, a capacity to feel and respond and act responsibly. It is taking care of, looking to the present and future welfare of a being. The mother's instinctive care of the infant is a genetic disposition to provide for a future—the future of the infant, the future of the species—as is the infant's instinctive disposition to seek and respond communicatively to others. Such preparatory responses in turn provide the shoots—Mencius called them "tender shoots of compassion"—for the growth of a mature and responsible life of symbols, mind, and human society.

The infant learns the reality of others and the world of physical objects through an empathic, symbolic act of what George Herbert Mead called "taking the role of the other." [26] Such role-taking presupposes the prior unities of individual organism and physical objects,

---

[25]Fantz, Robert L.: *Op. cit.*
[26]Mead, George H.: *Mind, Self, and Society.*

their opposition, and their interaction. Thus, in Mead's words, there is a "cooperation of resistance offered by physical things to the organism and by the organism to physical things." [27] In the manipulative phase of the act, the infant makes body-to-body contact with the physical object and feels directly its qualities. He feels its resistance quality as such, as simultaneously he feels his own hand's and body's resistance to its resistance. Among the first such objects that he encounters is the body of his mother. In his contact with it he experiences through his receptors of touch, in his muscles, and through his eyes, various textures, volumes, and actions; and he empathically reproduces them in his own neural and muscular system. He grasps that body with his mouth and hands; the parts of that body that he touches become continuous with his own. His hands move around that body and other bodies, handling them and creating them as felt objects with insides, outsides, and three dimensions. He becomes united with them by the imitative movements of eyes, hands, and muscular kinesthesis. In such behavior the infant primitively, empathically, takes the role of the other, a social act reinforcing and reinforced by the eventual development of signs and symbols.

Sign behavior is common among higher organisms. A sign is any stimulus preparing a response in an organism to respond to something that is not at the moment a sign.[28] A bee sees a certain patch of color and flies toward it seeking food. A dog hears its master's voice and responds by seeking affection. Sign behavior is not a direct, reflexive relation of stimulus followed by response. There is a process of mediation between stimulus and response, selectively directing response to what is not immediately a stimulus, and thus determining what shall be in the future both stimulus and response. Through responding to things as signs, the mediating organism controls in some degree its responses and the environment.

For the infant driven by vital needs, perceptions of qualities in the mother function as signs of the fate of these needs, signs of whether the infant will be fed, cuddled, etc. These qualities or sign vehicles

---

[27]Mead, George H.: *The Philosophy of the Act*. Morris, Charles W. (Ed.), with the collaboration of John M. Brewster, Albert M. Dunham, and David L. Miller. Chicago, University of Chicago, 1938, p. 187.

[28]Morris, Charles: *Signs, Language, and Behavior*.

are originally the kinesthetic tensions of the mother's body, her facial expressions, gestures of her arms and body, sounds of her voice, etc. The infant gets a direct feeling for these qualities, a feeling which leads him easily to associate them with, and take them as signs for, other things and events. Not only does the infant tend to take on those qualities—anxiety engenders anxiety, calm engenders calm, etc.,—but also the infant's system of personality and behavior begins in this first human relation to acquire its basic structure. When there is a consistent relation of mutual stimulation, warmth, and support between infant and mother, subtending all subsequent symbolic communication, the infant tends (other conditions being favorable) to become a friendly, communicative, realistic, effective, self-respecting other-regarding, independent, purposeful human being—in short, a fulfilled person.[29]

There is something more here, however, than empathic response and signs. What distinguishes *Homo sapiens* from other organisms is his capacity to intervene in the associational sequence of sign-mediation-response, his power to produce his own signs in a system of complex mediations, and his power to communicate. A chimpanzee can respond to an animal invading its territory by anticipating danger and by uttering a warning cry to its fellow members of the troop. But it cannot say, "The dangerous invader is there now; go in that direction," nor can it communicate this complex of signs. Man has the capacity for complex signification and for communication. We shall call such signs "symbols"—combined signs created and shared by members of a social community.[30]

This capacity on the part of man to communicate by means of complex symbols gives man great power. It enables him to cooperate with other men in coping with the natural environment, so that he can become, progressively, the master of a nature on which he depends for life. It also gives him power over his fellow man, while at the same time locking him into interdependence with others. Some of the basic conflicts of man are traceable to such conflicts inherent in his social

[29]For a sample of the large amount of evidence bearing on this proposition, see Hutt, Max L.; Isaacson, Robert L, and Blum, Milton L.: *Psychology. The Science of Interpersonal Behavior*, ch. 3.

[30]Morris, Charles: *Signs, Language, and Behavior*.

and communicative nature. Man's sociality gives him the power of creation and destruction, of life and death, over nature and the human species. The ultimate question for him is what he will do with such power, the power of himself.

When the infant begins to speak significant social symbols, biologic individuality, already socialized through nurture in a social community, advances to a new level. Every observant mother knows that early in life infants display markedly individual ways of responding to their worlds. Some are placid, some are high-strung, some are active. These innate, constitutional differences are inhibited, released, and modified as the infant responds to the expectations of the society and in turn shapes them. The infant develops in the institutions of family, neighborhood, school, etc. in which the roles expected of him are communicated to him through the language (meanings) of others. These meanings are not blindly registered and then acted on. Rather, they are modified by the infant's own system of needs and integrated with his system of symbols. As a developing system of needs and symbols, the infant organizes his symbols in accordance with the distinctive stamp of his emerging self, which in turn acts back upon the expectations, meanings, and selves of others. Thus the growing child is alternately open to the meanings of others, closed in his rejection, acceptance, and integration of those meanings, and once more open in communicating his meanings to others. In this dialectical rhythm his personality develops.

Thus, genetic individuality emerges into linguistic, socialized, personal identity. Individualizing comes through mutualizing, unity through opposition. In this creative process there is also destruction. For creation is selection of parts of the environment, organization of these parts into new forms, and elimination of the parts rejected. The body of an organism is created and recreated in this way; so is the personality of a man. The self openly receives the meanings of other persons, selectively rejecting some and retaining others. The retained meanings may disrupt and destroy those which already comprize the unity of his personality. In any case, they are integrated into his personality, and in the process the old organization is destroyed to make way for the new. In turn, the self acts back on the self of the other, expressing his meanings to the other and reciprocally changing, creating, and destroying the meanings that constitute the unity of his self.

Man as man, in his healthy state, keeps this dialectic in balance, receiving and expressing meanings, creating and destroying the meanings in both himself and others, individualizing and socializing meanings. Man is biologically equipped for doing so: his sense receptors, sense organs, and general readiness prepare him to receive the stimuli and meanings of others; his nervous system enables him to select and appraise what is preferred and what is not preferred; and his anatomical structure is the means whereby he responds to others and exerts the force of his own meanings and actions upon them.[31] Individuals differ genotypically in the amount and proportion of these biological components and hence in the behavior or temperament associated with them. Some are disposed to be more receptive, dependent, relaxed, and other-oriented; some, more interiorized and detached; and others, more active, dominant, and extroverted.[32] But every man possesses these tendencies and normally maintains them in appropriate dynamic balance. Their unbalance, the excessive development of one over another, because of internal (biochemical) or external (social and ecological) conditions, spells loss of identity and creativity.

Thus far we have considered the normal or healthy development of man's dialectical tendency in relation to other men. But the fact is that large numbers of men throughout history have not fully developed in this way. (Insofar as they have been human, they have participated in this process; but the humanizing process has been cramped and crippled.) Facing the dangers and deprivations of wild nature, and the oppressions and scarcities of class society, they have suffered from defective individualizing and mutualizing processes; their individualities have become weak or rigid, while they have either submitted to or dominated others. Their opposition to others has negated rather than affirmed the unity of their own selves, and their selves have not been able to sustain creative opposition. Their destructive powers have

---

[31]Morris, Charles: *Signification and Significance*, p. 8. I have modified Morris's model.

[32]Sheldon, William S., with the collaboration of S. S. Stevens: *The Varieties of Temperament*. New York and London, Harper, 1942.

superseded their creative ones. In short, the dialectical process by which man becomes fully human has been disrupted and aborted. What are the social causes for this?

The individual person is created and recreated out of the dialectical, social process. Throughout his life he remains dependent on and creative of those social relations, at once resistive and unitive, for his maintenance and growth as a person. Studies in neurosis and psychosis[33] and in feral children[34] provide evidence of indispensable need of the individual person for the social, symbolic process. George Herbert Mead, as we have indicated, was among the first scientists to describe in behavioral detail the process of role-taking via the significant or social symbol. He showed that in face-to-face, primary relations of the family and the game, one can observe the origin of mind, self, and society. Mead did not, however, consider the symbolic process in the institutions of men at work and the effects of the latter on their social relations, nor did he consider the environing economic order which sets the limits for the modes and values of social interaction in the institutions of society and determines the courses of the dialectical process working there.

For instance, the kinds of communication between slaves and slaves, masters and masters, and masters and slaves differ greatly, just as the kinds of communication between laborers and laborers, capitalists and capitalists, and capitalists and workers differ. Such differences are due to the different roles assumed by members of different classes in the processes of production and exchange. Roles are systems of reciprocal expectations.[35] As such they employ a system of communication. A worker in a factory understands, by meanings communicated to him by his fellow workers, his foreman, the factory manager, and (indirectly) his owner, that he has a certain role to fulfill, and normally he accepts it. (If he and his fellow workers refuse their roles, social chaos ensues in the factory; and if this refusal spreads to the society, a social revolution may result.) The owner likewise understands and

---

[33]The literature is extensive on this subject. As samples, see Mullahy, Patrick (Ed.): *A Study of Interpersonal Relations: New Contributions to Psychiatry.* New York, Hermitage, 1949; and Wortis, Joseph: *Soviet Psychiatry.* Baltimore, Williams and Wilkins, 1950.

[34]Gesell, Arnold: *Wolf Child and Human Child.* London: Methuen, 1941.

[35]Parsons, Talcott: *The Social System.* Glencoe, Free Press, 1951.

accepts his role. A given man fulfills different roles: in the factory he will act as a worker, while at home he becomes husband, father, etc.

The communication that defines such roles is more or less specific and fixed. Ultimately it is determined by the structures required to maintain the economic system. Thus, those who hold the power in a class society and have a vested interest in maintaining it will endeavor to contain and control communication within the bounds of established roles. In so doing they can control the behavior of the masses, keep it in established bounds, retain dominance over the economy, and thus secure their own position of wealth, power, and prestige. In European feudal society the primary means for such control was the church, interfused with other institutions like the state, law, etc. The church dominated the arts and the inherited tradition of literate ideas. A few priests and privileged lords could read and write; the masses, sunk in illiteracy, were thus directed in what to think, feel, and do. Under capitalism, however, with the upsurge of the printing press and the creation of electronic media, the ruling groups sought other institutional means to control communication among the masses. Education, news media, and entertainment became institutions touching the masses; hence the ruling groups have sought to control and use them for their own ends.[36]

If the primary needs of men are unsatisfied, there is a tendency to express the unsatisfaction, to communicate it to others, and to consider what might be done about it. Since historically most men have been unsatisfied, they have tended to talk about their needs, while the ruling groups have been preoccupied with keeping or extending the power they had. Thus communication among the masses has tended periodically to overflow the bounds set for it by the system of the economy, stimulated, of course, by certain material or technological changes that generated new roles. Such communication breaks free of

---

[36]On the relation of the ruling groups to the "professional celebrities," see Mills, C. Wright: *The Power Elite*. New York, Oxford, 1958. For an ample bibliography on the relation of government, industry, and the military to education, see Aptheker, Bettina: Higher education and the student rebellion in the United States, 1960-1969—a bibliography. New York, American Institute for Marxist Studies, 1969. For information on the control of the mass media by the upper class, see Domhoff, G. William: *Who Rules America?* Englewood Cliffs, Prentice-Hall, 1967, ch. III.

established roles. In it men express those deeper thoughts, feelings, and aspirations ordinarily attenuated or confined by role-determined situations. It is apt to arise where men share a common interest in warding off a common danger or working toward a common goal. In such situations men face common conditions and problems, have and recall and anticipate common experiences, undergo common oppression or enjoy common power, participate in common tasks, avoid common harm, and seek common good. Under such *common* conditions, men are driven to *commune*. Their communication serves the purpose of understanding and solving those common problems, of making meaning and significance out of those common experiences, of attaining common ends, and of enjoying common consummations.

By contrast, the communication among men in the ruling groups of class society is restricted to the maintenance of ego and power over others. "Honor among thieves" holds only so long as the thief believes it is to his advantage to honor the other thieves. There is an inherent antagonism among thieves that prevents deep trust and communication. Communication must be guarded, for one may be betrayed and lose one's all. Historically, for the masses, there was little to be lost, except life. When men reached the point of frustration where they ceased to care about their lives, then the barriers to communication fell, they expressed themselves freely, and revolutionary acts ensued against the ruling order.

Thus, history bears witness to a certain chasm between ruling groups and masses which human communicative powers have not yet succeeded in bridging. The peasants and nobility of sixteenth century Germany, the bourgeoisie and feudal aristocrats of eighteenth century France, the proletariat and industrial owners of nineteenth century England, and the peasants-workers and ruling powers in twentieth century Russia did not solve their antagonisms by communication. One might wish that it might have been so, and that it might be so now. But thus far in history, the material imbalances of human societies have so shaped men that those who monopolize the material and the power will not willingly give it up through creative communication with the masses, nor will the masses willingly accept the imbalance. Indeed, such communication is implicitly impossible when the instruments of communication are controlled by the ruling groups.

Yet peasant and nobleman might communicate about what did not touch their deepest interests. But when their antagonistic interests became explicit—the control of property, the right to crops and game, the determination of the law, etc.—then the clash of interests took precedence over communication. From the standpoint of class society, individualizing superseded mutualizing; opposition drove out unity; destruction triumphed over creation. The dialectic of such relations reflected the dialectic of human relations at the economic base. Similarly, the temporary truces and agreements reached through "negotiations" and communication between capitalists and workers can last only so long as the deepest interests of the workers are suppressed and do not break into the open. But when the workers demand what they really need—an adequate wage, international peace, medical care, authority over their own lives, cooperation for the welfare of all—and reject the roles of tool and commodity thrust on them by the system, then the myths of "freedom" and "affluence" which form the facade of "industrial harmony" will vanish and the antagonism of workers and owners will be brought into the open.

Here we encounter a major obstacle to man's fulfillment, a major cause of his alienation. Man as man is disposed to live and make his living in a social, communicative, cooperative way. He is disposed to develop his identity and individuality in mutual labor and communication with others; to refine, deepen and unify the sensitivities, understanding, and values of himself, others, and society in the struggle with opposed forces in nature and society; to create himself and others and his world through dialectical exchange; and to destroy what stands in the way of human fulfillment. At the same time, as Marx and Engels observed, such human development for individual person and society cannot take its free course so long as it is disrupted by the antagonisms of class exploitation, violence, and war. Part of the solution then is the elimination of classes.

Two trends are at work moving class societies toward this end. The first is a dialectical process dominated by a creative movement which progressively transforms men and their environment into more fulfilled human beings. This movement, in the United States, is most common among those groups alienated from the sources of economic and political power—the workers, the Blacks, the youth, the intellectuals, the poor. In their own day Marx and Engels saw this creative, healthy, solidifying movement among the proletarian masses. In 1844 the young Marx during his association with radical workers in Paris wrote of them:

> Such things as smoking, drinking, eating, etc., are no longer means of contact or means that bring together. Company, association, and conversation, which again has society as its end, are enough for them; the brotherhood of man is no mere phrase with them, but a fact of life, and the nobility of man shines upon us from their work-hardened bodies.[37]

Later in the same year Engels, setting down his observations of workers in England, reported:

> The working man is far more humane in ordinary life than the bourgeois . . . . the beggars are accustomed to turn almost exclusively to the workers . . . . in general, more is done by the workers than by the bourgeoisie for the maintenance of the poor . . . . the workers . . . . are more approachable, friendlier, and less greedy for money, though they need it far more, than the property-holding class.[38]

Why is this creative, humanizing, dialectical movement most common among the groups most alienated from economic power and most oppressed by it? The reason is not far to seek. For the bourgeoisie who hold power, privilege, and status, human living necessarily subordinates itself to the maintenance of that power and the system that sustains it. When men have what they consider to be a good thing, they will go to great lengths to keep or extend it. They will rob, steal, lie, plunder, torture, and kill on a small or large scale, if they are convinced that by so doing they might keep the values in property, money, and other forms of power which give to their lives satisfaction, meaning, and significance. To such values they have committed themselves supremely. Thus, a creative relation for such persons with other persons and the nonhuman world is severely circumscribed or ruled out. They are not driven by an interest in *creating* and transforming themselves, others, society, and nature so as to facilitate the fulfillment of all men. They are driven by *conserving* the privileged values of them-

---

[37]Marx, Karl: *Economic and Philosophic Manuscripts of 1844,* pp. 124-125.

[38]Engels, Frederick: *The Condition of the Working-Class in England in 1844,* trans. by Florence Kelley Wischnewetsky. London, George Allen and Unwin, 1968, pp. 124-125.

selves and the members of their small class. Members of a class ultimately loyal to their own status in that class cannot be ultimately loyal to their own *humanity;* hence they cannot be loyal to all the members of humanity.

By contrast persons belonging to the deprived classes have little if anything to lose in the way of property, money, and power. Their egos have not developed around an attachment to particular concrete goods or to a role or institution of social dominance. They are likely to be more free and open toward others, more responsive in feeling, more helpful to the needy, more communicative. And because, where social change is in issue, they have little more to lose than their chains, they are likely to produce the persons most prepared for a creative and humanistic transformation of society. If this were not true, we could never explain how human societies through history have basically improved; for basic improvements have never been originated by ruling classes.

In the dialectical process exemplified in the creative classes, the subprocesses of individualizing and mutualizing, opposing and unifying, creating and destroying, are all present. But the balance of these processes, in relation to one another among the creative class and in relation to the ruling classes, is distinctive. Among creative men who are members of a creative class, individuality develops, but always *with* instead of *against* other persons in the group, always in a *mutualizing* instead of in a *divisive* way. Opposition develops between members of the same creative group, but it is opposition balanced by unity, an opposition that diversifies and strengthens the unity of the movement instead of shattering and annihilating it. Similarly, such men exhibit both creation and destruction, but both serve to extend the power and human qualities of the group so as to construct a classless and human society.

In relation to the ruling, uncreative classes, the dialectical activity of the creative group takes a different form. There is a mutualizing process occurring between oppressor and oppressed: each, as Hegel pointed out,[39] is dehumanized. Such a mutualizing process, however, carries with it an opposing movement of separation and individuation.

---

[39] Hegel, G. W. F.: *The Phenomenology of Mind,* trans. by J. B. Baillie. New York, Harper and Row, 1967, p. 233.

Men are thrown together and drawn together by common interests; class lines and class consciousness develop. As class consciousness becomes clear, it also becomes clear that the mutualizing of ruling class and ruled class can only be superficial and temporary. For the members of the ruling class are dominated by an inhuman interest in exploitation, while the members of the ruled class are more disposed to an interest in human freedom. The two classes will individuate and polarize. While the ruling class will desire to maintain the individuation of the two classes to its own advantage, the ruled class as it becomes conscious will desire to destroy that individuation, that class war, in order to create a society devoid of classes, class war, and exploitation. Thus, the unity will be progressively undermined by opposition, until a new and more human unity is created.

A second trend—at work in the ruling class—is antagonistic to the movement of the creative class and is self-destructive. This process is constituted by the subprocesses of individualizing, mutualizing, opposing, unifying, creating, and destroying. But the interrelations of these subprocesses are quite different from the interrelations of processes among the creative class. In the ruling class, individualizing eventually predominates over mutualizing, opposing over unifying, and destroying over creating. For example, in the development of capitalism from its laissez-faire beginning to its recent stage of international monopoly, there has been a marked increase of mutualizing, unifying, and creating processes. Large factories, commercial systems, and cities have grown up, all singularly organized. This increase, however, has been accompanied by an increase in the separation of ruling class from ruled class, in the antagonism among individual persons, individual monopolies, and national groups, in the opposition between classes and between nations, and in the destructive processes released by the monopolies—imperialist wars, colonialism, the impoverishing of the domestic population, the waste of human and natural resources, deliberate obsolescence, pollution, crimes, neuroses, psychoses, etc. One may find occasional exceptions to this trend—for example, the "nationalization" of certain industries and services in capitalist countries like Sweden and Britain—but the trend is definite and long established.

Capitalism makes pecuniary and proprietary gain for self the primary motive for men. What happens, therefore, when men whose dominant interest is selfish and competitive accumulation and profit must associate and cooperate? If men cooperate, they do so primarily to achieve in the long run their individual advantage over others. (They also—but secondarily—come together for *human* ends.) Eventually individual and corporate rivalries break into the open. Mergers of individual enterprizes have, for a century, been the standard method of dealing with opponents. Today mergers of corporations to form conglomerates represent the method by which a large corporation deals with its competitor or potential competitor.[40] Military power and maneuvers often become auxiliary to this end. Such corporate oppositions and mergers cut across national boundaries.[41] At the same time the giant corporations bring under their domination increasing numbers of workers, drawing them into the cooperative operations of large organizations and subjecting them to their authority and exploitation.

Mutualizing is reciprocal changing and transforming of one person by another and of one group of persons by another. Such a process, as we have observed, separates by reason of its individualizing, but it also unites, by reason of exchange. In exchange we experience opposition—a world of persons and things that "objects" to us, as well as an experienced continuity and unity with that world. And both the opposition and the unity change; particular forms of them are created and destroyed. But opposition and unity, creation and destruction, always characterize our activity.

I live: I thus am a unity of individuality in space-time. I remember my past and anticipate my future. But the flow of my activity and experiences is cumulative. It is fed by the tributaries of other individualities with whom I enter into interactions as I work and communicate. If I have interests in common with another, if I work

[40]*Economic Concentration*. Hearings Before the Subcommittee on Antitrust and Monopoly of the Committee on the Judiciary, United States Senate, Eighty-Eighth Congress, Second Session, Pursuant to S. Res. 262. Parts 1-5a. Washington, D. C., U. S. Government Printing Office, 1964-1967. Mandel, E.: International capitalism and 'supra-nationality.' In Milliband, Ralph, and Saville, J. (Eds.): *The Socialist Register*. New York, Monthly Review, 1967, pp. 27-41.

[41]Baran, Paul A., and Sweezy, Paul M.: *Monopoly Capital*. New York, Monthly Review, 1966. Magdoff, Harry: *The Age of Imperialism*. New York, Monthly Review, 1969. Williams, William Appleman Williams: *The Roots of the Modern American Empire*. New York, Random, 1969.

with another, the mutualizing will tend to be unifying and creative, dominating the separative and destructive forces. If I work *for* another, the antagonism between the unifying-creative processes and the separative-destructive forces will be more intense; and while the former may suppress the latter, the latter may in time overthrow the former. Such overthrow on a large scale spells social revolution.

Preurban and urban men are drawn together in common interests by two compelling and generic associations, the family and the laboring group. The family is the product of man's social needs—his need for a sexual partner, his need for nurturance (to give and receive it), his need for communication, his need for a home place. The laboring group arises from man's need to live and to make a living by active and cooperative manipulation of the natural environment. In primitive societies these groups may be inseparable: the family or associations of families (clans, tribes) may constitute the laboring group. In primitive communal societies the mutual exchange in the family, the laboring group, and the social community subordinates, among its own members, opposition to unity, individualizing to mutualizing, and destruction to creation. Such subordination has been necessary to the survival and evolution of the species. In their dialectical relations with one another and nature, men recreate the material circumstances of their existence and create personality, society, and human values. They do not experience the split between values as produced and values as consumed, factual values and ideal values, and the war of one class against another.

But the quality of this unified and generic exchange is disrupted by the appearance of human relations in which one group uses the labor of another group as a commodity: a ruling class appropriates the social, value-creating power of men for its own private purposes. In class society the mutual exchange natural to the family and laboring group is subordinated to the dominance of the ruling class. Thus, while the mutual exchange continues among the workers and among the members of the family, its unity, mutualizing, and creativity are impaired because in their daily relations to the owners of the instruments of production the laborers are subjected to the forces of opposition, individualizing, and destruction. As a consequence, such forces affect the members of the family and the members of the laboring

group: the natural unity of the family and laboring group is undermined by the forces of exploitive opposition. Under the conditions
of human life and production prior to class society, the value of a
person was determined by his individual contribution to the life of
the family and the laboring group. But in class society his value is
determined by his contribution as a commodity in the market where
a portion of his contribution is appropriated by the members of the
dominant social group. The real value of man, however, derives
from his creative power, that which is the origin of his labor and
its products. The essential and nonrelative character of such labor
is that it creates both use values and exchange values in society, is
equal with all other particular kinds of labor, and is measured by the
expenditure of labor-power. And the law that determines the magni-
tude of the value of man's labor-power, as well as its products, is
the labor-time socially necessary for their production.[42] In short, the
true value of man's labor and its products lies in their human source,
use, and exchange.

Thus, while labor is a cooperative, mutualizing process which unifies men and whose value from the human standpoint is determined
in a communal society, in class society this social value of labor is
modified by the opposition and destructive relations of ruling class
and ruled. In the split of society into two classes and the consequent
separation out of the laborer from the productive process, the capitalist transforms the laborer from a man into a thing. He divides the
labor of the total group, money-wise, into value and surplus-value,
into wages and profits. This is the fundamental contradiction in
capitalism that Marx pointed out—masked, as he said, by the fetishism that ascribes to the commodities the real social character of human
labor and that leads man to worship an idol instead of the real creator.
In such a situation Marx foresaw that in the struggle of the forces of
opposition, individualizing, and destruction against the forces of unity,
mutualizing, and creation, the former will come under the control of
the latter as the private mode of production gives way to social ownership and control.

This division and disruption of the human dialectic among men

---

[42]Marx, Karl: *Capital*, vol. I, part I, ch. I, section 4, The fetishism of commodities and the secret thereof.

produces a pathology of personal behavior and of men's relations one to another. We have already spoken of the constitutional tendencies in men toward dependence, domination, and detachment—tendencies which in the humanly developing person are united and opposed in creative balance with one another and in relation to other persons. In society rent by class division, however, these tendencies become highly individualized, isolated, and antagonistic. The various forms of mental and social disorder exemplify such division. If there is mutualizing between them or with other persons, it is the mutualizing of dominant and submissive elements that is uncreative. The opposition between such elements is destructive; if it unifies, the unity is superficial and masks unresolved differences. Destructive relations, within the personality and between it and others, move into the ascendancy.

For example, excessive dependence on others has been fostered in all social systems based on the subservience of one class to another. The subordination of the slave to the master, of the serf to the feudal lord, of the industrial worker to the capitalist, has exaggerated the the receptivity of the masses of men and impaired their powers of thought and initiative. (The allied subordination of woman to man, child to adult, black to white, etc. has had corresponding effects.) It has fostered religions in which the gods, as heavenly counterparts of earthly rulers, have demanded absolute dependence upon them and obedience to them. Under capitalism it has begotten, as a secular successor of religion, an elaborate ideology of myths—economic, political, nationalistic, racial, male, etc.—which shape the minds and engage the loyalties of the dependent masses. In the relations of man to man, it has reduced the individual man to an echo of the dominant Other. It has crippled his capacity to detach himself from the oppressive influences of the world and other people and to choose and act upon his own choice.

European feudalism produced dependence in men on a massive scale by the development of a hierarchy of subordination and by an agrarian, barter economy which isolated the peasants and kept them at a low level of subsistence. It also produced a pathic dominance in the ruling classes, though this was early limited to a small number and later assigned to a special subclass, the soldiers. The early merchants who in the tenth century raised a challenge to this system[43] did so as men rejecting passive dependence in favor of active enterprize, and substituting individual enterprize in the cities for the passive coordination in the countryside. From its early to its recent stages, capitalism evolved increasingly intricate forms of cooperation between men, subduing their initiative in the patterns of industry. But capitalism introduced the principle of individual dominance into economic and social life: it favored all those who, endowed with a constitutional drive to act aggressively toward others and their natural environment, were prepared to break with the ties of tradition and exploit their world through manufacture, trade, geographical discovery, and scientific knowledge. The result has been a manic exploitation of men and nature by individuals, classes, and nations unparalleled in history—colonies, wars, poverty alongside plenty, advanced industry and technology, social chaos.

In addition to the pathic excesses of dependence and dominance, feudalism and capitalism also generated the excess of detachment. Monasteries and nunneries were large institutions in feudal times; and where the orders did not involve men in social work they nurtured the growth of the subjective and autistic mind—what may be called the medieval imagination. The solitary monk, the remote mystic, symbolized the alienation of the medieval peasant from a sense of creative participation in the land and the society, a peasant yearning for unity beyond this miserable and precarious life. But, whereas for medieval men the alienation of life was, while experienced, symbolized and sublimated by a group of men set apart, for men under modern industrial capitalism the alienation of life is directly and brutally felt, without any heavenly tranquillizer. The medieval peasant, for whom the lures of heaven and the terrors of an imaginary hell were very real, might lose this sense of loneliness in the assurances of his religion, with its opiate music and ritual. The modern proletarian has no such comfort; he cannot believe in God for, as Engels put it, since money is the god of this world, the bourgeois, having taken it from the worker, has made him an atheist.[44] So he

---

[43]Pirenne, Heni: A History of Europe. Garden City, Doubleday, 1956, vol. I, pp. 197-202.

[44]Engels, Frederick: The Condition of the Working-Class in England in 1844, p. 115.

drowns his loneliness in drink, or entertainment, or drugs, or any of the other diversions provided by the ruling class. If he is a worker who has ascended into comfort or affluence, and whose alienation, while economic at its base, appears to him only in all-consuming psychic forms, he may gravitate to any of the thousand "therapies" of the society—encounter, sensitivity training, gestalt awareness training, meditation, relaxation exercise, body movement, structural integration, bioenergetic analysis, fantasy, environmental and life design, sensory awareness, etc.

Under American capitalism we may observe the malignant growth of each of these activities—dependence, dominance, and detachment —in persons whose behavior appears to evince only one of them. There is, for example, the extremely compliant, receptive, submissive person who adapts easily to the demands of the large-scale corporation and becomes "the organization man," or who in a marketing economy becomes saleable and takes on what Fromm has called "the marketing orientation."[45] There is the dominant and domineering, self-made man who takes and acquires, oriented toward manipulating and using things and persons, the man who in the exceptional case becomes the top executive in the large business organization, the national politician, the military leader, in short, a member of the power elite. There is the withdrawn, isolated, antisocial personality who is not well suited to enter into the transactions of a capitalistic society either as a pliable follower or as hard, rigid leader. He is instead the man who lives to himself, who may hold down a job but who turns his feelings of alienation inward, an escape orientation that finds its specific expression in art, religion, mystical practices, drugs, the latest group therapy, etc.

But since every person is a mixture of tendencies of dependence, dominance, and detachment, closer observation will probably show that where in one person one of these processes has gone astray, so have the others. An example is the authoritarian personality. In some situations he appears submissive, weak, and dependent on authority; in other situations he appears dominant, strong, and independent; and all the while, following or leading a group, he feels alone, abandoned, and alienated and lives in a fantasy world. It is

[45]Fromm, Erich: *Man for Himself.* New York, Rinehart, 1947, pp. 67 ff.

true that relatively "pure" or "simple" types of psychotic behavior may be found, especially in the mental hospitals where the more vulnerable wreckages of our society are washed up. But even in those cases there may be a swing from mania to depression or from angry rebellion to delusional withdrawal. Man is a creative whole of working parts, and when something goes wrong with his creativity, all his parts are affected.

A creative person in a creative society maintains and develops his basic tendencies in concert, as individual persons maintain and develop themselves in concert, enhancing and strengthening one another. As these vital social relations break down, the vital relations within the individual person tend to break down. Hence, individual persons cannot be restored to their wholeness and creative health except as the basic divisions in society are mended. These must be mended by individual persons, acting together to change the conditions of their lives and the lives of coming generations.

The capitalistic organization of society could not succeed if it did not make use of and capitalize upon the tendencies inherent in men. Men naturally depend on other men; they desire to be in unity with them and to cooperate with them. In the advanced stages of capitalism today, capitalists have exploited these socializing, other-regarding tendencies of men. Elaborate and huge industrial and business organizations, the employment of large groups of managers and technicians, market research, advertising, propaganda, the engineering of public opinion in politics and the mass media—all bring masses of men into coordinated social activity and partially satisfy their need to belong and contribute to a group. Such coordination is achieved through coercion (work or die) and through deception (if you don't use this mouthwash, you won't catch a lover). Its prime motive is the power and profit of the power élite and hidden persuaders. Individuality is rendered subservient to the togetherness of the group.

This sociocentric tendency is of course not peculiar to the industrial, technological, and ideological system of highly developed capitalism. It threatens any system of technological industry involving persons in large-scale, highly specialized, and complex activities. It is a problem that under socialism has not been solved. But a major difference is that under socialism men in principle subscribe to a dialectical philosophy which balances social cooperation with individual initiative, while under capitalism the prevailing philosophy is individualism, or the egocentric tendency.

Thus while monopoly capitalism draws most men into large organizations and represses their individualities, at the same time it employs the ideology of "individual freedom" to secure loyalty to its system and hostility to socialism. All the while a few thousand persons, making the policies for the nation, enact the egocentric principle. They are the epigoni of the trust-builders and monopolists of the late nineteenth century. They operate by the rule of rugged individualism. They consider sympathy, mutual aid, and protection of the weak and disadvantaged fatuous and unnatural. While the freedom of men in the mass is confined and regulated by the institutions they control, their own freedom has a much wider scope of operation. When they speak of the nation's "vital interests," they mean of course their own egocentric interests. Such egocentricity has a natural and human base: men tend to be unitary, autonomous individuals, exercising some control over themselves and their environments. But in capitalists such egocentricity is maladaptive, exploitive, and destructive.

A human dialectic in man's relations to man maintains a creative tension between self-affirming and other-affirming tendencies, self-denying and other-denying tendencies, creative and destructive tendencies. In that dialectic man affirms himself over against other persons and the world, striving to remove and destroy in himself, in others, in external nature, and in his relations to others and nature, what would destroy his developing identity. To do otherwise, to conform to the forces pressing upon him, would end in his own psychosomatic decline and annihilation. At the same time he strives to affirm those integrative and supportive processes around and outside himself—processes creative of higher values in persons and their relations to one another, seeking to destroy what obstructs the development of others. As he affirms what is affirmative in himself and others, so he denies what denies human development in himself and others. To avoid such mutual affirmation—as in one of the pathic activities we have described—is in fact a negation of both self and others. The self-protective ego—using avoidance, repression, regression, projection, denial, etc.—cuts himself off from the sources of his strength. The other-protected ego, dependent on the group, becomes, as Emerson said, "a mush of concession." Neither can become a genuine person, dialectically creative of self and others.

Egocentric and sociocentric tendencies are opposites which beget one another. The one-sided affirmation of self is a symptom of unfulfilled relations with others. Overtly the egocentric person denies others. But in order to do so he must in some way depend upon their acceptance of his denial, and acknowledge and affirm them even as he affirms himself, since denial requires prior affirmation and since the recognition of the human in others presupposes a knowledge of it in oneself. But as the affirmation of the other is covert or repressed, so his affirmation of himself is repressed; in his conscious and active life he is not integrated with his deep and whole self. Thus, if he has occasion to express his affirmation of self and others, this must be done in a superficial or conformist way, in a way that touches not the unique, concrete depths of the other. Though overtly he appears to himself and perhaps to others as a self-made man, he is in fact in his alienation from himself dependent on the judgments of others. The affirmation of himself as self-made is a conscious compensation for the unconscious realization that he is not self-made and is in fact dependent on others (a fact he has not yet the courage to accept). This ambivalence requires him to perceive others as possessing overtly the conformist character that he possesses covertly. Appearing strong to himself, he sees others as appearing weak, though that weakness is a projection of his own unacknowledged conformity. Hence his élitist egoism requires the support of the conformist crowd. Such is the character structure of the men of the power élite of American capitalism. Lyndon B. Johnson and Richard M. Nixon are two recent examples.[46]

Similarly, the one-sided affirmation of others is a symptom of defective relations between a person and others and between a person and himself. The excessive affirmation of the other cannot be genu-

[46]Goldman, Eric F.: *The Tragedy of Lyndon Johnson*. New York, Knopf, 1969. An analysis of Nixon's ambivalences was given by Professor James David Barber before the 65th annual meeting of the American Political Science Association. *The New York Times*, September 4, 1969, p. 25. For a more critical study of Johnson, see Sherrill, Robert: *Accidental President*. New York, Grossman, 1969.

ine, for it leaves out of account and denies the self of the affirmer on whom the other depends for his welfare. Such self-denial requires that the self continue, if only in residual and repressed form. But as repressed and unfulfilled, removed from an interactive and grow-ing relation with the other, and dominated by the other, it remains undeveloped and separated. The self-denying self depends on the accepting of the other affirmed; so the denial cannot be genuinely affirmative. As it gives the appearance of conformity and affirma-tion of the other, the self becomes correspondingly frustrated in its depths, resentful, egocentric, and implicitly destructive. Being denied its own fulfillment in creative relations with the other, it also un-consciously denies the other. A genuine affirmation of the other would include, dialectically, a denial of the other, i.e., acceptance of his values and rejection of his disvalues. But such denial is itself de-nied insofar as the self has not integrated his affirming and denying tendencies with regard to his own self. He denies his own affirmation by apparently affirming the other; he affirms his own self-denial by really denying the other. He is an apparent conformist but a real egoist. Such a character structure is common among the masses of Americans who have been integrated into the system of capitalism as employees and who represent the inverse of the élite and ruling class.

With the rulers the egoism is open, the conformity is repressed. With the ruled the conformity is open, the egoism is repressed. Each class is a product of the other, each expresses the divisions and aliena-tions of class in his own way, each complements and reinforces the other like two pieces of a jig-saw puzzle. The rulers perceive in the masses their own conforming natures, which they must simultane-ously reject through their own selfishness and control through their own power. The ruled perceive in the rulers in public form their own repressed selfish desires acted out, which they dare not let come to expression in themselves except in fantasy or other privatized ways. Though ambivalent, the ruled accept their role as the ruled, while the rulers never question their right to rule. The system of economic power, wherein a few own and the others are owned, is overlaid with an elaborate system of interlocking roles which keeps the whole system going. The egoistic, dominant rulers depend on the self-denying passive masses in order to maintain their power. The sociocentric, dependent masses in their own way dominate what the aggressive rulers do; for the rulers depend on their approval to feed egos that function in isolation from creative, enriching processes within the self and between the self and others.

This description, however, is incomplete. Though it explains the stability of capitalism as a class society, it does not explain its change, disintegration, and evolution into a new and classless society. Some men belonging to the exploited and repressed class have rejected the role of conformist assigned to them by the system. As the crises of capitalism have deepened, other men have joined them. Increasingly the simmering discontent with the dehumanized society has boiled to the surface. In time a still larger group of the oppressed class will throw off their old role and begin to assume the role of free and self-governing men. As this process continues, men will approach the threshold of a revolutionary transformation of society.

But this transformation will not occur spontaneously and independently of human will, action, thought, and political organization. We must ask ourselves, what is the line of action that men can take to correct the pathology of human relations and create a human society?

Some do not acknowledge the existence of a problem, or wish to drift. While such men impede or resist creative change and constitute a part of the problem, they do not offer a theory for analysis.

Some men adopt an élitist, conservative, or cynical notion of man and of social change. They hold that only minimal and gradual changes should be made in society. Conservatives of the European, aristocratic kind, like Edmund Burke, stress tradition, social order, law, the loyalty of the individual person to the society, and genetic and social differences among men. American conservatism—such as that represented by Barry M. Goldwater—has by a quirk of history tended to take up and continue certain features of the eighteenth century British "liberalism." It stresses the economic, civil, and spiritual freedom of the individual, individual responsibility, and the dangers of too much government and (now) of the welfare state.[47] Such current conservatism is a thinly disguised ideology for big business,

---

[47] Goldwater, Barry M.: *The Conscience of a Conservative.* New York, Victor, 1960.

though it has a liberal veneer. In fact, as C. Wright Mills' analysis would indicate,[48] its psuedoliberalism is not needed to justify the economic and social order inasmuch as the public accepts a liberal view without serious question. Conservatism is consistently anti-Jacobin and antidemocratic. It is "republican" and hierarchical. It holds to the natural superiority and dominance of some men. It is élitist.

As if we did not have overwhelming evidence in history that conservatism has only confounded rather than solved social crises, it is inadequate on several other counts. First, its general debasement of human nature is not warranted by the facts. Second, it confuses the innate differences between men with existing social, economic, and personal differences, converting social power into real superiority and social impotence into inferiority. It is known, for example, that at least 12.5 percent of the population of the United States have the intelligence to earn a Ph. D.; only 1.5 percent actually do so.[49] It is known also that the distribution of income among individuals in the United States departs markedly from the distribution of abilities among individuals.[50] Third, conservatism's individualistic, egocentric view of man is contradicted by a great deal of evidence in the psychosocial sciences. Finally, the conservative's caution about social change, either by the masses or by government, betrays his real or imagined vested interest in élitism and his fear of loss of power over others. Conservatives do not trust the creative potential of men; hence they can never find the solution as to how men might actualize that creative potential.

By contrast, the liberals engaged in working in the traditional and established political parties believe that capitalism can be reformed and humanized and that in this way a human society can be created. They propose that more Blacks be aided to become capitalists, that social services like health care, education, and transportation be brought under complete government control, that welfare be expanded, that the government guarantee an annual income, etc. Such reforms will relieve the deprivation of important needs. They are

[48]Mills, C. Wright: *The Power Elite.*

[49]Wolfle, Dael: Intellectual resources. *Scientific American, 185*:43, 1951.

[50]Samuelson, Paul A.: *Economics,* 4th ed. New York, McGraw-Hill, 1958, p. 71.

preferable to the "business as usual" of capitalism. But they do not get to the root of the problem, the basis economic division of ownership and power. They treat symptoms and not causes. They leave the underlying, exploitive human relations of capitalism still standing.

Others—e.g., college students engaged in diverse confrontations and Blacks engaged in riots—believe that capitalism can be disrupted, disabled, and destroyed by their tactics. Insofar as they have an articulate philosophy, their views are represented by certain anarchists among them.[51] If not theoretical, and many are not, they exemplify the doctrines of anarchism in their romantic sentiments, their incitive rhetoric, their individualism and impulsiveness, their antiauthoritarianism, and their promiscuous use of terror and violence. Their actions may help to radicalize people, to alarm the ruling groups, and to produce particular reforms. But campus confrontations and ghetto riots, while they may produce victories in particular battles, do not win the class war. After the smoke has cleared, is there any doubt where the power lies? Anarchistic movements, moreover, have an inherent self-corroding character: men and women who believe in individual impulses and feelings as the final source and goal of society will not for long cohere and cooperate. They incorporate in their own chaotic, self-destructive way the egoism and individualism of the system against which they suppose themselves to be rebelling. Whereas the ruling groups have some command over the power they possess, the anarchists wish to "play with insurrection" and watch the flames spread. The organized egoists of the system are pleased to have disorganized egoists fighting them, for such a fight must be carried out with the weapons of brute power in which they excel and the weapons of ideas which they now monopolize. And in such a fight the ruling egoists know that no radical change is required of them and that they cannot by absolute opposition be dislodged from their positions of power.

Still others, in dealing with the dehumanization of American society, propose a solitary or communitarian escape from it. They believe that existing American society cannot be saved from its own self-destruction and is not worth saving, and that a fresh start must be made in the construction of a new society. An example is the Yippies, who preach

[51]Chomsky, Noam: *American Power and the New Mandarins.* New York, Pantheon, 1969.

"flower power," fun and games, no work, and the creation of a "counter-culture."[52] Such dissents from capitalism, by reason of their idealism, call attention to the hyprocrisies and defects of society and alert people to the possibility of alternatives. If these attempts blossom into communities, they may provide examples and intimations of the humanized society that is possible for men. But what probability of success does a utopian community have in the midst of a society based on the reign of large, interlocking corporations and a massive labor force geared into their working? These schemes of utopian communism are founded in a naive faith in pure feeling (or reason) and a self-centered oblivion to the struggle of working men to survive in industry, business, and agriculture. The escape artists, the utopians, speak and write as if history did not exist (utopian communisms have been tried in the past), as if present and future societies do not grow out of the past, as if a new society can be fashioned independently of the present material interests and struggles of men, and as if all men, being equally oppressed, were equally radical and equally prepared to repudiate the old society and create a new one. The fact is that history exists and moves according to definite material laws, that every future state of society grows out of a particular previous state of society, that men are divided by the class struggle and by class war, and that in this struggle some men are more radical and more prepared for material change than others. Hence the isolation of the utopians from the struggles that shape history is sterile.

Liberal reform, anarchistic disruption, and utopian escape fail to cope with the problems of the system in dialectical fashion and correspondingly to fashion in their own ranks the relations between men that will foster the strength and flexibility for victory. Liberal reform submits itself uncritically to the assumptions of the system; it integrates its thought and work into the existing authoritarian structures of a class society in economics and politics. Anarchists are blinded by their hatred of the evils of the system and see nothing to build on, nothing of the interplay of creative and destructive forces, of opposed classes, in capitalism. They are individualists, bent on annihilation of all that stands over against them, including other individualists.

---

[52]Hoffman, Abbie: *Revolution for the Hell of It.* New York, Dial, 1968.

Utopians, like the anarchists, are isolationists, but isolate themselves from society by abandoning it rather than by trying to shatter it. Like the liberals, they may seek integration with one another, but an integration that is separate and purified of the contaminated old society.

A progressive movement among men that advances a capitalistic society toward a socialist society and begins to transform it in radical ways must have two characteristics. First, its members must be united in the dialectical mode of union and opposition, of individualizing and mutualizing, of affirming and negating, so that individual persons in their relations with one another already begin to transform one another creatively in anticipation of a new society that will displace the old society of exploitative relations. Second, the members of the movement must be members of the most radical classes of existing society or must be dialectically united with them.

The progressive dialectic among men may be described in terms of self-criticism and criticism of others, where "criticism" is taken in the broad sense to mean holding anything up to a humanistic standard, judging how it measures up to that, and then taking appropriate action. A full criticism must be both positive and negative, affirming as good and denying as bad what is found in the self and in the other. The power to give and take this kind of criticism of self and others is generated and sustained in those situations where men are thrown by the necessities of human living into a common struggle to live and to fulfill themselves. In such situations men develop the trust and openness, the freedom and responsibility, the mutual care and concern, that mark them as authentically human. The primitive family group of a food-gathering or communal agrarian society, the workers engaged in a common task, the soldiers united in battle, the marooned band of travellers, the people enduring the common distress of natural disaster (flood, earthquake) or social deprivation (poverty, war)—in all such situations men sometimes (but not always) rise to the heights of their innate humanity and become greater as individuals and more responsive to others.

If this kind of transformation, this mutual humanizing of men, is to affect and transform a whole society, it must germinate in the largest and most oppressed class which alone has the power to overturn and transform the old society. Archimedes boasted that if he had a long enough lever he might move the world. Marx and Engels discovered the truly world-shaking idea that the lever for moving societies is an aroused and informed oppressed class. The great socialist revolutions created by the workers and peasants of Russia and the peasants of China—both in conjunction with radical intellectuals— proved that this idea was not mere hypothesis but a description and prediction of how social change takes place. The recent socialist revolutions in small countries like Cuba and Vietnam show the tremendous power of the oppressed class even in the face of imperialist opposition. Anarchists attribute such revolutions to nonauthoritative spontaneous uprisings. Bourgeois and reactionary people who have no feeling or idea of the dialectical community of oppressed people ascribe such revolutions to the manipulation of an élite—a way of reading history according to their own limited and class understanding of it. They do not realize that the great power in human history is the power of people when they are creatively opposed to what hinders and destroys them, and when they are creatively united and led in constructing their own human society.

IV

PHILOSOPHY, MENTAL HEALTH, AND HUMAN FULFILLMENT

Wᴇ ʜᴀᴠᴇ ʙᴇᴇɴ ᴘʜɪʟᴏsᴏᴘʜɪᴢɪɴɢ about man and his fulfillment, offering a humanistic concept of man and his values and employing philosophy in the process. In this chapter we shall turn to a specific aspect of the problem of human fulfillment, namely, man's mental health. At the same time we shall examine philosophy explicitly and propose what its relation ought to be to this problem. Mental health is selected as a problem because it occupies the attention of an increasing number of investigators in the world, especially as the level of material goods and services rises and the fulfillment of man appears more and more as a "mental" and "spiritual" problem as well as a physical and economic one.

A recent survey of the relevance of philosophy to mental health showed differences on this issue among United States philosophers.[1] Some said that philosophers can influence therapists indirectly, through ideas; others held that they can analyze the basic terms, language, and assumptions of therapists; still others contended that philosophers can collaborate with therapists. The present paper is an attempt (1) to restate our view of human nature, laying the ground for a theory of mental health, (2) to sketch a theory of mind and of mental health, and, (3) to define philosophy and indicate its relations to mental health.

The concept of mental health here is in part naturalistic and descriptive because it begins with the assumption that in order to know what the good of man is, i.e., what he ought to be, we must know what the major processes or functions of personality are. We must set forth the generic functions, the definitive characteristics, of personality,

---

[1]Morris, Charles: Philosophy, psychiatry, mental illness and health. *Philosophy and Phenomenological Research, 20*: 47-55; 1959.

which are such that to the extent to which a given individual person ceases to possess these characteristics he ceases to maintain personality. In short, to have a good personality, i.e., mental health, a person must maintain the generic functions of personality. Second, he must perform well those functions.[2] A person who acts destructively toward himself or who lives but does not live well lacks, to that degree, mental health.

Hence the concept of mental health here is (1) descriptive of the major functions that distinguish personality as such, (2) descriptive of what the major functions of personality aim at and hence of value, and (3) prescriptive of what the major functions ought to aim at and value.

In discourse about man as such, fact and value are implicit in each other. I understand "the major functions" of man to be generic functions or processes, and these characteristically aim at some value, some preferred state. Conversely, to begin with some concept of value, I take it, requires an eventual reference to what man is and can do. "Ought" refers to what *might* be in the future, what *would* fulfill or "make good" certain tendencies in the present, what is felt to be needed by the interpreter of the "ought," and what he is prepared to actualize. It is an advocacy of the continuance and development of certain present processes and is grounded in them. Thus, human nature as given constitutes some of the materials as well as the processes out of which the good life is constructed.

The procedure here for arriving at a concept of mental health is a continuous, dialectical, philosophical process—observing and analyzing meanings, reconstructing meanings, and actively exploring their consequences in concrete situations. We begin with an inheritance of a cluster of words like "good" and "well-being" and "health," which signify such referents as persons, acts, experiences, etc. By the selective use of these words, we observe their referents and learn the actual meanings in use. As we observe what these culturally produced and transmitted words signify, we make our own perceptions, judgments, and discriminations concerning better and worse. Thus we modify the meanings of traditional words. We then carry this modification to

---

[2]Hartman, Robert S.: The science of value. In Maslow, Abraham H. (Ed.): *New Knowledge in Human Values.* New York, Harper, 1959.

a highly conscious level, analyzing carefully the meanings in cultural use and reconstructing them. Then we return to concrete events, actively experimenting with them to determine by observation whether the consequences of the reconstructed meanings follow. For example, suppose we observe that in actual usage "good" among other things means acquisitive selfishness. Our analysis and reconstruction of this meaning leads us to assert that it means instead a certain amount of cooperative activity. We then create cooperative situations, observing them to discover whether the consequences we predicted do in fact flow from such cooperative activity.

With respect to the anthropological problem, the intervention of reconstructed, stipulated meanings is especially influential. Man studying himself, a subject taking itself as object, means a complex interaction and mutual influence of subject and conceived object and hence of value and conceived fact. The concept of what man "is" tends to be determined by the concept of what man "ought" to be. For example, certain defense mechanisms like fixation or repression are functions which serve the subordinate function of defense, but are dysfunctional for the whole personality. Although they may be found existing in many or even all men, a definition of what man ought to be, though taking account of these dysfunctions, would tend to minimize them in a description of what man "really" or generically is. Likewise, man's fulfilled or good nature tends to be defined as the future, idealized expression of his real, generic nature here and now. Knowledge of the good as the ideal in this sense tends to increase as knowledge of man's generic functions increases.

What are the major processes or functions of personality? The basic and overall process is the tendency to fulfill the generic capacities (tendencies) of personality in an integral way. Our inclusive need is to fulfill ourselves creatively and inclusively. What we can distinctively do is to effect and undergo, initiate and complete, learn and relearn, form and be transformed by, create and be created by, experiences in the direction of a unified fulfilled life for ourselves and others. This generic disposition-process may be analyzed into the following subprocesses:

(1) The process of expressing, forming, utilizing, and regenerating energies in as satisfying ways and with as satisfying results as possible.

Energy is a vector movement toward envisaged value: a need: a disposition to act with respect to some object positively or negatively valued. Some need-tensions are rendered quiescent through the energetic attainment of their goal-objects, and energy is spent; but man also needs new needs, new tensions, and new goals.

(2) The process of maintaining a characteristic form in space-time, in the midst of changes, diversities, and conflicts in both society and nature. Personality gets its individualized definition from a time-binding tendency: it remembers, conserves, selects, rejects, organizes, idealizes, aspires to, plans, and anticipates experiences. The persistence of its subjective aim gives it character. Every human individual, however young in years or primitive in condition, is a plurality of energies, driven and lured this way and that. But beneath these energies he is impelled to achieve his generic human identity and his own individual identity, even at the cost (often self-defeating) of anxiety and protective mechanisms.

(3) The process of securing effective means for expressing, forming, utilizing, and regenerating energies so as to actualize capacities for satisfaction. Successful purpose, and hence successful maintenance of the form of personality and fulfillment of its capacities, require a "serial program" of mean-ends relations and a "scheduling" of diverse activities.[3] The indispensable and principal instrument in this process is mind, or symbolic power. Similarly, mind is the principal instrument for developing the form and direction of the elements of the personality by which the drive to express its energies may be guided.

"Mind" here means both the functioning of symbols—special kinds of signs in the behavior of persons whereby meaning occurs—and the process by which new symbolic meanings are created. A person's mind is comprized by the meanings which his behavior exemplifies. (His potential mind is his potential meanings; but as Aristotle says his mind "is nothing until it has thought." [4]) A meaning is constituted by all the things, events, and relations that define a sign-situation. A sign is either (1) a stimulus outside an organism eliciting an incipient re-

[3]Murray, Henry A., and Kluckhohn, Clyde: Outline of a conception of personality. In Kluckhohn, Clyde, and Murray, Henry A. (Eds.), with the collaboration of Schneider, David M.: Personality in Nature, Society, and Culture, 2nd ed. New York, 1955, pp. 3-49.

[4]De Anima, trans. by J. A. Smith, 430a, 1.

sponse to what is not immediately acting as a stimulus—e.g., the sight of cooked meat elicits an incipient response to its gustatory qualities; or (2) an act of an organism that elicits an incipient response to what is not immediately acting as a stimulus—e.g., the hunger of a person elicits an incipient response toward cooked meat.

A person's mind is defined not only by the meanings exemplified in his behavior, but also by a process of innovating and integrating meanings. Mental behavior, as creative, includes the emergence of new meanings, their addition to those already in disposition or in effect, and the transformation and reintegration of this total set of meanings. This creative activity is *symbolic*. "Symbols" here mean signs which are produced by man, and are substituted for other signs. Symbols here are called "language" when they are used commonly by two or more interpreters in two or more situations according to certain rules of usage and combination.[5] Language symbols are plurisituational, interpersonal, and syntactical. Like the other animals man displays associative and Gestalt learning via signs, but he also creates, shares, and orders meanings—in social and political organizations, economies, technologies, sciences, arts, philosophies, and religions. In a word, man creates and recreates culture.

"Mind" refers to one component of the psychosomatic personality. The latter is defined as the system of physiological need-dispositions whose satisfactions are essential to survival and well-being, plus all the other secondary but generic dispositions that arise in the process of the symbolic socialization of the human infant. As symbolic system and symbolic creativity, mind is the way of relating, organizing, and directing other components of personality. Minding includes the legislative and planning functions of personality: it gives differentiation, integration, direction, and progression to the inchoately energetic, individualizing, purposive activities of the living personality . As through social, linguistic interaction, symbolizing processes emerge in the behavior of the infant and interlock with his somatic processes, the result is a growing, more or less unitary psychosomatic process called personality.

Thus "mind," and its correlate, "mental health," cannot be understood fully if taken in abstraction from its concrete and active function

---

[5]Morris, Charles: *Signs, Language, and Behavior.*

in the nexus of personality. Hence hereafter when we speak of "mental health" we shall be referring to the health of the whole psychosomatic personality.

"Mental health" here means (1) the maintaining of the equilibrium or system of the psychosomatic personality within and through change and conflict, and (2) the development of new and more effective system out of the materials of such change and conflict. "More effective" means better able to fulfill the generic functions of the human system. Mental health occurs to the extent that these functions (previously described) are maximized and brought to completion. Mental illness is the breakdown of system without replacement or the arrest of system without development. The difference between breakdown and arrest is one of degree: the two lie on a continuum defined by complete destruction at the one end and ideal fulfillment at the other. Also, "breakdown" is a relative term, for neither the psychotic nor the neurotic personality has lost entirely some minimal system of personality functioning. Rather, he has become a relatively ineffective system of activities.

The progressive ordering of personality which defines health occurs as personality is stimulated and reinforced by environs of events—interpersonal, societal, and natural. The psychosomatic personality is created, sustained, and developed in interaction with other personalities —as that interaction elicits needs (e.g., the needs of love and of esthetic satisfaction); provides the materials and the methods for the satisfaction of such needs (e.g., ideas and techniques); and forms the matrix within which such needs can be formed and expressed (e.g., communication). Language is the chief means by which the interpersonal stimulation, development, and satisfaction of these needs, and of the generic functions of personality as a whole, occur.

A social system or society is defined here as a group of personalities associated by a common language and common values and relatively permanent in time. A social system consists in both interpersonal processes and the conditions produced by these processes. An institution or a culture is a pattern of maintaining and transmitting a social system. Social systems secure their maintenance by the communicating of meanings (symbols-actions-referents), the reinforcing of certain preferred meanings (values), and the extinguishing of certain nonpreferred meanings (disvalues). Accordingly, social health means (1) the maintaining of the equilibrium or system of the interpersonal processes within change and conflict, and (2) the development of new and more effective system out of the materials of such change and conflict. A healthy society therefore not only maintains a certain minimum population of its individuals in their systems, but also supports them in their development. This support comes through interpersonal processes and conditions produced thereby, e.g., an economy, hospitals, schools, etc. Thus, no society can rise higher than the values that are created in its interpersonal processes of individual personalities and effected by common action. Individuals create society and society creates individuals. A leader is one who expresses the will of his group[6] and usually he expresses no less than his group demands of him, and no more than it permits. Thus a society sets the bounds of its own health. In *A Study of History* Arnold Toynbee has shown that thus far no civilized society has been able to maintain itself indefinitely. The reason is that no society has reached the level of development where its health-creating processes have become self-sustaining in a chain reaction and its individuals in interpersonal processes were able to control their growth in the direction of continuing human fulfillment.

Individuals and societies are ill to the extent that they fail to maintain or augment the personal, social, and natural conditions necessary to health. Societies break down and disintegrate because their component individuals have not sufficiently discovered and provided the conditions of individual and social health so that they can cope healthily with the changes and conflicts challenging their system and threatening their healthy existence. The problem of individual and social health is a primary theoretical and practical problem for men today. On its solution hangs the existence of man.

The sources of change and conflict for a society are both threats and opportunities, coming from inside the society, from other societies and from nature. These sources take the form of actual destructive forces (earthquakes, cancer, nuclear explosions) deprivations (lack of food, medical care, adequate housing, education), and constraining conditions (extreme hot or cold climates, the institution of military

---

[6]Homans, George C.: *The Human Group*. New York, Harcourt, Brace, 1950.

nationalism). Among the major societies today, the more affluent and powerful ones tend to threaten one another as well as the poorer societies. The poorer ones in turn are threatened by the powers of uncontrolled nature. Their efforts to bring these threats under control and turn them to advantages have often elicited additional threats from the more powerful social systems. Moreover, all the societies are threatened by nuclear, radiological, gaseous, bacterial war, large-scale destruction, and total human annihilation. And all the societies stand to benefit from the collective, constructive uses of atomic energy.

Only a collective, world society, maintaining and improving itself and its members through the minded, communicative, creative, and mutual fulfillment of needs and resolution of conflicts, can bring this collective threat under control and transform the intersocial antagonisms into intersocietal cooperation. This is the ultimate demand which haunts all discussion of mental health. There can be no secure, continuing, or hopeful health, either for individuals or particular societies, until the whole of humanity, ordered in a world society, achieves health. Thus world peace, as the absence of armed conflict or the threat of such conflict between persons and states, and as the presence of methods to deal creatively with conflict between persons and between states, is a necessary condition for man's health.

Such a society, moreover, must be linked in mutually sustaining relations to nature. Man came out of nature, is composed out of its materials, participates in its processes, and depends on its materials and processes for his existence and development. Eroded soil, denuded forests, polluted waters, vegetation sprayed with insecticides, slaughtered wildlife, lethal and deforming fallout—all constitute a threat to man's existence and health. Moreover, any man who is devoted to the fulfillment of the life-process in himself is bound to feel some obligation, however attenuated, with regard to the maintenance of wildlife so far as that maintenance is compatible with man's fulfillment. To survive and become healthy, man must produce and eat the food of nature, breathe its air, drink its water, clothe and shelter himself with its materials, etc. He must also find and make a place in nature where he has a place for the fulfillment of his "higher" needs. His body must have physical nutrients, and he must be physically rooted to earth and home, before his spirit can flower. As his body is biologically gratified, he must then discover or create a field for play, a grove for climbing and shade, a landscape for the delight of eye and ear and other senses, plain and mountain and water and sky for adventuorous and enjoyable action, and a world for contemplation and wonder.[7] For a million years man hunted and hacked and plowed his way through wild nature in order to make a household for himself and to humanize nature. But his success has overreached itself; now he finds that in humanizing wild nature and himself he has lost some of his own naturalness and hence those deeper roots of feeling and instinct out of which his very humanity grew. His task now toward himself and nature is to recover that deeper and wider humanity by recovering his earlier relations of intimacy, dependence, love, and awe toward nature.

"Mind" taken apart from its source and setting is an abstraction. Likewise individual "mental health" treated independently of its origin and effects in the body, society, and nature is an abstraction. Thus, mental health correctly understood is the social and ecological health of man taken as a species in a planetary environment. As an agent of action that is created by his environment and that helps to create it, the healthy person participates in and draws from a healthy system of activities and in turn contributes to its health. In such a dialectical relation, the maintenance and development of his own personal system supports the maintenance and development of other personal systems, the social system in which he lives, and the all-embracing ecological system of nature. Thus when we speak of a healthy person as "effective," we must mean effective in advancing the fulfillment of man as a species and in maintaining a livable and lovely home in nature.

Stated more fully, though summarily, some of the major attitudes of the healthy person are:

(1) Attitudes indicative of self: sense of belongingness, integrity, unity in variety (not divided, not monolithic), initiative, authenticity of goals, fidelity to goals, knowledge of self, trust of self, self-directiveness, freedom in devotion to a chosen calling, resourcefulness, adaptability, spontaneity (freedom from incapacitating inhibition or conflict).

---

[7]For evidence of man's ecological needs for grass, trees, etc., see Shepard, Paul, and McKinley, Daniel (Eds.): *The Subversive Science: Essays Toward an Ecology of Man.* Boston, Houghton Mifflin, 1969, pp. 115-139.

(2) Attitudes toward others: expressiveness, responsiveness, empathy, playfulness, detachment, critical judgment, effectiveness as a member of a group, respect for history, care for others, commitment to the welfare of the human species.

(3) Attitudes toward things: realism, imagination, appreciative esthetic responsiveness, tolerance of ambiguity, problem-centering (vs. ego-centering), responsibility for decisions and their consequences, effectiveness in problem-solving, dialectical understanding.

(4) Attitudes toward values: receptivity, discrimination, decisiveness in choosing values, keeping faith with what is chosen, courage in the face of adversity and failure, search for means to realize values, sacrifice for values, continuing inquiry into values, openness to new values, struggle against disvalues and evils, commitment to what transforms and creates the self and its values in the world.

These attitudes are clustered thus for convenience. The self is a unit of action directed toward other selves and things, and the character and quality of value extends all across this vector situation. Things become values when as means or ends they enter into the sphere of human purpose and choice. Nature becomes humanized when man treats it humanly, as human values become naturalized when they are embodied and realized.

The healthy person is a unique, free person, unfolding his powers in pursuit of the universal human values that transcend his particular situation, task, and life—the values of justice, love, truth, beauty, novelty, harmony, human development. The healthy person is in command of his powers. But he is also responsive to the powers around him that impel him to the improvement of all people—the inheritance of human history, the order and evolution of nature, the dear ones of his beloved community. He loves the good and hates the evil. He is passionately, rationally, actively, and persistently committed to fulfilling himself and helping others to do so, each in his own way, but each with and for others. He is grateful for the past, active in the present, hopeful for the future. He cherishes the child, for it symbolizes and incarnates all men: the opportunity of growth, the destiny of fulfillment. He is attached to each pleasure and task, immersed in it and enjoying it. He is also detached, able to stand off and see the whole of his life and human history and nature with humor, love, and an appreciation of its tragedies and triumphs. He is many things but one, contributing his oneness back to the flowing manyness and emerging oneness of the history of man. He is complex but simple. His work is play, his career is enjoyment, his freedom is necessity, his self is human society and the universe. As he reaches toward the heights, he seeks in his depths for the sustaining impulse and guide. He calls on his resources in feeling, action, and reflection to bring nearer the great dream. He gives his all; in giving he loses himself, only to find himself in the larger, longer, upward advance of mankind. In short, he loves Life, and is willing to spend his own life in living and if necessary dying for it.

Mental health has been defined as (1) maintaining of the personality system within and through change and conflict, and (2) the development of more effective personality system out of such change and conflict, more effective in advancing the fulfillment of man. Mental illness is therefore the opposite—(1) the breakdown of the personality system within and through change and conflict, and (2) the failure to develop new, more effective personality system in advancing man's fulfillment. Like its opposite, mental illness is psychosomatic. Fulfillment of "biological" needs such as hunger and thirst is a necessary, though not sufficient, condition for fulfillment of "psychic" needs such as love and creativity—consider the unhappiness of many affluent Americans. Conversely, a person may become purposeful and creative though suffering from biological deprivation—consider the slavery of Douglass, the impoverished youth of the hunchback Gramsci, and the harsh childhood of Dolores Ibarruri.

The mentally ill person has been cut off from that vital relation to others and the world which gives his life power, direction, and significance. The symptoms of such pathology are alienation, isolation, apathy, doubt, guilt, confusion as to identity and values, disgust, and despair. The mentally ill person suffers impairment in his life of feeling (he is hopeless, unloving, uncaring); in his life of action (he is weak of will, purposeless, inefficient, uncommitted); and in his life of thought (he turns away from remembrance, reason, and creative imagination). He may react to this frustration of his life need, to this loss of faith in himself and others, in several ways. He may withdraw into his own private habits, flattened feelings, and bizarre fantasies, wherein the fragments of his subjective life are unrelated to the world around him and lack purposeful identity. He may regress into the simple life of elementary impulse, sinking to a vegetative state. He may construct a fixed system of feeling and thought characterized by rigidity and hostility toward the world, and by ambivalent feelings of superiority and persecution. He may vacillate between attitudes of euphoric confidence and depression. All such reactions have been described in the pathology of psychoses.

Again, the mentally ill person, if his frustrations and conflicts are not so severe, may cope with them in ways learned from society and sanctioned in its institutional patterns. He may drift in listless and disoriented anomie. He may retreat into the symbolic life of scholarship and the arts. He may cultivate the indulgence of his biological appetites—hunger, thirst, sexuality, sensuality—and even cynically glorify his vulgarity. He may act out his aggressive, violent, and destructive impulses toward persons and property. He may become an authoritarian personality, submitting and conforming to those in power and dominating those not possessing power. Outwardly he may stress "law and order" while at the same time seeking his own self-advantage. He may take refuge in passive compliance with a group. The variety of such psychoneuroses in our society is great. But these examples will serve to show the extent of unfulfillment and at the same time the struggle against it. For all illness, as Virchow said, is a normal reaction to an abnormal situation.

The failure of man to cope with conflicts displays itself in various ways in various spheres. Conflicts within the personality system, such as conflicts between the tendencies of dependence, dominance, and detachment, may, if serious, produce the forms of mental illness called psychoses.[8] So far as the causes, contributing conditions, and consequences of this incapacitation are traceable to other persons, to the individual's interpersonal relations, and to the ecological conditions of society and nature, we can ascribe the illness to society as a whole. As yet we have no full science of the pathology of human societies, though Plato suggested the outlines of one, the Chinese sages like Mencius hinted at it, and the *philosophes* and utopians of the eight-

[8]Morris, Charles: *Varieties of Human Value.* Chicago, University of Chicago, 1956, pp. 141-142.

eenth and nineteenth centuries began to move toward it. Marx made the greatest advances toward it: he starkly revealed the etiology of the sickness of capitalist society, and boldly proposed a cure based on facilitating the healthy growth of proletarian power and the degeneration of capitalist power. Since him, sociology, which he helped to found, has not been the same, but it has not produced a full-grown science of social pathology. For, by reason of usage and a traditional individualism, we continue to locate illness only in the individual. The truth is that illness belongs not just to a man but to men, not just to a generation but to a historical process, not just to a class but to a relation of dialectical struggle between classes. For purposes of diagnosis, prognosis, and preventive and curative control, human illness is best defined as a certain disorganized, unproductive personal-social-natural complex on a world-wide scale.

Health is a dynamic equilibrium among men and between men and their environment. The simple identification of social illness with a class race or nation is no more adequate than the simple identification of bodily illness with a germ. We now know that the problem is not solved but rather compounded by the simple-minded effort to exterminate a race or nation or microorganism or virus. Every material entity or group of material entities sustains complex relations to its neighbors, and they to their neighbors, and so on. Blind efforts to destroy them produces far-flung consequences. For example, the indiscriminate use of pesticides and antibiotics in recent years has disturbed the delicate and protective balance developed over evolutionary time between organisms and other organisms and their environments. Competitors are thus reduced, opening the way for resistant species to expand. Established species of microbes and other populations develop new ability to survive the poisons; or they are replaced by new strains that are lethal to populations not yet conditioned and resistant to them. Predator-prey and host-parasite relations are upset. (For example, some birds prey on snakes, which feed on frogs that control locusts; if the birds of prey diminish, the increased number of snakes devour the frogs and the multiplying locusts destroy crops.) Moreover, toxic materials released into the environment move in cycles and return to man. As man makes and employs radioactivity, pesticides, and other poisons to deal with specific problems—such as killing peoples, insects, and germs—he sets in motion contaminants in the food chains that will return to plague him.[9] Such chains are not simply "biological." They are social, economic, and political, i.e., they have origins and consequences in the societies and nations of men. Every war between nations now being fought or about to be fought on the planet (in southeast Asia, in the mid-East) can have in the international cycle of economy and ideas repercussions for every other nation and for every living individual and individual to come. For nations now have the power to exterminate the whole species, and this power can be used in escalating international conflicts.

Thus in investigating the problem of man's mental health we must examine the conditions of society and society's relations to nature—the amount and kind of its food supply, its population, its ways of dealing with waste and sanitation, its medical care, its system of education, its economy and political system, its relations to other societies, its industry and agriculture, its system of practices, attitudes, beliefs, and values. Conditions of society and nature become pathogenic when they obstruct or destroy the fulfillment of man as individuals and as species. The curative plan for such conditions considers the consequences of certain actions upon the total system of healthy ecological relations in the long run. The noncurative and pathic response is some unconsidered applications of technology, for example, the exploitation of natural resources without plan for replenishment, and the expenditure of more than a trillion dollars from 1964 to 1970 for arms and armed forces.[10] The most diseased way of dealing with the diseases of mankind is the accumulation of atomic, chemical, and biological weapons by the nations, chiefly the United States. Such weapons are allegedly justified by reasons of "defense." But all the experts admit that no nation or person would survive their use. Thus the ultimate disease is the deliberate proliferation of diseases and death—a process whose only end can be to kill universally and irrevocably—unless a movement of masses of people, like those noble white blood cells, surrounds, immobilizes, and at last destroys these agents of death.

The only "defense" of human life where man has the power to de-

---

[9]Shepard, Paul, and McKinley, Daniel: *Op. cit.,* pp. 223-241.

[10]Arms Control and Disarmament Agency, reported in *The New York Times,* March 23, 1970, p. 8.

stroy all life on the planet in a few minutes is the defense of the planetary community. This means a joint, international control and reduction of weapons and a cooperative effort in solving the basic and planetary problems of men. Man maintains the integrity of his body in the face of other organisms and species by developing dialectical relations of balance which are variously benign, neutral, or antagonistic for the organisms involved. In a complex nature, the diversity in the kinds of organisms conduces to stability, in virtue of the mutual resistance and reinforcement of the various groups. Likewise in a world of many different societies (some 135 nation-states, with many more ethnic traditions) the procedure that is most viable is not direct destruction of social systems, but rather the development of relations of peaceful coexistence between states of different social systems and the transformation of these systems in the direction of a more human life for all. Where, as in Vietnam, an invading armed force like that of the United States attempts to impose its will on the people of another society, resistance of injury and destruction is natural and is justified, provided that the resistance is directed to the specific removal of the invader and does not spread as a destructive agent to the environment generally.

We turn now to philosophy and its relations to mental health.

The questions of philosophy were originally and radically *human* questions. In their drive to live and to fulfill their vital needs, men have encountered things, persons, and activities standing over against them—soil, waters, plants, animals, sun, rain, etc.—on which they depended for life. In their dealings with things, they were forced to come to grips with the causes, characters, and consequences of such things, to discriminate and relate their forms and properties, to classify them, to generalize the relations obtaining among them, to remember and forecast, to inquire into their kinds and functions. Survival required such knowledge of the *real*.

Likewise, in their interactive exploration of the world, needful men were forced to learn their import or *value*. The human practice that naturally leads out from the drive of need is selective and preferential. Not only must men designate things and their stimulus-properties; they must appraise them as satisfactory or not satisfactory, valuable or not valuable, for man's needs. Thus it is in men's deepest interest to know the causes and conditions and consequences of things as they bear on the values of things, and to develop general clues and laws as to how values can be created or controlled.

But men are not passive recipients of things and their values. They must gather, or hunt, or domesticate their food. They must participate in the creation of their relations to their fellow men. In their exchange with things they actively create a new relation between themselves and things; they must manipulate and control things and their values. Thus, they seek and make knowledge of *how to act* with regard to the world, in order to know it and in order to achieve the values they need.

Finally, men's knowledge of things, values, and required actions is called into question and may itself require to be tested. They thus turn to an examination of *knowledge* itself. Men discover that they must assess the bases for their observations and judgments about things, the evidence for their beliefs, and the methods for proving or disproving their beliefs. In short, in their interactions with things, men develop a dialectical way of thinking about things, going back and forth between things and their own needs and beliefs, and trying to improve their thinking.

At a certain point in history, philosophical thinking appeared as a natural extension of this kind of inquiry. It lifted to an abstract and general level the inquiry about things, values, actions, and knowledge. It generalized the inquiry into things and created ontology. It generalized the inquiry into values and created axiology. It generalized the inquiry into actions and created methodology. It generalized the inquiry into knowledge and created epistemology and logic.

This tie between philosophy and the natural inquiries of men appears in the origins of the earliest philosophies as we know them. The early Indian philosophers, the authors of the Upanishads, were concerned with the nature of the ultimate reality, the relation of the individual man to it, and man himself. Developed and subscribed to by men and even women from all classes, these speculations transformed the *brahma* or sacred power of the priestly sacrificial prayer into a cosmic and spiritual principle accessible to and inherent in all men. (Later Gautama Buddha and Mahavira reduced the cosmic and theistic questions to human ones.) In China Confucius and the

Taoists directed their attention to man's relation to his fellow man in the family and the empire, and to man's relation to nature. Such philosophies represented alternatives to the conventional morality, power politics, and disorder in man's social and natural relations. The earliest Greek philosophers, the Milesians, were interested primarily in nature; their interest was derived from widespread practical and scientific interests in their region and were antisupernaturalistic. All three of these adventures in philosophy challenged in various ways the traditional concepts of their societies, concepts popularly held and reinforced by political and religious authorities. All drew their impetus from laymen, and all were humanistic in emphasis. All appeared in a period of social change marking the increasing urbanization of society—in India the struggle between the warrior class and the priests; in China, the breakdown of feudalism; in Ionia, the rise of commercial towns outside the older empires. All sought for men general and stable orientations to man, society, and nature in a world of change and conflict. All were critical of prevailing notions and practices, and all proposed new syntheses of thought for the guidance of men's living.

The Indian philosophers, with their concern for the individual soul, developed a philosophy of man. Because of the distinctive focus of their interest on human relations, the Chinese developed primarily a moral and social philosophy. And as a result of their scientific interest, the Greek philosophers developed a philosophy of physical nature, thus initiating a motif that was widely exploited by western philosophers after the commercial revolution and the renaissance of Greek culture in Europe.

These philosophers were not specialists in religion or philosophy. They were living, reflective persons impelled to fulfill their needs in practice, to remove certain obstacles to those needs, to resolve problems that they faced in dealing with things, persons, and values. What is the good life? What are man, society, government? How do things work? These men had a reflective need, engendered in practice and nurtured by their new-found leisure. They needed not only to perceive, evaluate, and act on the world, but to order the perceived world in thought and to understand it as a unity. All men have a need for unity within themselves, with other persons, and with nature—the need of the individual to maintain equilibrium in change and conflict.

Unitary understanding is one way through which this need has sought to satisfy itself. The mystical feeling of oneness with things is another. Practical control of things is another. All of these ways toward unity are present in man's primary experience of dialectical adjustment with things. Only when society becomes specialized and men become alienated do these ways become separated.

Man needs to have his activities signify and reinforce one another; signification (meaning) is indeed the way in which a coherent, purposeful whole is created in the flux of activities. "Understanding" provides a stable structure standing under such flux. Man needs to "make sense" of what he senses, to integrate the elements of his own experience, and to order his life in a significant way toward the lives of others and nonhuman nature. This requires coherence and direction in the pattern of man's beliefs, meanings which lead to and guide activity. Basic beliefs pertain to the pervasive factors in human experience—the self, the world, reality, value, knowledge. Philosophical activity then is an examination, analysis, criticism, and reconstruction of such beliefs. It is the effort to clarify and integrate them. It is thus a necessary agent for achieving unity in human thought and in practice.

The first philosophers began with the common sense beliefs of the ordinary man; they analyzed, criticized, and synthesized them anew; and they offered their new thought as a guide to the solution of the problems at hand. The result was invariably antagonism between the philosophers and those whose personalities were identified with common sense beliefs and who felt threatened, economically or personally, by a criticism of them. Analysis and criticism of common sense beliefs, if radical enough, exposes the limitations of those beliefs—their vagueness, ambiguity, illusory character, invalidity, antihumanism, and origin in subjective bias or exploitive social conditions. Confucius was mobbed and imprisoned, the early Taoists lived outside society, Thales was scoffed at as a dreamer, Anaxagoras was thrown into prison for blasphemy, the record of the materialist Charvakas in India has been all but obliterated. From Socrates to Bruno, Spinoza, Marx, and contemporary men, critical philosophers have suffered persecution or death at the hands of political and religious authorities.[11]

---

[11]Dunham, Barrows: *Heroes and Heretics.* New York, Knopf, 1964.

Not all philosophers throughout history, however, have been critical and constructive. Most in fact have functioned to support and defend the existing economic and social system. They have done so either by leaving the basic beliefs of that system unexamined and uncriticized and engaging in some activity innocuous to it, or by accepting those basic beliefs and elaborating and systematizing them. Ruling groups have usually been able to count on or hire such lackeys in large numbers. Consider, for example, those many contemporary American philosophers who spend their time narrowly analyzing language and, whose analysis, following Wittgenstein's advice, "leaves everything as it is." [12] Such kept philosophers put themselves on the same side as the clerks, court officials, scribes, and priests of ancient empires, the side of the ruling groups who will not brook exposure of the fact that the emperor's ideological clothes are in rags and tatters. The establishment philosophers are the apologists for a sick, inhuman, and dying social system. They stand over against those philosophers who by social criticism, diagnosis, and prescription strive to help society become healthy.

Let us now examine more closely the relation between critical, creative philosophy and human health.

"Philosophy" in its nonacademic, nonspecialized sense means the general meanings of a person, basic to his character and determinative of the ways in which he perceives, feels, values, understands, and acts upon the things and persons of his experience. A person's "philosophy of life" is not just his basic ideas; it is those he is ordinarily prepared to act on. It is his basic beliefs. These beliefs pertain to: (1) the nature of his self, others, and the world—i.e., what will generally happen to him and the things in his environs when he or they act in certain ways; (2) the general ways in which he must behave in order to obtain an understanding of himself and his world, and the ways of testing that understanding; (3) the ways in which he must behave to realize values for himself and others; and the ways of understanding and validating such values. Named and examined in technical philosophy, these areas are called ontology, epistemology and logic, and axiology.

Technical philosophizing is to nonacademic philosophy as science is

---

[12] Wittgenstein, Ludwig: *Philosophical Investigations,* trans. by G. E. M. Anscombe. Oxford, Blackwell, 1958, p. 49e.

to a traditional craft or a customary way of dealing with a certain problem. It reflects upon, refines, and improves the uncritical beliefs and procedures. Technical philosophy discriminates and relates the areas and issues of philosophical belief; it clarifies, analyzes, and displays the typical, alternative ways of dealing with the issues; it compares these types by exposing unexpressed assumptions and inconsistencies; it probes into presuppositions, proposes new philosophical beliefs, argues for them and systematizes them, and tests them out through reason and experimental action.

A philosophical idea is a "basic" idea and, if involved in an attitudinal preparing of action, is a "basic" belief, insofar as it is an agent for determining other ideas, other beliefs, and, in general, mind. Mind is symbolic system and process. Philosophical ideas, if actively and not passively entertained, if operative and not inert, if believed in and thus acted on and not merely contemplated, are the determinative postulates of mind. They are the generic meanings which organize and direct the other meanings of mind. They are "generic" in the sense that they aim at an account of the defining characteristics of the human situation. They comprise the "meta-plan" regulating subordinate plans of personality. So far as such philosophical postulates make a difference to the symbolic system of mind, and mind affects the behavior of personality, philosophy makes a difference in human living. Studies in perception, personalities,[13] and cultures show that most men possess a philosophy in the sense used here—"an integrated and consistent personal attitude toward life or reality, or toward certain phases of it, especially if this attitude is expressed in beliefs or principles of conduct." [14] To determine what a person really is and what he will be, one must look to his active, living philosophy, i.e., the things he really believes in and therefore is reliably and predictably loyal to in practice.

A philosophical idea organizes responses. It does this in two ways. It grades the data coming to it so that they are graded up or graded down or screened out entirely as irrelevant. It also organizes the data it

[13]Whalley, Elsa A.: *Individual Life-Philosophies in Relation to Personality and to Systematic Philosophy: An Experimental Study.* Ph.D. dissertation. Chicago, University of Chicago, 1955.

[14]*Websters' New International Dictionary,* 2nd ed., unabridged. Springfield, Mass., Merriam, © 1959. By permission of G. & C. Merriam Co., publishers of the Merriam-Webster Dictionaries.

accepts by separating and integrating these data. Thus a person's philosophy defines his career or destiny. "Not merely to know, but according to thy knowledge to do, is thy vocation," said Fichte.[15] Man's vocation is to become something, to grow into a form of identity, or organize the elements of his life into a coherent pattern and direction. Philosophy, as the supreme organizing agent of mind, helps man to do this.

Since philosophy as here defined is intimately connected with human living, it can, and ought to, have three relations to the problem of man's mental health: (1) philosophy as a creative process exemplifies to some degree the pattern of mental health; (2) philosophy functions as the directive, organizing factor in mind and hence in mental health; (3) philosophy as inquiry into the nature of man, the world, and value is concerned to define the generic character of man and his values—and to achieve mental health men must fulfill that generic character.

Consider first the process of philosophy: seeking to formulate as generic meanings the categories of concrete human experience (change, matter, form, quality, etc.); assembling and examining the character of the data of common sense, the sciences, and the humanities (these data include the linguistic signs and the major elements making up experience); the emerging of insights concerning these generic meanings; formalizing these insights in language via description, classification, logical form, analysis to eliminate imprecision, explication by elaboration and argument, and coordination; applying the meanings to a variety of experiences, actual and imaginary; acting as guided by the meanings and observing the consequences to determine their relation to such action; making contact with recorded ideas and engaging in discussion with oneself and others to clarify, validate, correct, expose, and create meanings; continuous revising, transforming, and testing of such meanings.

The phases in this process have their counterparts in the pattern of mental health.

The search for generic meanings is a form of the search for identity. Unless a person maintains a common character in certain respects from situation to situation, he ceases to be. Kurt Goldstein has shown

---

[15]Fichte, J. G.: *The Vocation of Man,* trans. by William Smith. La Salle, Ill., Open Court, 1946, p. 94.

that persons who are mentally ill have difficulty in discriminating and conceptualizing similarities in situations.[16] "Fixation" at an early stage of development is another form of this difficulty. It is corrected by adaptability. But without form of identity adaptability becomes waxy. Further, the search for basic meaning is implicitly the search for self-knowledge. The philosophical person is not content with a specific identity of male, engineer, or American. He desires to be identified with the generic nature of humanity. He desires to be a fully developed man.

Assembling and examining the data of common human experience, the sciences, and the humanities has its correlate in mental health in a personality liberated from the narrow and unsocialized limits of feeling, thought, and action. The philosophical man is open to the variety of the world. He is not closeted in a narrow specialty. He is not confined to the flatland of established meanings. He lives in the currents of human activity and expression, where meanings are generated, integrated, and transformed.

The emerging of insights in philosophy is a feature of the process of growth in all healthy personality.

Mental health is the fulfillment of formative tendencies in persons. *We* become as we form our experiences. This means a minimum of dissociation of one part from another, and no rationalizing, projecting, or fantasizing. "Unuttered truths are poisonous," said Nietzsche.[17] To express is to make precise, definite, decisive; it is to create. Philosophical formulation is one way of doing this.

Philosophizing calls for elaborating the full meaning, in its detail and interconnection, and for disclosure of what is revealed to experience and reflection. A mentally healthy person has a style of elaboration too—he elucidates his life, brings it to light, gives it form, direction, and impact. This is the opposite of the involutional impotence of the sick person. His anxiety is diffuse, uncertain, apprehensive; his awareness is dulled and his development arrested.

Philosophical coordination of meanings is analogous to growing

---

[16]Goldstein, Kurt: Methodoligical approach to the study of schizophrenic thought disorders. In Kasanin, J. S. (Ed.): *Language and Thought in Schizophrenia*. Berkeley, University of California, 1944.

[17]Nietzsche, Friedrich: *Thus Spake Zarathustra*, 2nd part.

integrative identity for personality. The elements of experience are carried along together, the themes are maintained and orchestrated as they move. Nothing is isolated. For whatever is cut off from the circulating and developing system of life sickens and dies. Growing integration and comprehensiveness in philosophy has its parallel in the growing integrity of personality.

Creative philosophy requires that its meanings be applied to a variety of situations. Such application is a continuing test of generic and universal truth, and affirmation of the persistence of identity in change, a way of illustrating adaptability. In terms of personality, this is the reality principle. The final test of philosophical system and personality health is completion of tendencies in practice. It is the material embodiment of purpose.

For it is not enough merely to cogitate. One must act. The necessity for life, for action to affirm and sustain life, was the originating impetus of reflection and philosophical thought. "Ago, cogito, reago, ergo sum." One must be willing to step into the river. We ultimately judge a person by what he does, not by what he says. Similarly, we judge the wisdom of a philosopher by whether what he says is relevant to what we have to do—whether it illuminates, enlarges, and humanizes our thought and action. Such wisdom is forged, shaped, and sharpened by the hammer blows of action and the anvils of the world.

Making contact with recorded ideas and discussion with oneself and others, is, like action, a form of dialectical testing of ideas. Criticism and self-criticism break down the walls of egocentricity. They stir up and stimulate. They throw the stark light of a new perspective on our meanings. They give dimension and depth to our vision. J. B. S. Haldane once said that having a wife enabled him to acquire binocular vision and to see more deeply into things.[18] Through reflective acquaintance with the heritage of past ideas and through receptive and critical conversation, the philosopher and the healthy person are released from egocentric, provincial dogma; if they are sensitive and responsive, they can approach more surely to those recurrent, generic meanings that characterize all human experiences and all cultures. Hence they can approach more surely to themselves.

---

[18]Haldane, J. B. S.: Ch. 22 In *Living Philosophies*. New York, Simon and Schuster, 1933, p. 325.

Finally, the man of philosophy is always revising his vision, as the man of health is always developing. Continuous change and adjustment to a changing world is necessary for a healthy organism in a changing world. Moreover, just as a healthy man has the resilience to respond successfully to the various challenges of his environment, so a philosopher desires to deepen his understanding and widen his vision so that more and more of the world can be taken in and can find its place in his comprehension.

There is a second relation that philosophy has to mental health. The uncritical philosophies of life held by many direct and organize their activities and so partially determine the quality of their health. Critical, reconstructive philosophy can and ought to work to help men to improve their philosophies and in turn their health and the health of their societies. Relative to what it might be, the health of most men and societies today is poor. There are many causes for this. The incomplete, vague, ambiguous, fragmentary, inconsistent, rigid, superstitious, ineffective character of the philosophies which men hold represents one of the causes, and consequences, of their poor health, interlocked with many other causes. In most instances such philosophies are traditional religious supernaturalisms of one kind or another which divert men from genuine struggle with the problems of this life; or they are egocentric materialisms which isolate and brutalize men. In either case there is dehumanization in thought and practice. Men do not overcome their dehumanization by blind, furious action against their world, nor by mere contemplative thought. What is needed is a philosophy that will guide social action toward a more human order.

How can professional philosophers affect and improve the beliefs and behavior of the masses of men so that in turn these beliefs may function more effectively to secure the health of those men? (1) By developing among philosophers themselves, in collaboration with other students of human behavior, philosophical concepts that adequately characterize human nature and value and that are applicable to the solution of specific problems relevant to man's health; and (2) by discovering and effecting programs by which both these concepts and the method of philosophizing would be taught to persons throughout the world and implemented in practice.

It may be objected that philosophers will never agree with one another and that this proposal is utopian. It is true that a deep chasm separates the critical, radical, humanistic philosophers from the conformist, conservative, antihumanistic philosophers. Like other men philosophers side with one class or another. But massive agreement among philosophers has never been required for important social change. The critical question is whether sufficient numbers can be marshalled among the people and their leaders for a sustained movement toward a better social order. If the objection implies that philosophy can never be publicly and objectively verified, we reject the implication. For we have argued that man, the world, and values have an objective character and that they can be known through scientific and philosophical inquiry. What is the alternative? If men cannot in their philosophical efforts discover some things about themselves and their world and their fulfillment in it, then they are left with the chaos of competing social conventions, the bedlam of individual impulses and actions, the competition of demogogues, the tyranny of dictators, the armageddon of conflicting armies, and the final apocalypse of nuclear, chemical, and bacterial destruction.

As philosophers cooperatively turn their attention to the problem of man's fulfillment, and are supported by the developing sciences of man, society, and nature, the prospects of their reaching a consensus are much more promising than in the past. Philosophers are not normally specialized scientists, and scientists are seldom philosophical. But in the absence of philosophers who strive to make their work applicable to the problems of man, some scientists, concerned about the human implications of their work, have leaped into the breach to formulate the values and the guiding, overall visions for man. Sometimes their leadership has been bad (e.g., Edward Teller's), sometimes wise, useful, and humane.[19] In any case scientists, philosophers, and man as a whole stand to gain by this cooperation concerning the problem of man.

It may be objected too that such a plan is impractical. However, the activities of UNESCO indicate that cross-cultural communication among philosophers is feasible. Moreover, the great imperative for men now is to find ways to fulfill themselves. But in order to do this they require guidance of a general kind indicating the generic possi-

---

[19]Huxley, Sir Julian (Ed.): *The Humanist Frame.*

bilities of men and the generic path of fulfillment in whose framework all that is planned and done can be understood and evaluated. Only persons who are philosophical can provide this. And, if the human enterprize is to succeed, it is not enough to have a few philosopher-kings laying down such guidance as a fiat. Every person must be philosophical in this sense. And this entails a philosophical education centered on the problem of human nature and fulfillment; a limited scientific education is not sufficient. The role for the philosophers to play in this is leadership in providing such an education. One condition of world peace is a common, humanistic education for all peoples; and it is high time to plan for such.

Third, philosophers can and ought to be concerned about the problem of mental health, as it is implicated in the problem of clarifying, criticizing, and systematizing generic concepts like man and value. This concern is presupposed in philosophy at its primitive, common sense level, in the process of philosophy as I have described it, and in any effort philosophers might make with respect to arriving at a consensus and developing philosophy in education. However, not all professional philosophers today share this concern. In contemporary America, for example, most professional philosophers are interested in other questions. Analytic philosophers hold that philosophy is the analysis and clarification of the function or use of ordinary language. Logical empiricists maintain that philosophers properly should do a logical analysis of the syntax and semantics of scientific statements. Those following the method of phenomenology and existentialism seek intuitive insight and analysis of our intentions and lived experiences. Naturalists take the description and explanation of the "neutral" sciences to be the proper model for philosophical activity. Religious philosophies supplement one or another of these methods with the methods of supernatural faith and revelation.

In reaction against the *a priori* rationalism, speculative idealism, and unqualified supernaturalism of traditional philosophy, these philosophies are all in some sense pronaturalistic and prohumanistic. They all tend to seek to translate the traditional questions of philosophy into questions that can be investigated by men empirically and rationally. Thus they all reflect the secularizing, humanizing tendencies of modern societies defining the shifts from feudalism to capitalism and from

capitalism to socialism. They all have in various degrees "demytholo-
gized" modern thought and have produced useful insight and methods
in their various spheres.

At the same time they all reflect the individualism associated with
the bourgeois world and in particular the extreme individualism of the
disintegrative stages of western capitalism. In their theories of the
world of reality, knowledge, and value, they tend to be phenomenalist,
conventionalist, and arbitrarily restricted in scope. In their efforts to
secure moorings in choppy waters, they tie onto ordinary language,
or the language of science, or immediate experience, or the methods of
the sciences, or the deliverances of an ancestral faith, on the supposition that these will provide stable bases for philosophical thought.
They take these as foundational and final. They are uncritical and
conservative toward the historical, social, and ontological bases of these
supposed foundations. They do not probe into the ultimate presuppositions of their own materials and methods. They avoid facing the
fact that ordinary language, the sciences, human experience, and religious faith are all relative and limited, and that they are all created
and conditioned by institutions and forces of bourgeois, western European and American societies bent on preserving their own form against
the disruptive forces of socialism concentrated in other parts of the
world. All these philosophies are oriented primarily toward understanding the world, their own limited world, rather than toward
radically changing it. They do not pose the question of how language,
science, and experience might be used to transform man and the world
for the purpose of fulfilling all men. They do not inquire into the
monstrous inhumanities of their society or how these might be overcome. For that would lead in the direction of revolutionizing thought
and practice. But these philosophies are adapted to the establishment.
For example, Heidegger (whose view has a following among a number of American philosophers) says, "For the most part, Dasein ends
in unfulfillment, or else by having disintegrated and been used up." [20]
But he accepts this as a final "existential" fact. He never inquires into
the causes and correctives of this condition. He reports the sickness
and death of his society not as a doctor who describes and diagnoses

---

[20]Heidegger, Martin: *Being and Time*, trans. by John Macquarrie and Edward
Robinson. New York, Harper and Row, 1962, section 48.

(except as he speaks of "inauthenticity"), but more as a passive patient who reports to observers by *revealing* the symptoms of an illness endemic to this society.

The variety and partiality of these American philosophies are symptoms of the underlying disintegration of American society. Each approach retreats into the security of its own specialty and simultaneously escapes from the arduous, integrative, inclusive task of uniting the various parts of individual and social activity into a coherent, significant, humanistic whole. Such unity must ultimately be practical as well as theoretical. Thought is a guide to action, its only guide. And the most general and inclusive action requires a general and inclusive guide. That is analytical, critical, creative philosophy, aiming at the fulfillment of all men. Without such a humanistic, healthy philosophy, there can be no fully humanistic, healthy action or fulfillment. Thus the task of men in their practical drive to humanize themselves is to become philosophical. The task of philosophy in its theoretical drive to fulfill itself is to humanize itself in the practice of men.

PART TWO
THE HUMANISM OF MARX

V

HUMAN VALUE IN THE THOUGHT OF MARX

In the chapters just completed, we have expounded the meaning of humanism, and in the next three chapters we shall turn to an exposition of the humanism of Marx. The present chapter is a consideration of (1) some of the influences in the development of Marx's humanism, (2) what Marx meant by human value, a notion central to his humanism, (3) how man becomes alienated from himself and from his values, and (4) what man must do to recover those values.

The young Marx was deeply steeped in the religious idealism of Judaism and Christianity, a tradition which he inherited from his father and mother, his Gymnasium teachers, and his education in German idealistic philosophy at the universities. (We shall discuss in detail these influences in our final chapter.) Thus at an early age he was aware of the humanistic values proclaimed in these religions, as well as the problem of alienation (estrangement from self, others, the world, and fulfillment) as posed in the Bible, treated by theologians, and taken up by German philosophers, especially Hegel. Through his father and teachers, who followed Rousseau, Condorcet, and Saint-Simon, among others, Marx also received a strong indoctrination into the humanistic ideals associated with the French Revolution and the Enlightenment.

At the Universities of Bonn and Berlin (1835-1841), Marx came into contact with the powerful movement of German idealism, which in the four decades prior to Marx's birth had germinated a rich and suggestive body of ideas. A central motif of this movement was humanism. The great Kant had wrought a "Copernican revolution" by treating man as the center of the problem of knowledge. Kant emphasized the autonomy of human reason, the active and creative nature of man's mind, the futility of theological and metaphysical speculation, the generic character of man, as distinct from his mere empirical appearances, and the progress of mankind through history. All of these ideas turned up in Marx, as direct or indirect inheritances from Kant. Likewise, the influence of Kant's student Fichte on Marx is evident in his concept of man as a practical and social being who is self-creative, free, self-transcending, and dialectical in development. The deepest intellectual influence exerted on the young Marx was that of Hegel. While Hegel's philosophy took a theological and idealistic form, its essential content was humanistic. The young Hegel attacked the alienation in ancient and contemporary Christianity. In his maturity such alienation was depicted as the alienation of man's spirit or mind from itself—spirit nonetheless dialectically returning to its unity by means of a growing self-consciousness. But such spirit is the *Geist* of God himself. Thus Hegel, in an elaborate terminology, transformed the spirit of Christianity into the spirit of man, and theology into humanism.

In his Ph.D. dissertation of March, 1841, Marx boldly asserted his own version of Hegel's humanism, "the consciousness of man as the supreme divinity."[1] He appropriated Hegel's "self-creation of man as a process"[2] as well as Hegel's insight that man's objectification or alienation is the result of his own activity, which is in process of overcoming that alienation. That was the humanistic kernel of Hegel for Marx; he rejected the idealistic husk. For example, where Hegel spoke of *Entäusserung* (objectification), Marx substituted *Veräusserung* (selling). In Hegel human activity was always *mental* or *spiritual,* while for Marx it was essentially *natural* and *material.*

Later that year Feuerbach's *Essence of Christianity* appeared. It was a book which created a storm among the young Hegelians, of whom Marx was one. Feuerbach insisted on the sensuous test for all knowledge; he focussed on man, not God, and argued that it is man who creates God and not the other way around. Marx saw the power of this new materialism and empiricism. Yet he did not desert Hegel's

---

[1]Marx, Karl: Forward to thesis: the difference between the natural philosophy of Democritus and the natural philosophy of Epicurus. In Marx, K., and Engels, F.: *On Religion*. Moscow, Foreign Languages Publishing House, ND., p. 15.

[2]Marx, Karl: *Economic and Philosophical Manuscripts*, trans. by T. B. Bottomore. In Fromm, Erich: *Marx's Concept of Man*. New York, Ungar, 1961, p. 177.

grasp of the dynamic movement of things; he perceived that the concept of the dialectical activity of spirit is only a mystified way of exhibiting the natural and sensuous activity of men.[3] Yet only after he had passed through a number of developments did he work his way through to a synthesis of these two humanisms—that of Hegel, who epitomized the personal, organic, idealized humanism of Christianity, and that of Feuerbach, working in the individualistic, empirical, materialistic tradition of the French Enlightenment. Marx's synthesis was succinctly sketched in his *Theses on Feuerbach* in the spring of 1845.

At the end of 1842, under the stimulus of his work as an editor, the young Marx had begun to study the writings of the French on socialism and communism. Moreover, his experience with Prussian censorship and a law against wood theft helped to make his philosophical humanism concrete and practical. His "Critique of Hegel's Philosophy of the State" (summer, 1843) advanced this process. In that he attacked Hegel for being unrealistic: society is filled with contradictions—the state against the people, private interests against "socialized man," etc.; yet Hegel airily assumes a transcendent unity of all the parts. The Feuerbachian emphasis on the individual, empirical man is apparent here. At the same time the mention of "socialized man" and of labor as the basis of civil society portends a new departure.

In October of 1843 Marx and his new wife moved to Paris. There he met a great variety of democrats, radicals, revolutionaries, workers, artists, philosophers, writers, and other political dissidents, all imbued with the various humanistic hopes and schemes of the time. There Marx plunged into a serious study of socialism and political economy. To these fresh influences, both practical and theoretical, he brought his heritage of Hegel and Feuerbach and others, among them the thought of Moses Hess. Marx, as well as Engels, had met Hess in the fall of 1842, when Marx was editor of the *Rheinische Zeitung* at Cologne. Hess held that man generically is a social, productive being and that his alienation is at its root economic, stemming from selfish men who appropriate the social power through money and property. Hess was a philosophical communist. But he was also a

---

[3] *Economic and Philosophical Manuscripts,* last section.

cosmopolitan, and thought in terms of mankind as a whole rather than in terms of class.

Marx's "On the Jewish Question," written for the most part before he went to Paris, reflected these ideas. Why is the "heavenly" political life alienated from man's "species-life"? Answer: money, huckstering. Though religion has a "human core," it is nevertheless a form of alienation endemic to all political society. Man's species-life is fragmented into private interest and private property.

The great leap forward in Marx's humanism came in his "Contribution to the Critique of Hegel's Philosophy of Right," written in Paris at the end of 1843. This essay contains Marx's first mention of the proletariat. Robert Tucker claims that Marx got the idea straight from Lorenz von Stein.[4] If there was an influence, it was of the order of the influence of Saxo Grammaticus' story on Shakespeare's *Hamlet*. For Marx fused the idea of the proletariat with his other ideas about man, transforming the whole into a flaming philosophy for world-shaking action. In that essay Marx begins with the question of religious alienation. Recognizing once more the human essence of religion, though that appears in perverted and fantastic form, Marx observes that the illusions of religious consciousness are the symptoms of an alienated material situation. Criticism of the dehumanization in religion must become criticism of the political and economic conditions giving rise to such dehumanization. Thus, mere philosophy is not sufficient; there must be action. Marx breaks forth with a polemical cry, proclaiming *"the categorical imperative to overthrow all relations* in which man is a debased, enslaved, abandoned, despicable essence. . . ."[5] The power in history for achieving the fulfillment of man is not the Christian God, Hegelian Reason, or Feuerbachian Humanism. It is the proletariat—an utterly dehumanized class which Marx declares is destined to redeem all men because with its "radical chains" and its "universal suffering" it can free itself only by freeing all men. Humanism will thus become a living, militant faith as it is taken up and embodied by working men in a common struggle

---

[4]Tucker, Robert: *Philosophy and Myth in Karl Marx.* New York, Cambridge, 1961, p. 116.

[5]Marx, Karl: Contribution to the critique of Hegel's philosophy of right. Introduction, p. 50.

against the ruling class of capitalism. This indignant, caustic, incisive, optimistic work is like a ringing battle-cry. One can picture the young Marx, surrounded by the workers of a secret communist society in a smoke-filled cellar; and the young Marx is declaiming how philosophy must be realized in the action of workers, and how the workers must realize themselves through the guidance of philosophy. Marx found in the proletariat the real material and dynamic weapon for transforming the oppression of a society of private property and massive suffering. His humanism had come home to humanity. It had found a force and a hope in the toiling masses.

In Paris Marx for the first time became aware of the proletariat as a living power in history. Apart from that discovery, it is unlikely that the idea of the proletariat and the class struggle would have achieved prominence in his outlook. In his "Economic and Philosophical Manuscripts," written from April to August, 1844, Marx developed more fully the notion of alienated labor and made his humanism still more concrete. He characterized his position as follows:

> *Communism* is the *positive* abolition of *private property,* of *human self-alienation,* and thus the real *appropriation* of *human* nature through and for man . . . . Communism as a fully-developed naturalism is humanism and as a fully-developed humanism is naturalism . . . . atheism as the annulment of God is the emergence of theoretical humanism, and communism as the annulment of private property is the vindication of real human life as man's property . . . . They are . . . the first real emergence, the genuine actualization, of man's nature as something real.[6]

In *The Holy Family,* written in the fall of 1844, Marx with the collaboration of Engels attacked the enemy of "real Humanism," namely, *"spiritualism* or *speculative idealism."*[7] Criticism, says Marx, creates nothing; the worker creates everything.[8] Here Marx moved into a dialectical analysis of how the proletariat is unconsciously the destruction and dissolution of the propertied class, how in becoming conscious of its dehumanization it begins to act to abolish both itself

---

[6]*Economic and Philosophical Manuscripts,* pp. 127, 188-189.

[7]Marx, K., and Engels, F.: *The Holy Family or Critique of Critical Critique.* Moscow, Foreign Languages Publishing House, 1956, p. 15.

[8]*Ibid.,* p. 30.

and its opposite in wealth.[9] Here Marx was not—as in his "Contribution to the Critique of Hegel's philosophy of Right"—a German philosopher of the proletariat without a German battlefield. He was a philosopher who could proudly point out that "a large part of the English and French proletariat is already conscious of its historic task and is constantly working to develop that consciousness into complete clarity."[10]

Meanwhile both Marx and Engels were moving closer to direct immersion in the activity of the workers. Following a trip to England in the summer of 1845, where they studied economics and met Chartists and leaders of the League of the Just, they began *The German Ideology*. In that work Marx and Engels undertook to come to terms with their Hegelian heritage and to develop a material, concrete, historical approach to man. There they affirm that men are fundamentally material beings and secondarily conscious, and that becoming conscious of themselves and their world, men create their own life and history. This creation is social labor. Historically, however, men have become separated by private property (division of labor) into classes, the propertied and the propertyless. It is the antagonism of these classes which is the dynamic of history. Thus, communism for them is not merely an ideal. It is a material and world-wide force of the proletariat, "the *real* movement which abolishes the present state of things."[11]

The *Manifesto of the Communist Party,* begun by Marx and Engels in late 1847, developed this philosophy of historical materialism still further. It marked the culmination of a humanism which began with religious and philosophical idealism and matured in a philosophy, a party, and a program which has revolutionized the modern world.

Let us now examine more closely this philosophy of man and of human value.

All value for Marx has its source in human "self-activity"[12] or free labor. This self-activity or self-creation[13] is the creating of the

---

[9]*Ibid.,* pp. 51-52.

[10]*Ibid.,* p. 53.

[11]Marx, Karl, and Engels, Friedrich: *The German Ideology,* Parts I and III, R. Pascal (Ed.). New York, International, 1947, p. 26.

[12]*Ibid.,* p. 66 and passim.

[13]*Economic and Philosophical Manuscripts,* p. 139.

human self, human society, and the human world of natural objects—known, used, and assimilated to the needs and purposes of human beings in society. It is "practical-critical" and is the productive inter-action of man (as social) with circumstances, each changing the other.[14] Nature (soil, plants, animals, etc.) exists prior to the opera-tions of man upon it.[15] Moreover, ape-man may subsist in and through nature merely by consuming natural objects directly for his own subsistence (as in gathering fruits). But man becomes genu-inely human and objects acquire use-value (satisfy some human need) when proto-man "annexes [Nature] to his own bodily organs," [16] creates instruments or means of production, [17] and exchanges socially the use-value that he produces. Ape-man, like other animals, pro-duces his existence; man produces the means for producing his exist-ence. The former consumes nature in order to live (satisfy minimal needs). The latter consumes nature in order to produce, in order to live, in order to produce, in order to live productively. Man becomes man as he interposes his productivity between raw nature and his own needs. In doing so he makes products whose use-value is not just immediate and intrinsic, but is prospective and instrumental; he makes products that can be used to produce additional prod-ucts.[18]

In summary, value is a process by which man, social in his origins and makeup,[19] interacts with natural objects (unprocessed or already transformed by human labor), produces for his own productive use instruments of production, thereby increases use-values, exchanges such use-values with his fellow man, consumes use-values to satisfy needs, fulfills the demands of personal and social systems, and employs such fulfillment to facilitate this same process. The material con-sequences of this value-process are products—use-values, and, if com-modities, exchange-values. These are precipitates of the value process

---

[14]Marx, Karl: *Theses on Feuerbach,* I and III.

[15]Marx, Karl: *Capital: A Crititcal Analysis of Capitalist Production,* vol. I, p. 177 ff. See also Marx, K.: *Critique of the Gotha Programme,* pp. 15-16.

[16]*Capital,* vol. I, p. 179; and see *Economic and Philosophical Manuscripts,* p. 100.

[17]*The German Ideology,* p. 16.

[18]*Capital,* vol. I, pp. 177-184.

[19]*Economic and Philosophical Manuscripts,* p. 129.

—"crystalization[s] of social labor,"[20] "material expressions of the human labor spent in their production."[21]

The value process differentiates itself as the creation of the self of individual man, the creation (or humanizing) of natural objects (nature) in and through man's relations to them, and the creation of society in and through man's relations to other men.

The self is created in the following events:

(1) The impulsion (müssen) to live, develop, struggle with obstacles to living, and progressively order existence.

(2) The satisfying of the demands of subsistence by the producing of the means of subsistence.[22]

(3) The eliciting of man's "slumbering powers."[23]

(4) The evoking of man's sensitivities and needs, achieved through objectifying man's essence in human, social objects which in turn awaken specific senses.[24]

(5) The emerging, shaping, and directing of man's needs over and beyond the needs of subsistence. "This . . . is the first historical act."[25] Further, needs are satisfied in a psychosomatic system of needs and satisfactions.

(6) The emerging of consciousness, self-consciousness, consciousness of others and of natural objects (objectivity), language, and purposes.[26]

(7) The achieving of man's identity, his continuous self-becoming, and his humanization. "Free, conscious activity is the species-character of human beings." [27]

(8) The materializing of human labor through the human transformation of materials.[28]

The self's relations to others are created by and in:

---

[20]Marx, Karl: *Value, Price and Profit*, Eleanor Marx-Aveling (Ed.). New York, International, 1935, p. 31.

[21]*Capital*, vol. I, p. 74.

[22]*Ibid.*, pp. 179 ff.

[23]*Ibid.*, p. 177.

[24]*Economic and Philosophical Manuscripts*, pp. 131-134.

[25]*The German Ideology*, p. 17. See also *Capital*, vol. I, p. 171.

[26]*Ibid.*, p. 19; *Economic and Philosophical Manuscripts*, pp. 126, 130, 132; *Capital*, vol. I, p. 178.

[27]*Economic and Philosophical Manuscripts*, p. 101.

[28]*Capital*, vol. I, p. 180.

(1) The emerging of man's essential need for others.[29]

For, "the human essence . . . . in its reality . . . is the ensemble of the social relations."[30] It exists "only in community with others."[31]

(2) The humanizing of the man-woman relation.[32]

(3) The creating of the family and family-relations, and the re-producing of man.[33]

(4) The cooperative activity of human beings in production and reproduction.[34]

(5) The developing of the self's relations with others—love and trust—through reciprocal influence.[35]

(6) "The productive power of social labor," developing the capabilities of man as man.[36]

The self's relations to natural objects are created by and in:

(1) The transforming of the natural object from a mere thing to "a human, social object, created by man and destined for him."[37] This is the assimilating of natural objects into the context of human objective understanding, subjective appreciation, and human use. It is the transforming of things into values.

(2) The naturalizing or objectifying of human needs—the other side of the humanizing of natural objects.[38]

(3) The actualizing by the self of the possibilities of nature in thought and practice. "Living labor must seize upon these things and rouse them from their death-sleep, change them from mere possible use-values into real and effective ones."[39]

(4) The self's changing of the form of the materials worked over by man.[40]

---

[29]*The German Ideology*, pp. 19, 74; *Economic and Philosophical Manuscripts*, pp. 126, 129, 130, 138.

[30]*Theses on Feuerbach*, VI.

[31]*The German Ideology*, p. 74.

[32]*Economic and Philosophical Manuscripts*, p. 126.

[33]*The German Ideology*, p. 17.

[34]*Ibid.*, p. 18.

[35]*Economic and Philosophical Manuscripts*, pp. 126-127, 168.

[36]*Capital*, vol. I, p. 329.

[37]*Economic and Philosophical Manuscripts*, p. 132.

[38]*Ibid.*, p. 133.

[39]*Capital*, vol. I, p. 183.

[40]*Ibid.*, pp. 71, 178, 180.

(5) The producing of means of subsistence[41]—instruments and skills—which in turn create relations of production and exchange and give rise to institutions.

In his theory of man and of value, Marx rejects both idealism and mechanical materialism. Man is not a disembodied being squatting over the world from on high. Marx starts out from the "real premises" of "men, not in any fantastic isolation or abstract definition, but in their actual, empirically perceptible process of development under definite conditions."[42] Men are not ideal, spiritualized entities which happen to acquire bodies. They are objective beings in an objective world where there is reciprocal stimulus and response.[43] They are bodies—not inert, passive bodies moved by blind forces, but bodies that are passionate,[44] self-moving, and free in community. They are not billiard balls knocked about by circumstances, but active agents who change circumstances.[45]

Marx's view of man and of man's fulfillment (i.e., his value) is both materialistic and dialectical. Man is originally a biological being whose generic potentialities are materialized and formed, elicited and elaborated, differentiated and integrated, as man interacts with his social and ecological environment in his effort to live, to produce, to reproduce, and to fulfill his human needs. Man as man is in continuous creation: he creates himself and is created by others and his nonhuman world. "Circumstances make men just as much as men make circumstances."[46] He humanizes his natural body and naturalizes his humanity in his relations to others and to nature.[47] Thus man in his body-in-action, his body-in-productive-relations-with-others-and-nature. "As individuals express their life, so they are."[48]

This dialectical process of the unfoldment of man's material powers —a "practical-critical" process—is profoundly creative. Indeed, Marx characterizes it as "revolutionary."[49] For men make history. A Spirit

---

[41]*The German Ideology,* p. 16.
[42]Ibid., p. 15.
[43]*Economic and Philosophical Manuscripts,* pp. 133-134, 180-183.
[44]*Ibid.,* p. 183.
[45]*Theses on Feuerbach,* III.
[46]*The German Ideology,* p. 29.
[47]*Economic and Philosophical Manuscripts,* pp. 129-140.
[48]*The German Ideology,* p. 7.
[49]*Theses on Feuerbach,* I, III.

does not make it, nor do the concatenations of dead atoms make it. The process by which human life continuously transforms itself and its world precedes consciousness and determines it.[50] It is there before men become aware of it. Man is creating himself and human values long before he thinks consciously about doing so. Yet he can think consciously about his life and its creation. And he can discover how it is blocked in its fulfillment and how this blockage can be overcome.

Some humanists like Gajo Petrović have accentuated the "spiritual" or creative character of man's *praxis*[51] while other progressive philosophers like Donald C. Hodges[52] have accentuated the actual process of socially necessary labor. Both the normative and factual, the prescriptive and descriptive approaches to values may be found in Marx, for Marx intended to signify the dialectical union of man's creative needs and purposes with the objective materials of the world.

Leaving aside use-values (things that satisfy human needs) which are not created by human effort—e.g., air, virgin soil, natural meadows[53]—Marx holds that the value of an object is what is conferred on it by human labor-power expended in its production.[54] For if we look at use-values as exchanged, the generic feature that they display in common is that they are the products of human labor.[55] Thus specific use-values that can be exchanged in the satisfaction of human needs are a "congelation of homogeneous human labour . . . crystals of this social substance" of human labor-power.[56] Mark puts the accent on the social productive process of men, so that a thing or commodity acquires value as it becomes a "crystallization of social labor,"[57] "congealed labor-time,"[58] or the material expression of human labor.[59] The term "value" in its fullest sense covers this whole

---

[50]*The German Ideology*, p. 15.

[51]Petrović, Gajo: *Marx in the Mid-Twentieth Century*. Garden City, Doubleday, 1967.

[52]Hodges, Donald C.: Marx's contribution to humanism. *Science and Society*, 29: 173-191, 1965.

[53]*Capital*, vol. I, p. 40.

[54]*Ibid.*, p. 38.

[55]*Ibid.*, p. 74.

[56]*Ibid.*, p. 38.

[57]Marx, Karl: *Value, Price and Profit*. New York, International, 1935, p. 31.

[58]Marx, Karl: *A Contribution to the Critique of Political Economy*, trans. from the second German edition by N. I. Stone. Chicago, Kerr, 1904, p. 24.

[59]*Capital*, vol. I, p. 74.

situation: men working in dialectical relation with one another and nature to produce things which after social exchange satisfy human needs. (The "things," as shall see in a moment, may be vegetables or poems.) More generally, the term "value" means the all-round development of men through a creative, social process that fulfills men's needs. Men produce, exchange, and use particular values; but the creative process underlying and embracing these activities is man's drive for development and fulfillment.[60]

In more empirical and quantitative terms, value is measured by the socially necessary labor-time required to produce any given product, allowing for the cost of educating and training and replacing the worker. The value of a man is his labor-power—"a capacity or power of the living individual." [61] What is this? It is a certain fund of living energy, expressible in a great variety of ways. Since man is social, this fund of energy translates into the social means of subsistence necessary to maintain and reproduce man.[62] Maintenance is a function of individual human needs, and man's natural needs, as Marx remarks, are conditioned by the physical circumstances of his life such as climate, as well as by historical and moral ones.[63]

Those who argue that Marx demeaned man by describing him as an "economic animal" fail to understand that Marx simply gave an account of what he observed, namely, man as a power for transforming himself and his world by productive activity. The fact that most men spend this power in routine and demeaning activity was not Marx's fault. Yet it is a fact which the critics of Marx who so stress "culture" and "spirit" in man do not want to face, and for which they want to hold Marx responsible because he has called it to their attention. It is a fact which most honest working men can face; and it is but one step from there to recognition of the contradiction between man's creativity and this fact of its alienation.

In his early works Marx used psychological and phenomenological

---

[60]*The German Ideology*, pp. 15, 16; *Capital*, vol. I, pp. 399, 484, 490; *Economic and Philosophical Manuscripts*, pp. 98, 140; *Critique of the Gotha Programme*, p. 27; Marx, Karl: *Capital. A Critique of Political Economy*, trans. from the first German edition by Ernest Untermann. Chicago, Kerr, 1909, vol. III, p. 954.

[61]*Capital*, vol. I, p. 171.

[62]*Ibid.*

[63]*Ibid.*

language to characterize man. Later, after he turned to political economy, he adopted the more objective language of science. But even then he employed from time to time phenomenological expressions, so that there is no indication that he intended to abandon his earlier view of man as a creative being who might transcend the demands of the market economy. If this were not so, in fact, to what purpose would he have made his elaborate analysis of the workings of the capitalist system?

When Marx speaks in *Capital* of "the useful kinds of labour, or productive activities," as "a physiological fact . . . functions of the human organisms . . . the expenditure of human brains, nerves, muscles, etc.," [64] he means what he means by "self-creation" in his early writings. "Labor-power" is human power, the living and directed energy of man. As it produces food, shelter, clothing, etc. it has been thus far in history a *necessary* expression of man: to survive man has had to interact with Nature and "appropriate Nature's productions in a form adapted to his own wants."[65] But it is clear that at this level of biological survival labor-power as the source of value is not the final form of the expression of man's power. For human labor-power includes both "mental and physical capabilities,"[66] and unlike the activity of the spider or bee, it employs imagination, will, and purpose.[67] Thus man's generic power to create himself and his world may be used for purposes transcending survival.

Man is the "impersonation" of labor-power; his labor is a "manifestation" of that power.[68] In bourgeois society the elemental form which this expression takes is "the commodity-form of the product of labour—or the value-form of the commodity."[69] However, this particular form of man's living energy is not destined to rule over man forever. Instead of being subjected to the appropriation of his energy by others, man can cooperate to create "a new power, namely, the collective power of the masses.[70] Instead of becoming a com-

---

[64]*Ibid.*, p. 71.
[65]*Ibid.*, p. 177.
[66]*Ibid.*, p. 167.
[67]*Ibid.*, p. 178.
[68]*Ibid.*, p. 202.
[69]*Ibid.*, p. 8.
[70]*Ibid.*, p. 326.

modity, man can become a man. Instead of man living for the expansion of "existing values" of material goods, capitalist accumulation, and profit, material wealth can serve "the needs of development" of man himself.[71]

Instead of selling his power and having it consumed by the capitalist,[72] man can own his own life and soul and will expend his power as befits his inner creativity. The capitalist is interested only in the surplus-value of the worker, only in what he can extract from his creative power to produce goods that can be exchanged for a profit. In his greed he cares nothing about the length of life of labor-power. In his "were-wolf hunger for surplus labor," he "usurps the time for growth, development, and healthy maintenance of the body."[73] When, however, men organize to overthrow these relations of private property, when classes disappear, when the means to live are abundant, when labor as the creative expenditure of energy "is not only a means of life but life's prime want," when the productive forces have increased with "the all-round development of the individual"[74]—then men will live under a new law of life: they will create according to their talents, and consume according to their needs. Their prime need will be to create, and they will create to satisfy their own need and the needs of others. They will labor not merely to survive as bodies but to fulfill themselves as human beings. Their labor will be a labor of love—the love of life through continuous creation of their life and the life of others.

In his later years Marx referred to Milton as a man who in creating *Paradise Lost* was an "unproductive laborer" in the capitalist market, but who was nonetheless creative.[75] Indeed, the point of Marx's whole economic analysis is to show how the capitalist with his surplus-value has intervened between man's social, creative powers and his products, how "the fetishism of commodities" has blinded men to the fact that it is they who determine the relations of commodities,[76]

---

[71] *Ibid.,* p. 621.

[72] *Ibid.,* p. 184.

[73] *Ibid.,* p. 265.

[74] *Critique of the Gotha Programme,* pp. 26-27.

[75] Marx, Karl: *Theories of Surplus Value,* trans. by G. A. Bonner and Emile Burns. New York, International, 1952, p. 186.

[76] *Capital,* vol. I, pp. 72-73.

and how the life process of men will not be demystified "until it is treated as production by freely associated men, and is consciously regulated by them in accordance with a settled plan." [77] Such association and plan spell socialism. If man's creative labor to produce food, etc. is necessary for his survival as a body, then his creative labor to produce poems, etc. is no less necessary for his survival as a full human being.

Marx undertook this formulation of human labor-power in economic terms not only because he was working within the language of classical bourgeois economy, but also because he wanted to show how human value in its productive origins becomes alienated from its ends in human use, consumption, and fulfillment. He did this through the concept of commodity, or exchange-value, which presupposes the notion of "abstract" human labor as the common denominator of values produced for human exchange. Marx wanted to show not only the link but also the gap and contradiction between value in the form of productive activity and value in the form of products for human consumption and consummation.[78] For it is plain to anyone who will take the time to observe that while most men produce values they do not appropriate and use them in the same proportion. Something has been lost in the process. Men have been alienated from the products of their labor and consequently from themselves.

The explanation for this alienation lies in the workings of the economy of capitalism. Driven to live in an economy where the use-values for maintaining life are obtained through the exchange of commodities, and having nothing to exchange except his own labor-power, the laboring man sells himself to an employer.[79] How is the value of his labor-power then determined? Like the value of every other commodity, it is determined by the socially necessary labor time for its production. For a man, this means his means of subsistence and re-production. Note that "subsistence" is not fulfillment. For the latter is *not* required where a man is hired as a specialized "hand" or even

---

[77] *Ibid.*, p. 80.

[78] Ash, William: *Marxism and Moral Concepts.* New York, Monthly Review, 1964, ch. 1.

[79] *Capital,* vol. I, p. 167.

"brain" to do a work dictated by the exploitive purposes of someone else. Capitalist economics, that is to say, does not take into account humanism. The owner of this commodity in labor-power then puts it to work for, let us say, twelve hours per day. After six hours of labor the laborer has produced enough for the employer to pay for the cost of his maintenance, training and reproduction.[80] That part of the product produced in the remaining six hours is expropriated by the employer for his own use. In brief, in this kind of relation the value of the productive labor-power, in terms of exchange-value, is *less* than its use-value. The laboring man is used to *create* value over and above the mere cost of his maintenance.[81] In moral terms, he is "cheated" out of his labor; he is "robbed" of his living energy. In technical terms, his labor-time is expropriated in the form of the "surplus-value" of the capitalist who owns and commands his wage labor. Surplus value is possible because a few people can capture and utilize that labor-power which is the universal source of human values.

Marx thought of the value-process as being natural and as having the character of a natural law. He thought it was obvious to "every child" that if men did not work they would not live for long.[82] The ultimate good of man is the fulfillment of man's powers through social production. Action that, of all practical alternatives, most contributes to this fulfillment is right, and action that does not is wrong. As a naturalist or materialist in his ethics, Marx does not concern himself with an unqualified distinction between nature and man, between facts and judgments, between things and values. He does believe that value-predicates cannot strictly be ascribed to natural objects as such; such ascription borders on "fetishism,"[83] or treating values as if they have an eixstence independent of human purposes. On the other hand, he is not a subjectivist in value theory. "Value" for Marx signifies an objective process of productive interaction of the individual person with things and with other persons in which things, persons, and relations are created and transformed in such ways as to fulfill men. As a naturalist Marx thinks that a description of

[80] *Ibid.*, p. 171.

[81] *Ibid.*, p. 193.

[82] Marx, Karl, and Engels, Frederick: *Selected Correspondence*. Moscow, Foreign Languages Publishing House, ND., p. 251.

[83] *Capital*, vol. I, ch. I, sect. 4.

this process will suffice to show what value is. Although in a single paragraph he uses the words, "expropriation," "exploiting," "misery," "oppression," "slavery," "degradation," "revolt," "fetter," etc.,[84]—he considers that these words may have objective as well as subjective meaning, and his main intent is to show by description the process of value, the obstructions to it, and the ways to remove the obstructions. The primary mode of his language is designative, and its primary function or aim is to evaluate things and events and to incite human action with respect to them. When Lewis S. Feuer states that "technological necessity had for Marx the qualities of a finally beneficient deity,"[85] he distorts Marx. The human, natural process of productive activity is the ultimate value—and human reality[86]—for Marx. The technological class struggles at various stages of history are the ways in which this productive activity expresses its large-scale antagonisms and resolutions. Because man makes his own history[87] and "mankind always takes up only such problems as it can solve,"[88] it is *man,* making and using instruments of production, who creates the kind of society he has.[89] In *Capital* Marx repeatedly underscores the fact that men's labor has created tools, machinery, technology, capital, and private property; and the implication is continuous that the same labor can change the relations of private property.

Health for Marx is the progressive fulfillment of man's practical-critical capacities that comes with productive activity. It is psycho-natural-social health. The health of man is organic in this inclusive sense. Since ideas grow out of, organize, direct, and change the productive process,[90] all beliefs in a mechanistic fate or an omnipotent providence, or in a disembodied domain of ideas, are conditions of illness. Since "nature is man's body with which he must remain in a continuous interchange in order not to die,"[91] then philosophical

---

[84]*Ibid.,* p. 763.

[85]Marx, Karl, and Engels, Friedrich: *Basic Writings on Politics and Philosophy,* Lewis S. Feuer (Ed.). Garden City, Doubleday, 1959, xvii in Introduction.

[86]*Selected Correspondence,* p. 498.

[87]*Economic and Philosophical Manuscripts,* p. 39; Selected *Correspondence,* pp. 41, 498, 549; *Theses on Feuerbach,* III.

[88]*A Contribution to the Critique of Political Economy,* p. 12.

[89]*The German Ideology,* pp. 74 ff.

[90]*Selected Correspondence,* pp. 496, 505, 542.

[91]*Economic and Philosophical Manuscripts,* p. 101.

idealism which denies the primacy and coerciveness of bodily needs
is a sign of illness. Since man's productive activity is a natural transaction, wherein a part of nature, man, along with his objects, becomes humanized and man becomes more fully naturalized[92]—then
religious supernaturalism is a symptom or cause of illness. Since man's
productive activity is social and "the human essence . . . is the ensemble of social relations"[93]—then all isolation, enmity, subservience,
and exploitation of man in relation to man are pathic. Since man
collectively creates ideas, use-values, and exchange-values with his
brain and hands, all beliefs in the independent life and relations of
ideas and commodities[94] are mystifications of a disordered mind. Since
man is the creator of values and social relations, it is a delusion and
estrangement to think that commodities have a social law of their
own while man is only a material being. Since man's self-activity is
always revolutionizing the conditions of his life,[95] then all fixation of
ideas or forms of actions, all idolatry of the *status quo,* is indicative
of illness. Since *man* is the locus and man's fulfillment is the measure
of value, then all forms of "dehumanization" are conditions of sickness, both in the dehumanizer and the dehumanized.

In capitalistic society man experiences ill health and the loss or
"crippling" of his self-activity[96] when, as he cooperates with tools and
machines and other men and produces his life, he comes into conflict
with the relations of private property. Man's productive labor is
social and cooperative, but the products of his labor are exchanged
according to the principle of private ownership and exploitation.
Thus, in the exchange of the commodity of his labor, he is returned
less than the use-value he creates.[97] The difference is expropriated by
the capitalist in the form of surplus-value. This conflict, which takes
the social form of class struggle, is the conflict between social productivity and the private appropriation of the products of productivity.
(If we follow ordinary usage we cannot call it "stealing," for the
term in law and religion alike does not apply to it; hence the analysis

[92]*Ibid.,* pp. 100-101, 127, 129, 132 ff.

[93]*Theses on Feuerbach,* VI.

[94]*Capital,* vol. I, p. 72.

[95]*Theses on Feuerbach,* I.

[96]*The German Ideology,* p. 66; *Capital,* vol. I, ch. 14.

[97]*Capital,* vol. I, p. 193.

of ordinary language can never take us beyond ordinary capitalism.)

This conflict is the expression of man's alienation. It means that man is split off from the product of his labor, no longer at one with nature and with it, no longer owning it; that human value (including man himself and his products) is "objectified" in the form of things, products, commodities, to be bought and sold according to the principle of making money in the transaction, rather than using the commodities to fulfill human need; that man loses his unity with his means of subsistence; that he is alienated from himself by the constricting, exhausting nature of his work, and the separation of his production from genuine self-activity and enjoyment; that man is forced to work, not for the joy of creating, but in order to get the means whereby to satisfy other needs; that man is alienated from his "species-life," being compelled to enlist his whole life-activity in the service of animal subsistence and in the dehumanizing tasks of "detail labor";[98] that man is alienated from the means of production, including tools, machines, and other instruments of labor; and that man is alienated from other men by the division of labor, the "mutual cheating," [99] and the exploitation of private property relations.[100] In short, man experiences his own "devaluation"[101] for the sake of the power and glory of things. Money talks, through the mouths of those few who own and control it; and the mass of men listen and dance to those who call the tune. Thus, Marx portrays the pathology of man's productiveness, the occlusions in the arterial stream of the otherwise healthy body of society.

Marx believes that since by man came alienation and death, so by man also will come the resurrection of the dead and the return of alien man to his true human home. The cure for man's illness is (1) the removal of the causative conditions, and (2) the natural therapy of productive, social labor. To remove the conditions of illness, man must call upon the resources of health in his situation. Marx thinks man possesses at the roots of his being a natural impulsion to development, and that this is elicited and exerted in the face

---

[98]*Ibid.*, ch. 14.

[99]*Ibid.*, p. 164; *Economic and Philosophical Manuscripts*, p. 112.

[100]*Economic and Philosophical Manuscripts*, pp. 96-103.

[101]*Ibid.*, p. 94.

of adverse circumstances. It is at this point of conflict that consciousness is generated,[102] and is used to conduct man in recovering his lost unity with himself and the world of natural objects. The real is the rational, if by "rational" we mean the ordering process of man's productive activity. Man is ever impelled to "make sense" of his world, and thus to remove the "contradictions" that appear in his practice. This must be done by practice,[103] guided by theory. Man's real, healthy nature tends to assert itself in the face of obstacles: this is the anthropological basis for Marx's thesis that the forces of production overcome the "fetters" of the relations of production. The dialectical process in history is the transforming power of human practice writ large. Individual men collectively make history.

The key ethical concept in Marx is "development."[104] Man has a definite structure, a "species-life," a character that defines his humanity as creative growth; man's problem is to recover this. C. Wright Mills overdoes Marx's "historical specificity" and is in error when he says that "human nature, according to Marx, is not an unchanging, inevitable anchor-point for any existing or possible instiution."[105] When Marx speaks of "new men" and of founding "society anew"[106] he has in mind a return to (or progress toward) man as he really is in all the many-sided fulfillment[107] of his productive potential. Marx's anthropological "premises" are "men, not in any fantastic isolation or abstract definition, but in their actual, empirically perceptible process of development under definite conditions." [108] The goal of ethical thought and political action is "an association, in which the free development of each is the condition for the free development of all."[109] We cannot now know the full concrete content of such future development, but we can know that it will express the "species-life" of man's developmental nature.

---

[102]*A Contribution to the Critique of Political Economy,* p. 12.

[103]*Economic and Philosophical Manuscripts,* p. 149.

[104]*The German Ideology,* pp. 15, 16; *Capital,* vol. I, pp. 399, 484, 490; *Economic and Philosophical Manuscripts,* pp. 98, 140; *Critique of the Gotha Programme,* p. 27; Marx, Karl: *Capital. A Critique of Political Economy,* vol. III, p. 954.

[105]Mills, C. Wright: *The Marxists.* New York, Dell, 1962 p. 39.

[106]*The German Ideology,* p. 69.

[107]*Ibid.,* p. 22.

[108]*Ibid.,* p. 15.

[109]Marx, Karl, and Engels, Friedrich: *Manifesto of the Communist Party,* p. 31.

Man's immediate task is to break the bonds, to burst the "integument,"[110] of capitalist private property. It is to socialize the means of production and bring property relations into harmony with productive relations. The economic exploitation of the many by the few is the particular fetter from which creative man must now be freed. Capitalism is the particular "womb"[111] from which the new society must be delivered—"after prolonged birth pangs."[112] The root metaphor in Marx is productive labor, the joyful travail of the creator, the Promethean and Nietzchean suffering for the sake of a higher humanity, both here and now and in the future. This labor, moreover, is *social*. The primitive communal group, where the serpents of commodities and money have not entered, is also a root metaphor in Marx. The ideal is a world-wide commune of creators. Marx rescued the stone that the liberal and capitalistic builders rejected, fraternity, and made it the cornerstone of man's new home.

To criticize Marx for absolutizing (1) the economic factor in history and (2) the task of creating a socialistic economy now, is to mistake his particular for his generic emphasis. Marx was a philosopher as well as a man of political action. The emergence of man from the dark ignorance and slavery of "pre-history" into the full light[113] of intelligent social control and freedom, the turning around of the manifold "inversions" and the removal of "contradictions" of past and present, issuing in the unitary health of man and restoring man to the productive center of his life—that is the generic goal for man. But in practice, contradictions and problems must be solved step by step. The great task in capitalistic societies is to conquer and sublate the obsession with food and material goods by socializing and collectively controlling the means whereby these are produced and exchanged. That conquest by a social and industrial democracy is itself a manifestation of man's self-activity, but it also paves the way for creativity at a higher and freer level.[114] Egoism (status-seeking, the cult of the individual), tyranny (capitalistic or bureaucratic, centralized control of decision-making and the mass media), rigidity in

---

[110]*Capital*, vol. I, p. 763.

[111]*A Contribution to the Critique of Political Economy*, p. 13.

[112]*Critique of the Gotha Programme*, p. 26.

[113]*Economic and Philosophical Manuscripts*, p. 142.

[114]*Ibid.*, p. 140.

belief and practice (authoritarianism or sectarianism), schisms between theory and practice, overpopulation, nuclear war, economically undeveloped societies, automation, are specific problems too. But they will not be solved with optium value unless men collectively deal with them in democratic, creative ways for the sake of the release of man's creative capacities— "the capabilities of his species."[115]

Marx can be criticized for his failure to discern or foresee: the power of the non-economic and non-political factors in the life of man—biological forces; the symbolic origins and transformations of the minds and cultures of men; the force of social institutions and traditions, such as autonomous military and police powers; the sway of mass propaganda and advertising; instruments of destruction reared by technology—negations to end all negations; the narcotizing effects of mass media; and the inhibitory, repressive, perceptually and conceptually distorting effects of unconscious anxieties and habits. He did not comprehend in the nineteenth century the limits of man's control over his own history and development, though he knew of the stultifying influence of science and technology on men. He was aware that ideas and modes of action grow up "behind the backs"[116] of men, unknown to them in their full effects, and that circumstances change men in ways men do not imagine or will. He stood on the verge of seeing that if man does not arrest his social life at the level of an ant colony or blast it into oblivion, and if man has discovered and provided the proper conditions for optimum creativity—e.g., opportunities for individual initiative, responsibility, methods of consultation and consensus—then unpredictable perspectives will emerge opening the way for directing man into new forms of creative experience.[117]

What is to be the guiding factor in human evolution? Those emergent perspectives are most useful to man which enable him to know, and to relate himself effectively to, the conditions that control the further emergence of perspectives. Optimal freedom arises at this point, where man freely minds and effectively acts toward the

---

[115]*Capital*, vol. I, p. 329.

[116]*Ibid.*, p. 14.

[117]Jacobson, N. P.: Marxism and religious naturalism. *Journal of Religion*, 22: 95-113, 1949.

conditions necessary to the further freeing of his minding and acting. Perspectives and actions called "free" that do not produce this creative feedback can become obstacles to freedom in the above sense, when men who possess them purport to represent final truths and values for man. Their illusion is to mistake their own limited knowledge and control for the wider power of a creativity that under certain conditions frees them from such limits. When Engels says that freedom consists in the knowledge of natural laws and decisive control over things[118] he is correct so far as freedom is in part the displacement of ignorance and subjection with knowledge and control. But he does not recognize, except perhaps implicitly, that the natural law of man's development—the liberation of creative powers—as far as some now have insight into it, issues in knowledge of things and knowledge of that law itself, which knowledge man does not now have.[119]

Contrary to common belief in this country, Marx's concept of human value and health, for all its distinctiveness, is the inheritor and transformer of a long line of humanistic thoughts and systems in western culture. These systems might be called "naturalistic" insofar as they affirmed that man as a part of nature can and should realize his natural and human possibilities. But many have been at the same time supernaturalistic and in that respect have not accepted a humanistic solution to man's alienation. This humanistic line of thought is illustrated in the Jewish, prophetic, preexilic concept of man; the individualistic philosophy of Aristotle and the communal, though static, philosophy of Plato; the Stotic concept of the unity of man and man and man and nature; Jesus and early Christian thought; the millennialist Brethren of the Free Spirit; the Cathari and Waldenses; Francis of Assisi and radical Franciscans; the pantheists; the apocalyptics who followed Joachim of Fiore; Thomas Aquinas, in spite of his conservativism; Wycliffe, the Lollards, and John Ball; the spokesman for the Flemish, French, and English peasants in revolt; the great German mystics; the Gottesfreunde and Brethren of the Common

---

[118]Engels, Frederick: *Anti-Dühring. Herr Eugen Dühring's Revolution in Science.*, 2nd ed. Moscow, Foreign Languages Publishing House, 1959, p. 157.

[119]Wieman, Henry N.: *The Source of Human Good.* Chicago, University of Chicago, 1946. For Engels' fallibilism, see *Anti-Dühring,* ch. IX.

Life; Huss, Münzer, and others in the left-wing of the Reformation; the humanists of the Renaissance—Dante, Erasmus, Leonardo da Vinci, Thomas More, Francis Bacon, Campanella, Bruno, Shakespeare, Montaigne, etc.; Dutch and English revolutionary thought; Levellers and Diggers; the thinkers of the Enlightenment; humanistic leaders of the French and American revolutions— the list goes on through many figures and nations to modern times. When R. H. Tawney described Marx as the "last of the Schoolmen," [120] he was referring to Marx's opposition to the middleman and to excess profits, and to Marx's labor theory of value. But this theory, as we have seen, entails a natural and social view of man and his health. Marx continued and advanced this tradition, which, though variously mixed with individualism, supernaturalism, and class society, came down from ancient times. That ancient tradition held, not without ambiguities and mystifications, that man is a participant in nature and society, and that his good life lies in the fulfillment of his essential nature, here and now, among other men, and in nature.

Taking account of their differences, there is a strong similarity between some thought in contemporary American psychology and psychiatry and the views of Marx on human nature, value, and health. What they stress in common is as follows: man can be understood and fulfilled by his own study and control of his natural, social, critical behavior; the natural dispositions of man to be productive and social are primary and predominant over dispositions to be unproductive, destructive, and antisocial; man's fulfillment consists in the elaboration and integrated consummation of these productive dispositions; man's environment, natural and social, elicits or inhibits such dispositions; man thus can learn to control and guide his fulfillment as he controls and guides these dispositions of transaction with environing men and nature; and man can improve in this power to fulfill himself. To the extent that contemporary thought is melioristic about man, it shares most, if not all, of these definitions and postulates. It thus stands in contrast to that fatalism, religious or secular, which views man as the victim of his own inadequacy, of an omnipotent deity, or of inexorable physical forces.

---

[120]Tawney, R. H.: *Religion and the Rise of Capitalism.* New York, Penguin, 1947, p. 39.

However, Marx's humanism differs from all of these. It is revolutionary. It realizes that man's true fulfillment requires a thorough transformation of society. That means that the working class of men must displace the ruling class with a cooperative social order in which each man contributes according to his abilities and each receives according to his needs. The means for this transformation may be peaceful and ought to be so; if violence is introduced into the struggle, then it is introduced primarily by those who monopolize the tools of violence and who are accustomed to using them in maintaining and extending power. The transformation must be human, social, and total. It must be of, by, and for the people. It must be impelled by the people's real human needs and must proceed socially by fulfilling those needs through changing the material and social environment. The revolution cannot be effected by mere formal education or by anarchist violence. The source of the revolution must be real men moved by the need and ideal of fulfilling themselves; and the end of the revolution must be men's fulfillment itself.

VI

MARXISM AND HUMANISM

IT IS IMPORTANT to elucidate Marxism still further, by showing more specifically how it arose in reaction against its humanistic predecessors and how it is distinguished as a materialist, dialectical humanism from rival humanisms.

Marxism is a humanism in its origin, method, and goal. By "Marxism" here we shall mean primarily the leading concepts expressed by Marx. By "humanism" we shall mean any system of thought that makes man the agent and tester of knowledge and value. Of course, there are many other Marxist thinkers, the principal ones being Engels and Lenin. Marxism is much more than humanism in the sense defined; it is science, practice, and a way of life. Our focus here, however, will be on the humanistic character of the thought of Marx, though to examine that thought leads us necessarily into questions of practice.

The historical origin of Marx's thought lies in the whole complex of natural and historical conditions which produced him. Here we should consider the course of western civilization, Marx's family life, his education, the economic, political, and cultural forces at work on him, and the like. (See the final chapter.) We have already mentioned the immediate and primary philosophical causes of Marx's thought in the work of Hegel and then Feuerbach. With the great heritage of the Enlightenment and Christianity behind him, Hegel fused the questions of how man can become perfect and how Jesus became divine, i.e., he fused the basic questions of philosophy and religion. His answer lay in tracing man's unfulfillment or alienation back to its source. In the terms of the secular Enlightenment, this source is the world-spirit; in religious terms, it is the spirit of God. But Hegel was sufficiently humanistic to see that these are one and same, and that, moreover, man's spirit is an expression of the divine world-spirit. It follows, then that any alienation which man experiences must be the self-alienation of the divine world-spirit as it works out its destiny in the consciousness of man, progressively achieving its freedom through self-awareness.

This was an explosive idea, explosive because it located the force of progress and freedom not only in the world but also in man. But the logic of its development was hidden under the shell of religious philosophy.

Feuerbach smashed that shell. What emerged was the embryo of the world-spirit transformed into man—real man, natural, material, and human. In Feuerbach it was shown that man is the being who is alienated, not God, and that God is in fact the reflection of man's alienation and not the other way around. Man has alienated himself from himself by projecting his highest attributes onto God. Nonetheless, Feuerbach, limited by the mechanical materialism that he had taken over from the French *philosophes,* clung to certain mystical vestiges like "love" and "religion." He started, but did not complete, the revolt against Hegel.

In his *Theses on Feuerbach,* written in 1845, Marx proposed to negate and supersede the negator. Hegel spoke of a dialectical, spiritual humanism; Feuerbach, of a materialistic, sensuous, humanism; and Marx, of a dialectical, materialist humanism. Where Hegel referred to a thought process in God, Marx referred to a real historical process among men. Where Feuerbach advocated sensuousness, Marx insisted on practice. Where Feuerbach held on to the isolated human individual, and Hegel absorbed man in the divine whole, Marx argued that the human essence is social and interactive. Where both Hegel and Feuerbach believed that religion belongs to man's essence, Marx maintained that religious sentiment is always a social and particular product. Where Hegel said that God makes history and Feuerbach countered with *"contemplative* materialism," Marx proposed that *man* change society by revolutionary practice. Where Hegel aimed at the Kingdom of God in the state and Feuerbach took as his standpoint "civil" society, with individuals in abstract relations one to another, Marx affirmed: "the standpoint of the new is *human* society, or socialized humanity." [1] In short, Marx's humanism—the critical, crea-

---

[1] *Theses on Feuerbach,* X.

tive synthesis of Hegel's and Feuerbach's humanisms—was dialectical, practical, social, and revolutionary. Thus, while the *historical* origin of Marx's humanism may be traced to his predecessors, its real origin (humanism grounded in the facts of nature itself) must be *man,* i.e., both his real possibilities for fulfillment and his decisional tendency to realize those possibilities.

Earlier, in his article, "Contribution to the Critique of Hegel's Philosophy of Right. Introduction," written at the end of 1843 and 1844, Marx had discussed the question of how critical, revolutionary theory can in fact make connection with human practice in shaping history. He said:

> Theory is capable of gripping the masses as soon as it demonstrates *ad hominem,* and it demonstrates *ad hominem* as soon as it becomes radical. To be radical is to grasp the root of the matter. But for man the root is man himself.[2]

He goes on to show that the German criticism of religion, which is "the premise of all criticism" and indicates that *"Man makes religion, religion does not make man,"*

> ends with the teaching that *man is the highest essence for man,* hence with the *categorical imperative to overthrow all relations* in which man is debased, enslaved, abandoned, despicable essence. . . .[3]

If man is "the root of the matter," and if his "essence"—definition, ideal, or active principle—is human, then for Marx there is no alternative: man is commanded unconditionally to become a fully concrete man. What Marx is saying is that man's nature is such that when his thought reveals to himself his needs and their necessity for fulfillment, then he will be obliged (müssen) to follow their impulse and to overcome obstacles that stand in their way. This notion of Marx's that self-knowledge leads to self-fulfillment in action is a materialist transformation of Hegel's notion that self-consciousness increases freedom. The notion also conveys a faith in the great power of theory, theory that "becomes a material force as soon as it has gripped the masses." [4] Here Marx implicitly rejects the view that a small elite minority can "lead" or "direct" the masses to their own revolutionary fulfillment,

---

[2]In Marx, K., and Engels, F.: *On Religion,* p. 50.
[3]*Ibid.*
[4]*Ibid.*

and the view that history automatically carries the masses to fulfillment. As Marx and Engels put it in several different places,[5] men
make their own history, by applying their own thought to themselves
and their own specific conditions. This view of man and his possibilities for human improvement by himself is thoroughly humanistic. Man
makes himself.

In the same article, Marx considers the question of how man might
achieve his fulfillment, specifically, the question of the "emancipation"
of the German nation through revolutionary activity. With the Reformation and the French revolution in the background, he takes it for
granted that such a change must come through a class. But which
class? A merely political or partial revolution, such as the French and
American revolutions, in which one class liberates only those who
share in its advantages, cannot be adequate. Only that class which
merges itself with the needs of the masses, which makes its claims and
rights the claims and rights of all, which makes itself their general
representative, can emancipate society. For this task, mere idealistic
energy and feeling are not sufficient. The emancipating class, to act
for the generality, must be "the incorporation of the general limitation,
a particular social sphere must be recognized as the *notorious crime*
of the whole society, so that liberation from that sphere appears as
general self-liberation." [6] The emancipating class must concentrate
in itself the defects of all society, standing over against a class whose
oppression is obvious. In short, there must be negative and positive
class representatives of man—those who represent man's negation of
man, and those who, embodying man's suffering and revolutionary
nature, represent the negation of that negation. Marx then describes
this positive, revolutionary class; it is

> a class with *radical chains*, a class of civil society which is not a class
> of civil society, an estate which is the dissolution of all estates, a sphere
> which has a universal character by its universal suffering and claims no
> *particular right* because no *particular wrong* but *wrong generally* is per-
> petrated against it; which can invoke no *historical* but only its *human*

---

[5]In *Economic and Philosophic Manuscripts of 1844, The German Ideology,
Theses on Feuerbach, The Eighteenth Brumaire of Louis Bonaparte,* and *Selected
Correspondence.*

[6]Marx K.: Contribution to the critique of Hegel's philosophy of right. Introduction, p. 50.

title, which does not stand in any one-sided antithesis to the consequences but in an all-around antithesis to the premises of German statehood; a sphere, finally, which cannot emancipate itself without emancipating itself from all other spheres of society and thereby emancipating all other spheres of society, which, in a word, is the *complete loss of man* and hence can win itself only through the *complete re-winning of man.* This dissolution of society as a particular estate is the *proletariat.*[7]

The *human* ground and motive of revolution in this passage should be noted with care. It is often asserted, in ignorance or in malice, that Marx and the Marxists want class struggle and revolution because they like discord and violence, because they believe that might makes right, because they take bloody conflict to be an ultimate force in history, etc. Nothing could be further from the truth as far as Marx was concerned. In the first place, Marx and the Marxists did not invent class struggle and revolution; they simply observed it and tried to describe, forsee, and control its course. In the second place, they sought to trace this struggle to its roots, i.e., to man. What is society but a vast struggle of man against himself? Many men had seen this, from some of the Jewish prophets to Machiavelli, Hobbes, and Rousseau, and many humanists had proposed diagnoses and solutions. Here Marx proclaims the existence of a suffering class which, because it embodies no particular wrong but the wrong of the human *species* inflicted on it, is alone capable of acting for the species and, hence, liberating it.

Stated negatively, no particular civil class can act for mankind because it has no general interest. It has no general interest, except perhaps in an ideal or sentimental sense, because it has a particular stake in preserving its status in the civil order. It has something to lose. But the proletariat, as Marx and Engels stated in the *Manifesto* of 1848, have nothing to lose but their chains. Here these chains are called *radical.* That means that man is enslaved *at the root,* and that, therefore, when the slave undertakes to overcome the conditions of his enslavement he will "overthrow all relations" in which he is debased and not merely certain civil relations in civil society. In short, those members of classes who already have a commitment to a class society cannot lead the way into the emancipation of man: they are already committed to the forms of man's enslavement. Conversely, those who

---

[7]*Ibid.,* pp. 56-57.

are totally wronged and alienated will, when adequately aroused and informed, rise up, as Marx and Engels say in the *Manifesto*, and "the whole superincumbent strata of official society" will be "sprung into the air." [8] That is because proletarian change must be a radically *human* change in society. It is not because in God's providence the meek will inherit the earth, or because like Rousseau's noble savage man is born good but is everywhere in chains. It is because the depth of dehumanization in the proletarian class is so profound that in order to shake off its shackles totally it must demolish its dungeon totally. That is, it must necessarily sweep away "the conditions for the existence of class antagonisms and of classes generally, and will thereby have abolished its own supremacy as a class." [9] For man to free himself, he must free all men. Marx here maintains the grand Hegelian vision of the whole human species, interconnected and united, acting to free itself.

In the *Economic and Philosophic Manuscripts of 1844*, Marx examined the question of "alienated labor" and concluded:

> If the product of labor does not belong to the worker, if it confronts him as an alien power, this can only be because it belongs to some *other man than the worker*. If the worker's activity is a torment to him, to another it must be delight and his life's joy. Not the gods, not nature, but only man himself can be this alien power over men.[10]

Thus, as man sets the problem, so man also creates the solution to the problem. The dynamics of this process take the form of class struggle, which is to be understood through the materialist conception of history. Marx's article on Hegel's philosophy of right (written in 1843) shows an awareness of the state with its classes as a form of human alienation. Only when revolution is rooted in radical needs, he asserts, can a revolution be radical. Here there is a natural linkage of the human to the material and economic. In the *Economic and Philosophic Manuscripts of 1844* Marx says: "Communism, as fully-developed naturalism, equals humanism, and as fully-developed humanism equals naturalism." [11] When private property has been superseded, "only here has what is to him his *natural* existence become his *human* exist-

[8] *Manifesto of the Communist Party*, p. 20.
[9] *Ibid.*, p. 30.
[10] *Op. cit.*, p. 79.
[11] *Ibid.*, p. 102.

ence, and nature become man for him. Thus *society* is the consummated oneness in substance of man and nature the true resurrection of nature—the naturalism of man and the humanism of nature both brought to fulfillment." [12]

"On the Jewish Question," also written in 1843, likewise criticizes civil society, notes the contradiction between it and the real species man, and calls for revolution. These early works prepare the ground for and anticipate the later works which expound historical materialism—*Theses on Feuerbach,* written in 1845; *The German Ideology,* written in 1845-1846; *Manifesto of the Communist Party,* written in 1847-1848; and *A Contribution to the Critique of Political Economy,* written in 1859.

Some argue that in his later work, i.e., his researches in political economy, Marx deserted his youthful humanism. For example, Robert Tucker contends there are two Marxisms—the Marxism of early writings, which picture man as a self whose sole alienation is subjective, and the Marxism of the later writings, wherein "the idea of the self seems to disappear" [13] and everything, including alienation, becomes societal. But there is no sharp break here; there is only a shift in emphasis and movement from concern with the end, which is man and his development, to the means, which are material conditions as they shape and are shaped by classes struggling against one another. What Tucker, like many critics, fails to grasp is the essential social and material—i.e., environmental and historical—character of man. They can understand the humanistic tone of Marx's early writings because they echo the spirit of the eighteenth and nineteenth century Enlightenment that produced the liberal imagination in Europe and the United States. But they retain an individualistic and idealistic concept of man. They fail to grasp Hegel's unitary and dialectical drive, as well as the realistic outlook of materialism. For to grasp the two together one would begin to see what Marx was aiming at.

For Marx, man from the beginning is social; he is engaged in collective practice. To believe, as liberals have done since the Enlightenment, that we begin with discrete, independent, individual men and that the problem is to reform the external conditions of nature and so-

---

[12]*Ibid.,* p. 104.
[13]Tucker, Robert C.: *Philosophy and Myth in Karl Marx,* p. 165.

ciety in order for man to develop as he ought to be—that is an illusion. It leads to a second illusion, namely, the belief that to speak of alienation in and by society (as Marx does) loses the real man. There is "moral escapism at the core of Marx's thought," says Tucker. He is "collectivizing the process" of self-change, both self-alienation and self-disalienation, and is "evading the issue of individual responsibility for self-liberation." [14] It is true that Marx and Engels in their efforts to describe the whole sweep of history and to prescribe action for the movement of the working class did not focus primarily on the individual person. It is true also, as Engels pointed out in his letter to Bloch (September 21-22, 1890)[15] and proved by his own statements, that he and Marx overstressed the economic side of history, and thus understressed other sides, such as the ideological, which is in part a function of individual initiative. But there is, in fact, no sharp dichotomy between the economic and ideological, the individual and social or, indeed, any other pair of categories, as a dialectical understanding of the world requires. "Men make their own history . . . under circumstances directly encountered, given, and transmitted from the past."[16] Individual men make one another and their world, and their world, natural and social, makes them.

The liberal, individualistic view of man, which must necessarily be a reformist humanism, is an error of a limited class approach to man. As Engels says, the "eternal reason" of the French philosophers of the Enlightenment "was in reality nothing but the idealised understanding of the eighteenth century citizen, just then evolving into the bourgeois." [17] Just as the wealthy Renaissance merchant and his patronized thinker thought of fulfilled man as his own idealized self, so the eighteenth century monarch and his *philosophe* thought of fulfilled man as the defeudalized member of a civil society, with personal and property rights before the law. For the latter, "freedom" was the great rallying cry. What it meant was the free economic enterprizes of a small class, and the formation of a parliament of those few as the political means of making secure its economic freedom. This notion of humanism is still

[14]*Ibid.*, p. 242.

[15]Marx, Karl, and Engels, Frederick: *Selected Correspondence*, p. 500.

[16]Marx, K.: *The Eighteenth Brumaire of Louis Bonaparte.* Moscow, Foreign Languages, ND., p. 15.

[17]Engels, Frederick: *Socialism: Utopian and Scientific*, p. 34.

the dominant one in the United States today, though it is disguised by phrases like "fredoom of speech" and "freedom of religion" and by the actual operation of an evolved free enterprize, namely, monopoly capitalism.

Like the French philosophers, the Utopian socialists were interested in the emancipation of all classes and all humanity. But while they saw that the bourgeois world was itself irrational and unjust and extended their criticism to its institutions—e.g., private property, marriage, and religion—they were equally ineffectual. Instead of working to reform existing institutions, they withdrew from them, establishing their own experimental colonies, principally in the New World. These socialists had little grasp of existing historical conditions and of the movement of those conditions. They saw only what was negative and antihumanistic, like many today who draw corresponding conclusions about the imperative for opting out of present society. Not relating their knowledge and action to present society, they could not be realistic and objective about it; for objectivity is always relative. The result was a dreamy, highly idealized, universal humanism which had at best only transient success in the rural interstices of a capitalistic America. For all its claims to absolute truth and justice, such socialist humanism was splintered into hundreds of fragments in both theory and practice. It lacked force because it lacked linkage with the real forces of history. It could not be effective because it was not scientific. Yet it expressed a dynamic idealism that was absent among Jewish, Christian, Greco-Roman, and Renaissance humanism—the latter including "utopias of calm felicity" [18] like those of Thomas More and Campanella. This dynamic idealism had already been voiced in the great tradition of German philosophy. What it needed to acquire power was a material and historical basis. That was indicated by Marx and Engels and provided by the militant proletariat of the late nineteenth and twentieth centuries.

Historical materialism, as Engels called it, was not only a great discovery in science, a discovery which Marx jointly attributed to Engels and himself,[19] and which Engels attributed to Marx.[20] It was also a

---

[18] Manuel, Frank E.: Toward a psychological history of utopias. In Manuel, Frank E. (Ed.): *Utopias and Utopian Thought.* Boston, Beacon, 1967, p. 72.

[19] *A Contribution to the Critique of Political Economy,* p. 13.

[20] *Socialism: Utopian and Scientific,* p. 53.

great advance in humanism. For it laid bare to location and study the forces which shape man, and which he in turn must shape and direct if he is to become more fully human. In short, it *materialized* and *historicized* man. Whitehead remarked that physiology put mind back into nature.[21] Marx put mind back into man, man back into history, and history back into nature. Today some of us may take this view of man and the universe for granted. But it is by no means universally shared. In Marx's own day many educated people did not believe that man makes his own ideas. Rather, they agreed with Hegel, man merely manifests what the Absolute Spirit expresses in him, or he registers and associates the impact of sensations on him from a mechanical, determinate, and all-determining world. For both idealists and mechanical materialists, moveover, it was thought that "ideas" would change the world and humanize man; "education," even for the French materialists, became the great panacea. Comte, Mill, and other humanists placed their faith in it. But as Engels observed, no one asked where the ideas come from.[22] Many today still operate on the assumption that ideas spring full-blown into their minds quite apart from their own brains, bodies, families, societies, and material environments. On the other hand, the materialists, who recognize that men are products of circumstances, forget that it is men who change circumstances, and that "the educator himself needs educating." [23] Man lives and moves and has his being in the sea of history; but that does not mean that he must drown there.

Still further, these events flow and have a definite direction: man lives in the movement of historical events, which create him and which he in turn creates. The agency of this creation is not some material or spiritual force hidden to man, but an observable process in man's midst. It is the class struggle.

Marx did not discover class struggle. Rousseau, who argued that the inequality of men is due to the passage of primitive man to collective production in agriculture and metallurgy, and hence the division of labor and property, was on the verge of the discovery. He wrote:

---

[21]Whitehead, A. N.: *Science and the Modern World*. New York, MacMillan, 1926, p. 213.

[22]Engels, Frederick: Karl Marx. In *Reminiscences of Marx and Engels*. Moscow, Foreign Languages Publishing House, ND., p. 23.

[23]*Theses on Feuerbach*, III.

Thus, as the most powerful or most miserable made of their force or their needs a sort of right to the goods of others, equivalent according to them to the right of property, the destruction of equality was followed by the most frightful disorder; thus the usurpations of the rich, the brigandange of the poor, the unbridled passions of all, stifling natural pity and the as yet weak voice of justice, made man avaricious, ambitious, and evil.[24]

In this passage, also, Rousseau anticipated the Marxist notion of base and superstructure, though the base for him is the material struggle of social groups while the superstructure is the "passions" which, in a society of inequality, are all deviations from true man.

Saint-Simon saw in his own day a conflict between the working, deprived "producers" and the "idle" classes of princes, household officials, bishops, marshals, prefects, and landowners.[25] In broader terms, he stated this conflict as the "oppression" of the poor and the deprived by the luxurious and the rich.[26] Although, because of his own charitable and optimistic nature, Robert Owen did not apprehend the deep antagonism between the ruling capitalist classes and the working classes, he nonetheless saw the more general conflict between individual and cooperative modes of industrial production and government.

Marx's historical materialism is abumbrated in the early writings. The notion of conflict or contradiction in the material basis, formulated in *Theses on Feuerbach*, sets the stage for other conflict. That such conflict must lie in social practice, i.e., in the relations among classes, is indicated in the same work when he describes the human essence as "the ensemble of the social relations," and when he declares that when men change circumstances they engage in "revolutionizing practice." In Marx's famous article on Hegel's philosophy of right, the notion of the proletariat appears. And then *The German Ideology* and the *Manifesto*, and at last *Capital*, brought the notion to full expression. It is a simple notion: that man must eat and clothe and

---

[24]Discourse on the origin and foundations of inequality among men. In Rousseau, Jean-Jacques: *The First and Second Discourses*, trans. by Roger D. and Judith R. Masters. New York, St. Martins, 1964, p. 157.

[25]de Saint-Simon, Henri: First extract from the "Organizer" 1819. In de Saint-Simon, Henri: *Social Organization, The Science of Man and Other Writings*, trans. by Felix Markham. New York, Harper and Row, 1964, pp. 73-74.

[26]*Ibid.*, p. 74.

shelter himself before he does anything else, and that the material conditions of production and exchange of a given society determine all other relations in that society, namely, the social, political, legal, religious, and the rest.[27]

We correctly say that Newton contributed to physics a study of physical bodies, by setting forth some laws of universal physical motion which have been confirmed in practice. Similarly, we may say that Marx contributed to humanism a study of man's activity by setting forth some laws of universal human activity which have been confirmed in practice. Neither thinker was correct in all he said. But the great merit of each was that, relying on his predecessors, he formulated highly general and simple laws which explain a large number of past observations and predict future behavior of the class of phenomena in question.[28] The primary difference, of course, is that while Marx's "laws" provide a generalized description of past history, once men become consciously aware of such "laws" a new factor is immediately introduced into history to modify in some degree in the future those laws. That new factor is the awareness and the changed practice to which it leads. This, of course, is what Marx intended, and it spells the ethical or prescriptive dimension in his descriptive work. The point for him is not merely to describe or interpret the world but to change it. Description is justified so far as it points to prescription; thought must serve action; science must serve man. Marx's science is always humanistic in its goal, and his humanism always has science as its method. But the method of science can never be bloodless and neutral, if only for the reason that it is carried out by flesh-and-blood human beings. Those who believe that it is neutral, whether they be scientists or politicians, are only deceiving themselves. As the production and political use of the atomic bomb showed vividly to scientists themselves, the scientist is a man, repeatedly making decisions as to values. The question always is whether those values, relative to practical alternatives, advance man's welfare or do not.

A law of an individual person, of a society, or of human history

---

[27]Engels, Frederick: Karl Marx's funeral. In *Reminiscences of Marx and Engels*, pp. 348-349.

[28]For the influence of Marx's thought on modern economics, see Horowitz, David (Ed.): *Marx and Modern Economics*. New York, Monthly Review, 1968.

has a peculiar status not shared by a law of physical bodies. What human beings and physical bodies have in common is that both behave in regular ways. A law, in fact, is just that, a regularity in behavior, given certain conditions. But unlike physical laws, human laws are relatively responsive to change. That is to say, human behavior is subject to change by conscious understanding and manipulation, which when formally precise and systematized become science. Physical bodies appear to be driven by a certain inherent and relatively inescapable compulsion to behave tomorrow as they behaved yesterday if conditions remain more or less constant. It is not quite so with human beings. It is true that there are certain *general* laws of our being which define our *human* nature and which, so far as we remain human, we cannot escape. But over and beyond them, we are under no strict compulsion to behave tomorrow as we behaved yesterday. In fact one of the general laws of our being is just this, that we can achieve "insight into necessity" [29] when conditions are favorable, i.e., we can be free. One of the built-in conditions of man's "nature" is this possibility for increasing insight and hence increasing self-change. It is a variable in the human equation, i.e., a quantity that fluctuates within certain limits. Man's distinctiveness lies in this: that whereas with physical bodies "conditions remain more or less constant" (prior to man's own interference and control), in man's case there is no certainty that conditions will remain more or less constant for the reason of man's possible insight and change of nature and self. "Natural laws" —i.e., regular past behavior extending into the future—can be disturbed because man has in him the capacity for modifying such laws, both within him and in external nature. The critical question then becomes whether man realizes this possibility for insight, for change of himself and nature, and how he does so. We can say that under previously existing class societies, when man's potential insight and self-changing action still remained slumbering, he had such-and-such a nature, i.e., enslaved, debased, exploitive, etc. But we can also say that his *free* nature, that part of him which sets him apart from physi-

---

[29] Engels, Frederick: *Anti-Dühring*, p. 157. Engels is quoting Hegel. This translation reads, "freedom is the appreciation of necessity." But John Somerville has pointed out that the original reads: ". . . ist die Freiheit, die Einsicht in die Notwendigkeit." Somerville, John: Marxist ethics, determinism, and freedom. *Philosophy and Phenomenological Research, 28*: 20, 1967.

cal nature and animal nature, was as yet undeveloped—that, in short, he was not yet *human*.

That is what Marx meant by writing in *Capital* that beyond the realm of necessity "begins that development of human power, which is its own end, the true realm of freedom, which, however, can flourish only upon that realm of necessity as its basis." [30] At this point, Marx says, labor passed the point where it is required "under the compulsion of necessity and of external utility." Man's freedom then is this: "that socialized man, the associated producers, regulate their interchange with nature rationally, bring it under their common control, instead of being ruled by it as by some blind power; they accomplish their task with the least expenditure of energy and under conditions most adequate to their human nature and most worthy of it." [31] Engels expresses a similar notion.[32]

What this means is that on the one hand man is impelled to be and become himself, to achieve freedom through cooperative reason and collective practice, to become independent (but not separated) from the hidden influences of society and nature. This impulsion of man to close the gap between his essence and his existence does not mean that he will. There is no guarantee in this concept of man, or in any of Marx's writings, which suggests that the victory of man over antihuman forces is inevitable—though the polemical writings necessarily proceed on faith and hope in such a victory.

On the other hand, Marx's view of man—while holding that man is internally, by his psychosomatic makeup, and externally, by the material conditions and forces of history, impelled to fulfill himself—leaves man open and exposed to those conditions and forces. There is a grand drama in Marx's picture of history. The more sensitive man is to the grinding power of impersonal forces working "behind his back," the more freedom he begins to acquire over them. But this freedom is destined to remain abortive and futile unless it issues in action to grapple with that fate which seems to be destroying men. Thus full freedom means to act—to unite thought and action, criticism and practice, in revolutionizing society. Thus, while the free man appears to be ex-

---

[30] Marx, Karl: *Capital,* vol. III, pp. 954-955.
[31]*Ibid.*
[32]*Socialism: Utopian and Scientific,* p. 73.

posed to the buffeting of external conditions and its blind laws, he over-comes history by internalizing it in his own revolutionary behavior. This is what is meant by the repeated expression in the early writings, "Men make their own history." The real battle in society is that be-tween the imposed "necessities" of a history dominated by the be-havior of a class system in which men are not aware of the nature and direction of their struggle, and the generic necessity of man to be a creative, social being. This latter necessity is the need for freedom. But this necessity is, at the present stage in history, only a latent neces-sity, a need and demand pressing for realization. It cannot be realized apart from taking account of present and past regularities in society, i.e., the drift of events and the "laws" that appear in them. To know such regularities and to act to transform them for the welfare of man is the union of objective with subjective necessity. It is the road of revolution and freedom.

The goal of Marx's humanism is inseparable from its method. The method is humanistic and dialectical. "Humanistic" here means of, by, and for man; "dialectical" means interactive, struggling, creative of good, destructive of evil, progressive in the highest human sense. While "humanistic" cannot be taken apart from "dialectical," "hu-manistic" expresses the content of the method and the goal, while "dialectical" expresses the form and movement of method and goal. The method and goal, moreover, are two indistinguishable aspects of a single process. Since man, social man, is the primary instrument and material for creating the goal, which is man himself, the very act of self-creation (*Selbstveränderung*) is both means and end, both method and goal. So far as man's human qualities diminish or disappear from his present activity— as in fragmented, routine, monotonous, or other-wise alienated work—the end of human life has to that degree been degraded. For the end is in part this very man whose labor has been degraded.

How is Marxist humanism distinctive, in contrast to other forms of humanism? How does it differ from conservative, liberal, and an-archist humanism, from religious and pagan humanism, from ancient humanisms, both east and west, and from modern humanisms?

(1) Marxist humanism is preeminently concerned with *all of man*

—his bodily, sensuous, passionate, active, intellectual, spiritual, personal, social, decisional, determinate, responsible life. This is a humanism that has not merely a contemplative or scholarly interest in man, but a concern for his welfare and fulfillment. And since the concern is with the *total* man and his *total* fulfillment, the concern itself must be *total*. For a man cannot be totally concerned about another man without simultaneously and in like degree being concerned about himself. Thus, in the depth of its commitment, Marxist humanism is in principle the equal of other humanisms. It shares a common perspective with much anthropology, psychology, and philosophy on the many dimensions of man and the possibilities for his realization of a life that is rich, varied, and full. Religious humanism, such as that proclaimed by Pope John XXIII and Pope Paul VI of the Roman Catholic Church, is in fact a formidable rival to Marxist humanism. What religious humanism lacks, however, is a single-minded totality of commitment to the total fulfillment of man. It is often divided and weakened not only by its hierarchical and elitist institutional structure, but specifically by its feudal, capitalistic,[33] and conservative character. Marxism in its institutional structure has also been deviated from its vision and total commitment. But the point is that Marxism in its essential foundations was and continues to be a revolutionary philosophy whose commitment is defined precisely by total criticism and total radicalization of man and his world. We can think of many national and religious heroes in the past and present who were not Marxists. But as a movement committed to man's total liberation, Marxism in the last one hundred years has surely distinguished itself not only among modern rivals, but also among other forms of humanism in the past. This demonstration of Marxism's success is not due merely to its faith in man; the humanistic elements of the great religions have always had that in some degree. It is due primarily to Marxism's openness to the sciences, its incorporation of the findings of science in its view of man and the world, and its union of this sounder and fuller view of man with the passion and action of commitment. Thus, Marxism was able to be more thoroughly and authentically humanistic

---

[33]Aptheker, Herbert: *The Urgency of Marxist-Christian Dialogue.* New York, Harper and Row, 1970, pp. 136-137.

than the great religions because, unencumbered by supernaturalism, it started afresh with a naturalistic outlook on man, an outlook that opened the way for a clearer and deeper vision of man.

(2) Marxist humanism is concern with *all men*. It is inherently democratic in its notion of what men are and what they ought to be. It stands over against all humanisms which are elitist and exclusive. It takes man, in the context of his fellow man, history, and nature, to be the final judge of what is real, true, and valuable. But by man it means in addition to the species man, each member of the species individually and in association with others. That does not mean that all men are equal in power or ability. But it does mean that each expresses the human essence and is essential to others and to the fulfillment of the species, both as exemplar and participant.

"Man" in Marxism means those generic features, such as sociality and creativity, which make man and together distinguish him from other species, though in each individual these features are variable and relative. For example, each person is characterized by sex, age, and "racial" characteristics. Thus when Marxism speaks of "man," it means to include in principle female, male, young, old, and black, white, yellow, and red. Ideally Marxism sets itself adamantly against any and all arbitrary discriminations and exclusions of certain persons from the human species. In its opposition to members of the oppressing class, it strives to change or destroy certain persons, not because it is malevolent toward a particular class of men, but on the contrary, because it seeks in this and other ways to maximize the good life for as many persons as possible, including the privileged few—if they be willing to work for humanity—along with the deprived many.

Marxism has been accused of being a truncated humanism because it calls for the overthrow of the ruling class and because like the religions it rejects those who do not embrace it. But the class struggle with its violence, as Marx and Engels pointed out in the *Manifesto,* is not something the Marxists invented or initiated. It is an age-old fact, the major expression of man's inhumanity to man. The problem that every honest humanist must pose for himself is: What is to be done about such inhumanity? Marx was aware that in the past various humanistic approaches to the problem had been found wanting: philosophy, religion, law, morality, national wars, etc. The problem remained. It is not a question of how we can preserve the dignity, liberty, etc., in short, the humanity, of the dehumanizing and dehumanized classes. For the humanist who is not an elitist but a genuine, thoroughgoing humanist, the question is how we can preserve and enhance the lives of the largest number of persons in the long run.

This is thus an objective question, if one begins with the criterion of man, man as a species, composed of all his individual parts, present and future. As a man, a Marxist must feel sorrow for the injury and destruction done to any man. "Nothing human is alien to me," Marx was fond of saying. But the objective question is how to minimize such sorrow and destruction, both for oneself and for others. Here the final appeal for thought and action must lie in conditions and events. There is, according to the Marxist view, an objective, humanizing process taking place in history. It is inherent in the way in which people make their living. Marx saw it going on primarily among the industrial workers of Europe in the nineteenth century. The humanizing forces are at work to retire from history the dehumanizing forces. It goes without saying that if the humanizing forces in this struggle dehumanize themselves, they will defeat themselves. But struggling to remove the conditions of one's dehumanization, especially the class of men who preside over those conditions and profit from them, is not dehumanizing. On the contrary, it is the only choosable alternative for a man who strives to be human. The self-styled "humanist" who is indifferent to this struggle or criticizes it wants to escape the real dehumanization that is taking place and is to that extent himself dehumanized. Marxist humanism rejects other forms of escapism, such as a utopian humanism which holds that all men can be changed solely by persuasion. On the other hand, it rejects the notion that swallows up human forces in the blind movement of events—a notion that in its own way denies the power of humanism by denying the power of man to know and direct his world and himself.

In the bold tradition of Hegel, Marx insisted on a "total" man, on a "totalizing" movement for both individual man and man as a whole. Hence, he was unalterably opposed to all divisions and alienations within man and his immediate relations to others—alienations which he specified at length in the early manuscripts. He was also opposed to the alienations in the larger society—what he called "alienated labor" in the early manuscripts, and what he traced in detail, for both cause and effect, in *Capital*. Marx was the passionate enemy of all partiality and brokenness in human life, in both the individual and society. He had a hunger for unity—for the integrity of the person in the integrity of society in the integrity of history and nature. Hence it followed that he must be active in overcoming the divisions and alienations in man. To love man means to fight for him, to help to shape the future by healing the broken present.

(3) Marxist humanism is *scientific*. That means that it is not only oriented to man as his own value and end. It understands the conditions and causes, the mechanism of events, that are relevant to man's existence and welfare and that determine his present and future states. That means that Marxist humanism has linked up with the most potent instrument that man has discovered in his million-year history on this planet. That means that Marxism is the most powerful and influential humanism to appear on the face of the earth. For all their insight into man and their good intentions toward him, prescientific humanisms could not begin to match this power. The accomplishments of Soviet, Chinese, and other forms of socialism in the past fifty years are testimony to that power.

What is the mechanism of this power? Man is a material force, Marx argued against Feuerbach, that is engaged in "human sensuous activity" or "practice."[34] This practice is interactive, taking in the world by perception and manipulation, transforming it, and in turn being transformed by it. This dialectic was grasped by idealism, but only abstractly. Man thus in practice proves the truth, the truth *for him*. He proves, he tests, he discovers and creates—*himself*, i.e., himself in relation to the world, and the world in relation to him. Marx acknowledges the materialist doctrine that circumstances change men; but he adds—and this should never be forgotten—that "it is men that change circumstances."[35] This latter, which must be "practical-critical" activity, is called *"revolutionizing practice."*

But here Marx is describing the scientific method in its most generalized form and in the context of man's deepest needs and propul-

---

[34]*Theses on Feuerbach*, I.
[35]*Ibid.*, III.

sions. Science in essence is human practice. That seems very plain when we think about it. But much of what passes for science today in class society has become a perverted science, a pale imitation of the real transformation of the world in the service of man's needs. It is for profit, war, and racism, not for justice, peace and equality. Yet when Marx thought of man he always thought of man in this revolutionary-practical relation to the world, and when he thought of practical-critical activity, i.e., science, he thought of man. The two were inseparable for him. The power of science is really the power of man, acting out of the fullness of his commitment to man, to truth, and to the proving of truth by his social practice. To prove the truth is to prove man. For the truth, the whole and genuine truth, is not some function of a bare, abstract proposition. In its broadest and most human sense, the truth is the growing totality of men's responses to the world, rendered consistent and mutually reinforcing, and progressively brought into kindred relations to the world. The truth is the truth *for man,* i.e., for the total ensemble of individual living human beings now and in the future, in relation to their world. Hence that social practice through which truth is created must be total— i.e., revolutionary activity must involve all of mankind and be worldwide.

For man who is a multidimensional and creative being, meaning cannot be reduced to a method of propositional verification, nor can truth be limited to a function of individual propositions. Man needs and seeks not only propositions that designate the properties of things, are empirically meaningful, and on investigation turn out to be true. His very survival requires such propositions—consider, for example, the propositions of medical science. But he also needs and seeks meanings that express dispositions and feelings and ideals, that appraise values, and that prescribe actions. These meanings, too, may have their own "truth" or adequacy to the conditions they signify. (Only a narrow, fetishized science and philosophy divorced from the real needs of the masses of men and serving a special class treats these as "nonsense" or secondary.) Moreover, man needs and seeks an organized and developing system of all the meanings which emerge in his living—a system of meanings which are mutually supportive, which

create and give form to the intention of his life, and which always
signify a frontier of creation beyond the boundaries of established and
coordinated meanings.

Such a system of diversified and integrated meanings comprizes
the very structure of personality. Moreover, man needs to bring this
system of personal meanings into interaction and dynamic integration
with other personality systems. He needs to bring these personal and
social systems of meaning into creative interaction with the world of
nonhuman nature, aiming at the unfolding and integration of new
meanings. This whole process, by which meaning is created, differentiated, integrated, and transformed in a growing system, is the process
of man's development as individual personality and society. Particular
designative, appraisive, and other truths as adequate to particular
conditions emerge within the process. But they are modified by other
particular truths and by new truths. Consider, for example, how our
knowledge of man himself has been modified by our developing
knowledge in the physical and biological sciences.

The creation and modification of truths is not some historical
process to which man is passive witness or puppet. *Man is at the
center of it as its primary cause, striving to fulfill himself.* In this
process man aims not only at particular truths for dealing with particular situations—for surviving and passing beyond the demands of
survival. He aims also at an inclusive and integrated system of truths
as he aims at an inclusive and integrated life. He aims at his own
development and the development of other men in their common developing world of nature. He aims to be true to his destiny, to be a
true man. In the process of fulfilling this larger meaning and truth
of man, the search for particular meanings and truths must always
be provisional and instrumental.

(4) Marxist humanism discriminates *means* from *ends* and strives
to relate them so that each signifies and requires the other. It is
intensely focused on *all* of man and on *all* men, is committed to man's
fulfillment, and in using a dialectical, scientific method in understanding man is able to grasp the conditions and relations that define man.
Thus, more than prescientific humanisms, or nonscientific humanism,
or humanisms which are attenuated by a supernatural outlook, it can
discriminate the goal, which is man's full realization and represents

a final and intrinsic value, from all other instrumental considerations. Thus, Marxism in principle can put into proper perspective all the spheres, conditions, and activities of man's life—e.g., in economics, material needs, consumption, commodities, money, production, technology, planning; in politics, state and the apparatus of government, democracy, centralization, political parties; in cultural life, institutions and systems of education, public media, ideologies, etc. Marx was ever insistent that all these factors are to be subordinated to man, and he repeatedly decried the perversion by which means are turned into ends, man is devaluated, and *things* are made the be-all and end-all of man's life, the process by which man is transformed into a commodity. One of the main aims of *Capital,* in fact, is to show how this latter process leads to surplus-value, the institutionalized blood-letting of labor by which capital survives.

Marx argued that all these conditions must be seen and treated for what they are, i.e., as means to achieving the one thing needful, the free association of men. What is required is that all existing dehumanizing conditions must be negated. But that negation is only the first step. The next step must be one of transformation of conditions into the positive means for man's fulfillment. Thus, atheism, which is the negation of man's primary ideological alienation, and communism, which is the negation of private property, are not enough. "Communism," writes Marx, "is the necessary pattern and the dynamic principle of the immediate future, but communism as such is not the goal of human development—the structure of human society."[36] Later he says, "Communism is humanism mediated with itself through the annulment of private property. Only through the annulment of this mediation which is itself, however, a necessary premise—does positively self-deriving humanism, *positive humanism,* come into being."[37] The point is not that communism is not important, but that in the long run its function is to serve the fulfillment of men.

(5) Marxist humanism is *revolutionary*. It should be contrasted with *contemplative* humanism, or *conservative* humanism, which

---

[36]*Economic and Philosophic Manuscripts of 1844,* p. 114. The editor comments: "Under 'communism as such' Marx here means crude, equalitarian communism, such as propounded by Babeuf and his followers."

[37]*Ibid.,* p. 164.

knows nothing of the principle of *practice,* of changing present circumstances, of negating and superseding those circumstances in the direction of man's progressive improvement. The humanism of the Enlightenment, like certain liberal humanism today, sees man as a set of definite qualities and possibilities which are given, are placed in a social and natural environment, and require only the manipulation of that environment to achieve the heavenly city. It does not grasp the method of dialectic. In this it is half-way like the conservative view of man which at the same time claims to be humanistic. For the latter, unlike the liberal view, holds that the environment ought to be kept more or less constant; but in common with the liberal view it adheres to the notion that man's nature is in some degree independent of its active relations with other persons and the world. Individual man, in both views, is a given quantum. For the conservative, that quantum is fixed; for the modern liberal, the quantum is changeable, but the change is primarily a function of circumstances.

Such views of man reflect, of course, class positions in society. A man sees mankind through the lens of his own activity and experience. Marxism, more than any previously existing humanism, takes the point of view of the ordinary man who must struggle with his physical and biological and social world in order to live; who must oppose, co-operate with, and transform that world; who, in short, must revolutionize it. (Chinese Taoism, more than any pre-Marxist philosophy, had a dialectical approach to man and nature; but it did not apply this to history, nor is it clear how it was revolutionary. The records indicate that it was mystical, and there is some evidence that in its alchemy, for example, its scientific outlook was obscured by its mysticism.) More than any other humanism, Marxism thus puts itself directly on the side of the broad laboring masses of humanity—what Marx and Engels called in the *Manifesto* "the immense majority."[38] Not only that; Marxism roots its theory of historical change, that is, its theory of man and man's progress, its humanism, in that immense majority. Marxism in its humanism takes man seriously, it takes him in the average, the "divine average," as Whitman said, and it takes him in the mass, at the point where certain activities are most frequent, obvious, and preponderant.

---

[38]*Manifesto of the Communist Party,* p. 20.

If one were to study a certain species of oak trees, let us say, with the intent of producing a definitive description of them, he would assemble as large a sample as possible of individual trees and take note of certain recurring and common properties, i.e., of the defining essence to be found in every individual tree. What was not thus common would have to be discarded. For example, one would not include the characteristics of dead or dying trees, nor would one include diseased trees. One might examine good or near-perfect specimens in order more clearly to define the essence in question. But one could not determine the characteristics to look for in such specimens until one had first clarified the notion of essence by examination of a wide range of individual trees. Further, the good specimen is always simply an enhanced case of the ordinary or normal (frequent) case—which means that the potentiality for "good" or fulfillment is contained in each individual in the species. The same applies to a study of man. Elitism has no place in an empirical science that aims at definition.

But humanism has to do with what *ought* to be as well as with what *is*. Marxism's defense of its value theory is a naturalistic one. It finds that the vast majority of men choose to live and to develop themselves through dialectical exchange with other persons and the nonhuman world. It does not argue with this drive and tendency. It accepts it, it joins with it, it tries to clarify and facilitate it.

A clarified account of the laboring activity of man shows that it is revolutionary. Here Marx showed his genius—the genius that sees through the appearance, which millions of men have observed before, and penetrates to the underlying essence and dynamics. A dictionary provides this meaning of the term "revolution":

> The overthrow and replacement of a government or political system by those governed. . . . The essential idea of *revolution* [in this definition] is a change in the form or government or constitution, or a change of rulers, otherwise than as provided by existing laws of succession, election, etc.; while such change is apt to involve armed hostilities, these make no necessary part of a *revolution*, which may be accomplished without a battle.[39]

---

[39] *Standard Dictionary of the English Language*, international ed. New York, Funk and Wagnalls, 1958.

Marx's *revolutionieren* carries the Hegelian notion of annulment, absorption, and supersession, i.e., creative transformation. But Marx saw that the Hegelian notion, while powerful in its abstract form and threatening enough to the bourgeoisie, was still more powerful if applied concretely to existing property relations and alienation of real labor. The liberal or conservative humanist, who thinks of man as an isolated unit and individual, tends to think that the notion of revolutionary activity is something that Marx and Marxists tack onto man for certain purposes of power or expediency. This view is directly opposite the truth. For Marx man is in the deepest springs of his nature a revolutionary being. He is continuously changing the "form" and "constitution" of his environment, and thus continuously changing himself. Thus, we can say that Marx was more deeply empirical, more deeply human, than most other humanists. Other movements claiming to represent man have been intensely militant and destructive in the defense and spread of their faith—e.g., Islam during its early centuries, and Christianity during the Inquisitition and the crusades. But these militant movements were directed by economic and political elites and were in fact engineered for antihumanistic ends. Marx's humanism is of quite the opposite kind. It locates the moving and constructive power of history. Man's problem then is one of becoming conscious of who he is, potentially, and of discovering the method by which he can realize that potentiality. The method is to be true to himself, i.e., to engage in social, revolutionizing practice.

That practice does not begin in a vacuum. It begins where man confronts an environment which has alienated him, but upon which he depends. Revolutionary practice must begin with the concrete, specific conditions that stand over against man. It must know them, select and reorganize them, and transform them in the direction of a world that progressively removes destructive contradictions and in the process fulfills man.

(6) Marxist humanism is *progressive*. This characteristic follows from its revolutionary character and is inherent in its Hegelian awareness of constant change and development. The one constant in man's universe for Marxism is man's dialectical development in a world that develops with him. Thus, Marxism must be opposed to all fixities in thought and practice. This is the reason why Marx and Engels fought

so strenuously traditional morality and psychology, which endeavored to enshrine certain "eternal" structures as the fixed content of man and his goals. Likewise the genuine Marxist must always beware of confusing means and ends, for the reasons already discussed. The end is man, and man's genus is creativity, a process that necessarily leaves him ever unfinished and keeps him open to the future. Here Marxism utilizes the basic principle of science, which is self-correction. Science is ever correcting, transforming, and improving its insights by a dialectical process between scientists and the world and among scientists themselves. It aims at bringing its statements into a certain mutual fit with external reality and one another. Marxism aims at the same general goal, so far as the perspectives and responses of men are concerned. But it can never rest contented at any point, for the process of man's development, at the level of the individual person and the level of the species, can never be completed. Marxist humanism cannot therefore be a system; it must refer to a process, and that is why its ultimate test and fulfillment lie not in a doctrine but in totalizing, revolutionary, social practice.

VII

MARX'S HUMANISM VS.
SARTRE'S EXISTENTIALISM

W<small>E MOVE NOW</small> to a clarification of Marx's humanism by examining Jean-Paul Sartre's effort to integrate his own existentialist humanism with Marx's Marxism, and by expounding what we believe would be Marx's response. Sartre's work is always revelatory of man and society and has been an influential form of humanism in the postwar world of western Europe and the United States. Hence, such an examination can serve to make clear not only Sartre's effort to develop an existentialist Marxism, but also by contrast Marx's materialist Marxism.[1]

In his two works, *The Problem of Method* and *Critique de la Raison Dialectique*,[2] Sartre attacks both the thought and practice of Marxism, and attempts to restore the existential individual to Marxism, claiming that "Marx's own Marxism" had an implicit demand for an existential foundation.[3] Since the issue of freedom is so critical and other issues turn on it, I propose here to deal with it and to show that Sartre's concepts of freedom and of related phenomena are incompatible with Marx's.

Sartre holds that the individual is always free at any moment to negate and escape from the determinations of his environment. In contrast with his position in *Being and Nothingness,* he acknowledges

---

[1] For another critique of Sartre's existentialism, see Parsons, Howard L.: Existentialism and marxism in dialogue. In Aptheker, Herbert (Ed.): *Marxism and Alienation.* New York, Humanities, 1965, pp. 90-124.

[2] Sartre, Jean-Paul: *The Problem of Method,* trans. by Hazel E. Barnes. London, Methuen, 1963. Sartre, Jean-Paul: *Critique de la Raison Dialectique, précédé de Question de Méthode,* Tome I, *Théorie des Ensembles Pratiques.* Paris, Librairie Gallimard, 1960. For an exposition of the latter, see Desan, Wilfrid: *The Marxism of Jean-Paul Sartre.* Garden City, Doubleday, 1966.

[3] *The Problem of Method,* p. 177.

that the environment influences choice and that man and the environment interact. And he correctly draws the conclusion that the freedom of detachment only relocates man in the inert world of isolated, unsocialized, serial individuals. Sartre writes that "being is the negation of knowing and knowing gets all its strength from the negation of being."[4] In short, I know the world—material objects, persons—but in knowing it I transcend it; and that is my freedom. Here Sartre's position on freedom is of the same kind as Whitehead's: man is internally determined but externally free.[5] This can mean at least two things: either (1) I feel that my thoughts or actions are not caused by internal or external forces; or (2) ontological description simply presents me with the fact of an undetermined act of choice.

Marx's answer to these methods is to rely on the methods and findings of the sciences. This means, as Marx says, that "just as our opinion of an individual is not based on what he thinks of himself, so can we not judge of . . . a period of transformation by its own consciousness"[6]—although understanding of the consciousness can yield some comprehension of the circumambient conditions that produced it. What then is the character and role of consciousness in history? Or, to put the problem in terms posed by Sartre's position, what is the relation of mind to body? Marx and Engels held that both body and mind are functions or activities; that mind is a reflection or internalizing of the body's encounter with other activities including the activities of other men with their patterns of work, exchange, and language; that the reflections of consciousness consist in the patterns of sense data, to which are added conceptual patterns within the brain; and that consciousness then has its effects in bodily activity precisely because the organ of mental activity is the brain, which is located in the body.

By Engels' own admission, he and Marx did not lay enough stress on the "formal" side of ideological notions, i.e., the ways and means by which their content, derived from the economic base, are "mediated."[7] This mediation, Engels observes, is always by thought, i.e.,

---

[4]*Critique de la Raison Dialectique,* p. 131.

[5]Whitehead, A. N.: *Process and Reality.* New York, Macmillan, 1929, p. 41.

[6]*A Contribution to the Critique of Political Economy,* p. 12.

[7]Marx, Karl, and Engels, Frederick: *Selected Correspondence,* pp. 500, 540.

the activities of the world impinge on the sense receptors and the brains of individual men and are accordingly transformed. Over a period of time, therefore, the material world "has gone through its own independent course of development in the brains of successive generations."[8]

Two observations are relevant here. First, Engels points out that ideologies—in the sense of political, juridical, and other notions—are false, i.e., they represent collective, symbolic ways of disguising class conflicts in the society. Engels assumes, as most people with the slightest good sense assume, that false ideas cannot lead to freedom. Therefore he and Marx directed much of their analysis and polemics against existing bourgeois ideology, false notions which clothed themselves in the mantle of "eternal truths." It follows that truth is the pathway to freedom; as Engels put it, quoting Hegel, "freedom is the appreciation [*Einsicht,* insight] of necessity."

Second, the phenomenon of freedom in human history does not occur automatically and independently of man's own effort and intelligence. The act of freedom is complex. It presupposes a psychosomatic personality generated within a group of men who in their exchanges with nature and their interpersonal, symbolic relations have created an ongoing culture of meaningful practices that sustain and transform the culture. An individual person moves under the propulsion of a need toward an environment that is indifferent or hostile to that need. He pays conscious attention to the elements and relations in that problematic situation; he poses alternative lines of action to himself, calling on the resources of memory and imagination; he projects the consequences and evaluates them relative to certain criteria of value; he takes into account the perspectives of others, directly or indirectly; and he chooses and settles on one line of action and tries it out.

Sartre himself with characteristic insight into the phenomenon of man describes the stages in this whole complex act. But he insists on putting asunder what Marx had joined together, namely, man and his objective world. For Sartre the free act of *praxis* is at its core undetermined. He cites Marx in support of his view.[9] But there is

[8]*Ibid.,* pp. 540-541.
[9]*The Problem of Method,* pp. 85-87.

nothing in Marx to indicate that he believed the principle of causality might ever be suspended, even for the sake of man, whom he valued more than anything else. For Marx man and nonhuman nature represent continuous but different processes; man is simply the physical world biologized, and the biologized world humanized, with a dialectical relation with the various levels of things and events around him. Man's freedom cannot escape the natural order, broadly conceived; it is the freedom to understand it by being in touch with it, sensing its items and patterns, and reorganizing those patterns through imagination, nerves and muscles, tools and machines, and communication and cooperative action with other men.

Freedom in Marx's and Engels' sense is freedom from rule by unknown powers within and without man, powers that lead to scarcity, deprivation, exploitation, suffering, violence, and destruction—in a word, dehumanization. It is the freedom that only the knowledge of the environment and of man himself can bring, when accompanied by appropriate action. Such action, says Engels, means that men "accomplish their task with the least expenditure of energy and under conditions most adequate to their human nature and most worthy of it."[10] Freedom in this view is a dialectic of negation and affirmation, of the movement from ignorance to knowledge and from the suppression of men's creative powers to their liberation. On the scale of history, according to Marx, this dialectic takes the form of forces which organize themselves around the productive means of any given society. He sought to show that the "necessity" of classes, their antagonism, and all the consequences that follow therefrom are in fact relative and conditioned by the tie of such classes to "particular, historic phases in the development of production," and that such "necessities" can be overcome.[11] Following Marx, it would be as incorrect to say that "History" causes this kind of insight or any particular insight, as to say that it can be explained by a strict mechanical causation.

For Marx, insight (or "comprehension," to use Sartre's term) is the consequence of a particular conjunction of conditions, *including* the effort and the project of the individual person and his brothers

---

[10]Engels, Frederick: *Socialism: Utopian and Scientific,* p. 73.
[11]*Selected Correspondence,* p. 86.

and sisters to fulfill their needs. Marx suggests that what distinguishes man among other organisms and physical bodies is that he is capable of a dialectic with himself, with other men, and with the natural world in such form that, through social sign-processes, he can grasp and foresee the pattern of events, and through tools and machines he can begin to control them. Thus, the *true,* as contrasted with the *apparent,* necessity of history is the movement of this dialectical power. So long as man is man, this is a necessity, since it is the law of his species-life.

There is no guarantee independent of man that this movement realize itself. But given the pattern of past history, the tendency of man's needs to overcome obstacles through practical, critical, revolutionizing activity, and the capacity of men to respond to ideas relevant to their needs, Marx felt that the odds were in favor of man's development. Freedom as the insight into necessity means, as Engels points out, bringing one's thought into conformity with what is.[12] But in the case of man this includes man himself as he might be, in his generic nature. "To be radical," said Marx, "is to grasp the root of the matter. But for man the root is man himself."[13] To grasp the root is progressively to become the root, i.e., to grow in both knowledge and being. And on man's part that requires knowledge of himself, of others, and of the world.

Sartre argues that when Marx states in *Theses on Feuerbach* that "circumstances are modified precisely by man and that the educator must be himself educated," this is either a tautology, making the educator a product of circumstances and education—"or else it is the decisive affirmation of the irreducibility of human *praxis.*"[14] By this latter he means "the irreducibility of the cultural order to the natural order."[15] If by "irreducibility" here Sartre means that as a sign-creating, projecting, time-binding creature man is different from animals, then many, including Marx, would agree. In fact, in a strict phenomenological sense, nothing can be reduced to anything else: things just are what they are. But if he means, as he sometimes ap-

---

[12]*Anti-Dühring,* p. 157.

[13]Contribution to the critique of Hegel's philosophy of right. Introduction. In *On Religion,* p. 50.

[14]*The Problem of Method,* p. 87.

[15]*Ibid.,* p. 152.

pears to mean, that man "surpasses" or "transcends" the categories of nature, broadly conceived—then he has departed from Marx. And to this extent Marxism does not become mechanical materialism as Sartre insists. Marx simply remains what he claimed to be, a humanistic naturalist or materialist for whom the essential dialectic of man is not a *praxis* originating with the individual and thrown against the world but an interpenetration, unity, and opposition of the individual man with other men and the world. When Marx said in argument with Feuerbach that the human essence "is no abstraction inherent in each single individual" but is "in its reality . . . the ensemble of the social relations,"[16] he did not negate individuality, but rather underlined its social character and foundation. In rejecting Feuerbach's "abstract" and "isolated" human individual who is united with other individuals only by some kind of "genus" or "internal dumb generality,"[17] he simultaneously rejected Sartre's primordial individual, and his Platonic recognition of freedom in the other which is "le commencement de l'humanité." [18]

Marx's own position on man's nature and freedom is set forth in his *Economic and Philosophical Manuscripts*. Man is a species-being, says Marx, who makes the human community and other communities his object in both a practical and theoretical way. Likewise, "he treats himself as the present, living species," i.e., "as a *universal* and consequently free being." [19] (By "free" here Marx means not limited with regard to the extent of objectification.) In the terms of George Herbert Mead,[20] man takes or can take the role of *all* things in their contexts, both in thought and action. His "generalized other" can take account of an unlimited number of other perspectives and by "importing the social process" it enables him to view himself from the viewpoint of the species. The universal character of man's species-life, according to Marx, derives from the range of his interpenetration with the whole of inorganic nature. Man senses, forms, acts toward, manipulates, and transforms that nature; he thinks about, uses, and enjoys it. "The physical and mental life of man, and nature,

---

[16]*Theses on Feuerbach*, VI.

[17]*Ibid.*

[18]*Critique de le Raison Dialectique*, p. 453.

[19]*Economic and Philosophical Manuscripts*, p. 100.

[20]*Mind, Self, and Society.*

are interdependent." This means, says Marx, "that nature is inter-dependent with itself, for man is a part of nature."[21]

How does this quite explicit naturalism allow for freedom? The quality of freedom is inherent in the species-life of man, which is productive—"life creating life." Unlike the animal, which is its own activity, "man makes his life activity itself an object of his will and consciousness." This determination of man is not one "with which he is completely identified"—i.e., man surpasses mere animal activity through his directed consciousness. Although Marx did not point out what Mead later observed, it is through the mechanism of the signifi-cant symbol, socially derived, that this consciousness of life activity— "life creating life"—becomes possible, coupled with the physical in-struments by which man changes his world. Marx put it very gen-erally: because man is a species-being, he says, "his own life is an object for him." In short, man aims at the community of universality and internalizes that perspective of universality and freedom in him-self. Marx then summarizes the meaning of man's free activity in contrast to the activity of animals. Animals produce "what is neces-sary for themselves and their young," but "only in a single direction"; man produces universally. Animals produce "under the compulsion of direct physical need"; man produces when freed from such physi-cal need "and only truly produces in freedom from such need." Ani-mals proluce things belonging directly to their bodies; man is free as he confronts his product. Animals are limited by the needs and the standards of the species to which they belong; man can produce "in accordance with the standards of every species." This species-life of man is not an existential fount that leaps up out of nothingness; it is simply "the species-character of human beings." [22]

I believe that what basically divides Sartre from Marx—the divi-sion that accounts for arguments over individuality, freedom, histori-cal causality, etc.—is the question of the nature of man. It is possible for Sartre to argue with some persuasiveness that he follows Marx because there are many passages in Marx and Engels indicating that man has no "nature," fixed and eternal, and that as man makes him-

---

[21] *Economic and Philosophical Manuscripts*, p. 101.

[22] The quotations in this paragraph are from *Economic and Philosophical Manu-scripts*, pp. 101-102.

self and history he transcends all conditions and categories of the past. But a closer reading will show that these passages are criticisms, often highly polemical, directed at the existing fatuities concerning man and morality—criticisms aimed against the reigning idealistic ideologies and their efforts to keep man "in his place." Marx and Engels appeal not to some far-off and formless state of affairs in which each man "turns on" spontaneously like a religious mystic, or a Left Bank intellectual, or a Frisco hippie. They appeal to man as he is *in posse,* i.e., to man in his species-life, the communal life of conscious men interdependently developing with one another and the rest of nature. When Marx wrote that the task of the working class is not to realize ideals but "to set free the elements of the new society with which old collapsing bourgeois society itself is pregnant," [23] he underlined the fact that man's fulfillment comes not out of nothing, but out of existing trends and relations. Included here is the conviction that man in his essence is profoundly social—a conviction that should not surprise us, coming from a socialist. In spite of many qualifications in the *Critique,* Sartre considers man's individuality in its *praxis* as prior to society. Sartre struggles courageously to show how "real communication" is possible. But he oscillates between a description of sympathetic role-taking, in which the self appears really to grasp the feeling-acts of the other directly, and a Humean account which builds up the other by analogy, but leaves the essential self untouched by the other.

Who is correct, Marx or Sartre? In recent years scientists have demonstrated the vital importance of maternal care in the development of the child's psychic health.[24] To discover that the mother's body comes before the child's body, that the child's body both prenatal and postnatal develops in intimate interaction with the mother, and that the child's body precedes the emergence of its psychic activity in the form of human feelings, purposes, and language—this now seems no unusual discovery. Yet Sartre's position does not take it into account. But it is empirical confirmation for the Marxist no-

---

[23]Marx, K.: *The Civil War in France.* Moscow, Foreign Languages Publishing House, 1952, p. 97.

[24]As one source, see Bowlby, John: *Child Care and the Growth of Love,* 2nd ed., edited by Margery Fry. Baltimore, Penguin, 1965.

tions that material bodies in relative motion comprise the real,[25] that mind is an emergent level and function of matter, and that "mankind must first of all eat, drink, have shelter and clothing, before it can pursue politics, science, art, religion, etc."[26] When Sartre (in Desan's words) asserts that man's hunger-need, though defined as a negation of external nature, is "ultimately provoked by man himself and not by nature"[27] and that therefore dialectic begins with man— he makes his point by splitting man off from "nature." If man is not a *spiritus ex nihilo,* but an organism that evolved with the environment as a communal primate species over millions of years, creating language, hunting, agricultural and industrial tools, the wheel and boat, domestic plants and animals, and cultural patterns which in turn created him—then the sharp distinction between man and external nature breaks down. Man, of course, continues to carry the initiative and hence responsibility in this dialectic of human nature with nonhuman nature. And that Sartre should point this out so forcefully is probably the chief contribution of his thought. But his picture of man and man's freedom is overdrawn: it is that of a needy creature, aggressively driven to negate the negating scarcities of nature.

Consider, however, a mother and infant: the infant is hungry, the mother gives it suck. Who initiates the dialectic? The mother is a nature prior to the infant, dominated by processes prior to her own conscious intent. She is also a *human* nature, initiating activity and responding to the infant's activity. While prior to the infant's humanity, her humanity is expressed in a bodily way. And in making contact with the infant's body her body begins to humanize his nature, whose emerging human nature then begins to affect her own. The complex mechanism of breathing illustrates the evolution of a delicate adjustive activity of organism to environment. Similarly, the evolution of colors and visual forms, alongside eyes, is evidence of the objective existence of knowledge in nature. A kindred mutual creation occurs in humanized sexual relations and in man's interaction with nonhuman nature, i.e., in his communal labor. Man can have per-

---

[25]Engels in *Selected Correspondence,* p. 342.

[26]Engels, Frederick: Karl Marx's funeral. In *Reminiscences of Marx and Engels,* p. 348.

[27]*The Marxism of Jean-Paul Sartre,* p. 83.

ceptual and cognitive contact with the bodies of human and non-human nature and transform them precisely because his body was generated in and by nature and is sustained by the bodies of nature. His communal species-life is simply the bodies of nature specialized, i.e., humanized.

The evolution of the body of man not only provides us with a link between mother and child and hence between man and man, throwing some light on how mind is nurtured and sustained by matter and material relations. It also indicates the solution to the origin of human society. For Sartre, who does not accept evolution,[28] society is never really accounted for, except by the fiction of "common freedom." If we are to follow the principle of simplicity, and Descartes' principle of clearness and distinctness, the evolutionary explanation seems indicated. Man is social because, like his contemporary cousins, the primates and mammals, his ancestors were social—i.e., his body like theirs is brought forth alive, is sensitive, responsive, and interdependent toward others in his species, and communicates with them.[29] In short, both individual man and the human species have their origins in objective conditions, the conditions of a social, historical life which has interwoven itself with the planetary environment. Marx wrote: "Men make their own history, but they do not make it just as they please; they do not make it under circumstances chosen by themselves, but under circumstances directly encountered, given, and transmitted from the past."[30]

Although Sartre acknowledges statements like this and appears to agree, he nonetheless insists that man is "the only factor actively managing history"[31] and claims that man at any moment is free to escape from the processes of history.[32] In a word, he clings to a dual-

---

[28]*Ibid.,* pp. 84-85.

[29]Engels, in his posthumously published pamphlet, "The Part Played by Labour in the Transition from Ape to Man," was groping toward establishing a connection between man and preman. His efforts to do so by noting the gregariousness of our simian ancestors, the freeing of the hand, and the influence of labor on communication, have acquired some support in subsequent studies by anthropologists.

[30]*The Eighteenth Brumaire of Louis Napoleon,* p. 30.

[31]Odajnik, Walter: *Marxism and Existentialism.* Garden City, Doubleday, 1965, p. 139. The quoted words are Odajnik's translation of Sartre's.

[32]*Ibid.,* p. 160.

ism in thought that, in order to preserve a bourgeois notion of freedom —the notion that freedom is godlike independence of and power over the world—tears man's free activity from its social, biological, physical, and evolutionary context. Sartre does not appear to grasp fully the elementary principle that "life is not determined by consciousness but consciousness by life."[33] The subjective life of man remains for him man's real life. But as Marx put it succinctly, "a non-objective being is a *non-being*."[34]

Sartre's subjectivistic and idealistic tendencies are evident in his discussion of the dialectic, which, he holds, operates in and between men as a "lived reality,"[35] but is in nature only hypothetical. While for Marxism the world is independent of our thinking, at the same time it is always a world *for us*. As Lenin said, "human knowledge develops from ignorance," and "millions of observations not only in the history of science and technology but in the everyday life of each and every one of us . . . illustrate the transformation of 'things-in-themselves' into 'things-for-us' . . . ."[36] In his *Critique of the Gotha Program,* Marx stressed that *nature* is "just as much a source of use values . . . as labor," and that man's labor is a "manifestation of a force of nature, human labor power."[37]

As for the dialectics of nature, there is considerable evidence that the processes of nature move in dialectical fashion. Of course Marxism accepts the concept of emergent orders and the differentiation between dialectical processes at the physical, biological, and psychosocial levels. The opposite view that man only finds what he looks for in nature is contradicted by the fact that organisms, including man, are born and nurtured by natural processes and that information systems evolve within organisms and coordinate organismic activity with external processes of nature. It is true also that man's distinctive dialectic, which Sartre describes as moving from need toward environment by way of unifying comprehension and group practice, interacts with natural processes and thus introduces a new direction and quality

---

[33]*The German Ideology,* p. 15.

[34]*Economic and Philosophical Manuscripts,* p. 182.

[35]*The Marxism of Jean-Paul Sartre,* p. 74.

[36]Lenin, V. I.: *Materialism and Empirio-Criticism.* Moscow, Foreign Languages Publishing House, 1952, p. 99.

[37]*Op Cit.,* p. 15.

to the otherwise unconscious processes of nature. In giving an accou.
of that communistic society in which private property would be positively superseded and man's labor and the materials of labor would
be redeemed from their alienation from man, Marx writes:

> The *human* significance of nature only exists for social man, because
> only in this case is nature a *bond* with other men, the basis of his exist-
> ence of others and of their existence for him . . . The *natural* existence
> of man has here become his *human* existence and nature itself has be-
> come human for him.[38]

The mutual influence of the psychosocial on the one hand and the
biological and physical on the other is a fact that Sartre must miss
to the extent that he continues to hold to a Cartesian bifurcation of
spirit and body. But it is plain in the *Theses on Feuerbach* (written
in 1845) and his afterword to the second edition of *Capital*, published in 1873, that for Marx the dialectical is a *human* method. It
is plain also that man stands at the center of history capable of transforming it if he can only learn how its processes work, and that when
Marx refers to "circumstances" and "the existing state of things,"
he means that whole fabric of history in which man's critical-practical
activities have interwoven themselves with the structures and processes
of tools and machines. This is why the revolutionary transformation
of man must be both ideational and environmental, philosophical and
technological.

Finally, Sartre's deviation from Marx's thought appears in his views
on alienation. He broadens both the existentialist and Marxist notions
of alienation by defining it as a breach between man and his world
which breaks out the moment man freely acts. Alienation appears, in
fact, to be a category inherent in man's *existence*—and to this extent
it perpetuates the alienation between the *Pour-soi* and the *En-soi* of
Sartre's early existentialism. Sartre says that the antidialectic rises up
when man's individual *praxis* encounters the inert, i.e., any series of
passively united men,[39] or any man-made totality, such as a picture,
a machine, or a tool.[40] Man's oppressed labor, his participation in
a class, constitute a form of the inert that drags down his social *praxis*

---

[38]*Economic and Philosophical Manuscripts*, p. 129.
[39]*The Marxism of Jean-Paul Sartre*, p. 80.
[40]*Ibid.*, p. 75.

and nullifies it.[41] The source of such alienation, however, is man's very act of creating, wherein as soon as he creates in *praxis* he discovers that he is alienated from his creation, i.e., impeded by its otherness, its determination.[42] One form of this alienation is the "antiman," whom man by his social *praxis* brings into being. In seeking to control both his material and human world man "others" his world, and it in turn rises up to resist his free movement. In addition to the exploitation that he suffers under the property relations of capitalism, the worker feels the force of the humiliating "look" of the bourgeois, which turns him into an object. Only when workers in sufficient numbers are aroused to a common class consciousness and in turn make the bourgeoisie aware of their objectifying "look" does the latter acquire a class consciousness. By his psychological analysis Sartre enriches the traditional "materialist" account of alienation, but in the process he clings to a Hegelian concept of alienation.

For the Marxist, the primary impediment in the path of dialectical activity on the part of men is the existing mode of production (the capitalist one), the relations of production (private property), and the ruling class (capitalists). The antagonistic power consists in the new forces of production, i.e., the machines and the working class, whose relations are essentially cooperative. As they develop they come into increasing antagonism with the existing property relations presided over by the capitalist class. It is true that class consciousness is an important and necessary factor in the whole complex of events required to move society from capitalism to socialism. And the whole point of Marxist political activity was and is to develop such a consciousness as a way of building history toward this issue. But Marx and Engels did not stress it as the *major* factor, and in their studies they were inclined to concentrate on the movement that grows up "behind the backs" of men in history. Even in the early writings of Marx, such as the *Economic and Philosophical Manuscripts,* where the premises of humanism are laid down, the stress is on the *material* basis of alienation.

"We shall begin," says Marx, "from a *contemporary* economic fact. The worker becomes poorer the more wealth he produces and the

---

[41]*Ibid.,* pp. 106-108.
[42]*Ibid.,* p. 106.

more his production increases in power and extent."[43] The human worker is devalued in direct proportion to the increase in value of things. Thus, "the object produced by labor, its product, now stands opposed to it as an *alien being,* as a power *independent* of the producer . . . . this product is an *objectification* of labor."[44] Marx goes on to elaborate the consequences of this primary alienation in the form of alienation from nature, from the act of production and from man himself, from man's own species-life of universality and freedom, and from man's fellow man.[45] In *Capital* this same notion, refined and concrete, reappears in the form of the fetishism of commodities. The economic source of alienated labor is commodity production, the key is surplus-value, and the alienation of man is now described as "material relations between persons and social relations between things."[46] Alienation consists not in what man thinks but in what he does. Objectively, man acts like a commodity. The supersession of this action must be an opposite action. It must be practical-critical activity. While this means the negation of the conditions of commodity production and of the class which presides over surplus-value, it does not in principle mean the introduction of a new alienation in the Marxist sense. It is true that revolutions and socialisms generate many problems, among them the problems of human conflict, misunderstanding, and separation. But in a socialist society, the problems are of a different order. Institutional structure, for example, may arise, as Sartre points out, founded upon the oath and the *Terreur,* and bureaucracies, with their monopoly of power and special privileges, may spread. Such phenomena, however, indicate not that the Marxist notion of alienation as alienated labor is mistaken, but that it is incomplete for explaining and coping with the problems of human living.

Sartre's notion that in the very act of "totalizing" our worlds we alienate them is true. But it is true within the conditions of a world of capitalism where the many can never be one *within those conditions* and where class struggles against class in a world of scarcity.

---

[43]*Economic and Philosophical Manuscripts,* p. 95.
[44]*Ibid.*
[45]*Ibid.,* pp. 98-103.
[46]*Capital,* vol. I, p. 73.

Only in *one* world, where classes have disappeared and the dominant mode of living is cooperative, where the "totalizing" of each enhances and reinforces the "totalizing" of all, can this kind of alienation be superseded.

If we take Marx's thought as the criterion of Marxism, we cannot therefore call Sartre a thoroughgoing Marxist, particularly where the concept of freedom is in issue. And this is the critical issue, for it is on this point that Sartre proposes to correct Marxism. "Marx's own Marxism," Sartre writes, "contained implicitly the demand for an existential foundation for the theory."[47] It is true that Marx did not develop anthropology and that some alleged Marxists have committed the practical and theoretical mistakes of which Sartre accuses them— mechanical materialism, the loss of man as a free and telic creator, *a priori* dogma, "lazy" and "sclerotic thinking," lack of a psychology and sociology that take account of the subrational and creative forces in the individual in interaction with his complex world, the ossifying and brutalizing of institutions, and so on. Sartre's work represents a counter-movement against such errors. But in overstating the case for the opposition it fails to achieve the necessary synthesis. Sartre's radical individualism, his location of the "original dialectical movement in the individual,"[48] his unabated *negativité*, his alternation from moods of euphoric freedom to depressed fatalism, his idea of pure indetermination as the heart of freedom—all of these are alien to Marx, who believed in the freedom of man's *praxis* without compromising his naturalism, and who was steadily optimistic about man's history.

In the United States we admire Sartre because of his passionate and devoted defense of the individual person, in both thought and practice. But that is in part because we come out of a society which exalts the individual and at the same time frequently turns him into the selfish, possessive, and nauseated person whom Sartre so vividly portrayed in his early work. It is also because we live in a political tradition in which individual resistance to institutional tyranny has some standing and esteem. Marx understood and appreciated the individual too. But he saw something larger and more lasting, the associa-

---

[47]*The Problem of Method,* p. 177.
[48]*Ibid.,* p. 161.

tion of individual men intimately related in the creative power of thought and practice. Man is free, and, as Sartre insists with Marx, human life and action is deeper than knowledge and, in that dimension, irreducible to knowing.[49] But man is free only in that association. The freedom of detachment always issues from it and refers back to it, and is in fact a moment in the process. Sartre points to the dangers, the dehumanizations, the terrors in a system of thought and practice that tends to lose the individual. But the problem that we face is our own society, with its thought and practice. It is a good thing to call for the concrete and creative individual in Marxism. As for us Americans, it would be a better thing to rescue the individual from capitalism. There, one's starting point cannot be the Sartrean individual, bereaved of all except his own comprehension. Such an individual may be dramatic, but is not enduring. An institution, as Sartre points out, endures; but it may not be creative. The alternative is the creative group, which maintains the freedom of the individual within the power of the group—a group whose power derives from the creative individuals working in concert against the conditions of their oppression and toward the conditions of their liberation and fulfillment.

---

[49] *Ibid.*, p. 14.

PART THREE
MARXIST HUMANISM AND
SOCIAL QUESTIONS

VIII

SOCIALISM AND DEMOCRACY

ONE OF THE IMPORTANT SOCIAL questions for men in the contemporary world is that of democracy. The world-wide revolutions against feudalism in recent centuries have been impelled by entrepreneurs and merchants as well as by peasants and laborers. Both groups have chafed under the restrictions of feudal authority in economic and political areas. Both have pressed for wider distribution of power in these areas. The first broad success in these revolutions was the emergence in Europe of a capitalist economy, which carried with it the creation of a political order based on the rule of the bourgeoisie. This order was "democracy" in the first modern sense of that term. But the democracy of capitalism excluded the peasants and laborers from political power, just as capitalism excluded them from economic power. The result was that the peasants' and laborers' revolts, begun in the fourteenth century, continued into the nineteenth and twentieth centuries. Capitalist democracy was little better for these exploited groups than feudal autocracy. In the face of the oppression of wage labor and imperialism, they demanded freedom to determine their own lives. Hence the proletarian-peasant movements culminating in the great socialist revolutions of the twentieth century. These revolutions were essentially broad demands for socialism in the economy and for a people's—not a class'—democracy in political life.

Since the rise of socialist movements based on Marx's thought, the defenders of capitalism and capitalist democracy have represented socialism and socialist democracy with the grossest distortions. These have been called tyranny, totalitarianism, fascism, brutality, antihumanism, antidemocracy, etc. Since 1917 the fears and illusions connected with anti-Bolshevism have dominated the minds of most Americans—fears and illusions cultivated by leaders in government, the economy, the military, the mass media, education, law, religion, etc.

and taken up by the masses. During the cold war from 1945 to the present the mood of anticommunism among Americans has been sustained and intense, with a virtual blackout of Marxist ideas in the schools and vast economic and military actions abroad, in Korea and Vietnam, for example, to contain or roll back communism. Thus when one speaks of socialism, most Americans do not understand what is meant, and, moreover, they associate it with all that is the opposite of democracy as the rule of the people. It is therefore important to clarify the meaning of socialism and its relation to democracy.

For the truth is that socialism and socialist democracy represent a threat to the limited, class-based, self-seeking "democracy" of capitalism, as well as a fulfillment of the democracy of those Americans who falsely associate capitalist democracy with their salvation and socialist democracy with their destruction. Socialism and genuine democracy are intimately related. They demand one another. If one truly understands and practices socialism, by the same token one understands and practices democracy. This is democracy of, by, and for *all* the people. That is why the defenders of capitalism want to distort it. For a widespread understanding of socialism and its democracy would number the days of capitalism. It would in time do away with "a democracy for the minority, only for the possessing classes, only for the rich." [1]

When I maintain that socialism and democracy demand one another, I refer to both (1) the actual workings of socialism and democracy and (2) the theories of socialism and democracy. People who believe in and try to practice true socialism as a working system, who try to follow the logic of its idea and to discover the conditions required for its fulfillment, demand democracy. As socialism develops its essential characteristics, democracy in like proportion develops. A given society that is socialistic in outline and general direction may be temporarily or partially undemocratic; decisions may be taken by the leaders without consultation of the people and in defiance of their will and their welfare. But on the whole and in the long run a society cannot properly be called socialistic to the extent that it is not democratic. Socialism means public ownership and control of the techniques and instruments of production—more broadly, an association of free men creating their own lives and their relations to their social and material

---

[1] Lenin, V. I.: *The State and Revolution.*

world. To the extent that this creation is exercised by public, collective deliberation and action, democracy obtains. On the theoretical level, therefore, socialism envisages the time when formal democracy, like all superstructures, will be transformed and people will govern themselves *directly*. Thus Marx spoke of "the self-government of the producers." [2] And while Lenin wrote of "the equal right of all to determine the structure and administration of the state," he foresaw a time in a fully socialized society when men would *"become accustomed to the observance of the elementary rules of social life . . . and to observing them without force"*—"when all the members of society, or even only the overwhelming majority, have learned how to govern the state *themselves."* In such a society, thought Lenin, the democratic "state" would wither away. [3]

Conversely, democracy in its deepest sense demands socialism, both in fact and theory. It is true that partial or spurious democracy has in fact been associated with the increasing concentration of economic and political power in the hands of a small group of capitalists. In Nazi Germany many of the barbarities committed were sanctioned by legal procedure and popular vote. In the United States the crimes of war, racism, and poverty are all perpetuated through the institutions of "democracy." Yet many people, confronted with the fact that these decisions are in fact made by a few people, would acknowledge that real democracy is not at work. Moreover, it is not democracy as such that produces monopoly capitalism or fascism, but rather the relative weakness of democratic forces and the relative strength of antidemocratic forces. On the other side, as democracy develops, what happens? Democracy means the collective participation of people in making and executing decisions intended to advance their welfare. Such participation or self-government arises out of the demand of people to meet their basic needs and fulfill their all-round human existence. Such a demand in turn tends toward a demand for the removal of exploitive institutions and the establishment of collective control of the techniques and means of production. The history of socialist revolutions since 1917 makes evident this connection, namely, that under certain conditions the democratic dispositions of people

---

[2]Marx, Karl: *The Civil War in France,* p. 90.
[3]*State and Revolution,* pp. 83, 74, 84.

demand the forms of socialism. It is evident also that the perpetuators of bourgeois forms of democracy do not necessarily demand socialism—quite the contrary. But democratic theory, as defended here, demands it; for the full significance of democratic ideals like liberty, equality, fraternity, and peace can be realized only in a socialist society.

In addition, this factual-theoretical connection between socialism and democracy carries with it an imperative or *moral* connection. When I say that socialism demands democracy I am doing more than merely describing a psychological, political, or historical fact or a theoretical connection. I am proposing a connection that ought to prevail; I am arguing that socialist systems ought to be and that, implicitly, they ought to be democratic.

When I speak of "socialism" or "true socialism" I am of course stipulating an ideal definition, one that I believe *ought* to prevail, one that I *demand*. However, some people believe in or demand socialism, but do not believe in or demand democracy. Some demand democracy but do not therefore demand socialism. Still others are opposed to the demands of both socialism and democracy. On what basis, then, do I define socialism and democracy in such ways that they demand each other? The fundamental basis is the concept of man and of man's fulfillment defended in this work. Man's fulfillment is the final demand, the categorical imperative. All these other demands—socialism is demanded; socialism demands democracy; democracy is demanded; democracy demands socialism—are derivative demands, hypothetical imperatives. They derive their forces as demands from the force of this categorical demand that man be fulfilled, and from the demonstration that they are the necessary means by which to achieve man's fulfillment. I have already explained and argued for the concept of man and his fulfillment basic to my exposition. Here I shall indicate how socialism and democracy in their interdependence are necessary means to man's fulfillment.

Socialism and democracy as ideas have a long history, which we shall only briefly review here. They have changed and evolved through the centuries, reflecting changing conditions. Athenian democracy, when the term "democracy" first came into use, cleared the way for unprecedently large numbers of men to participate in the affairs of government. Even so, citizenship restrictions barred most males and all females from such participation; and the popular assembly could not propose laws or control the business of government. Likewise, the notion of common ownership in ancient Athenian society was limited by class structure: Plato argued in the *Republic* that a necessary condition for securing the unswerving loyalty of the guardians to the welfare of the society was to arrange that they held no private property. The early Christians, we are told, held all things in common, and seem to have ordered their lives by discussion and friendly persuasion, a form of primitive democracy. But it was a small and short-lived experiment. Christian, Stoic, and other Greek ideas find their way into the view of Thomas Aquinas and others that royal power derives from the people and can if abused be legitimately restricted or abolished by the people. With the dawn of the Renaissance utopias begin to appear, envisaging in various forms and degrees ideal socialistic societies in which men live harmoniously together.

Not until the modern period, however, did these two great ideas, socialism and democracy, begin to assume mature form. Under the stimulus of the rise of capitalism and the development of science, the Renaissance, the Industrial Revolution, the English and French Revolutions, and the Enlightenment, they spread. Democracy as a modern bourgeois idea emerged in response to the demands of the merchants, entrepreneurs, traders, bankers, townsmen, emerging propertied groups, and others of the new class. They demanded political and economic freedom in the face of the restrictions of vested feudal and ecclesiastical interests. The demand for democracy came out of the need of the rising propertied and capitalist class for political power and authority. John Locke in England was a representative spokesman of this demand. God has given the earth to mankind in common, Locke argued.[4] There, in a state of nature, all men are free and equal. They can "order their actions and dispose of their possessions and persons as they see fit, within the bounds of the law of nature, without asking leave or depending upon the will of any other man." [5] Thus men enter into political society only by their own consent,[6] and even

---

[4] Locke, John: *The Second Treatise of Civil Government. An Essay Concerning the True Original, Extent, and End of Civil Government*, V, 25.

[5] *Ibid.*, II, 4.

[6] *Ibid.*, VIII, 95.

after government is formed the people retain a natural right to dissolve it.[7] Locke's labor theory of property,[8] though individualistic, pointed in the direction of socialism; for what would Locke have said if he had seen, as Marx did, that the labor of most men is appropriated by a usurping class? But Locke was speaking for a class, the new insurgent property owners.

Socialism as an idea emerged in response to a more widespread and deeper need. That was the need of the peasants, the new industrial working class, and the urban poor, for a social order that would wipe out their oppression under both feudalism and capitalism. This need encompassed both political and economic demands for a transformation in society. For these groups saw that through existing institutions they had no prospect of seizing immediate political power. At the same time they saw that only a radical change in the existing state of affairs, i.e., an economic change, could secure to them any meaningful democratic self-rule. Thus, the socialistic ideas of John Ball, the Taborites, Thomas Münzer, Winstanley and the Diggers, Babeuf, Owen, Saint-Simon, and Fourier, all anticipated a broader and fuller democracy than that imagined and achieved by their contemporary capitalistic class.

It was, in fact, the pressures from these broad, oppressed classes in society which helped to sharpen the humanistic demands of the new propertied classes and which provided the mass base for the success of the latter's revolutions.

Initially, these proto-socialists, seeing no basis for building an ideal society in the society around them, looked backward to early Christianity for their model. Later, with the opening of the New World, they looked westward. But the idea of a socialistic society, conceived in the ancient slave society, born under the oppressive conditions of feudalism, and nurtured amidst the miseries and upheavals of capitalism, began to grow toward maturity in the nineteenth century. What had been a mere religious dream and remembrance of things past for the feudal utopians now became a practical possibility. If partial and bourgeois democracy were possible, why not full proletarian-peasant democracy? But just as the capitalist had to fight with kings and popes

---

[7]*Ibid.*, XIX.
[8]*Ibid.*, V.

for their power, so the new working class must fight for their power against their exploiters. Through the theory and practice of socialism, the urban and rural masses would finish what the capitalists had begun: they would extend and realize fully the ideal of political democracy by achieving economic power by and for the whole people. In their demands for utopian socialism and primitive democracy alike, and for the abolition of class distinctions, they anticipated the Marxist view which demands the simultaneous destruction of both economic and political exploitation and the simultaneous creation of both socialism and democracy.

Let us consider now how socialism demands democracy.

Socialism, building itself upon the humanistic tradition of the past, has always claimed to be the inheritor and fulfiller of the democratic tradition. In the modern conception of democracy, freedom and equality are basic concepts. Locke's conception of freedom was that no man should be "subject to the inconstant, uncertain, unknown, arbitrary will of another man." [9] In practice, this meant for him and his followers freedom from the tyranny of absolute monarchs and large landowners. Politically, it has meant in the Anglo-American tradition the freedom of a properly qualified (property-qualified) citizen to vote or to run for political office. Even today, millions of citizens in the United States cannot exercise this freedom because of conditions of racial discrimination, local poll taxes, literacy tests, residency laws, and the like. But even if universal suffrage, only a relatively recently ideal of democracy, were to prevail, freedom of the ballot would still need to overcome economic inequalities and slaveries in order to give itself any full democratic significance. In the past bourgeois freedom has meant the freedom of the businessman from government interference and his own freedom to employ and exploit the labor of others. Today in America to this freedom has been added the freedom of the large corporation to receive the support of the government and the military, and the freedom to exploit foreign labor and resources.

Socialism envisages an ideal society that has done away with classes and class antagonism, "an association, in which the free development of each is the condition for the free development of all." [10] Thus,

---

[9]*Ibid.*, IV, 22.
[10]*Manifesto of the Communist Party*, p. 31.

the freedom conceived of in socialism is not negative, not instrumental alone, and not primarily political. It is the positive freedom of man's fulfillment. It is "its own end." [11] And it cannot be political in the old sense which presupposes the parliamentary, legal, forcible control of one class by another. It is instead the everyday exercise of man's powers, in cooperation with other men, in the control of the conditions of their relations with another, with tools and machines, and with external nature, in the direction of human fulfillment.

In the theory and practice of the bourgeois state, political freedom serves two functions. First, it secures to the ruling groups the opportunity to express and facilitate their economic power in the political sphere. Woodrow Wilson once remarked that while in the past businessmen manipulated the politicians behind the scenes, they now enter directly and unashamedly into the affairs of government. Second, political freedom serves the function of screening the great masses out of participation in the making and execution of governmental policies. Several factors may be counted on to produce this latter result: legal disqualification of voters, ignorance of the people, confusion and misinformation about the issues effected by news and propaganda controlled by the minority, the perpetuation of myths about the existence of "democracy," "freedom," "the Free World," etc. Thus emphasis is placed on verbal freedoms—freedom of speech, press, assembly—because it is not anticipated that these freedoms will be used by the masses. Bourgeois political democracy is based on property relations. Accordingly it cannot be broken until those property relations are broken. Under bourgeois democracy, freedom to think, act, and decide is a function of ownership. Power at last comes down to economic power, and freedom is a form of power. Accordingly, freedom cannot be extended to all until ownership is extended to all, and men cannot be equal in opportunity to develop until their economic opportunities are equal. Full freedom, in short, is the very antipode of economic exploitation. Freed *from* that, men may then be freed *for* their own development. Because ultimate power then ceases to be economic power, since that power is collectively shared and controlled and no man can use it to exploit the freedom of another—socialism aims at the most complete form of democracy.

---

[11] *Capital,* vol. III, p. 954.

Under capitalism, which divides and alienates men from one another and from themselves, bourgeois democracy sets aside "freedom"
as an isolated value. Like a pure and precious jewel, it is cut, polished,
and displayed for praise and adulation. It is not intended by the ruling groups that it be used by the thinker in his criticism of society or
by the working man in his effort to improve his conditions. Socialists
aim at taking this jewel out of its display case and putting it to use in
cutting away the fetters of man. Socialists want to use it to reflect,
magnify, and analyze man's slavery, and to foresee the way to this
fulfilled future. For socialism, freedom, as concept and practice, is
fundamental and not peripheral for man. It is not something to be
set aside as a stratagem to be used by the ruling class in maintaining
its power, or a privilege or luxury conferred upon the masses, to be
indulged in under the prescribed etiquette of those conferring it. It
is instead a power, a force for historical change for man, essential to
his fulfillment as man and hence both a means and end of socialism.

Under bourgeois democracy the concept of "equality" was a protest
and a program for a few, rather than a prescription and program for
the many. When a British thinker like Harrington spoke of "equality,"
he meant "equality of estates," in which interpretation he was followed
by Locke, Madison, Hamilton, and others. Like the concept of "freedom," this definition helped to boost the rising landowners into power
and to break royal rule. But it also excluded the vast mass of the unpropertied from effective political power. When the American founding fathers declared that "all men are created equal," they did not
mean by this an unqualified suffrage for all. Just as the British Parliament claimed the right to represent the whole Commonwealth, so the
American Congress claimed the right to represent the people. Among
the French, who stressed equality more than liberty, the Declaration
of Rights and Duties of Man and Citizen states at the very outset:
"The rights of man in society are liberty, equality, security, and property." "Property" here hung like a millstone around the neck of
"liberty," "equality," and "security." The party of Babeuf realized
this when, three years later, in 1796, it wrote: "The aim of the French
Revolution is to destroy inequality and to re-establish the general welfare. The Revolution is not complete, because the rich monopolize
all the property and govern exclusively, while the poor toil like slaves,

languish in misery, and count for nothing in the State." [12] As R. H. Tawney has shown in his classical study, *Equality*, "equality" is meaningless unless it includes economic opportunity and security.

The historical irony of bourgeois democracy, operating in the context of laissez-faire capitalism, is that it progressively negated the very ideals of liberty and equality which were its rallying cries. In the eighteenth century, as a new economic movement restive under the restrictions of feudalism and mercantilism, capitalism asserted the revolutionary premise that no government shall limit the freedom of individuals engaged in business and trade. But as capitalism grew, and as capitalists acquired increasing industrial and political power, more and more persons were necessarily denied such freedom, including lesser capitalists themselves. Thus, while the man of small capital in the business world, and the man of small resources in the political world, might in nineteenth century America reasonably hope to rise in power, by the twentieth century monopolies in both economics and politics had excluded him. Business and political opportunities were closed to him, and "liberty" and "equality" had little concrete meaning in these spheres. The eighteenth century "liberal" had become a twentieth century "conservative." Pursuing the "liberty" and "equality" of a few, he had destroyed them for the many.

The theoretical error of Locke, Ricardo, Adam Smith, Turgot, and other agrarian physiocrats—an error necessitated by their own class perspective—was to picture men as "free and equal" in some ideal state of nature, independent of the existing slaveries and inequalities of men in society. Such slaveries and inequalities they traced to the class immediately above them; and in opposing *their* social organization they set themselves against *all* forms of social organization and government as hindrances to the civil liberty of the individual man. A similar error is committed by the bourgeois liberal of today. Although he may, like a New Dealer, recognize the need for a social solution of social problems, he views the problems of freedom and equality independent of their economic setting. Thus, he does not see that the freedom of the Negro in the United States varies directly with his economic power.

Socialism aims at providing and guaranteeing this economic freedom

[12]Cited in George, Charles H. (Ed.): *Revolution: Five Centuries of Europe in Conflict.* New York, Dell, 1962, p. 411.

and security. For it, the democratic ideal of equality means that through the humanistic attitudes of citizens, the collective ownership and control of property, and law and its enforcement, society will guarantee to each individual person the education, knowledge, skills, tools, opportunities, and all else needed for his own free development. Socialism aims to remove the main stumbling block from bourgeois democracy, namely, the inequalities of power and opportunity that spring from a system of exploitive property relations. It aims to give concrete and universal meaning to the concept of equality by equalizing, and thus destroying, property relations, i.e., by socializing the instruments and processes of production.

The idea, "From each according to his ability, to each according to work performed," means, as Marx explained in *Critique of the Gotha Programme*, a common or equal standard applied to all men, namely, labor. This means not only that all men will have freedom or opportunity to engage in creative labor as able; it means also that they *must* work. As a man works, he will be rewarded: he who does not work shall not eat. Thus, the exploitation of another man through the hire of his labor is prohibited. While this is a standard that is, under socialism, to be applied to all men equally, it results as Marx observes, in inequalities: some men will be married while others are not, some men will have more children than others, etc. There is the additional difficulty of measuring and applying the standard of "labor."

The formula, "From each according to his ability, to each according to his needs," [13] transforms the equal standard of labor into the broader standard implicit in it, namely, the equal standard of human development. In the ideal of socialism, each man is to live productively in relation to other men and the world in accordance with his unique individual powers and endowments, expressing his productive capacities and at the same time contributing to the development of others. In order to do this, his various needs must be provided for—his need for food, bodily safety, and physical health; his need for trusting relations with others, nurture, love, and belongingness; his need for a free and autonomous identity; his need for cooperation; his need for skills, habits of work, and valid vocational objectives; his need for the mutual confirmation of others in play, work, love, and social planning; his

---

[13] *Critique of the Gotha Programme,* p. 27.

need for symbolic expression and creation; his need for a philosophy providing standards of judgment and orientation to things of greatest significance.

All of these needs can be subsumed under one need—the need for creative development. All men are born equal and are equal in the sense that they share this generic, essentially human need, expressed in different styles and forms and thus requiring different conditions for its fulfillment. Socialism declares that all men *ought* to be equal, that they have an equal *right* or claim to be fulfilled. And socialism then becomes a collective effort to guarantee this equal right of different development. It does so by democratically planning and providing a human and natural environment that will nurture every individual of the human species in his development. This does not mean that some amorphous, mysterious "state," with magical and affluent largess, confers upon individuals all the finished goods and services of a utopia. It means rather that as a necessary function of his own fulfillment the individual person acts to help others achieve their fulfillment. He cannot receive according to his needs unless he also gives to others according to their needs. Such giving—to close associates, to children, to contemporaries, to future generations—rises out of the nurtured recognition of a common human identity in other persons alongside a healthy respect for their differences in temperament, endowments, and needs. The sense and practice of fraternity, in short, is fundamental in socialism.

In this appreciation of fraternity, socialism seeks to supply what is conspicuously absent from bourgeois parliamentary democracy and its economic counterpart, capitalism. In both theory and practice, capitalism has stressed the self-interest of the isolated and self-sufficient individual pursuing his own private, pecuniary, and material goals in a competitive and acquisitive market. The broad, *human* fulfillment of the individual person, social service, and mutual aid are, in such a perspective, only adventitious values, if indeed they are recognized at all. Likewise, parliamentary democracy has never made anything but a token pretense to acknowledge fraternity as a central value. The British emphasized liberty, the French equality, and Americans both. For the roots of such democracy lay in the individual landowner, entrepreneur, trader, and the like, each bent on protecting and defending his economic rights by political means. Because both capitalism and parliamentary democracy were built on the principles of individualism and egoism instead of socialism and altruism, they were doomed to fail in fulfilling their own ideals of liberty and equality. Men cannot develop freely and equally unless they express a common concern and care for one another. But the system of private profit and exploitation in economics, and the system of oligarchic power, struggle, and compromise in politics, are contradictory to such a fraternal feeling and practice. Thus, those who believe that the United States government can conduct a foreign policy in Asia, Africa, and Latin America that will fraternally identify itself with the needs of the suffering masses there, are expecting the circumstantially impossible. Some have even dared to ask why the United States government does not relieve the condition of its own colonials at home, the Negroes, Indians, Mexican Americans, Puerto Ricans, and other oppressed minorities, or why it does not make war on the poverty of some one-fifth to two-fifths of its own people. To seek a true answer to these questions would lead them back to the foundations of the whole politico-economic system.

The classical theory of capitalism relies on the mechanism of the market to distribute goods and services, to determine values, to check individual excesses, and to harmonize individual interests. Fellow-feeling, cooperation, social unity, and fraternity have very low priorities in capitalism's scheme of things. In theory, they are, like charity and all social services, supposed to flow as natural consequences from an aggressive and prosperous collection of citizens, each pursuing his own individual material interests. But in practice these social services —schools, hospitals, care of the handicapped and aged, transportation, communication—all are greatly neglected, as a survey of American society will show. The theoretical error here is to split man into two parts, "material" and "spiritual," and to identify the material part with his individuality and the spiritual with his altruistic dispositions. The practical error, which in fact precedes the theoretical and which the theoretical aims to justify and reinforce, is the organization of society in such a way that the individualistic, material dispositions of man are rewarded while the altrustic ones are not. This is a consequence of the class structure of capitalism. The result is the production of large numbers of deformed persons—skilled and energetic in their "egotistical calculation," inept and weak in their sympathetic and cooperative impulses. Society, with solidarity, mutual aid, and social purpose, was in some mysterious way supposed to arise out of the actions of such atomic individuals. An "invisible hand," "moral sentiments," or "natural law" were supposed to be the agents of this transformation. But the bear that in this fairytale is supposed to be transformed into a prince remains a bear. The "public interest" remains a mere fiction as long as the fundamental interests of men are private interests.

Political theory followed a similar line of argument. James Madison started out with the assumption of "factions" in society. The great problem of government then for him became how to protect both individual rights and the public good against the domination of minority and majority factions. If we ask why the public could not protect itself against such factions, the answer is that in Madison's premises no such public, with a unitary sense of its own good and the power to secure that, exists. And in this Madison was realistic: in his society "factions" (classes and subclasses) existed, antagonistic to one another, vying in the market and in politics for power. Consequently he proposed the republican principle and the system of checks and balances in government. These, he argued, would "enable the government to control the governed" and "oblige it to control itself." [14] The premise here is isolated and antagonistic individuals and groups; the conclusion is a mechanism for compromising and balancing the diverse claims and interests. Fraternal democracy does not appear in the conclusion because it is not in the premise.

Hence, the highly vaunted principles of suffrage, the multiparty system, parliamentary debate, majority rule, and so on become ways of adjusting collisions between factions. Even in Madison's society, "majority rule" in Congress meant in fact minority rule, for the majority of the people did not have a voice or hand in determining the course of their civic affairs. And "majority rule" becomes an even greater farce when the dominant faction in a society is a powerful group combining business, military, and political interests supported by the mass media which in large part reflect uncritically their views and thus sterilize in advance the seeds of dissent.

---

[14] *The Federalist*, 10, 51.

Democratic theory that developed more or less independently of capitalism tended to found itself on the idea of fraternity. During the Peasants' Revolt in 1381, John Ball, speaking for the peasants, artisans, and unskilled laborers, revived an ancient Christian argument: "Are we not all descended from the same parents, Adam and Eve?" The implication is plain: all men are and ought to be brothers and sisters in one family: freely, equally, and democratically sharing benefits and responsibilities. In the next century the Taborite radicals —democrats, free thinkers, primitive communists—proclaimed the pooling of goods and the equality of men based on the belief in the common origin and nature of men. Münzer and other Anabaptists took up this cry in the sixteenth century, and it was echoed by the Diggers and Radical Levellers in the seventeenth century. In 1649 Abiezer Coppe wrote:

> My most Excellent Majesty (in me) hath strangely and variously transformed this forme. . . . *I overturn* . . . . who ever you are, that oppose me, the Eternal God, who am UNIVERSALL Love . . . . I, the eternal God, the Lord of Hosts, who am that mighty Leveller, am comming . . . to Levell in good earnest . . . . Loose the bands of wickednesse, undo the heavy burdens, let the oppressed go free, and breake every yoake. Deale thy bread to the hungry, and bring the poore that are cast out (both of houses and Synagogues) to thy house. Cover the naked: Hide not thy self from thine owne flesh, from a creeple, a rogue, a begger, he's thine owne flesh. From a Whoremonger, a thief, &c. he's flesh of thy flesh, and his theft, and whoredome is flesh of thy flesh also, thine owne flesh.[15]

In the eighteenth century Rousseau resumed the theme of man's fraternity, but in a pagan, more sophisticated form. This was developed in the nineteenth century by utopian socialists in Western Europe and Russia, and by romantics like the American Walt Whitman.

In all of this precapitalistic thought, rising in reaction against the oppressions of feudalism both sacred and secular, the fraternal image served as a potent weapon to juxtapose to the established hierarchy of privilege and depredation. The cry of equality, the levelling of all orders and estates, was aimed at demolishing the whole entrenched system from king and pope down to villein and serf. The demand for freedom naturally followed in its train, for to *be* equal men must be

---

[15]Cohn, Norman: *The Pursuit of The Millennium*. Fairlawn, Essential, 1957, pp. 357, 360, 362.

freed from a system imposing inequality on them. But it is important
to note that these demands of equality and freedom were, in the
mouths of the lower, dispossessed classes, far more radical and extensive than similar demands made by the rising bourgeois class, though
the two were often allied. The bourgeoisie wanted freedom for their
own class. They could not, and did not, honestly demand and fight
for the freedom of all classes. But the great masses of men had nothing
to lose but their common sufferings and chains and a world to win in
a common revolt. Freedom and equality for them were more than
freedom and equality to conduct their economic and political affairs
as they saw fit; for they had no such affairs. Freedom and equality
had to mean a new order entirely, and hence the wiping away of *all*
classes, both the ruling feudal groups and those enslaved to them in
the bondage of inequality. Consequently, the demands for freedom
and equality were deeply rooted in a fraternity of suffering, struggle,
and hope. To declare that all men are brothers simultaneously challenges the presumptions of class society and rallies the oppressed to
unite in destroying those presumptions and their tangible institutions.
With the rise and maturing of capitalism, the growing army of the
industrial workers took up this demand for a universal, classless society.

Thus, bourgeois democratic theory could be relatively clear about
what it wanted and how to secure it: the enemy is feudal domination,
and this can be defeated by the freedom of the entrepreneur in the
market and the equality of the propertied in parliament. The democracy of the masses—reaching into the depths of men's souls and leading them to die heroic deaths by the hundreds of thousands in scores
of peasants' and workers' revolts—has tended to be vague and visionary. Even when they managed to free themselves temporarily from
the tyrannies of their masters—sharing all goods in common and collectively running their own affairs—they have not appeared ready
for the instituting of the fraternal principle. Nonetheless, there is no
other viable and humanistic alternative than that of the people learning how to live together through repeated failure and effort.

Marx and Engels argued that all movements in the direction of a
society of equals living according to fraternal principles were doomed
to miscarry so long as there was no proletarian class. Hence, the
peasants' revolts and the utopian experiments in socialisms could not

draw upon large masses of people, unified by common conditions of work, exploitation, and class interest, to carry through their ideals. Socialism and its concomitant of full democracy are possible, in short, only when the social principle has developed and spread among masses of people—associations, trade unions, cooperation in industry, commerce, and the like.

This observation is true. But it should not lead us to assume that the passage of years automatically produces advances in socialism and democracy. Industrialization produces changes in modes of human living which are propitious to the adoption of socialism and democracy. But in advanced capitalisms it produces also countervailing forces like the control of the mass media, the new military-industrial-political complex, and the manipulated psychology for the organization man. Moreover, under socialism, it is evident that the transformation of human attitudes, beliefs, and values is much more difficult than Marx and Engels imagined. Here the role of ideas and of intellectuals is critical, and the problem of humanistic education is a central one. The break-up of the systems of capitalism and feudalism is now proceeding with accelerating momentum. The crucial question facing us is how to mobilize human resources in the struggle against poverty, hunger, disease, homelessness, unemployment, overpopulation, illiteracy, ignorance, prejudice, apathy, passivity, inertia, individualism, exploitation, hopelessness, authoritarian attitudes, alienation, and all other nonhuman and inhuman conditions. This is a question that cuts across all countries, backward or advanced, socialistic or capitalistic, though clearly the problem differs in content and form from place to place.

An essential factor in the solution of this question is the development of an adequate theory of socialism and of democracy. Socialism and democracy, if they are to be effective as ideas, must be built on a sound theory of man, of man's fulfillment, and of the conditions required for man's fulfillment. We speak of a "science of socialism," but we have many steps yet to take in constructing such a science. That science would proceed according to the general pattern of all sciences. It would propose hypotheses about the character and conditions of man's realization as man, put such hypotheses to the test in concrete situations, observe and analyze the results, and revise the hypotheses accordingly. The science of socialism can not be developed by a few esoteric experts in isolation from their subjects. On the contrary, the very concept and practice of socialism, as we have tried to show, demands democratic decision and implementation concerning values. It demands that the people, through collaborative discussion and action, form and transform their values. This means that the leaders of socialism—whether they be in socialist, capitalist, or feudal countries—must interact with the people in an effort to elicit and reinforce their creative and cooperative dispositions. The problem is to educate the people in such ways that they *educate themselves* through cooperative, productive activity. This means that the educators—i.e., the leading socialists —must themselves be educated. Lenin declared: "The local Soviets, depending on time and place, can amend, enlarge and add to the basic provision worked out by the government. Creative activity at the grass roots is the basic factor of the new public life. . . . Socialism cannot be decreed from above. Its spirit rejects the mechanical, bureaucratic approach; living, creative socialism is the product of the masses themselves." [16]

Many conditions are required for this creation. A primary condition is the development of the democratic process, including criticism and self-criticism, within political groups. The undemocratic notion that one man, or a group of men, have the complete and final answers to the problems of a society, must be eradicated. Self-criticism must cease to be a ritual for ratifying a prior decision of leaders. It must be a response to the demands growing out of the people's needs themselves and expressed by the people themselves. Leaders must examine themselves and their colleagues in the light of what the people need and not what the leaders want or what they think the people need. How is this possible? Only by continual direct contact and discussion with the people, so as to discover what they really feel, think, and need.

It is tautologous to say that mankind is composed of individual men and that only individual men can achieve human fulfillment. But it is important to repeat this, because leaders, as well as those led, often

---

[16] Reply to a Question from the Left-Socialist-Revolutionaries, at a meeting of the All Russian Central Executive Committee, November 4, (17), 1917. Lenin, V. I.: *Collected Works.* Moscow, Progress, 1964. vol. XXVI, pp. 287-288.

think of men in the mass, and because some think that the fulfillment of the individual person occurs automatically once certain conditions obtain. The authoritarian personality in fact believes that fulfillment must be *forced* upon people and that this is achieved by conformity to a social pattern and by suppression of individual values. The theory of socialism does not deny the use of force. But it holds that force must always be temporary and instrumental and that the ultimate force of history lies with individuals who themselves, in association, make their own history. Socialism in this sense demands democracy, not as an afterthought, but as a necessity. Engels observed that the workers "like everyone else . . . must learn by their own experiences, from their own mistakes." [17] The true socialist in the long run trusts the people because he trusts himself and finds strength in human struggle against exploitation and deprivation. But the authoritarian distrusts the people and sees them as weak because he distrusts the weakness in himself. The one is ultimately the counsel of hope and democracy, the other of despair and tyranny. That is why among revolutionary socialists like Marx, Engels, and Lenin we find repeated denunciations of dogma and sectarianism and calls for flexible thought and leadership responsive to the needs and conditions of people. In the words of Mao Tse-tung, "Dogmas are more useless than cow dung. Dung can be used as fertilizer." [18]

Socialism as a method of organizing natural resources, human labor both physical and mental, and processes of distribution and exchange of goods, requires democracy both as *condition* and as *ideal*. Democracy is a *condition* necessary for the achievement of socialism, because unless the large majority of people choose socialism and act to realize it, socialism will never be achieved. As an ideal economy, socialism also envisages the fullest kind of democracy and requires such a democracy for its fulfillment.

No less important for the growth of socialism is the development of a relevant philosophy, a "science" of socialism that will be true and will be powerful because it is true. Thus Marx called for a philosophy

---

[17] *Selected Correspondence,* p. 490. See also p. 473.

[18] Quoted in Payne, Robert: *Mao Tse-tung, Ruler of Red China.* New York, Schuman, 1950, p. 270.

that would be the "head" of the emancipation of man, just as the proletariat would be its "heart." [19] If fraternity is to be more than a utopian dream, man must find out how to act fraternally to create a society wherein fraternity is an everyday and living principle. Marx and Engels provided a guide for such revolutionizing action, and seventy years later Lenin and his comrades put that into effect. In October of 1917 man thus passed from the dream of fraternity to its first conscious, organized, large-scale reality.

But every new achievement of man in practice creates new problems, in both practice and theory. Marx and Engels initiated, but did not fully develop, a social theory of man. They occupied themselves with working out the theory of historical materialism and with laying the ground for revolutionary action. Their writings shed little light on the specific problems of a socialist and democratic order. In *The German Ideology,* and particularly in *Marx's Economic and Philosophical Manuscripts,* may be found the germs of a social anthropology. This latter work is of particular interest now because it speaks to the resurgent humanistic concerns of socialists today. Such socialists are aware that effective social action in producing the fulfilled socialist man must proceed from sound social theory. They realize that non-Marxist studies have much to contribute to the construction of such a theory. To be richly scientific, socialism must assimilate and use such studies.

We turn now to a consideration of how democracy demands socialism.

In its broadest sense democracy is the mutual self-government of a given group of people. Such government is carried out to the extent that the people of the given group exercise their intelligence cooperatively in the solving of their common problems. "Government" here means controlling, ordering, ruling; and the method of ruling is mutual intelligence. Here we are speaking of democracy as "a way of life," although the formal procedures of traditional democracy, such as voting, majority rule, and the like, may accompany democratic practice, but are not always necessary for it.

Democracy is the mutual and collective rule of the people. It should be contrasted with the rule of one or the few over the many. Generally

---

[19]Contribution to the critique of Hegel's philosophy of right. Introduction.

speaking, no matter how intelligent or experienced, no one man or group of men can be as wise or effective in ruling a group as can the members of that group. The reason is that the rule of one over many, in order to effect any kind of collective behavior, such as work, tends to become overloaded with decision-making and directives, to centralize power, and to make mistakes difficult to correct. Ordinarily, the best-informed persons about the conditions of specific jobs are those who do the jobs. They are also ordinarily the most discerning of the needs and demands in such situations and the best able to suggest and carry out specific improvements. The rule of one person cannot be democratic no matter how perfectly he acts to express the intelligent will and solve the problems of the group. For the rule always remains *his* rule, *his* decision, *his* action. If, on the other hand, he deliberates and consults with the people, then he *represents* them; and to that degree a representative democracy is approached.

Democracy should also be contrasted with the rule of the majority. Normally in democratic decision-making the majority will prevails. But that is not because a vote is or must be taken but because the characteristic method of democracy is *consensus*. In such a method the minority views (usually more than one) are integrated so far as possible with the dominant ones. This integration occurs through free, full interchange of perspectives and deliberation. A simple counting of votes is undemocratic procedure if the voting does not grow out of a collective, serious consideration of the problem at stake and a genuine, frank exchange of perspectives on the various aspects of the issue. It is not uncommon to hear people boasting that a certain decision was taken democratically, when in fact what they mean is that parliamentary procedure was scrupulously adhered to—although the persons of the group did not freely and fully participate in discussion and collective deliberation on the question. The reasons for their not participating may have been apathy, ignorance, fear of reprisal, factional intrigue, or the habitual tyranny of the few, within the group or above it. Similarly, a specious consensus can pass for a real consensus.

Democracy should be contrasted with mob rule. It is, instead, the collective use of intelligence, and so is opposed to the collective use of passions and prejudices. If as Plato argued democracy were necessarily the rule of the appetitive element in man, then most if not all intelligent men would repudiate it. If men discover that they can solve their problems more effectively through the use of collective intelligence, they will tend to prefer such a method. There is considerable evidence that this is so. To the extent that it is so, men prefer democratic methods to antidemocratic ones.

For a group to be called democratic in the sense here, it is not necessary that all persons in the group in question take part in decision-making and execution of decisions. But to the extent that all do, to that extent democracy occurs.

Moreover, the democratic use of inelligence does not mean that the best decisions are always made. Intelligence is fallible in individual and collective forms; it may be used little or much, and it may be directed to good or bad ends. Under the influence of panic or demagoguery, democracy may degenerate into mobocracy. Further, the collective intelligence of a democratic group may decide to confer irrevocable power upon one or a few man. In that case the consequence is not democracy but the abrogation of it. Again, a democratic group may repeatedly fail to solve its common problems—e.g., war and poverty—whereas these *might* be solved in ways not yet tried. The supposition of those who believe in democracy is that in the long run the least fallible method of dealing with collective problems is that of collective intelligence in action. The cure for the weaknesses of democracy is not less democracy, but in fact more democracy. For the same reason the corrective for an error in science—where the same general method is employed—is continued application of the method of science. The democratic method, like the scientific method, is self-corrective. To increase the probabilities of correction, information, analysis, and diversity of initiative and perspective must be increased. For democracy, this means that its safeguard lies in intelligent, vigilant individuals who are undergoing continuing intellectual and personal development in their social practice. Thomas Jefferson understood this.

The democratic method applies to the problems *common* to a group, though it may also be used in the solution of a private problem. The method of democracy is not a panacea, and does not displace individual effort, thought, decision, and action. On the contrary, the strength of a democratic group depends on the skills, perspectives, and developed intelligence which the constituent individual members bring to it.

Critics of democracy focus on the fact that in practice the rule of the people often means the rule of passions and the abandonment of intelligence. ("Your people, sir, is nothing but a great beast!") They hold that even if people use intelligence collectively in the solving of their common problems, that intelligence may be uninformed or otherwise inadequate. Usually, these critics of democracy propose some kind of rule by "experts." The theory of rule by experts has been defended by various arguments—"natural superiority" (Plato, Hitler), "divine right" (James I), and the effectiveness of trained scientists or engineers (technocrats). We can dismiss appeals to elitism based on some form of self-evidence: such appeals are vague and conflicting, and offer no method for public testing. But what of those persons who appear superior to ordinary men by reason their scientific training, skill, and knowledge? Is not science the systematic use of expert intelligence in the solving of problems? Thus we come to the question of what the relation ought to be between scientific experts and the people ruling themselves democratically, i.e., by the use of collective intelligence.

One such possible relation is that the experts shall rule the people. In this relation the intelligence and initiative of the many are sacrificed to that of the few. Another possible relation is that the people shall rule the experts. Here, the specialized wisdom, training, and experience of some of the people are sacrificed to the unspecialized perspectives of the many. A third possible relation is interaction and cooperation between experts and people: the experts provide specialized knowledge and skills in the determination of both ends and means for the solution of the people's common problems.

In actual fact the dichtomy between experts and people is only an apparent one. For experts are themselves people, sharing common human needs and problems; and many people have specialized perspectives and skills in consequence of specialized training, experience, and reflection. The educational problem posed here is that of educating people both in a general, humanistic way and in some specialty. Suppose, for example, that the people of a community raise and discuss the question of whether to create a school. A democratic treatment of this problem would mean the following. Highly specialized experts would be consulted as to the ends and means involved—psychologists, sociologists, ecologists, city planners, building constructors, architects, educators, etc. So far as possible their ideas would be communicated to the others in the community, in detail and in ordinary language that could be understood by the unspecialized. Their ideas would be subjected to the discussion, criticism, and evaluation of others. These others would express a variety of perspectives and judgments coming out of a variety of backgrounds and vocations. Almost every adult, and every child of school age, would know from experience something about schools, or learning, and would be able to express something, if ever so little, about the general question of which values are to be taken as the ends in the creation of the school. Almost every adult would possess special perspectives to contribute to the discussion of means for reaching these ends. Once a consensus was reached on these questions, decision would be taken to create a certain school, and a plan would be drawn up. The execution of the plan would then demand the cooperative effort and adaptation of the plan. In this latter process the democratic process is necessary to the most effective fulfillment of the plan. (Specialists from other communities might be employed to carry out the plan; and in that event a democratic relation between them and the community members supervising the carrying out of the plan would be worked out.)

The democratic method is not applicable to all human problems, and where it is applicable it is not always applicable in the same degree. A technical problem as such, calling for the adaptation of means to some given end, demands the technical knowledge and skill of a select few (who themselves may work democratically). For example, the question is posed as to the most healthful and efficient heating and ventilating system for a given school. ("Healthful" is already defined, and the general plan of the school is already given.) An adequate answer to this question requires expert knowledge and skill. Similarly, the captain's decisions as to the management of a ship are not taken democratically, though he normally consults with his chief officers, engineer, navigator, and others before making many of his decisions. A family with small children cannot be conducted with a great degree of democracy, for the children lack the experience to qualify them as participants equal with adults. Nonetheless, the good parent seeks and takes into account the expressed perspectives and needs of the children in making his decisions. Likewise, an emergency situation, calling for an immediate decision by one person or a few persons, precludes democratic consideration by the group. For instance, a natural catastrophe strikes a group, disruptive violence is inflicted on the group by another group, or the group's life or welfare is threatened by forces from within itself. In such cases, and in all cases where decisions cannot be taken democratically, the important question is whether the ultimate goals served by the decisions—the building of the school, the ship's purposes, the values of the family or of the group preserved by emergency action —exemplify or facilitate basic human values. And such values of the common life in the long run can best be determined by the judgments and deliberations of people themselves, discussing and making decisions democratically. In such a process the people surely can use the help of experts—anthropologists, psychologists, axiologists, etc. Here we are not forced to choose between experts and people. Instead, we can achieve the most fruitful outcome by cooperation between people and experts with regard to producing the common good. The determination of this common good as the end of human life should precede, undergird, and surround all special, technical, expert, and emergency decisions, presupposing such good as their general and continuous end.

This same concept of democracy provides the answer to the problem of the relation between "representatives" and the people represented. The old formula was that government rests on the consent and will of the governed, a formula that presumed a separation between the two. As long as this separation exists, genuine representation is impossible. Yet direct democracy is not possible in groups beyond a certain size. The division of a large group into small groups where face-to-face discussions involving every member can take place, can effect the conditions for democracy in a "cell." But cells can interact with other cells only by means of representatives. A good representative in such cases is one who accurately reflects the interests of his group. This reflection is possible as he directly, sensitively, and recurrently listens to his group. Large-scale democracy does not eliminate the principle of representation, but indeed requires it. But effective democracy demands that the representative does not stand apart from the people but is in fact *one of them*. Precisely because he communicates with them and feels and thinks *in common* with them he can re-present their perspectives in other contexts. The formal principle of "recall" rests on the recognition of the fact that elected representatives may not represent the people's interests. But it is a negative and abstract principle. The solution to this problem is a close, concrete, working relation between the representative and his group. And this must be secured and developed by a demand from both sides to maintain and deepen communication.

Similarly, democracy does not rule out the principles of centralism and leadership, but in fact requires them. As in an organism that is planfully directed the cells require a central system of coordination, so the small groups of democratic men require a central directive agency responsive to the information from the cells. In every group of any size leaders naturally appear as particular persons through whom the collective interests of the participant individuals are expressed, organized, and implemented. The question is whether a leader is good or bad, democratic or undemocratic—whether he facilitates the solution of the common problems of the group. We are not here faced with the question of authority vs. no authority but with the question of kind of authority. And again this is not a question of a dichotomy, but a question of where a given leader is to be placed along a continuum. For every leader must cooperate to some degree with those led and to that degree must be democratic.

A good leader (1) directly communicates with the people led and learns what their problems and perspectives are; (2) helps them to articulate, organize, and assess these problems and perspectives; (3) contributes to the solution of their problems by his participation in discussion of those problems and by making available to them his specialized skills; (4) helps to cultivate resourcefulness and self-sufficiency within the group and among its individuals; and (5) becomes himself progressively dispensable as the members of the group themselves acquire more power to express and fulfill their interests. In these ways a leader is effective, i.e., he elicits the energies and loyalties of his group. And in these ways his leadership is humanistically justified.

There is justification of experts, representatives, and leaders alike insofar as they assist in the fulfilling of the needs of the people in ways that the people without them cannot do alone and directly. In groups where this creative relation between experts and nonexperts, representatives and represented, and leaders and led breaks down or never adequately develops, bureaucratism and tyranny, apathy and submission, grow up. In such groups authority and responsibility become concentrated in the few. Hence such groups are always weaker than democratic ones, because they rely heavily on a few people, whereas democracy draws out and organizes the strength of the many. And their leaders must always compensate for this weakness by the use or threat of coercion in order to achieve goals which are decided on at the center and from which the group, commanded to obey, must feel alienated.

As the rule of collective intelligence, democracy presupposes that the people will be educated, i.e., experienced in the use of reason in the solution of their problems. The people cannot exercise and keep supreme power and cannot rule themselves in their own interest if they lack the tools, the knowledge and skills, necessary for solving their problems. A relatively primitive, simple democracy, with a relatively primitive collective intelligence, can solve the problems of a relatively primitive society. For example, during the national liberation movements of recent decades, soldiers and peasants have effectively used democratic methods to solve such problems as waging guerilla warfare, organizing the economic life of villages and armies, and effecting land reforms. But problems of a more advanced stage of society demand a more advanced level of education. Problems like the development of water supply, agriculture, transportation, and industry require specialized training of many different kinds for their effective solution. They require the education of the people in scientific ways. Because such education and the implicit democratic demands that tend to accompany scientific education have been lacking in those underdeveloped countries where socialist revolutions have occurred, the methods of building socialism have sometimes been undemocratic in the extreme. In this vacuum, bureaucratism and tyranny have sometimes flourished. The people's education, both scientific and humanistic, has not kept pace with industrial and technological demands and advances. Hence the mentality of the people has often not been prepared for technological changes or has positively resisted such changes. The difficulty of changing from primitive to technological agriculture is a case in point. In addition, rigid, compulsive, and authoritarian attitudes have appeared in many institutions—industrial, commercial, and even "scientific"—where the attitudes implicit in an authentically scientific and humanistic education have not yet displaced those carried over from a primitive period.

The justification for democracy is human and pragmatic. It is an established principle of human experience that to the extent that a person participates in making and implementing decisions affecting his own interest, he will understand the decisions and their consequences more clearly, assume more initiative and responsibility in putting the decisions into practice, experience more satisfaction from his activity and defend his interests more effectively, than if he does not so participate. Men feel identified with what they themselves create and with the process of its creation. They indeed create their identity in such a process. They care about what they do and produce to the degree that they put themselves into their decision-making, their plans, and their acts. A sense of a bond of interdependence and ownership arises at those points where man voluntarily moves out toward the world and other men to create new things and relations. But when such decisions are made by other men and orders for action are handed down by those other men, men do not feel "in it." They feel alienated from the action they undertake, even if it means the production of food or some other vital necessity. Their morale and efficiency are relatively poor. And if they have enjoyed a previous taste of freedom, they will resent still more the coercion and control of their free, self-initiating, and self-controlling activity.

This same principle, that participation in decision and planning increases productivity, applies where two or more people are engaged in solving a common problem. It is indeed reinforced by the principle that collectively men can solve their common problems more effectively than they can separately. This is an old principle, required for the organization of every human group and society. A society, so far as it coheres as a unit, is a set of cooperating individuals working for common values. Democracy aims to make this cooperative principle explicit and conscious, to develop intelligence in the organization and maintenance of the public life. Man is necessarily and naturally a social creature. When he interacts and communicates with other persons under certain favorable conditions, his mind and personality are formed and transformed. New perspectives and modes of action are created in consequence of such interaction—perspectives and modes of action not previously possible for individual persons separated from such interaction. The deliberation and action of men in a group, when conditions are favorable, elicits their interests, talents, experiences, and perspectives. It stimulates and reinforces their drive in solving the problem before them. It generates *esprit de corps* and morale. It evokes, corrects, integrates, and develops individual perspectives, and through common speech and action makes such perspectives the common property of all. Thus, it simultaneously nurtures individuality and group solidarity. Individuality stimulates and enhances the energies, the life of felt quality, and the intelligence of the group, and this group life in turn determines how effectively its problems will be solved.

All men share with others certain common, generic needs—hunger, thirst, bodily safety, etc. One of these needs is the social need, a need whose satisfaction not only possesses intrinsic value, but whose exercise is instrumental and necessary to the satisfaction of all other generic needs. Another is the need for creative activity as man determines the conditions of his life in his relations to the natural world and to other persons. Democracy as a form of social, creative activity provides outlet for man's social, creative needs. Democracy is man's natural, *human* way of life, his home. Separated from that way of life, through which he becomes his true self and is fulfilled, man becomes an alien.

How can this free, equalitarian fraternity of men come about? Only as men begin to establish the material and social conditions which are the necessary base for such a creative fraternity of individuals. When one defines those basic conditions, one defines socialism.

Believers in socialism assume that if people as a society own the means and control the activities of production, in the long run they will do so in their own interest and for their own good. They also assume that people in the long run know what they need and what their own fulfilled good is. Both of these assumptions are shared by believers in democracy, which in common with socialism puts its final faith in social man and his intelligence.

Historically both "socialism" and "democracy" have carried both narrow and broad meanings. Under the narrow meanings, determined by the limitations of class thought, each tended to be confined to a special sphere—democracy to politics, socialism to economics. But under the broader meanings the kinship of socialism and democracy becomes plain and it is difficult to find where one ends and the other begins. In its narorw sense, socialism has been thought of as an extension, into the economic sphere, of the democratic principle of politics. Thus, it has been called "economic democracy." But democracy as a human method for solving common human problems directly implies a total socialism. For the democratic method is collective intelligence, planning, and fulfillment of plans, and this is precisely the method of socialism, which requires collective *ownership* of basic tools and resources as well. Similarly, socialism in its broad, humanistic sense—demanding that man be fully social and cooperative in his productive life—directly implies free, equalitarian, fraternal democracy as a way of life. Socialism and democracy meet at the point where they answer the question, Who shall rule the people, and how? Their answer: the people shall rule, by cooperative intelligence. Intelligent problem-solving always involves a plan of action. Whoever may originate the plan, it is the people who must be consulted as to its value, as to the subordinate plans, and as to their roles in carrying out these plans. And it is the people who must in the end carry out the plan.

In conclusion, the relations between democracy and socialism can be understood by considering the relations between the psychosocial activities of men and the economic materials and processes of their lives. These two sets of activites interpenetrate, so that a full definition of each eventually leads to the other. Historically, the term "democracy" is connected with a bourgeois tradition which concentrates on man's expression of ideas, speech, writing, discussion, deliberation, debate, enactment and interpretation of laws, and the like—in short, on man's mental and social activity defined as popular self-government. As we have observed, the bourgeois definition of democracy delimited it to a small class, while the dispossessed classes of Europe broadened and deepened that definition to embrace the economic context of man's life. And with the establishment of the first socialist country in the U.S.S.R. in 1917, this deepened concept of democracy, developed in

Marx, Engels, and Lenin, achieved its first concrete form. Since the time of Marx and Engels, however, the term "socialism" has referred mainly to the economic processes and conditions necessary to man's development. And just as in the U.S.S.R. the imperative economic demands for collectivized farms and factories and machines took precedence over the "higher" values, so the literature on economics has greatly overshadowed humanistic studies like those on democracy. Nonetheless, the definition of socialism has reached out to include the psychosocial activity of man. We see now in Europe and the United States a new convergence and dialectic of these two traditions, democracy and socialism. Humanists from different backgrounds are turning their attention to Marxism, while Marxists are undertaking new studies in humanism.

To anyone who cares to look objectively at the achievements of people in socialist countries—from the older and larger ones, like the Soviet Union and the People's Republic of China, to the younger and smaller ones, like the Democratic Republic of Vietnam and the Republic of Cuba—the durable humanistic achievements are immediately evident. Within the limits of the economy, the socialist society satisfies the basic necessities of people—food, shelter, clothing, health and medical care. Labor, available to and expected of all able adults before retirement, is carried out under humane conditions. The other needs of the human personality are provided for through opportunities for education, vocational study, recreation and rest, and cultural development. Those numerous multitudes hitherto neglected or abused in most "civilized" societies—children, women, ethnic and racial minorities, the aged and infirm, the retarded, the handicapped—know the dignity of human life and development. A yearning for peace and justice among nations pervades the people— a yearning indeed shared by the great masses everywhere in the world, whatever the government. These achievements are not perfect; socialists have never claimed that they are. They are flawed by scarcities in the economy, injustices in human relations, inefficiencies, outworn habits from the past, frailties of character, etc. But they mark an unprecedented turn toward humanization in the history of mankind on this planet. And they could not have occurred apart from the devoted labor and thought of masses of people—that is, their democratic participation. No tyrant or party boss can order such achievement; they are the creations of democratic and socialistic persons working together for human ends. And they are signs that promise to Americans what they might achieve if they would actualize the socialist potentialities inherent in their own democratic heritage and institutions.

The psychosocial activities and the economic activities of men can move and develop in dialectical relation to one another. Concrete economic processes of an oppressive society produce the economic, biological conditions of deprivation and suffering. Such conditions are always accompanied by psychosocial conditions—ideas, attitudes, emotions, convictions, idealized values, plans of action—which can transform those otherwise mere biological conditions of animal fate into conditions of unrest, resentment, and potential revolutionizing activity. When these revolutionizing ideas and attitudes become widespread and achieve a critical mass—as is possible under modern conditions of communication—men can and do act to change their economic conditions. In short, democracy of a crude, inchoate kind— "rough, strong, impatient of formulas, contemptuous of sentimentalism," in John Reed's words[20]—arises to take those conditions into its own hands. Guided by great and sometimes vague, visionary ideas, men can and do act to change economic conditions and to create a new society. This society in turn, over a period of years and generations, can transform the minds and social relations of men, deepening and widening and refining their democracy. And that new democracy, productive of new ideas, attitudes, and values, can act back upon the established social habits and economic traditions.

It is a truism to say that men must act to bring mind and matter, collective human decision and economic life, into fruitful relations, so that economy releases the physical and mental powers of men and so that the freedom of men reacts to strengthen the material base of their lives. But orthodox, static, undialectical, or fatalistic thinkers forget this and assume that democracy automatically develops once the first steps of economic socialism have been taken. Such thinkers try to imprison this creative, dialectical process of human development—demo-

---

[20]Reed, John: *Ten Days That Shook the World.* New York, Random House, 1960, p. 179.

cratic socialism—in fixed economic, political, and intellectual forms. They quote great thinkers of the past to prove their points. But no one man, or group of men, can anticipate the problems and conditions of all men. Nor can they foresee what new perspectives the creative association of new generations will bring forth.

It is now increasingly acknowledged by socialist thinkers that they have neglected scientific investigation of the psychosocial side of this dialectic—i.e., the origins, nature, functions, changes, conditions, and humanistic control of ideas, beliefs, attitudes, values, and other activities of mind, personality, and interpersonal relations. It is evident to them that the economic base and framework of socialism does not in itself guarantee the optimum, healthy, and creative development of persons. It is further evident that such an economic base cannot itself function effectively apart from that healthy and cooperative state of mind and action which we have called "democracy." Hence what is needed is research concerning the character of healthy personality, the conditions that obstruct the development of such personality, and the conditions that conduce to its development. As we have indicated, such research must be conducted in connection with actual experiments which enlist the cooperation and initiative of the people, leaders, and experts.

On the other side, democratic theory has tended to develop in independence of economic considerations. Following the same tradition, psychological and social studies of personality, in the United States, for example, have made some important advances, but have neglected the economic context and base in the formation of personality and values. But a number of students of man are turning to these economic considerations.[21]

Thus, we see now in Europe and the United States a new convergence and dialectic of these two traditions, the liberal-democratic tradition and the Marxist one. A new trend in European socialist countries promises to bring socialism and democracy into new dialectical relations. On the level of practice, this trend in the United States is expressed in the growing demand on the part of many groups—Blacks,

---

[21]A pessimistic wok of this kind is Seligman, Ben B.: *Permanent Poverty. An American Syndrome.* Chicago, Quadrangle, 1968. An optimistic work is Cleaver, Eldridge: *Soul on Ice.* New York, McGraw Hill, 1968.

the poor whites, youth, women—for participation in important decisions. On the level of theory, this trend is expressed in the growing interest of scientists in problems of personality, human nature, human conflicts, human values and related issues, as revealed in studies in anthropology, psychology, sociology, history, literature, philosophy, and the like.

Are such humanistic studies a threat to socialism? They are if they divert scientists and men from the task of creating or improving a system of socialism through improving men, and of improving men through creating or improving socialism. Studies can advance socialism still another step if they open the way to the creation of men who are more profoundly democratic and healthy than before, and who can therefore discern and bring into being the conditions for a better social order. Socialism demands democracy and democracy demands socialism. And in this mutual and evolving demand we find the basic pattern for the creative fulfillment of individual man and human society.

IX

TECHNOLOGY AND HUMANISM

O<small>UR CRISIS TODAY</small> has been described as one of technology against
humanism, science against the humanities, and machines against man.
However, these are abstract ways of describing the crisis. When we
speak of technology, science, and machines, we cannot point to concrete, independent things apart from man. These are not beings with
hearts and limbs and brains of their own. It is always living men
who make and use technology, science, and machines. Thus, the
crisis is a crisis of conflict between men themselves—between those
who make, control, or use technology for certain values, and those
who do not share those values. The crisis is a crisis of human values,
a conflict between persons and groups. Ultimately, in the United
States, this is a conflict between classes—between (1) a small group
of men who own and control the major power of technology—the
corporate capitalists, their executives and managers, and most of the
scientists in the country who are in their pay—and (2) the mass of
men who do not own or control the power of technology. Yet the
conflict is not so simple. For while a small group of men own and
control technology, the great mass of men cooperate in the making
and using of technology. Further, the great mass of men acquiesce
or participate in the values associated purposely or adventitiously with
the elite-controlled technology: money, war, racism, affluence and
poverty, political oligarchy, bureaucracy, competitive individualism,
commercial entertainment, the despoliation of nature, etc. At the
same time many men are in revolt against such values. They feel
that their bodies and souls are violated and besmirched by such values.
Consciously or unconsciously, persistently or sporadically, they strive
toward values of another kind; the fulfillment of human needs, peace,
equality, justice, democracy, cooperation, and the collective care of
nature. Thus, the crisis of men is a crisis of values, a struggle between

those who pursue dehumanizing values and those who cherish humanizing values—between those who love appetite, power, and money, and those who love people.

What is important is that this conflict of values takes the form of technology and social organization around classes of men. We are urban creatures who owe our survival and welfare to the advanced development of technology sustained by the specialized labors of many men integrated around scientifically developed machines. Indeed, the achievement of the dominance of the human species on the planet occurred only as men advanced from the simple weaponry of the nomadic hunting and fishing stage of Paleolithic life to the advanced weaponry of the Neolithic period, the domestication of plants and animals, the settled life of agrarian communities, and eventually cities. In the two millennia (5000-3000 B.C.) immediately preceding the great urban revolution that marked the beginning of human history, a large number of discoveries in applied science laid the basis for "civilization" as we know it today. These were: artificial irrigation using canals and ditches; the plow; the harnessing of animal motive-power; the sailboat; wheeled vehicles; orchard-husbandry; fermentation; the production and use of copper; bricks; the arch; glazing; and the seal.[1] These technological advances (for technology in a broad sense is applied science) were both cause and result of the organization of society into ruling and working classes. Technology made possible an increase in food and the other necessities of life, as well as in the refinements of "culture." It also brought in its train all the problems of urban, industrial life from which contemporary man still suffers—class antagonism, war, extremes of rich and poor, social division and alienation, political tyranny, religious superstition, etc. Let us turn then to an examination of the problems of men today as seen in the context of modern technology.

The meaning of the transformation of agrarian societies into industrial societies is well known: machines; the harnessing of natural power (water, coal, steam); factories and the making of cheaper and more numerous commodities in factories; modern cities; a system of distribution of manufactured commodities; an increase in population;

[1]Childe, V. Gordon: *Man Makes Himself*. New York, New American Library, 1951, p. 180.

the rise of a new kind of national state; the mechanizing of national wars; and the centralized control of industrial and social processes.

The meaning of the "postindustrial" revolution is not so well known: the systematic application of scientific theories and methods to industrial and other problems. We may also call this the "scientific"[2] or "technological" revolution, since "technology" means the application of theoretical knowledge to the development of technique (working method) usually in industry or the industrial arts. The modern technological revolution developed gradually—in an industrial society of synthetic chemistry, atomic fission, electronics, automation, and cybernation. It has resulted in a postindustrial society growing out of industrial society and gradually changing it: a relative shrinking of the extractive industries (hunting, fishing, agriculture, forestry, mining); an increase in service occupations (trade, finance, real estate, sales, recreation, government, travel, education, health); an increase in professional and scientific groups; an increase in the role of theory in society and in intellectual institutions; an increase in organization, population, centralized control, nationalism; and the application of advanced technology to national and international wars.[3]

Since the industrial and technological revolutions have overlapped and since many recently industrialized societies will skip over some stages of nineteenth century industrialism, we shall refer in this paper to the conditions and problems generated by both kinds of revolution insofar as technology is in issue. According to one prediction, which takes income per capita as the index, in the year 2000, 40 percent of the world's population will live in postindustrial societies (in the United States, the U.S.S.R., France, West Germany, Benelux, Great Britain, East Germany, Poland, Czechoslovakia, Japan, Canada, Scandinavia, Switzerland, Italy, Israel, Australia, and New Zealand) and in advanced and mature industrial societies (in Spain, Portugal, Austria, Yugoslavia , Albania , Greece, Bulgaria, Hungary, Ireland,

---

[2]Snow, C. P.: *The Two Cultures and the Scientific Revolution.* New York, Cambridge University, 1961. In vol. I of *Capital,* in the next to the last chapter, Marx mentions among the trends of capitalism "the conscious technical application of science." But as Snow points out, such application was not large-scale until relatively recently.

[3]See *Daedalus,* issued as *Proceedings of the American Academy of Arts and Sciences, 96,* No. 3, for a discussion of these tendencies.

Turkey, Mexico, Argentina, Colombia, Venezuela, Chile, Taiwan, South Korea, Hong Kong, Malaysia, one fourth of Latin America, one-third of the Arab world, one-half of S.E. Asia).[4]

Technology is not confined to the problems of industry, however. In the general sense it is the application of thought to any technique in an effort to improve that technique. And a technique is a developed way or method of doing something, of attaining an end. Man is *par excellence* the technician. To live and to create himself, man must be receptive to his environment, think about it, and manipulate and dominate it. To do so, he contrives procedures or techniques. And to attain and assure his ends—food, water, clothing, association with others, objects of esthetic delight, etc., he endeavors to improve, by practice and thought, the effective execution of such procedures. Hence in the course of things he becomes a technican, and, with the application of reflective methods to technique, a technologist. What is known as "science" consists of techniques of inference, prediction, and control, as well as specialized techniques of self-correction of those techniques. The science of chemistry, for example, which evolved out of primitive cooking, medicine, metallurgy, etc., and then the fantasies of alchemy, transcends its predecessors by virtue of its power to correct and improve its technique. Probably all techniques insofar as they are successful (e.g., playing or composing music) involve some self-correction, i.e., mutual influence of observation and reflection relevant to some end. But scientific technique is a highly developed and systematized self-corrective technique on both formal and empirical levels. Technology which employs the techniques of science has produced and will produce changes in human living which not even its eighteenth century enthusiasts could foresee.

The term "science" here, as in ordinary language, is used loosely. Whitehead has pointed out that "the greatest invention of the nineteenth century was the invention of the method of invention."[5] Invention is not the whole of science; but the methods of careful observation and experiment are an important part of it. Men have been

---

[4]Kahn, Herman, and Wiener, Anthony, J.: The next thirty-three years: a framework for speculation. *Daedalus,* issued as *Proceedings of the American Academy of Arts and Sciences, 96*: 716, 718, 1967.

[5]Whitehead, Alfred North: *Science and the Modern World.* New York, Macmillan, 1926, p. 41.

inventive throughout history, but in the nineteenth century they became consciously and systematically so. Thus, the methods of controlled and self-correcting observation more and more entered into the habits of professional groups. That is, technological method spread. Today, a housewife who shops observantly and critically has begun to pass from mere technique, in the direction of improving that technique by the application of self-correcting methods that anticipate systematic science.

The modern technological application of theoretical science to the manufacturing processes of large industry has its recent origins in the long revolution of capitalism against feudalism. As early as 1100 A.D. the first merchants began to open up trade routes between Europe and the East and Constantinople, and even before then men in the West had applied water power to industrial processes like milling grain, sawing timber, and pumping blast furnace bellows. The new economy was this-wordly, sensuous, empirical, practical; it relied on the manual skills of workers and engineers to build ships, machines, and tools. Even after the manuscripts of Greco-Roman and Muslim science were discovered and translated in the West and the revolution in theoretical natural science was launched in the seventeenth century, men made no large-scale effort to link rational theory with the empirical practices of the economy. Industrialists were satisfied with their own machinists and designers; after all, they produced results, and the industrialists were pragmatists. Bacon and Saint-Simon had foreseen how science might be applied to "the relief of man's estate." But the royal landowners and the entrepreneurs were concerned with their own power and profits and not the welfare of mankind. However, the growth of industry in the nineteenth century nurtured a new attitude: the large numbers of men brought together in the cities as wage laborers began to demand a share in the products of their own industry. The growth of a middle-class and of a technological and professional educational system, first in Germany, began to bridge the distance between abstract thought and concrete application. Moreover, some industrialists had discovered that the science of chemistry might be applied in manufacture. The democratic revolutions of the nineteenth century tended to force a fusion of theoretical science, traditionally associated with aristocratic and intellectual classes, and technology, carried forward by lower-class groups.[6] Thus, while the masses of men have in their demands helped to stimulate the technological revolution, and have through their labors created it, they are today threatened by this very creation of their own needs and labors. That is the central contradiction of modern American society. The source of the contradiction is that the mass of men do not control for their own fulfillment what they have created. It is controlled by a small class of men interested in accumulation, profit, power, and status.

We have spoken of man's use of technique as a necessary means of survival, and of the systematic improvement of technique, or technology. But it is an error to think that man is only, or essentially, a technician and technologist. He concerns himself with technique in consequence of a prior tendency—a need and demand for values, for forms of fulfillment. This need finds expression through man's symbols —his creating of signs to signify valued and intended things that are absent and future. Man is futuristic, valuing, creating activity. He projects, promises, and commits himself to a valued future. Accordingly he becomes concerned with present means to future ends. He signifies means-ends relations (sowing-reaping, machine-finished product) in which the envisaged end functions as a guiding factor controlling present conditions and means. Thus, the original and primary function of technique and technology is to serve man in his creative activity. To become preoccupied with particular conditions, ends, means, and techniques is a diversion and perversion of our fulfillment. It is a loss of our full human creativity.

There are techniques of the practical arts (farming, fishing, mining, cooking, weaving, pottery-making), of the fine arts, of the theoretical and applied sciences, of logic, of the social arts and sciences (such as economics and politics), of religion, of warfare, etc. In the United States a great deal of money is made by the writing of books or the conducting of schooling in the techniques of how to win friends and influence people, how to make a million dollars in the stock market, how to succeed in business, how to get into the college of your choice, how

---

[6]White, Lynn, Jr.: The historical roots of our ecologic crisis. In Shepard, Paul, and McKinley, Daniel (Eds.): *The Subversive Science. Essays Toward an Ecology of Man*, p. 343.

to be a better sexual partner, "how to get thinner once and for all," "how to get and hold a woman" ("Do not try to reason with a woman, just manipulate her in her feelings"). We now have a book "in non-technical, narrative form" which presents the "techniques of joy"—"pushing, nudging, bumping, wrestling, guided fantasy, 'acting-out', talking, silence, and non-verbal communication." Since some of these techniques "may be emotionally dangerous without professional guidance," we are advised to seek the help of technicians themselves to possess certain joys.

It is important to keep this range of techniques in mind. For many identify technology with the improvement of industrial processes and products, and, thanks to the techniques of idea-manipulators, forget that vast and profitable sciences (technologies) have developed in the areas of buying, consumption, political processes, advertising, etc. There is the view also that techniques and technicians are somehow "value-free" and not responsible for their antihumanistic accompaniments or consequences, a view that derives from an artificial separation of the sciences and humanities. In this chapter the term "technology" will normally be used in this broader sense. With that sense, we can more clearly see the relation of technology to humanism.

The modern technological revolution in industry has produced an unprecedented set of interconnected problems: a rapid and large increase in world population; a relative decrease of food supply and arable land; the problem of discovering and transforming for human use natural resources and energies; the despoilation of the land, the polluting of air and water, and the upsetting of the chemical and climatic balances in the ecological environment; urbanization, with its crowding, overstimulation, loss of privacy, interpersonal conflict; impersonal organizations of industry and business; political centralization and bureaucracy; the development of new genocidal weaponry, including thermonuclear, chemical, and biological warfare; new forms of imperialism; increasing demands on education; mass culture; leisure time; rapid institutional changes (in family, school, business, industry, science, etc.); revolutions based on a sense of national or racial identity.

Men have responded to industrial technology and to the problems created by it in a variety of ways. (1) They have drifted and remained indifferent to the problems, willing to accept the values generated by technological changes and to seek immediate gratifications. Here we can find many of the passive middle class of United States society as well as many of the hungry, diseased, illiterate poor of the world. (2) They have violently and blindly rebelled against the problems, aiming to vent their hostility and resentment against the oppression they feel, but lacking a clear direction for change toward new values. Here are the riots and insurrections occurring in the cities of the United States. (3) They have sought to separate themselves from the possible human values of the technological society by escaping from those values. Such escape may be effected by remaining in the society and dutifully performing certain social and technological functions, but by repressing awareness of the problems and seeking satisfactions in a world of entertainment, fantasy, sports, and other private "diversions." Here are large groups in affluent societies who find forms of escape, provided and encouraged by decision-makers, relatively cheap and accessible. Escape may also be effected through physical removal of oneself from the society—emigration or movement to the countryside or hinterland to establish a Utopian community. (4) They have sought to control the conditions of their technologies, institutions, communities, or societies in the interest of an established or aspiring elite. Such control is aimed at conserving traditional ways and values, and at repressing and resisting change in the direction of more democratic sharing in decision-making, in responsibility for such decisions, and in the fruits of such decisions. Here we find the owners and controllers of wealth and power in feudal and capitalist societies, as well as the politicians with vested interests and special privileges in socialist societies. (5) They have sought to control the conditions of their technologies, institutions, communities, or societies in democratic ways in the interest of the great masses of people. Here we find the successful revolutionary movements of modern times which have borne fruit in the socialist nations and are continuing to bear fruit in countries like Vietnam.

These ways of responding to technology and its problems are not of equal value. They compete for the loyalties of men and they do not with equal effectiveness solve the problems. Moreover, as we have observed, technique and technology are always instrumental to values to which men are implicitly or explicitly committed. The question of evaluating responses to technology can be answered only as we answer the question, What human values should technique and technology serve?

Let us begin with some elementary definitions. "Value" in the general sense will here mean anything relevant to the fulfillment of a human preference or interest. Thus a specific value may be something toward which a person actually shows a preference ("preferred value"). It may be sought and cherished ("positive value"), or shunned and destroyed ("negative value"). It may be something which satisfies an interest ("satisfying value"). It may be something which in fact fulfills a real human need ("human value"), independently of whether or not it becomes an explicit and preferred object of interest. And it may be symbolized as a value ("ideal value") or not. An individual person's satisfaction of his interests in a mutually reinforcing way is "personal value." The mutual reinforcing of personal values is "social value." The mutual reinforcing of nonhuman conditions and man's personal and social values is "ecological value." Because man is a preferential activity fulfilling itself, in process of creating or *realizing* value, the life of value may be studied objectively. But it includes a commitment to a future which transcends present value-facts and aims at the creation of new value-facts.

The standard which we propose for directing and judging technology is that of "human value," i.e., values that in fact fulfill real human needs, both personal and social. Man can value (prefer, be satisfied with, symbolize as ideal) and has valued a great variety of things—luxury, ascesis, homicide, torture, slavery, illusion. But there is evidence that some values conduce to man's life and fulfillment on the whole and in the long run, while others do not. Such evidence is to be found in a certain consensus throughout many cultures in human history and in the sciences that bear upon man's behavior, including those sciences concerned to discover man's real human needs, personal and social, as distinct from illusory needs. (A "need" is an unstable condition and drive to stabilize it; a real human need is such that its deprivation means deprived humanity.) Furthermore, the evidence that all men have a primary propensity for life and personal and social fulfillment is indicated in the struggle of men in history to live and live better, as well as in psychological studies in depth of both deprived and fulfilled personalities.[7]

This standard is here called "generic humanism." "Humanism" means: pertaining to values (forms of fulfillment) that occur in human experience, that are known to man's observation and reflection, that can be changed and improved by man's thought and action. "Man" is here taken in the broadest sense to include all men in the long run. "Generic" means, a certain *genus* of man distinguishing him from what is nonhuman, as well as a certain corresponding *genus* of fulfilling activity distinguished from purely preferred or satisfying values. Studies in the biological and psychosocial sciences indicate that man is defined by a certain biological structure with corresponding functions, and that he satisfies the needs associated therewith in certain ways in a social and ecological context of a certain kind.[8] To this extent man has a certain objective *genus*—a value-realizing nature aiming at generic values, which in their specific realization are functions of the variables of biological constitution and of social and ecological context. Such generic values indicated by the sciences are also found recurrently expressed in the great symbolized, ideal values —the philosophies and religions—of past and present cultures.

Man is a psychosomatic being with an underlying genotype that survives and develops in interaction with the things and persons of his social and ecological environment. Whatever his specific need may be (hunger, need for others, etc.), he is required to satisfy it by a receptive, active, and sensory-reflective response to the world. He needs continuously (1) to adjust to things and persons by letting them act on him; (2) to act upon things and persons and to control them to some degree; and (3) to perceive them in sensory form and relate the sense data in such ways as to act upon, and be acted upon

---

[7]It would suffice here to cite revolutionary literature. But we may also refer to studies done among American white middle class persons by Erich Fromm, Karen Horney, A. H. Maslow, Carl Rogers, and Harry Stack Sullivan.

[8]The fact that scientists do not agree on a precise list of needs is overshadowed by a converging consensus on needs. Probably most would accept most of the needs listed by Ashley Montagu: oxygen hunger, hunger, thirst, fatigue, restlessness, somnolence, bladder pressure, colon pressure, fright, pain, internal excitation, feeling of nondependency or aloneness, and general need or tension. Montagu, Ashley: *On Being Human*, pp. 50-51.

by, things and persons in the environment. When these three basic needs work together to maintain the person in dynamic balance and growth, they represent the inclusive need of creativity.

The three categories of need-action-value may be called receptivity, dominance, and detachment.[9] They can be oriented toward self or others. They are, respectively, functions of basic components of the somatic organism: endomorphy (the digestive viscera), mesomorphy (bone, muscle, connective tissue), and ectomorphy (nervous tissue, skin).[10] These somatic structures in turn are the expression of the structural genotype of the organism.[11] Thus both the similarities and the differences in the values of individual persons may be explained by consideration of the interplay of these somatic variables as they function in relation to the natural and social world.

Technique is a developed, habitual action of dominance: it is control of things or persons exerted toward some end. Technology is the theoretical effort to improve technique. Hence the central humanistic question for technology is: How can technical and technological dominance more effectively serve the realization of human values?

Contrary to Jacques Ellul and others,[12] technique and technology as such are not bad. They are in fact values; men require them to live, they practice them, they find them to be satisfying, they symbolize them as values. The categorical value that men find in technique and technology is dominance; men enjoy controlling things and persons and dominating them: they enjoy perfecting procedures to certain ends. Dominance is not bad in itself; it is not necessarily domination (domineering)[13]—e.g., a man controls his car (is dominant over it) in order to enjoy the scenery and to go to the seaside to relax. The larger questions are: What ends and other values are being served by

---

[9]Morris, Charles: *Varieties of Human Value.* I have used the term "receptivity" instead of Morris' "dependence."

[10]Sheldon, William H., with the collaboration of Stevens, S. S., and Tucker, W. B.: *The Varieties of Human Physique.*

[11]Sheldon, William H., with the collaboration of Dupertuis, C. Wesley, and McDermott, Eugene: *Atlas of Men.* New York, Harper, 1954, p. 19.

[12]Ellul, Jacques: *The Technological Society,* trans. by John Wilkinson. New York, Knopf, 1964.

[13]Morris, Charles: Technique and human value. Unpublished paper for the Symposium on the Technological Society, The Center for the Study of Democratic Institutions, Santa Barbara, California, 19-23 December, 1965.

technology? Who controls the technology and determines its ends and consequences? Who shares in the goods and services of economic technology? Technology is a "threat" only insofar as the values of dominance restrict, repress, or displace the development of other human values like those of creativity, receptivity, and detachment. From studies of college students' preferences in the United States, Norway, India, China, and Japan about 1950[14]—partially repeated in recent years[15] and supplemented by recent data from Poland and Hungary[16]—there is evidence that most people do not prefer a way of life in which the values of dominance are highest. Most in fact prefer ways of life which favor detachment (or social restraint and self-control), with the values of dominance and receptivity, or some combination of receptivity, dominance, and detachment also preferred. "Enjoyment and progress in action" is a value for most people, but not a preeminent value.

Industrialization as carried out under capitalism concentrates industrial technology and dominance in the hands of a small class, a dominance which spreads from the economic base to the whole society. It was the great merit of Marx to see this: "all means for the development of production transform themselves into means of domination over, and exploitation of, the producers." [17] He saw also the rising counter-movement of the dominated class in the direction of a non-dominating, democratic society. But under socialism also, as we have seen, the struggle of some to dominate others is carried on from the political base and from there through the whole society. It is a struggle that is not entirely explainable in economic or political terms, for it goes on within socialism and within ruling groups. Stalinism as practiced does not reestablish the doctrine of original sin or the recent "scientific" view (a secular version of the former) put forth by Lorenz, Ardrey, and Storr that man is an aggressive, domineering animal. But it does lead us to inquire more radically into the causes of dominance and submission in men. In The People's Republic of China, for example, we have seen a struggle of those supporting a

---

[14]Morris, Charles: *Varieties of Human Value,* Ch. 3.

[15]Morris, Charles: Technique and human value, p. 21.

[16]Varga, Karoly: The view of life of Hungarian students. *The New Hungarian Quarterly, 10:* 22-45, 1969.

[17]Marx, Karl: *Capital,* vol. I, p. 645.

"cultural revolution" to "recapture" the Party leadership from those "taking the capitalist road." The alleged dominance is not economic or technological. It has to do with "education, literature and art and all other parts of the superstructure not in correspondence with the socialist economic base. . . ." [18] The revolution claims to be directed against Party bureaucrats and demands the dominance of the masses. Similarly, the situation in the Czechoslovak Communist Party in the postwar period has been described as follows:

> The incorrect line of the leadership changed the party from a political party and an ideological alliance into a power organization which became very attractive also to egotists avid for rule, calculating cowards, and unprincipled people.[19]

Protest against the dehumanizing effects of dominance—industrial, political, or otherwise—is evident in nearly all societies throughout the world today. The protests take different forms, have different goals, and reach different levels of consciousness.

In the more advanced capitalist industrial societies (United States, Japan, Canada, Scandinavia, Switzerland, France, the German Federal Republic, Benelux, Great Britain, Italy, Israel, Australia, New Zealand), the protest tends to take the form of intellectual criticism, political opposition, or direct action like demonstrations and strikes. In the industrially advanced socialist societies the protest tends to be intellectual, as it does in less industrialized socialist states. At times, of course, the protest in some of these countries has involved both intraparty and extraparty political struggle and direct action.

In the less industrialized capitalist societies (e.g., Spain, Greece, Argentina, Columbia, Venezuela, Chile), the forms of protest are similar, though protest may be borne more fully by the industrial working classes and the peasants and involve their repression by ruling groups.

In the poorly industrialized societies, protest is directed against the local landlords and foreign industrialists engaged in exploitation. Such

---

[18]Central Committee of the Chinese Communist Party: Sixteen points. August 8, 1966.

[19]2,000 words to workers, farmers, civil servants, scientists, artists and everyone. Issued in Czechoslovakia by "a group of leading intellectuals." *The New York Times,* July 21, 1968.

has been the situation in many of the sixty-odd nations, chiefly in Asia and Africa, which since World War II have emerged from colonial status. In a number of such cases, as well as in Latin American countries, the protest has taken overt revolutionary form.

As nations become more industrialized and integrated, protest tends to take intellectual and political form rather than the form of direct, collective, destructive action. As societies pass from a partially industrialized state to an advanced industrialized state, they develop three kinds of protest against industrial dominance: revolutionary peasant-proletarian, proletarian-political, and political-intellectual. These are not mutually exclusive. For example, the revolutionary peasant-proletarian protest includes political and intellectual forces, but the peasants and proletariat represent its base.

Also, protest in an advanced capitalist society is qualitatively different from protest in an advanced socialist society. In the former, many protesters reflect the qualities of the capitalist system: they are liberal, reformist, romantic, anarchistic, etc.; and if they are realistic they know that a basic source of the dehumanization is a dominant economic class in control of technology. In the latter (aside from C. I. A. collaborators) many protesters know what it means to live in a socialist society as contrasted with a capitalist one; hence the protests tend to be focused on politicians, bureaucrats, managers, technicians, and others whose policies have had dehumanizing effects. The proletarian revolution which Marx foresaw in industrialized western Europe did not materialize, and "the self-government of the producers" which he anticipated under socialism has not been perfected. But it should be remembered that at the heart of Marx's teaching was a call for a radical transformation of human living. Marx had in mind a humanistic order which would release men from the constrictions of special groups bent on dominating the society in their own interest. Or as Lenin put it, the task of the revolutionary proletariat is "to *break up* at once the old bureaucratic machine . . . to reduce all officialdom to naught." [20] To prevent this domination, Marx and Lenin saw that the control over industrial and technological processes and indeed over all social processes must be appropriated once and for all by the people themselves.

---

[20]Lenin, V. I.: *The State and Revolution,* p. 42.

The devolopment of dehumanizing technology today has prepared the way for a reaction against it, just as the development of nineteenth century industrial society generated the forces of its own criticism. In incipient postindustrial societies like the United States, the growth of population, the disappearance of dispersed agrarian communities in favor of crowded urban centers, the expansion of scientific, professional, and service occupations relative to skilled and unskilled workers, the spread of education and cultural pursuits, the increase of leisure, affluence, consumption, and opportunities for sensate pleasures, have all developed in people a vague consciousness of the repressed values of receptivity, detachment, and creativity. These changes have made people increasingly aware of the dominance of their lives by forces they do not control and, correspondingly, of their own frustrated self-determination. Under this advanced capitalism the traditional values of individual dominance, made possible for a number in the "free market" of an earlier day, have given way to the values of an intensified, disguised corporate dominance. Nostalgia and hope for such "freedom" have led to the rise of reactionary groups opposed to the welfare state, the labor movement, the income tax, World War II, communism, the United Nations, etc.[21] An "inner-directed" society has become "other-directed." The dominance of the nineteenth century European industrial ruling class—which Marx and Engels described as "naked, shameless, direct, brutal exploitation"[22]—has taken on an additional characteristic masking the exploitation of subordinate classes at home and abroad. That characteristic is social, political, and ideological manipulation of masses of people through large, impersonal organizations in industry, business, the service occupations (especially education), the sciences, the professions, and the mass media. The influence of the governmental-military complex is interwoven into these organizations—e.g., more than one-half of all scientists and engineers are involved in military work. Corporate capitalism in the United States has produced affluence for 7 percent of the population, comfort for 50 percent, and deprivation and poverty for

[21]Lipset, Seymour Martin: The sources of the 'radical right.' In Bell, Daniel (Ed.): *The Radical Right.* Garden City, Doubleday, 1964, pp. 333-334.

[22]*Manifesto of the Communist Party,* p. 11.

43 percent.[23] Hence the task of masking its exploitation is easier than in the earlier period: the middle or "comfortable" stratum of population is much larger, the poor are more dispersed and less visible to most, and the instruments of emotional and mental manipulation are more comprehensive and effective.

Most Americans have not focussed on the nature and causes of this corporate dominance, but increasing numbers are aware of it. The Negroes, the unemployed, the poor, the unskilled and semiskilled workers, the draftable students, have felt it directly. Young people, facing entrance into a society they know to be conformist, impersonal, and repressive, have led the way in rebelling against it, though their rebellion has often been either blind, destructive, passive, retreating, or indulgent. Many have protested against the system by stressing the ideal and actual values of individual receptivity and detachment—the cultivation of sensuous enjoyment and detachment from institutional ties and responsibilities. The new hedonism of the hippies, of happenings, of be-in's, of inner exhilaration, expresses this rejection of a social order which threatens the diversified and free fulfillment of the individual person. Herbert Marcuse's work is popular among such American youth, not so much because of its revolutionary Marxism, as because of his emphasis on instinctual pleasure vs. repression and on the values of individual "immediacy" vs. "organized *domination*."[24] He articulates the revolt of the youth against dominance in favor of receptivity and detachment. Protest is also expressed in patterns of dominance, as seen in the militant actions of some youth; but some of the militancy is aimed at the balanced values of a democratic order.

Throughout its history class society develops ever more elaborate and subtle forms of social dominance. Thorstein Veblen pointed out how the military and priestly coercion of barbarism evolves into the more complicated economy of business enterprize. The predatory class creates a culture of exploit, aggression, emulation, invidious comparison, prowess, trophies, booty, conspicuous leisure, conspicuous consumption, etc.[25] Social status emerges to reflect economic power.

[23]Conference on Economic Progress: *Poverty and Deprivation in the United States. The Plight of Two-Fifth of a Nation.*

[24]Marcuse, Herbert: *Eros and Civilization.* Boston, Beacon, 1955, p. 36.

[25]Veblen, Thorstein: *The Theory of the Leisure Class.* New York, Macmillan, 1899.

Patterns of value feature self-assertion as primary—not as direct, naked power over others, but in the oblique forms of wealth and leisure. Thus, what was and continues to be unchecked economic dominance over other men is supplemented by a *display* of dominance.

In the early stages of capitalism in America the drive for dominance meant the ruthless use and extermination of plants, animals,[26] and men, and the reckless, wasteful manipulation of land, minerals, waterways, and whatever materials the capitalist could lay his hands on. "Wealth is virtue," as one of Balzac's characters puts it in *Père Goriot*. Capital in the form of money and surplus-value becomes an essential means for the growth of such dominance. "Accumulate, accumulate! That is Moses and the prophets!"[27] In the later stages the accumulation of material objects—material "goods"—has become an object in itself and is held up for popular admiration. In the early stages the possession of material goods both as material objects and as social values is impossible for the masses. But advanced capitalism makes such objects available to large groups of people, and hence what was previously only admired at a distance is increasingly possessed and enjoyed. In this, capitalism in western European countries and the United States has gradually opened the eyes of large numbers to the realization of its values of material accumulation and material display. It has incorporated the workers into its system of values.[28] By means of its rising productivity and the tendency to level its materialistic ideals (Fords become surrogates for Cadillacs, suburban homes for estates, frozen foods for maids, mass-produced clothes and coiffures for privately produced ones, television for special entertainment, inexpensive boats for yachts, artificial perfumes and shampoos for natural ones, etc.)—many noncapitalists have been converted to the values of capitalism, even though they remain wage earners.

Moreover, in this way the revolt against dominance in favor of receptivity is somewhat appeased. For in its more affluent stages capitalism is able to blur the distinction between those who control

---

[26]The increase, misery, and exploitation of the surplus population is compared by Marx to "the boundless reproduction of animals individually weak and constantly hunted down." *Capital*, vol. I, p. 643. Marx also took note of how the farmers in their greed ruin the soil. *Ibid.*, p. 265.

[27]Marx, Karl: *Capital*, vol. I., p. 595.

[28]Marcuse, Herbert: *One-Dimensional Man*. Boston, Beacon, 1964.

the economy and those who do not. Politicians serve as the facade of the empire of high finance. And a politician, as Americans demand, must mingle with the people and be one of them. Through its advertizing and its political programs capitalism is able to convince large masses that the happy way of life is the life abundant in material goods. If men in the past objected because their lives were dominated by others and because life was all work and no play—then today those who do not object do not see the dominators and can proceed to enjoy their beer, their television, and their sports. There are few desires, longings, or forms of fulfillment which the system of corporate capitalism has not tried to capture, promote, and commercialize: surfriding, sky-diving, space exploration, sports cars, clothes, cosmetics, nudism, drugs, painting, music, sculpture, cinema, drama, polymorphous sexuality, pornography, gambling, etc. (When a reform group wishes to "legalize" one of these hitherto underground or undeveloped activities, what it usually means is that it wishes to open up the field for exploitation by money-making groups other than the "criminal" ones now operating it. It wants an Open Door Policy in the exotic land of the heathen.) Two experts have predicted that among the technical innovations likely before the year 2000 (presumably in the United States) are controlled super-effective relaxation and sleep; improved capability to "change" sex; competitive synthetic foods and beverages; nonharmful methods of overindulging; extensive and permanent changes in features, figures, complexion, skin color, and physique; and programmed dreams.[29] Such innovations may satisfy some. But those who submit uncritically to such technological "advances" are already candidates for this new colonization, already in need of an opiate and a new "spirit" for a "spiritless situation." Thus new opiates become the new religion of the people.

Why is dominance, as exercised through technological control by a few, antihuman and bad?

(1) By virture of a monopoly of power in the hands of a few, technological dominance deprives the large masses of men of the primary human value of creativity. Dominance in itself is not the primary human value. It is necessary for survival and fulfillment. But in the context of the full human being functioning healthily in society and

---

[29]Kahn, Herman, and Wiener, Anthony, J.: *Op. cit.*

nature, dominance functions alongside receptivity and detachment as a mode through which man creates and fulfills himself and others. Hence when dominance is singled out by a few men as their ruling life-principle and is used to dominate other men, it becomes dehumanizing. It deprives those men of initiative, self-determination, cooperation, and responsibility. A "welfare state," whether capitalist or socialist in outer form, is therefore bad to the extent that decisions and their execution affecting all members of the society are monopolized by a few. However wise the few, they cannot become the creators of the many; undemocratic, they can only become the manipulators and dominators if not the destroyers of the many. This is the very contradiction of man himself, who in his real and axial being is a self-creator.

(2) Dominance, whether exercised by the few or the many, when it takes precedence over values like receptivity and detachment, becomes shortsighted and destructive. All obsession is ruthlessly exclusive. In allowing themselves to be dominated by the drive to manipulate and control the things and persons in their world, men lose sight of the other needs of their natures. They also become blind to the needs and demands of others, the conditions of the nonhuman environment, and the consequences of their actions. History and its creative reflection, literature, are filled with the lesson that those whom the gods would destroy, they first make mad with the lust for power. Insofar as the American imperialists, the latest madmen on the scene, attempt in Vietnam to put a humanistic face on their crimes of genocide, they do it in the name of "freedom," "democracy," "justice," etc. But such slogans are only mockeries of the fact that in their greed for dominance they cannot begin to feel and understand the passions and ideals of the Vietnamese people. To dominate others is to treat them as objects—inanimate, usable, expendable for one's own driving purposes. Correspondingly, natural objects like land, water, plants, and animals are stripped of their humanistic meanings and values, both instrumental and intrinsic, and are wantonly destroyed in pursuit of the all-consuming end of dominance. The same exploitive attitude shows itself in the industrialists who pollute the water and air with waste products and the lumbermen of California bent on destroying

magnificent beauty and two thousand years of natural history for the sake of power over nature, men, and the almighty dollar.

The value of dominance, like any other value, becomes a confused and self-defeating value if isolated from other values in the dialectic of a creative life. For if a man dominates a person, a plant, an animal, or another natural object to the exclusion of appreciating and understanding it, its own autonomous being and life, its own qualities and forms and movement, disappear. Total domination ends in destruction. And what can this mean except that the dominator is driven by his own self-destructive tendencies? A creative person, by contrast, is dominant and receptive, active and thoughtful, attached and detached; he preserves the dialectic of creation, being dominant and destructive only for the sake of a fuller life for himself and others in the long run. He maintains the generic human values of receptivity, dominance, and detachment in dynamic and flexible balance, in himself and with other persons and the world.[30] Some values must always be lost, forsaken, and destroyed. But the guiding principle of his life is the optimal creation of all men.

(3) Technological dominance, by arrogating to itself the central position in the determination of human culture and its values, produces an unhealthy imbalance. A social system based on the dominance of a class which maintains and extends its dominance through the elaboration of technology cannot purposefully and systematically direct its technology toward humanistic ends and thus keep in balance all the values of human existence. The United States, for example, spends more money on chemical and biological warfare than on cancer research, more on the space program than on poverty; and while it can devote $30 billion per year to the Vietnam war, more than ten million of its people go hungry. The pattern of dominance, competitiveness, and acquisitiveness, ingrained in the ways in which people earn their living, pervades the society. It suppresses the values of sensuous responsiveness, release, relaxation, enjoyment, emotional warmth, tenderness, compassion, etc., and the values of perceptual acuity, sensitivity, delicacy of response, self-control, self-awareness,

---

[30]In Charles Morris' studies of values preferences in the United States, India, Japan, China, and Norway, this "way to live" was on the average the best liked way. See Technique and human value, p. 24.

imagination, etc. More important, it displaces the dynamic, integrating, spontaneous, growing, life-affirming drive of the healthy person with the static, piecemeal, mechanical, arrested, death-oriented tendency of the unhealthy person. It distorts personality and culture. Nietzsche, who is often misrepresented as a proponent of a dominant, ruthless will to power and nothing more, described this kind of distortion: "human beings who are nothing but a big eye or a big mouth or a big belly or anything at all that is big. Inverse cripples I call them.[31]

Various psychological studies show that what characterizes the sick person and society is just this deviation from life.[32] The courage to grow, to venture, to enter into new relations and integrate new meanings and values in a give-and-take exchange with things and persons, is given up. In their insecurity men seek the regular, the orderly, the tightly controllable. This mechanism is deep-seated. It can be observed in the magic and religion of primitive times, and in the mythologies and rituals of ancient slave society and feudalism. In industrial and preindustrial societies the mechanical and the technological have provided the main outlets for this neurotic need. Science applied on a massive scale to industry and business, capitalistic efficiency, bureaucratic system, political "machines," vast military organizations, total war, the Protestant ethic, the "repetition compulsion," the obsessive character, other "mechanisms" of defense, the authoritarian personality—all express and appease this need. Men become preoccupied with routine techniques, organizational procedures at their place of work and at home, machines and gadgets. For like the *lares* and *penates* these give protection against the new, the strange, the unknown, and the unpredictable in man's spirit and in his society and world. In industrial society men derive a sense of satisfaction and accomplishment by driving a car, doing "paper work," putting the shop and desk in order (reward: status, money), making house and yard neat by using the many machines they have been induced to buy (reward: status), shopping, paying bills, etc. Men often lavish more care on their food, clothes, houses, yards, cars, machines,

---

[31]Nietzsche, F.: *Thus Spoke Zarathustra.* In Kaufmann, Walter (Ed.): *The Portable Nietzsche.* New York, Viking, 1954, p. 250.
[32]See, for example, the references in footnote 7.

and tools than on persons. They are often more interested in the means, the techniques, the act of controlling, then in the ends. In the United States life, liberty, and happiness are vaguely presumed to be the ends; but how many people are lively, free, and happy?

In the complex and uncertain world of capitalist industrial society, men are tempted to turn to and deal with the inorganic and inanimate, the vegetative and the animal, because their technique and technology there can give them that tidy and narrow order that they compulsively seek, but cannot find, among genuine and creative human beings. If they deal with human beings, they endeavor to reduce them to the level of things, where, in good "scientific" and "political" fashion, they can be enumerated, correlated, consensualized, and controlled. Likewise, in this process of dehumanizing others, they themselves become dehumanized. They learn how to subordinate their own purposes to the efficient running of a social machine. They manipulate and shift their technique to suit its demands. In such a way they become successful workers, leaders, social and natural scientists, market researchers, military men, politicians, bureaucrats, concentration camp managers, organization men, and citizens. And many are proud of their conformity to the system. For example, Hubert Humphrey "has been called an opportunist by some, for which he has, as always, a fast answer: 'What's wrong with taking advantage of the opportunities?' . . . 'Politics of the old days—when you pitted one group against another—it's out, it's obsolete,' he said not long ago. 'Hell, I'm an organization man'."[33]

Erich Fromm has argued that man's love of the mechanical and the dead is not an inborn instinct, but is a secondary reaction to the frustration of his primary love of life.[34] He has also asserted that "the spirit of capitalism, the satisfaction of material greed, is conquering the communist and socialist countries."[35] This is misleading. There are persons, institutions, and policies in socialist countries stressing dominance over people and the environment through technique

---

[33]Sherrill, Robert, and Ernest, Harry: *The Drugstore Liberal*. New York, Grossman, 1968, pp. 10, 29.

[34]Fromm, Erich: *Man for Himself*, pp. 210-216.

[35]Fromm, Erich: The application of humanist psychoanalysis to Marx's theory. In Fromm, Erich (Ed.): *Socialist Humanism*. Garden City, Doubleday, 1965, p. 215.

and technology—bureaucrats, managers, technocrats who see man only as an economic, technical animal. But the general spirit that pervades socialist societies, as compared with the spirit of capitalist societies such as the United States, is more cooperative, balanced, peace-keeping, and humanistic. In no socialist society on earth is the preoccupation with over-kill, megatonnage, imperialist dominance, guns, violence, and the instrumentalities of death so virulent as it is in the United States. Does not the United States society represent the supreme example of how capitalism, generating technology as a means for its own expansion, comes to be dominated by its own empty and destructive techniques of dominance?

Nevertheless, Fromm's statement may be taken as a warning and is *à propos*. The utopian and revolutionary socialism that arose between 1789 and 1848 was a reaction against the dehumanizing, deadening "order" of the conservative Tories and feudalists, on the one hand, and the equally dehumanizing and fixed order of bourgeois liberalism. The theory of the latter gravitated toward materialism, but it was mechanical materialism, which missed the communal and dynamic character of human life and history. Marx saw how the processes of industry isolate, mechanize, and destroy men; but unlike the utopians, he also saw the promise of industry for man's humanization, both in the cooperativeness which it engendered, and in its promise of the liberation of men from necessary labor. The point of proletarian revolution was to release men from the repressive conditions of the feudal and bourgeois order, but to do this through industry. Socialist societies have thus always struggled with the problem of maintaining the revolutionary, humanistic vision while developing and subordinating industry and technology to it. In political terms, this is the problem of creating a genuine democracy among people who know their real human needs and who have the knowledge and the technological and other means to fulfill them.

But the achievent of humanism is not easy. Analysts like J. J. Servan-Schreiber have recognized the growing American dominance of the western European economic community through investment and management. United States corporations in Europe control 15 percent of the production of consumer goods—radios, television sets, and recording devices; 50 percent of semiconductors; 80 percent of computers; and 95 percent of integrated circuits. The answer proposed to the "dynamism, organization, innovation, and boldness that characterize the giant American corporations" is "creativity"—which for Servan-Schreiber means more effective corporate capitalism in Europe.[36] Servan-Schreiber accepts the fundamental dogma of capitalist technology; the humanistic values and consequences of technology are shoved into the background. Is it not clear by now, however, that neither technology nor capitalism is a god that will guarantee men a good life, but that, on the contrary, both pose a serious threat to man? The major theoretical alternative to the antihumanistic technology of capitalism in western Europe is the humanistic technology of socialism. But whether this can become a practical alternative, a real possibility, depends on the exemplary success of humanism in existing socialist states in eastern Europe and throughout the world. People prefer the goods and services of industrial and postindustrial technology, capitalist or communist, to little or no technology. But as real human beings they also prefer a humanistic technology to a nonhumanistic one.

In these terms Lenin's view that "without a revolutionary theory there can be no revolutionary movement"[37] means that the values and goals of social change must be fully clarified—not abstractly, but in concrete criticism of current conditions. What is to be said and done will vary from society to society. But change cannot be revolutionary unless it is basic, and therefore criticism must be basic, i.e., must cut to the assumptions, the philosophical roots, the beliefs concerning man, history, the world, values, and methods, which dominate the society. When they "occupy" university buildings and "confront" the authorities American students imagine that they are making a "revolution." But many repudiate theory and "ideological garbage" (meaning any ideology), and the consequence is far from revolutionary. But the development of a widespread, informed, radical consciousness among Americans—hitherto preoccupied with the immediate and pragmatic—would indeed be a step in the direction of

---

[36]Servan-Schreiber, J. J.: *The American Challenge,* trans. by Ronald Steel. New York, Atheneum, 1969.

[37]Lenin, V. I.: *Selected Works.* Moscow, Foreign Languages Publishing House, 1950, vol. I, p. 227.

radical social change. That consciousness would have to direct itself not only to capitalism but to the whole problem of the dialectics of humanism and technology. In this sense the revolution for Americans must be a double one, just as citizens of socialist countries must now save themselves from the potential distortion and dehumanization of their own technology.

To do this, socialists must recall to themselves the fundamental humanistic root and inspiration of their philosophy. The great drive of Marxism is the removal of all exploitation of man, the elimination of dominance as the principal motive in human life, the creation of a social order in which the generic possibilities of men for receptivity, dominance, detachment, for enjoyment, control, and thought, for individual resourcefulness and social restraint and concern, can develop in concert. Compare this philosophy, for example, with the antihumanistic philosophies of fascism and nazism. Mussolini boasted of "a human will dominating the will of others," of the "will of the few, if not, indeed of one," of "that highest expression of human power which is empire," and of war which "puts the stamp of nobility upon the peoples who have the courage to meet it."[38] Hitler brazenly preached and sought to put into practice the doctrine of the superiority of the "Aryan" race and the folkish state. He rejected the equalitarianism of democracy and Marxism in favor of the "aristocratic principle" of "the most superior men." He called for the destruction of the weaker and inferior peoples by the stronger and superior ones. "Mankind has grown strong in eternal struggles and it will only perish through eternal peace."[39] Mussolini and Hitler, in theory and practice, trampled on most of the values that make men distinctively human. They exalted the values of cruel and destructive dominance of one man or one group over another. Contrast this apothesis of force and violence with the attitude of Marxist-Leninist socialism:

> We set ourselves the ultimate aim of destroying the state, i.e., every organised and sysematic violence, every use of violence against man in general . . . . striving for Socialism, we are convinced that it will develop

---

[38]Mussolini, Benito: *The Doctrine of Fascism.* In Somerville, John, and Santoni, Ronald E. (Eds.): *Social and Political Philosophy: Readings from Plato to Gandhi.* Garden City, Doubleday, 1963, pp. 424, 427, 437, 431.

[39]Hitler, Adolph: *Mein Kampf,* trans. by Ralph Manheim. New York, Houghton Mifflin, 1932.

into Communism; that, side by side with this, there will vanish all need for force, for the *subjection* of one man to another, and of one part of the population to another, since people will *grow accustomed* to observing the elementary conditions of social existence without force and without violence.[40]

Democratic control and direction of technology, whether under capitalism or socialism, must begin in specific institutions. The most basic of these institutions are industrial plants and in particular the plants providing what is vital to the economy—food, machinery, electrical power, chemicals, oil, iron and steel, coal, certain metal goods, automobiles, aircraft, etc. Hence, under American capitalism industrial democracy is a necessary step toward a democratizing of the whole economy. If industrial workers permit themselves to be governed by those of a small class who own them, their labor, and their products of labor, they cannot expect to be freed from the burdens of unemployment or the threat of it, war, and social strife. If, however, they organize to demand increasing control over the conditions of their lives in the plants and participation in the increasing productivity of the new machinery—automated and cybernated—[41] then they will take an important step toward a democratizing of the whole society. For the character and course of the economy and the society are determined in large degree by the character and course of the basic industrial plants. As they become genuinely democratic, political, educational, and other institutions will tend to become democratic. A democratic spirit among the workers would *ipso facto* move in the direction of a socialized economy, providing for broader participation of the broad masses of the people in decision-making and in distribution of goods and services.

Changes in specific institutions must and will be distinctive for distinctive situations. But certain general principles of social action apply to all such situations as men endeavor to make technology more humanistic and to shape it to serve the whole range of human values. Some of these principles are as follows:

(1) All of the people to the extent of their ability shall have access

---

[40]Lenin, V. I.: *State and Revolution*, p. 68.

[41]*U. E. Guide to Automation and the New Technology*, New York, United Electrical, Radio and Machine Workers of America, ND.

to knowledge about themselves, their values, proposed decisions on technological policies affecting their values, and the consequences of such policies for themselves and others.

Corollary: All formal education should make questions of value basic and pervasive.

Corollary: Specialists in knowledge about human beings and human values, technology, planning, leading, etc. should communicate and discuss with the people affected, the technological policies proposed and affecting thm in their institutions.

Corollary: No group, independently of such communication and discussion, should make technological policy.

(2) All of the people affected should, in consequence of such discussion, decide upon and determine a course of action with regard to instituting or changing technological policy.

(3) All of the people affected, after the instituting of technological policy, should discuss, evaluate, and, if decided, change or eliminate such policy.

(4) Institutions (families, schools, unions, government, etc.) should be organized so that the democratic-scientific methods of solving value-problems become established and habitual.

Corollary: Nondemocratic, authoritarian, elitist, impulsive, traditional methods of problem-solving shall be eliminated.

X

RACISM AND WAR IN THE UNITED STATES

W<small>E HAVE SHOWN</small> that the democratic doctrine of the sovereignty of all the people requires the socialist doctrine of the public owner-ship of the basic resources and productive instruments. Capitalism, which lodges economic power in a few, can never give rise to a demo-cratic political system; it is, moreover, destructive and dehumanizing. To illustrate capitalism's undemocratic and dehumanizing character, we now turn to a study of the racism and war inherent in it.

Our thesis here is that in the United States both racism (chiefly that directed against the Afro-American) and exploitive war, as forms of man's inhumanity to man, are products of an inhuman economy and social structure, and that we cannot eradicate one without eradi-cating the other. To eradicate each we must eradicate the economy which requires and supports both. Only in a genuinely socialist economy and democratic society will the twin monsters of racism and war vanish.

In the society of the United States, racism and war (here "aggres-sive" or exploitive war) have developed as institutionalized, mutually reinforcing features of the society. The society most similar to ours in this respect was that of Nazi Germany, whose massive destruction of six million Jews and whose war against the western powers and the Soviet Union was unparalleled in history. In both cases the racism and the war were the interpenetrating products of an economic and social system which breeds racism and war, namely, capitalism. For capitalism is the systematic exploitation of man by man, of ruling class by ruled class; it promotes acquisitiveness and selfish gain at the expense of human development and mutual aid; it rewards the aggres-sive individual and deprives those who by accident of economic con-dition or temperament are not so aggressive. The driving motive and activity of men under capitalism is the expansive production and accumulation of material goods—the domination of nature and men by means of tools and machines, for the sake of satisfying the wants of the individual person without regard for the wants or welfare of other persons. Charles Peirce called its chief principle "the Gospel of Greed."

As an economic and social system, capitalism divides society into two groups, the ruling class and the ruled class, both of whom compete for domination over nature, instruments of production, and society by competing for the economic, financial, and political power which represents such control. The ruling class seeks a greater share of the profits from the industry and natural resources it owns and controls. The ruled class seeks a greater share of its wages. Thus, in the struggle for existence and for material goods both classes necessarily concentrate on producing the goods that satisfy elementary needs (food, shelter, clothing) or, in a more advanced stage of capitalism, induced needs (gadgets, luxuries). The genuine needs of man, such as authentic communication, creativity, and cooperation for the welfare of all, are suppressed. Men are dehumanized into owners and owned, into commodities to be exchanged, into instruments of production to be used, into materials to be shaped for another's ends.

Western capitalism has passed through a series of developments which have, in their own inner demands, given rise to war, slavery, and racism. Early capitalism began in medieval towns settled by free serfs who had escaped with their craft tools from the countryside and who in the face of common needs and competition from other craftsmen organized guilds. The guilds owned their own capital in houses and craft tools, and sold the goods they produced. Gradually, however, specialized merchants took over the function of selling and buying goods, introducing a commerce that transcended the local neighborhood and seeking large profits in long-distance trading operations. As a result towns began to enter into new relations; individual towns began to specialize in production, but also, realizing their common opposition to the landed nobility, united against the latter. The result was a growing burgher class. The division of labor among the towns stimulated the growth of manufactures, which in turn rose on the base of the expanding population and accumulated capital. Thus, both the merchants and the manufacturers developed movable capital, i.e., capital convertible into money and thereby capable of generating new capital by means of investment in new economic enterprizes. In the process they outstripped the guild economy which was tied to "estate" capital and which lacked the expansive power of the former. The new economy was greatly accelerated by dramatic maritime discoveries and the extension of commerce to Africa, the East Indies, and the Americas. For that new commerce brought in new products, large quantities of gold and silver (new money), and competition among nations of manufacturers and merchants in a world market.[1]

In the most rapidly expanding period of capitalism, in the seventeenth and eighteenth centuries, commerce and navigation outran manufacture in their development. The demand for domestic protection for manufactures through duties and for their foreign protection through monopolies brought the merchant into the ascendancy over the manufacturer. The system of colonization required a favorable balance of trade for the colonizer and a merchant marine to protect its waterways in the world market. During this period the competition of the major maritime nations for trade routes, territories, raw materials, markets, and profits was intense and protracted. The result was a series of wars, "the sport of merchants," between the colonial powers —first Spain and Portugal, and then the Netherlands, Britain, and France.

In their expanding domination of territories and peoples, the early capitalists pursued three policies: extermination, trade, and enslavement. In North America both trade and extermination were practiced toward the native Indian population, with extermination predominating as trade became unprofitable and as the Indians resisted. In the end the Indians were virtually destroyed and reduced to an impoverished people living as outcasts. Here the driving power was the appetite of men for land and wealth. From the seventeenth century onward the Americas offered the most promising opportunities for the new European merchants. Trading companies organized by merchants and men of means obtained huge pieces of land there by appropriation or royal grant, and then induced people from Europe to settle and develop the land so that they might buy and sell with

---

[1]Marx, Karl, and Engels, Friedrich: *The German Ideology*, pp. 43-58.

them at a profit. The big merchants also relied on the white settlers to deal with native Indians. The attitude of the white settlers toward the Indians (with some notable exceptions, like Roger Williams and William Penn) was entirely commercial: since they could not be easily enslaved, they were exterminated. The attitude common among many frontiersmen was, "The only good Indian is a dead Indian."

Until the nineteenth century capitalism did not require large masses of industrial workers; its chief need was for craftsmen and farmers, and this need was supplied by white Europeans. They came to America lured by a better material life and bourgeois political and religious freedom. But many came under the coercion of mercantile capitalism with its demand for cheap labor. Indentured servants bound themselves for a four- to seven-year term to get their passage paid. At one point kidnappers roamed the streets of London seizing men, women, and children to send to America as bondservants.[2] The massive exploitation of labor did not commence until capitalism developed on a large-scale in America, first in the plantation system and later in the advanced industry of the nineteenth century. The plantation system created black slavery, a slavery that might have been based on white or Indian labor except for prior historical conditions.

The origin of black slavery lies in capitalist colonization in Africa and the development of the slave trade in African Negroes. Started in 1442 when a captain of Prince Henry the Navigator received ten Blacks and some gold dust in exchange for some Moors, the trade provided vast commercial profits. Between 1680 and 1780 the British imported into their colonies in America and the West Indies 2,130,000 slaves.[3] For every one hundred Negroes shipped from Africa to the West Indies, not more than fifty survived to be effective laborers.[4] Scholars estimate the total number of slaves landed alive in the Americas to be between fifteen and fifty millions or more, while many millions more died in raids and wars.[5]

Slavery is an ancient institution, but in no other period in human

[2]Huberman, Leo: *We, The People*. New York, Harper, 1947, pp. 11-12.

[3]Ingram, John Kells: Slavery. In *Encyclopedia Britannica*. Chicago, William Benton, 1959, vol. XX, p. 780.

[4]*Ibid.*

[5]Davidson, Basil: *The African Slave Trade. Precolonial History 1450-1850.* Boston, Little, Brown, 1961, pp. 79-80.

history did it grow so rapidly as it did among the leading capitalist-colonial nations of the eighteenth century. What is remarkable is not only its dehumanization of millions of Negroes, but also its development as a logical extension of an economic system represented as necessary and just. What kind of economic system is it which systematically must traffic in human beings? Wage laborers always knew they were exploited under capitalism. But the hunting down of African Blacks, the branding of them, the throwing of them into irons, the transporting of them across thousands of miles in the hulls of overcrowded and unsanitary ships (where they were sometimes packed in cells three feet high, with little or no light), the stripping of them of all identity, family, history, property, and human rights, the selling of them into chattel slavery, the working of them in fields from sun up to sun down six days a week, year after year, the absolute pauperizing of them in body and soul—what else reveals so starkly and conclusively the depravity of the capitalist system? Nothing else—except the capitalism of the fascist state with its murder of millions of human beings, its totalitarian repression and coercion, torture, concentration camps, gas chambers, crematoria, slave labor, and genocide of "inferior races." In the case of American slavery, the murder was relatively slow; in the case of fascism, relatively quick.

Racism in its minimal form is the disposition to reject, debase, and dominate another people on the basis of what is perceived and labelled as "racial" differences, and this often leads to coercion and to war. Conversely, exploitive war requires some sentiment of group superiority, often racial. A people claiming to be superior may live aloof from their putative inferiors, peaceably tolerating them; but if conditions are favorable—economic deprivation, hatred, desire for wealth, inflammatory ideas—they may actively endeavor to dominate those inferiors. A common way of imposing domination is coercion and, where this is organized and armed, war. Whether the dominated are killed or not depends on whether the conquerors wish to use them as slaves. The domination and enslavement of a particular race may not lead to a large, systematic war. The colonial racists who took Negroes from Africa into slavery did not always take them by force or raids on villages; they often relied on the forays and wars of local tribes to obtain captives.[6] Once slavery is established, of course, it is maintained by corecion, by the war of the ruling class against the ruled and all others who threaten it. When slaves run away or revolt, the police of the state make war on the disrupters of its "law and order."

By a complex series of events, the system of slavery and racism in the southern United States led to the bloodiest war in its history (nearly 500,000 deaths). Underlying the military conflict were intense class struggles: northern industrialists as well as small southern farmers competed with southern cotton plantation owners; slave labor in the South tended to lower the wages of the industrial workers in the North; northern industrialists and independent farmers of North and West clashed with slaveholders for the control of the western lands. In the showdown, the slaveholders would not yield their class power peaceably, nor would northern capitalists tolerate their chief competitors without open warfare upon them. The white laborers joined in this war to destroy slavery, and "boasted it the highest prerogative of the white-skinned laborer to sell himself and choose his own master."[7]

The purpose of exploitive war, like that of active racism, is the subjection of a people and their territory. The wars of ancient racist empires aimed at the acquisition of slaves, whose labor in turn supported the imperial societies, though many of the conquered were killed. The Nazi theory and practice of racism went hand in hand with the theory and practice of world conquest through exploitive war. It led to both the enslavement of millions and the systematic extermination of whole peoples unmatched by ancient empires.

The similarities between the American system of racism and war and the Nazi system of racism and war are not accidental. Both social systems were highly developed, industrial, technological, monopolistic economies of capitalism, dominated by the interlocking interests of a few thousand men in industry, the armed services, and

---

[6]Wiedner, Donald L.: *A History of Africa South of the Sahara.* New York, Random House, 1962, p. 58.

[7]Address of the International Workingmen's Association to Abraham Lincoln, published in The Bee-Hive, London, January 7, 1865. In Marx, Karl, and Engels, Frederick: *Letters to Americans 1848-1895.* New York, International, 1953, pp. 65-66.

government who were determined to acquire, hold, and extend their power not only over the major economic, political, legal, and other significant institutions of their own society, but increasingly over the whole world. In each case money, the gun, and the law collaborated to achieve the goal. In each case a specially selected "race" was chosen to bear the brunt of oppression and to suffer brutalization at the hands of a ruling class whose insecurities called for a scapegoat and whose demand for profits required a victim. One German firm in the time of the Nazis, calculating the cost of maintaining a concentration camp prisoner and the income from his clothes, gold fillings, and ashes, arrived at "an average profit of 1630 marks per person." The Krupp industries used more than 100,000 slave laborers, and other German firms were implicated in the profits from slave labor and mass killings, many of them connected with American capital. Likewise American slave owners made billions of dollars from the labor of slaves. In both cases "race" or "color" became the badge of inferiority. Indians, Negroes, and yellow peoples were considered impure, and the impure peoples were treated as colonials at home and abroad. In both cases war became an instrument of national policy for subjecting inferior peoples (the Nazi war against the allies; the United States Indian wars, Mexican war, Spanish-American war, Korean and Vietnam wars). In both cases communism was conceived as the devil incarnate and vast resources were mobilized to destroy it.

"Race" in the popular usage is a loose and imprecise term. Anthropologically speaking, there is no "Aryan" or "Jewish" race. Because of the difficulty in establishing it with physical precision, many anthropologists have in fact abandoned the concept of "race." But "race" (Italian *razza,* Latin *generatio,* lineage, breed) has served men's purposes, in spite of its imprecision. Sometimes identical with the concept of family stock, clan, tribe, or nation, it has designated a group of people with a common set of physical traits. Since Paleolithic times, for the purpose of safety and survival, people have been required to distinguish between their own familiar kind and strangers. One of the most immediate and easy ways to do this (but not the only way) was by the discrimination of skin color, on a scale of white-black. For relatively light-skinned peoples, such as the Indo-Aryans, this distinction became early associated with a still more primitive distinction and symbolism. For primitive man, whether living in the forest or open plain, day became associated with sunlight, life, and good, while night became associated with darkness, death, and evil.[8] Thus in the contacts of these light-skinned peoples with dark-skinned peoples, as in the Aryan invasion of India, this primitive dualistic symbolism offered an ideological justification for their superiority. The dualism of light and dark, of good and evil, later appeared among the Persians and the Pythagoreans, from whom Plato probably acquired it; and thence it passed into Christian thought.

The moral and religious symbolism of color in Christianity was developed in medieval painting,[9] though it was not fully applied to race until the development of maritime commerce to Africa and Asia and of the slave trade. Under the lead of Calvinists for whom the distinctions between God and the world, good and evil, salvation and sin, and the elect and the damned were sharply drawn, an ideology emerged which portrayed the Negro, Indian, and Oriental heathen as cut off from the grace of God and from God's rewards for the elect in this life—enterprize, thrift, austerity, cleanliness, and profit. Christian missionaries among the colored peoples in Africa, the Americas, and Asia found that the latter did not conform to their economic (capitalist) moral standards, and so condemned them as inferior. Thus the Protestant ethic along with Catholic casuistry, both nurtured in the western colonial nations, was a reflection and self-fulfilling justification of the stratified society of capitalism. Their neat dualism sanctioned the white, rich, Christian capitalist at the top of the social order, while the colored, poor, pagan slave remained at the bottom, each ordained by an almighty God to his appointed place in the universe.

Slavery has flourished since early civilizations, i.e., the first class societies, but its concrete form has been a function of the particular social structure which created and sustained it. The Greek slave could accumulate property and small savings with which he might buy his liberty. The Roman slave in the second century A.D. received cer-

[8]Eliade, Mircea: *The Sacred and the Profane,* trans. by Willard R. Trask. New York, Harcourt, Brace, 1959. Gergen, Kenneth, J.: The significance of skin color in human relations. *Daedalus, 96:* 390-406, 1967.

[9]Bastide, Roger: Color, racism, and Christianity. *Daedalus, 96:* 312-327, 1967.

tain legal protections and his manumission was facilitated. Greek, Roman, and later European serfdom did not allow chattel ownership, and the Christian theology of feudalism viewed the serf as occupying a position in God's order, albeit a lowly one. While the Koran decreed humane treatment for slaves, captives not monotheists suffered castration and loss of their rights in person and property; as early as the eleventh century most of the slaves taken in this way in North Africa were Negroes.[10] But the slave did not become a chattel and color did not become a tabu there; black-white relations were based on class, not color.[11]

For nascent capitalism, however, the slave, as something seized or bought like ivory or gold, transported in ships, sold at a profit, and bound for life as a chattel to his owner, could not be human. He was thus pictured as a beast. Later, as the mercantile monopolies developed and generated conflicts between themselves, with their colonies like those in the Americas, and the revolutionary, new bourgeoisie and proletariat of industry, this extreme ideology changed. Now the colored man was pictured as only an inferior human being. Since the Civil War the colored man in the United States has been regarded by an increasing number as equal but separate—a belief that only thinly masks the older notion of his inferiority. The tenacity of this belief is revealed in the fact that in the Deep Southern states complete segregation obtained in more than 90 percent of the schools in 1967.[12] And the social function of this belief is still what is was in the seventeenth century: to justify the profits of a ruling class. In 1967 Negro families in the South on the average earned $2,265 less than Negro families in the North, while white families in the South on the average earned $1212 less than white families in the North.[13]

Slavery in the United States has a distinctive history. In 1619 a Dutch ship sold some Guinea Negroes to tobacco planters in Jamestown, Virginia. The number of Negro slaves in the colonies increased

[10]Wiedner: *Op. cit.,* p. 46.

[11]*Ibid.,* pp. 469-470, 472. Brown, Leon Carl: Color in Northern Africa. *Daedalus, 96*: 464-482, 1967.

[12]Watters, Pat: Introduction, *Lawlessness and Disorder.* Atlanta, Southern Regional Council, 1968.

[13]Perlo, Victor: Relevance of Marxist economics to U. S. conditions. *Political Affairs,* 48 (No. 2): 45, 1969.

slowly. In the 1690's the white servants in the South outnumbered the Negro slaves. About that time, however, planters in South Carolina began to concentrate on the production of rice in the swampy coastal areas. Negroes were judged to be suitable to the steady, all-year-round work in the hot climate. More important, slave labor was cheap. As late as the 1790's a good field hand could be bought for $200, and the cost of maintaining him for a year on a small plantation was only $30 to $40 (it was half of that on the large plantation). Moreover, slaves could be hired out, and after their cotton lands had worn out, some states, like Maryland and Virginia, bred slaves for profit.[14] In the 1790's the state of Virginia contained 200,000 Negro slaves. In 1863, the year of the Emancipation Proclamation, there were 4,000,000 slaves. Slavery had become a profitable institution. It was a billion-dollar business.

The driving forces in the development of black slavery in the United States were economic—the demand of people for goods, the desire of entrepreneurs for profit, the available natural resources, the available labor supply, the manufacturing machines and processes, and the conditions of the economy that permitted and encouraged the exploitation of natural resources, labor, machines, and market for the profit of the entrepreneurs.

The demand for clothing is universal. Moreover, in the industrial revolution generated in western Europe in the eighteenth century, increasing numbers of people possessed not only the demand for, but also the power to purchase, cheap and usable clothing. For many reasons, cotton clothing could be produced and sold cheaply and could satisfy the demands of people. The British East India Company, founded in 1599, had given the British a monopoly on the raw cotton grown in India, and gradually cotton grew to be a competitor with wool for the spinning and weaving machines developed by English inventors in the eighteenth century.

In the United States, where land was abundant and very cheap, the dominant motive in the economic sphere was money-making, and the rich, virgin land, easily obtainable, was adaptable to this purpose. In many places it was more profitable to diversify the products produced, both for family use and for sale. But in other places, such as

---

[14]Huberman: *Op. cit.,* pp. 165-166.

the South, it was often more profitable to concentrate on the production of a single crop in a large-scale, year-round operation, i.e., in a plantation. In the seventeenth century rice and tobacco were the principal crops grown on southern plantations. The profit from these crops was great—the combined result of the favorable land and climate, the cheap labor, the industrial processes, and the freedom of capitalist enterprize to use nature and human beings for profit.

The southern climate is the most suitable in the world for cotton-growing. The weather is hot in summer, with ample rainfall. The growing season is long. The picking time, autumn, is dry. The short, frosty winters destroy the pests. For the early white settlers the land was easily accessible. It was cheaper to move on to new lands rather than to fertilize the used ones. The slave owner could take his own labor force with him, whereas white laborers were not so movable. He was all set up to move his operation. Moreover, he had to. To get the maximum out of his investmtent in human laborers, he had to keep them at work continuously. So he followed the lure of new lands southward and westward from Virginia. Thus the institution of slavery tended to reinforce the year-round, large-scale operation of the one-crop plantation.

The raw cotton had to be processed for shipment. In 1793 invention of the cotton gin, which separated the cottonseed from the lint, made this possible. Meanwhile the textile mills in England, the northern United States, and France were ready to card, spin, and weave the cotton into the fabrics that were in such great demand. By 1860 the production of cotton had increased by a thousand-fold over what it was in 1789. Thus, when the slaves were freed, the southern plantation owners lost two billion dollars' worth of property.[15] The cotton industry had generated an economy in the South in which one out of three persons was a black slave. And the legal abolition of slavery did not change the underlying system of capitalism; it simply moved the Blacks into the ranks of the poor farmers and wretched wage laborers.

The slaveholders in the United States in 1850 numbered about 350,000. Of these, those holding fifty or more slaves totaled less than 8,000. But, they comprized a ruling class who owned the best land and exercised a dominant ideological influence through their control

---

[15]*Ibid.*

of local, state, and national governments, newspapers, churches, schools and universities, and the opinions of professional persons. That ideology reflected the prevailing situation of the black slave: it held that the Negro is either an inferior human being or a subhuman being. That ideology in various forms persists today among many Americans, reflecting the pervasive discrimination against the Negroes in economic and social life. The discrimination and the ideology are both the products of an economic system in which money-making and profits are the chief end of human life and human beings become the means to that end. As long as men are treated as means by other men, then the most vulnerable among the oppressed will suffer the most. For the colonial nations of the seventeenth, eighteenth, and nineteenth centuries, the oppressed groups were the defenseless peoples of the Americas, Africa, India, the East Indies, and the mainland of Asia. For the British industrialists of the nineteenth century, the oppressed groups were poor and ignorant factory workers, women, and children at home, and the natives abroad. For the American plantation owners in the southern United States for 250 years, the oppressed group was the African Negro, imported, hired out, and bred as a commodity. Because of their enslaved position before legal emancipation, the group most vulnerable to oppression in the United States in the last century has been the Negro people. For in passing from chattel slavery to a lower caste status in the society, the Blacks have continued in deprivation and discrimination and are thus open to the severest forms of oppression in the society.

Some statistics will indicate some present-day consequences of black slavery under capitalism. In 1967 the median family income for Negroes was 59 percent of the white median income. Thirty-four percent of all Negroes, compared with 10 percent of all whites, were below the poverty level in 1967. The unemployment rate for non-whites was 6.7 percent for 1968, almost twice that for whites.[16] In 1966 the number of substandard housing units occupied by nonwhites was 1.69 million.[17] In 1968, 75 percent of the whites between the ages

---

[16]Recent trends in social and economic conditions of Negroes in the United States (prepared by Herman P. Miller and Dorothy K. Newman). Bureau of Labor Statistics Report 347, July, 1968. Washington, D. C.: U. S. Government Printing Office, 1968.

[17]U. S. Bureau of Labor Statistics and U. S. Bureau of the Census, in a publica-

of twenty-five and twenty-nine had completed four years of high school; 58 percent of the Negroes in that age group had.[18] In 1966 7.4 percent of Negro males and 17.9 percent of white males had completed college.[19] In 1952 there were six million potential Negro voters in the South; five southern states disfranchised seven million people by the poll tax. The total number of registered Negro voters in 1968 was a little more than three million.[20] Negroes comprize 14 percent of the Americans dying in the Vietnam war and less than 5 percent of members of draft boards.[21] In 1967 the life expectancy for the white male under the age of one was 6.7 years greater than that for the nonwhite male, and 6.9 years greater for the white female.[22] If we multiply 6.7 times 22,000,000, the number of Negroes then living in the United States, we get 147,400,000, the number of years of life of which these Negroes are being deprived. If seventy years is taken to be the average length of life (it is a little more than sixty for the nonwhite male), then this means that the equivalent of more than two million black lives have been lost over a seventy-year period. This is genocide.

If we seek the causes of this mass injury and destruction to human life, we find that they do not lie in the inherent inferiority of the Blacks or the decrees of an Almighty God—causes alleged in the past by large groups of whites and still clung to by reactionary mentalities. The most direct causes lie in the economic system which begets and fosters the war of the ruling class on the oppressed classes, and racism. Poverty, unemployment, poor housing, inferior schools and education, disenfranchisement, a high disease and mortality rate—all are the direct results of a society of capitalism whose leaders in the industrial political, military and other sectors devote their energies and the nation's resources to the accumulation of wealth and power for them-

---

tion issued in October, 1967. Cited in Glazer, Nathan: The Negro's stake in America's future. *The New York Times Magazine,* September 22, 1968, pp. 30 ff.

[18]See footnote 16.

[19]See footnote 17.

[20]See footnote 17.

[21]See footnote 16.

[22]Department of Health, Education, and Welfare, Public Health Service: *Vital Statistics of the United States.* Cited in U. S. Bureau of the Census: *Statistical Abstract of the United States:* 1969, 90th ed. Washington, D. C., U. S. Government Printing Office, 1969, p. 54.

selves. They impede democratic planning to achieve justice in the production and distribution of the nation's resources for the meeting of the people's real needs. In 1969 the Congress appropriated 66 percent of the national budget for military and defense-related purposes, and 16.5 percent for health, education, and welfare. This figure is only one of a legion of indicators of the institutionalized dehumanization in American society.

It is sometimes asked: "Why must the economic system be the main determinant of black oppression? Is it not possible to correct the injustices done to the Blacks and other groups by means of legal, political, and other means?" The question overlooks the fact that the institutional life and thought of a society tend to reflect and reinforce the relations into which men enter in their economic life.

In the American colonies law allowed that a black bondservant might be held by a white owner for life, while a white bondservant could be held only for a term of years.[23] The original United States Constitution recognized the distinction between "free persons" and slaves, and in acknowleging poll taxes and property taxes in Article 1, Section 2 (3), it implicitly accepted the economic base of political power. The Fugitive Slave Laws, the Missouri Compromise, and the Dred Scott case simply elaborated legally what the ruling groups believed to be the intent of the Constitution. Amendments XIII, XIV, and XV, which freed the slaves and gave the Negroes the right to citizenship and voting, were the consequence of a civil war. But they did not alter the profiteering, exploitive habits of the ruling white class, who still demanded the cheap, ignorant, and passive labor of the Negro. The law, as repeatedly confirmed by the Supreme Court (e.g., Plessy v. Ferguson), employed fictions like "separate but equal treatment under law" to justify segregation. The law of the white ruling class, moreover, was frequently used as a positive oppressive weapon against the Black. For example, during 1938-1948, in thirteen southern states, where Negroes comprized less than one-fourth of the population, fifteen whites and 187 Negroes were executed for rape.[24] The disproportionate penalty for Negroes for rape shows the

---

[23]Franklin, John Hope: *From Slavery to Freedom,* 1st ed. New York, Knopf, 1947, pp. 70 ff.

[24]Dombrowski, James A.: Execution for rape is a race penalty. *The Southern Patriot, 8* (No. 9) : 1-2, 1950.

tendency of the ruling class and its legal allies to seek for signs of its own violence among its victims, to project its own violence onto them, and to expiate its own guilt by making them the scapegoat for violence. This might be called the Reichstag Fire complex.

The political oppression of the Blacks paralleled their economic and legal oppression. Reduced to property before the Civil War, Negroes experienced a brief period of freedom after the three critical constitutional amendments of 1865, 1868, and 1870. Between 1869 and 1876 sixteen Negroes were seated in the Congress and several others had titles to their seats but did not gain them.[25] Many were elected to their state legislatures.

But the economic pattern of capitalist exploitation soon asserted itself. After the war northern industry experienced a great boom. Investors and speculators made vast profits in lands, mines, factories, and railroads. Corruption abounded; Boss Tweed and his cronies stole $75,000,000, and Congressmen commonly received their payments from industry. The South was corrupt too, but blamed the corruption on the disfranchised Negroes. After a few years of wild freebooting, up to the panic of 1873, a new monopolistic capitalism emerged, based on corporate interlocking investment in coal, steel, oil, and copper. Big business crushed the robber barons and grafters, provided stability of investment to the petty bourgeoisie, accomodated itself to the new labor unions, withdrew the Federal army from the South, and restored political control to southern property.

The northerner capitalist saw the impoverished South as an opportunity for new enterprize, but in the competition for the cheap labor of Black and white alike, he embittered the planter-capitalist of the South. The latter, moreover, saw the laboring class controlling the vote and enabled to redistribute his remaining wealth in land, while he himself was required to pay through taxes the burdensome costs of the war and of reconstruction. As Negroes proved themselves capable of free labor and education, southern industry recovered. But the wealthy and powerful white classes opposed the restoration of the Negroes to their full citizenship. The Freedmen's Savings and Trust Company went down under white discrimination and corruption. The

---

[25]Du Bois, W. E. B.: *Black Reconstruction.* New York: Russell and Russell, 1935, p. 627.

Freedmen's Bureau, supported in its first year by Negro rents, failed to obtain much land for the propertyless exslaves. Negro wages were low and Negroes could buy little land anyway. From 1868 to 1876, however, the political demand of the Negroes for a greater share in the ownership of land grew.

In the face of this demand for universal suffrage, three forces, themselves in part antagonistic to one anther, formed themselves: the small, poor capitalist from the North; the southern planter impoverished by the war who resented the "carpetbagger"; and the poor white man, peasant and laborer and bourgeois, who opposed both big capitalists and Negro workers, but who would cooperate with capitalist planters against northerners and Negroes. In the struggle for power, then, intrigue, alliances, enmities, corruption, and violence ensued. The immigrant northern capitalists, who accepted the ninetetenth century notion of a free, informed, organized, and voting labor force, lacked acceptance among white laborers and capitalists. The southern planters lacked capital and political knowledge; and the freed Blacks lacked land, education, and the vision of their role as a laboring class. In the strife a new form of racist ideology appeared in organizations like the Ku Klux Klan.[26] In 1876 the Supreme Court, infused with the thought of men in alliance with big business, rendered innocuous the Fourteenth and Fifteenth Amendments.[27] In the same year a bargain between big business and the South was struck: the Republican Hayes, on becoming President, would by the withdrawal of Federal troops allow the planter capitalists to control South Carolina and Louisiana, while the Southern landholders and capitalists would assume control of black labor.[28] The result: "an exploitation of labor unparalleled in modern times, with a government in which all pretense at party alignment or regard for universal suffrage is given up."[29]

Thus, by a "counter-revolution of property" the freed black slaves were forced back into new forms of oppression, those of the share tenant, the sharecropper, the industrial wage laborer, and the poor independent farmer. The Blacks effectively lost their vote; in 1920

[26]*Ibid.*, Ch. 14.
[27]*Ibid.*, p. 691.
[28]*Ibid.*
[29]*Ibid.*, p. 630.

only seventy thousand of them in the South voted. After the Civil War, thousands of them died by mob violence, many by lynchings, and untold numbers of them perished from starvation, malnutrition, disease, and the other adversities to which American society subjected them. Similarly, the racist ideology which accompanied slavery was revived in new forms. Newspapers, books, stage, motion pictures, and radio programs all tended to portray the Negro as inferior. Thus politics followed economics, and ideology reflected both.

Black enslavement and segregation were the consequences of an economic system in which capitalists found it profitable to create and maintain a cheap labor force. In the South the post-Civil War segregation was also supported by the poor white laborers, who feared the competition threatened by an educated and skilled group of Negroes. Capitalism when successful creates a sense of loyalty to capitalism in the capitalist. It generates a self-image that identifies itself with the successful functioning of the system and that resists threats to the system as threats to self. It likewise generates in its wage laborers an insecurity as to their future and a fear of other laborers who might take their jobs and their livelihood. It thus sows the seeds of hostility and scapegoating. Blacks in the South have therefore suffered retardation in their economic, social, and educational development because of the combined antagonism against them on the part of the capitalists and the white wage laborers and farmers. Though the white wage laborers would have improved their wages and working conditions by a unionized effort to upgrade *all* workers, white and Negro (since the low Negro wages pulled theirs down)—their actions were governed by the anxieties, fears, and prejudices fostered daily by the deprivation and oppression in their work and in the newspapers, books, sermons, and other media whose ideas were determined by the dominant class.

To understand the oppression of the Black, we must see it as a special and intense case of insecurity and violence pervading a whole social system—not always conscious and deliberate, but ever present, latent, and ready to break out in one form or another.

As a spacious, virgin land, with a temperate climate of stimulating cyclonic storms, abundant and variegated in natural resources and occupied by relatively few Indians (estimates vary from half a million to a million), the country which became the United States offered a "golden" opportunity for Europeans imbued with the spirit of capitalism. Initially they came to the New World to claim its lands and extract its booty. Most settlers came seeking freedom of enterprize in city or on farm, and a better material life. Soon the combines of merchants and industrialists sought profit in trade with the colonies. The exploitive tendencies carried to the continent by men of acquisitive drive and predatory appetite were thus reinforced by the physical environment and by the socioeconomic system of a capitalism which was at first mercantilist and then, in the nineteenth century, industrial. Vast areas of land, untapped natural resources (water, water power, fertile and arable soil, minerals, animals, a climate neither arctic nor tropical), isolation from the competing societies of the Old World, plus an inventive capitalism[30] whose advancing techniques enabled men to exploit those physical factors—all produced an unparalleled activity and dominance over the physical environment. This drive to dominate ran rampant through the country for many decades. Its appetite grew by what it fed on. What men acquired they wished to keep and increase.

The results of this rampage are well known among scientists: the despoiling of the land and the land's plant and animal life (the cutting down of seven-eighths of the forests, without replacing most of them); the damaging of 200 million acres of land on the Great Plains (one-half of the tillable land); the extermination or near-extermination of many animal and bird species; the arrant seizure of vast lands by private individuals and by government; the pollution of air and water and soil; and the creation of crowded, unhealthy, and ugly cities. But these results must be seen in relation to human beings. The genocide of millions of Indians; the deprivation and suffering of many more millions of poor wage laborers, shopkeepers, farmers, and sharecroppers; the drafted American soldiers who died or were wounded in wars to extend or defend capitalism; the exploitation of the peoples of Mexico, Cuba, Puerto Rico, Nicaragua, Guam, the Philippines, Hawaii, Alaska, the Virgin Islands, Panama, Santo Domingo, and many other countries, by either direct military invasion or "dollar diplo-

---

[30]Burlingame, Roger: *Machines That Built America*. New York, Harcourt, Brace, 1953.

macy" or both; the extremely high crime rate in the United States[31]—
all are the results of a historical pattern of anxiety, aggressiveness, and
violence whose equal is difficult to find in the history of modern
nations. The enslavement and ghettoizing of millions of Negroes was
one strand in this pattern.

The pattern was, of course, evident in European capitalism. Dar-
win had inadvertently given it a description in the subtitle of *The
Origin of Species:* "The Preservation of Favored Races in the Struggle for Life." William Graham Sumner, the spokesman for Social
Darwinism, would later formulate its working principle: "Root, hog,
or die." The rigor of life in the frontier settlements, the hardships of
the pioneers, the competition in the entrepreneurial and commercial
cities, all tended to subordinate or eliminate the weaker and more
vulnerable portions of the population. But the base of the whole
society was economic, i.e., the domination of a growing working class
by a growing owning class. Before the Revolution a small clique of
wealthy men, merchants and planters, controlling land and trade,
conflicted with the mass of laborers, mechanics, and farmers.[32] With
the development of large industries in the nineteenth century, a working class emerged whose interests clashed with those of the owning,
industrial class. Class warfare appeared as a determinative force on
the national scene during the Jacksonian era, when the industrial
workers of the eastern cities joined with the pioneers, farmers, small
planters, and country shopkeepers to oppose the banks, money lenders,
industrialists, and monopolists.[33] But the workers faced special adversities in organizing themselves, and their history was "checkered with
strikes and violence."[34] The growth of the large corporations in the
last two decades of the century produced intense strife between capital
and labor; from 1881 to 1905 thirty-seven thousand strikes occurred,[35]
with bloody consequences, but also significant gains for the workers.
The struggle of laboring men to achieve and hold their rights revealed

---

[31]Department of Justice, Federal Bureau of Investigation, *Uniform Crime Reports for the United States.*

[32]Nevins, Allan, and Commager, Henry Steele Commager: *The Pocket History
of the United States.* New York, Pocket Books, 1956, p. 74.

[33]*Ibid.,* pp. 172-173.

[34]*Ibid.,* p. 296.

[35]*Ibid.*

in a stark way the desperate violence of the capitalist. Had not the Blacks under slavery felt this violence? Had not the plantation owners of the South fought a costly war to defend their slave system? Had not northern capitalists responded by a defense of their industries, protective tariffs, and centralized banks? American capitalists have fought viciously to acquire, maintain, and extend their rights in property.   · ·

Such fighting has not been confined at home, against Indian, Negro, and wage laborer. It has been carried abroad to many parts of the globe. The nation that has taken more square miles of its own continental territory by military conquest than any other nation[36] has become the leading military power and aggressor in the world today. Such aggression is the arm of a capitalism in its highest stage, marked by monopoly and imperialism. It has as its purpose the profitable domination of lands, rivers, seas, air routes, and peoples. Thus the military-industrial-intelligence system of the United States has insinuated itself into the world economy. United States business has a foreign market in Europe, Africa, Asia, Latin America, and Canada that is more than $100 billion or two-fifths the size of its domestic output of farms, factories, and mines, with foreign sources of earnings more than one-fifth of the domestic nonfinancial profits. At home, one hundred corporations own 55 percent of the total net capital assets; abroad, forty-five of these account for almost three-fifths of all direct foreign investment. Such corporations exercise a community of interest through their control of the financial centers of power, their monopoly of the military contracts, and the mergers of their domestic businesses with foreign-oriented businesses.[37] The recent growth of multibillion dollar conglomerate corporations controlling a variety of industries is monopoly capitalism in its most powerful form.

Business receives the support of the government and its military arm to make its foreign investment successful. For the exploitation of foreign resources and peoples requires political and armed power. Thus the military establishment expends 55 percent of the national

---

[36]Mills, C. Wright: *The Causes of World War III.* New York: Ballantine, 1958, p. 63.

[37]Magdoff, Harry: Economic aspects of U. S. imperialism. *Monthly Review,* *18:* 10-43, 1966.

budget (1967), maintains 3.5 million troops at home and abroad and
1.2 million civilian employees, and controls 31 million acres of land.[38]
It is America's largest corporation, in league with many other corporations. In 1968, through the legalized forms of government, it
provided business with $44 billion in defense contracts, only 11 per-
cent of it through formal advertising and competitive bidding.[39]
Twice as much money ($80 billion a year) is spent on defense as on
private investment—a fact that illustrates the contradictions within
capitalism; for in the imperialist domination of lands and peoples,
capitalists have created problems of hunger, slums, inadequate medical
care, inferior education, etc. which spell deepening exploitation at
home and riots in the streets of many cities.

The military establishment exercises increasing ideological control
over business. The leading one hundred defense contractors employ
2,072 retired military officers.[40] The military power extends into major
American universities, where it commands their resources for war research, including research on biological and chemical warfare.[41] Thus
in many cases it is difficult to determine where the military institution of "government" ends and the institution of "private" business
begins. The truth is that under capitalism there can be no genuinely
"social" or "public" institution. All institutions are ultimately controlled by some private group, and the most powerful of these are
the private monopolists. Dominance by a private group means submission by one or more private groups.

Government serves as the facade and justification through which
the military-industrial complex operates. The military establishment
is America's largest corporation—in theory, an agent of the government, but in fact, along with other corporations, the dominant policy-
maker of government. How else are we to explain the undeclared,
undebated, and enormously expensive war in Vietnam—unopposed

---

[38]Friends Committee on National Legislation, *Washington Newsletter,* No. 289
(January, 1968).

[39]Yarmolinsky, Adam: In Wiesner, Jerome B., and Chayes, Abram (Eds.):
*A B M: A Report Prepared for Senator Edward M. Kennedy and the American
Public.* New York, Harper and Row, 1969, p. 149.

[40]*Ibid.*

[41]Hersh, Seymour M.: *Chemical and Biological Warfare: America's Hidden
Arsenal.* New York, Bobbs-Merrill, 1968.

by three presidents, the Congress, and the courts? Politically, the military-industrial complex exercises its authority as an institutionalized organization within the established government; there is a Department of Defense, a National Security Council, and a host of other such agencies. It also exercises influence among Congressmen, most of whom are lawyers or businessmen who have a direct interest in the preservation and expansion of their businesses and capitalism in general.[42] Finally, the military establishment relies on an "invisible government" of the Central Intelligence Agency, the nine agencies comprizing "the intelligence community" (the Federal Bureau of Investigation, etc.), and many other agencies and persons.[43] The decisions and policies of these bodies are made independent of public scrutiny and control. In its efforts to displace liberal or progressive governments and establish reactionary ones, this "invisible government" has been active in China, Taiwan, Iran, Egypt, Costa Rica, Burma, Indonesia, Laos, Vietnam, and Guatemala. In some instances (Iran, Guatemala) it helped to overthrow governments. In the case of Vietnam, by its support of the dictator Diem, it helped to prepare the way for the eventual full-scale war of intervention by United States forces.

Thus American imperialism throughout the globe has opposed many movements working against capitalism and toward socialism. The Truman Doctrine, the Marshall Plan, the military encirclement of the Soviet Union, wars in Korea and Vietnam, anticommunist legislation, etc.—all the weapons of the cold war—represented attempts of American imperialism to secure its sway and to halt the progress of the peoples. But the forces of socialism and national liberation have fought back, as well as the oppressed groups of Blacks and others within the United States. As the last refuge of world imperialism, American imperialism is still strong, as in Latin America,[44] but it has been halted and defeated on many fronts.

A recent study states that "violence has truly become a part of our unacknowledged (or underground) value structure."[45] It refers

[42]Mills, C. Wright: *The Power Elite*, pp. 248-249. See also *U. S. News and World Report, 62* (No. 15): 44, 1967.

[43]Wise, David, and Ross, Thomas B.: *The Invisible Government.*

[44]Gerassi, John: *The Great Fear in Latin America.* New York, Collier-Macmillan, 1965.

[45]Graham, Hugh D., and Gurr, Ted R.: *Violence in America: Historical and*

to discontent among specific groups, like labor, the Blacks, ethnic groups, and opponents of wars. It also acknowledges that "force and violence can be successful techniques of social control and persuasion when they have extensive popular support." But it fails to understand the shifting and persisting patterns of violence in the broad causal context of the economic and social system—a system in which the primary end is personal profit, wealth, and power under capitalism, and in which the sanctioned means to that end is aggressive action that does not stop short of violence. It overlooks the institutionalized, legalized violence of the military-industrial-governmental complex.

In the individual person, violence has its sources in deprived needs and frustrated impulses and in an environment that elicits the expression of those impulses in violent forms. Capitalism in America has been a fertile breeding ground for both of these sources. Its competitiveness, its individualism, its aggressiveness, its planlessness, its irrationality, its institutionalized greed and selfishness, its waste, its vast expenditures on war, have all produced widespread want and deprivation among large numbers. From the period of the early settlements and the frontier to the present-day crowded cities, American capitalism has fostered a social milieu which has allowed rather free expression of the frustration which it engenders. Americans have two kinds of needs: those which are generic to every person—the needs for food, for avoidance of bodily injury and pain, for association with others, for communication, for the creative development of one's powers; and those artificial needs ("wants") induced by the conditions of the society—acquiring material goods, displaying signs of status, dominating others, marketing and selling oneself and others, consuming, hoarding. The pervasive deprivation in American society, touching all persons and groups, is the deprivation of the needs for communication and creativity. This deprivation is part and parcel of the nature of capitalism, which sets man against man in a struggle for wealth and power. The deprivation of the hunger-need, while not so extensive as under European capitalism of the nineteenth cen-

---

Comparative Perspectives. (A Report to the National Commission on the Causes and Prevention of Violence). Washington, D. C., U. S. Government Printing Office, 1969, vol. I, p. 56.

tury, still affects some ten million people; and many millions in addition are malnourished because of lack of information concerning an adequate diet. Hunger affects the unemployed and the partially employed—those who lack the skill and training to acquire steady and adequately paying jobs. Deprivations in the needs for clothing, shelter, protection against injury (rats, violent criminals, police brutality), and protection against disease fall upon those members of the working class who are confined to living in urban ghettos or in town and rural shanties. This material deprivation is the consequence not of scarcity and technological backwardness, but of an inhuman system of production and distribution. Statistics for manufacturing in the United States in 1966 show this. The value of manufacture was $251 billion; the total payrolls of clerical and manual workers was $117; thus the owners got 115 percent of what the workers got.[46] The rate of surplus-value has been rising rapidly over the past fifteen years and has been accelerated by the profits from the Vietnam war. The comfortable and affluent classes—capitalists and well paid wage-earners—do not suffer from material deprivations, but instead measure their lives by the wants generated in them by the system. Through the public media of newspaper, television, and radio they are induced to want more goods and services, more opportunities for "winning," and more money. And they remain unhappy because no amount of affluence can satisfy either their artificial wants or their generic needs.

Since there is in most Americans a deep-seated deprivation and frustration concerning the "spiritual" needs of man, there is a corresponding disposition of aggressiveness in them. A similar disposition develops in groups deprived of the satisfaction of their basic physical needs, as it does in those deprived of the satisfaction of their wants, however artificial these may be.

A fundamental contradiction—a contradiction of capitalism—has lain at the base of American society since its inception. That is the contradiction between its promise and its practice, between the ideology of democracy, with its humanistic ideals, and the antihumanistic system of capitalism. European immigrants to America have viewed it as the land of opportunity where the poorest man might be free and become rich; for them the New World was a New Jerusalem and

<hr>

[46]Perlo: *Op. cit.*, p. 43.

they were the people chosen by God to reap its harvest by dint of conscientious work. But only a few really entered into that promised land of material abundance; for most the promise was only incompletely realized. The reason was that, even in a country as affluent in natural resources and technology as the United States, the relations of production and exchange under capitalism are such that a few own and become rich, and most are owned and remain poor. The rise of a comfortable middle-class in recent decades has not essentially altered this division; and in the last forty years the basic pattern of distribution of income has not changed. Now, as then, 5 percent of Americans earn 20 percent of the nation's income, while the poorest 20 percent earn only 5 percent of the income.[47]

Although the level of living in America in volume of goods and services has been higher than in most countries of the world, Americans have tended to measure themselves by their ancestral promise. This promise included the eighteenth century Lockean revolutionary dream of liberty, equality, and property, or, in the language of the Declaration of Independence, life, liberty, and the pursuit of happiness. The promise included a spiritual component, an aspiration toward human dignity, fulfillment, justice, and brotherhood. As formulated by the Founding Fathers, it only equivocally included the dark-skinned peoples; the Continental Congress, for instance, rejected Jefferson's denunciation of slavery in an early draft of the Declaration of Independence. However, the dream of equality touched all elements of the population—the lower classes more deeply than the upper classes, since they were more oppressed in body and soul. But it was contradicted by the brute facts of a growing capitalism. The result: continuing frustration and frequent outbursts of violence. For the promise of America included also the hope and the insistence that the New Jerusalem would be ushered in not in a thousand years or in a hundred years, but in a lifetime. Americans have believed in the imminent coming of their earthly fulfillment, a reward that would come with hard work. When they did not see that coming, they grew restless, resentful, and angry. And, in an environment in which overt and ruthless action on the environment was the ruling response—a

[47]Gans, Herbert J.: The 'equality' revolution. *The New York Times Magazine,* November 3, 1968, p. 37.

pattern dictated by capitalism—that anger tended to spill over into overt, aggressive action.

The most potent and continuous form of this aggressive action has been the institutionalized warfare of entrepreneurs, big industries, and their legalized instrument, the national government. This began with the raids of the crew of Columbus on the land and the Indians (some of whom he took as prisoners) and continued through the appropriation of the frontier territories, the war on Mexico, the Spanish-American war, the military and economic control of many countries such as Mexico, Cuba, Puerto Rico, Nicaragua, Guam, the Philippines, Hawaii, Alaska, the Virgin Islands, Panama, the Dominican Republic, and the like. The warfare for lands, resources, and markets at home and abroad was not merely an expansionist drive for conquest. It was an inherent and necessary part of a system which set capitalist against capitalist and capitalist against laborer, which produced cut-throat competition, corporations, monopolies, and imperialism, which resulted in the oppression of labor in low wages and inhuman working conditions, widespread violence against unions, powerful antilabor feelings among the populace induced by capitalist ideology, and, as an inherent feature of this oppression of labor, the oppression of the Negro.

The position of the Negro must be seen in the context of this repressive social and economic system which assigns specific places and functions to unskilled, uneducated, impoverished and depoliticized sections of the population and which develops an ideology of discrimination to reinforce its hierarchy of productive relations and social status. The force and violence exercised against the Negro in the living conditions of the ghetto, schools, jobs, the armed services, etc. must be seen as one feature of a whole social system of institutionalized force and violence.

The economic aspirations that the white immigrants to America brought with them in the seventeenth and eighteenth centuries were essentially of two kinds: the postfeudal ideal of the small, independent, self-sufficient landowner, and the ideal of the merchant and small manufacturer. Up until the Revolution, most Americans were English colonists and thus derived their economic goals from the agricultural and commercial traditions of the mother country. The ecology of the new continent fostered these aspirations, which shared in the principle of "free enterprize" and which eventually produced revolt against the mercantilist restrictions of the mother country.

Capitalism, in the form of well developed manufacturing, wage labor, savings, credit, investments, etc. did not emerge until after the Revolution. Before that small farming, lumbering, and maritime activities dominated in New England, small and large farming and small-scale manufacturing in the middle colonies, and farms and large plantations in the South. Thus the South, with its rapidly growing plantation system, especially in cotton, was the major source of exploited labor. After the War of 1812 and the creation of protective tariffs, factories began to flourish in New England and New York; and workers, forced to labor twelve to fourteen hours daily for five dollars a week, formed unions and supported the Jacksonian revolt against the national bank.[48] Not until after the Civil War, however, with advent of big industries and the great acceleration of immigrants (from 1870 to 1910 twelve million came) did the class struggle develop to the level that it had attained in Europe. Still later the emancipated Negroes began to pour into the cheap labor market and to assume their position as "free" laborers at the low end of the social scale that they have occupied ever since. Ideology played an important role in assigning them this position.

American society was created in an open, undeveloped, unstructured wilderness by diverse immigrant groups with diverse economic, political, social, and religious traditions. The culture was not something given and inherited; it had to be created *de novo*. It is true that the predominating numbers of English settlers up to the Revolution lent a coherence to the culture, and that after that Americans were inspired by the ideal of economic and poltical freedom. But the situation in the land of diversity and opportunity generated at the same time insecurity in the immigrants as to their social identification. This insecurity did not afflict the settlers of the prosperous middle colonies in the middle of the eighteenth century, as Crèvecoeur's testimony shows. But as industrial capitalism expanded in the nineteenth century, the insecurity implicit in the life of the wage earner deepened and developed most acutely during the periodic depressions and in-

---

[48]Nevins and Commager: *Op. cit.,* pp. 173-174.

dustrial warfare that marked the career of capitalism. The insecurity was not confined to industrial workers; it affected all who felt the threat of losing jobs, savings, property, or social status. To cope with their insecurity and maintain some sense of stable identity in the midst of economic and social uncertainties, many men adopted an ideology of super-patriotism. As immigrants or offspring of immigrants, they were disposed to overidentify with Americanism; the system of capitalism intensified this overidentification. This aggressive patriotism required its "enemy" at home and abroad, its "subversion" and "treason," its Alien and Sedition Laws of 1798 against critics of government, its use of conspiracy laws in the 1830's against striking labor, its Know Nothing Party of midcentury against Irish Catholics, the Ku Klux Klan against the Negroes, and the Palmers and Hoovers and Mc-Carthys and Birchites against the communists.

This authoritarian ideology—rigid, extropunitive, dichotomous, moralistic, ambivalent toward authority, institution-oriented, resistant to ambiguity and instability, dependent on "fate," anxiety-ridden, projective, scapegoating[49]—was strengthened by a Puritan sense of mission, a conviction of being the chosen nation with a "manifest destiny," a strong feeling of distance from Europe and of freedom from equals and competitors, a low level of tolerance among the moralistic immigrants competing for jobs and political power, the pluralism and anarchic freedom of many groups, the economic struggles of owners and working classes, and the long tradition of violence and defiance of law in American life. The ideal of equality in the setting of a rampant capitalism has motivated most men to become authorities in their own right at the expense of others; it has produced a common social type, the authoritarian personality, characterized by "violence, anarchic impulses, and chaotic destructiveness in the unconscious sphere."[50]

Coming to the United States, many European immigrants felt freed from the Old World constraints of economic mercantilism, political monarchy, established religion, social classes, intellectual aristocracy, esthetic elitism, and legal order. In time Americans created their own

---

[49]Adorno, T. W., Frenkel-Brunswik, E., Levinson, D. J., and Sanford, R. N.: *The Authoritarian Personality*. New York, Harper, 1950.

[50]*Ibid.*, p. 675.

institutions for these various domains. But many shared the conviction that they were freed once and for all from the heavy hand of the European ruling group; that governments and laws exist to serve men and continue through the consent of men; and that therefore at any moment men might legitimately take into their own hands the law. Today, when the military-industrial-political complex has taken power, an increasing number of people are asking how this authoritarian power over the people can be broken.

Thus three levels of violence can be distinguished in the history of American society. The first is the legitimatized violence built into the structure of industry and government—the violence daily practiced in the exploitation of labor in urban industry and on southern plantations, the employment of the police power to protect the interest and property of the ruling classes, and the use of violence in pursuing a policy of imperialism toward other countries.

The second is the violence exercised by groups more or less independently of class lines. In the face of change or threat of change in their established values, power, and status, certain groups, often prosperity-based, have given vent to strong and irrational feelings of hostility against minorities—ethnic groups, religions, atheists, socialists, communists, intellectuals, big government, big-city finance, the welfare state, the labor movement, the income tax. Made anxious and insecure in their position by the uncertainties of the social and economic system which they patriotically defended, such groups feared the loss of status which they had achieved or to which they aspired. They aimed their frustration and suppressed hostility against scapegoats both at home and abroad.[51] These people derived from varied strata in the population—filio-pietistic groups seeking to recover a fading claim to status, the new immigrants in search of status, the newly rich (the millionaires, the small independent businessmen, the storekeepers, the small manufacturers), and the workers low in socioeconomic status, education, and success.[52] The same system which generated discontent in such groups also protected itself by directing that discontent away from its real source and toward innocent but

[51]Lipset, Seymour Martin: The sources of the 'radical right.' In Bell, Daniel (Ed.): *The Radical Right.*
[52]*Ibid.*, pp. 336-350.

vulnerable groups. The reasons why American workers have never formed a massive, militant, Marxist party are too complex to recount here; we have dealt with them elsewhere.[53]

The third kind of violence has come from the members of the working classes engaged in a struggle for existence and the improvement of their existence. The violence of the black slaves and the industrial workers has at times been considerable.[54] But over-all it has been infinitesimal compared to the violence expended by the other groups in defense of the ruling order. Also, the legitimatized violence of the ruling groups, along with the coopted violence of the middle and lower classes in support of that violence, is designed to maintain an exploitive system; whereas the violence of the Blacks and the workers has been an attempt to resist, reform, or displace it with a humanized economy and society. When we speak of "violence," it is important to discriminate between these two types. The latter can be justified if, compared with other alternatives, it most effectively brings about the human values desiderated. The former type of violence can never be justified.

Racism as an attitude and idea is a form of mental violence. It is more than prejudice, which has been defined as "thinking ill of others without sufficient warrant."[55] It is something more than the assumption of inherent racial superiority of one race and the inferiority of another race. It is a conviction in the desired or achieved domination of the allegedly superior race over the allegedly inferior race. And it it often accompanied by action to implement that conviction. We cannot suppose that the southern plantation owner sat in the shade of his veranda, sipped mint julep, and merely contemplated the notion of white superiority and black inferiority. On the contrary, what concerned him was the *practice* of making profits off the sweat and blood of his Negro slaves. Thus those who seriously hold to racist ideas are persons filled with hatred for the "inferior" race. Hatred is an emo-

---

[53]Parsons, Howard L.: The influence of Marx's thought in the United States. *Praxis, 3*: 264-275, 1967.

[54]Aptheker, Herbert: *American Negro Slave Revolts.* New York, International, 1963. Foner, Philip S.: *History of the Labor Movement in the United States.* New York, International, 1947.

[55]Allport, Gordon W.: *The Nature of Prejudice.* Garden City, Doubleday, 1954, p. 7.

tion that desires to bring injury and destruction to the hated object. A racist is bent on oppression and destruction of members of the race which he hates. The long-range upshot of racism is genocide, if the opportunity presents itself. The presence of this destructive impulse in racists has been documented by studies in the structure of their personality type.[56]

Before the slave trade began, Europeans supposed no natural inferiority in the African Negro.[57] But the great growth of the slave trade, slave owning, slave breeding, and slave labor required a myth to sanction the dehumanizing of the Negro. That myth therefore dehumanized the Negro, so that practice might seem "right." It is easy to understand why slave traders and slave owners would adopt such a myth. But why would most white Americans develop prejudice against the Negro? We have already indicated the answer: the deprivation of men in their bodily and psychic needs (such as their needs for creativity and cooperation) generates frustration and a disposition to hatred, aggressiveness, intolerance, and discrimination. Such deprivation arises in a society marked by competitiveness for material goods and psychic rewards, and by class antagonism. Such a society, in short, creates persons disposed to intolerance and discrimination. Once that disposition is created, it will find outlet in the sanctioned attitudes and ideas of the society. If the ruling groups propagate the belief that the Negro is inferior, frustrated people will tend to adopt and to act upon that prejudice. Studies in social distance indicate that most Americans, including members of ethnic minorities, believe in a similar pattern of separation between ethnic groups, with the Hindus, Turks, and Negroes having the greatest social distance.[58] Thus American society generates a pecking order defined in part along "racial" lines; and deprived people who are compelled to peck tend to peck as social roles and institutions indicate.

For two and one-half centuries prior to the Civil War, the Negro, stripped of his humanity and property, was at the bottom of the pecking order. A century later he is still there. The primary cause for this is not his color or the prejudice that interprets color as a sign

[56]Adorno, et al.: *Op. cit.*
[57]Davidson: *Op. cit.*, p. 5.
[58]Allport: *Op. cit.*, p. 37.

of inferiority. The primary cause is the system of production and the roles and institutions generated by it. The productive system of capitalism requires that some persons fill the role of unskilled, poorly paid workers in industry and agriculture, that some fill the role of living in poor housing, attending inferior schools, etc. Social habit and attitude dictate that the Negroes fill such roles. Such roles are reinforced by a conservative and authoritarian temper in many members of the society, who respond to Negro discontent with such roles by calling for "law and order."

In American history the fullest weight of oppression and prejudice has consistently fallen on the Negro. The reasons for this, as we have tried to show, were not accidental. The dynamics of developing capitalism required in its early stages the plunder of the African continent, and later, in the advanced stages of mercantilism and colonialism, it required slave-trade and the mass employment of slave labor on large plantations, just as it required armies of industrial workers in the cities. Still later, and to this day, the economic system required cheap and menial labor in both North and South (despite the vaunted advances in technology) as well as willing cannon fodder for its racist wars.

The prejudice against Negroes will not be fully lifted until the material oppression that demands the prejudice is lifted. The major victims of class war will not be saved from war until the class war itself is wiped out. As Marx said, "Labor cannot emancipate itself in the white skin where in the black it is branded."[59] This does not mean that the freeing of men from oppression must be solely an economic or political process. What men do on the job and in political campaigns is determined by their beliefs, and their actions in turn determine their beliefs. Efforts to improve the economic position of the Negro are important but are not enough. For a living or even an affluent wage for the Negro in the present system would still leave him oppressed by uncreative and alienated work in a manipulated culture. Economic change must move on to strike at the roots of the essential oppression of all workers in the society. An ideology of class struggle and of humanistic hope must inspire economic and political action. At the same time, an equalitarian ideology alone is insufficient.

---

[59]Marx, Karl: *Capital,* vol. I, p. 301.

Without struggle toward a radical humanization of the whole system, ideology will fall short and will leave its adherents disillusioned. At best it will provide only token gains, as the Negroes discovered when they learned that the gains to which they were recently guided by the liberals, the social scientists, and the churches—the legal gains in voting, use of public facilities, and education—were not far-reaching. Radical thought and radical action must go hand in hand and develop each other.

At this point the futility of the ideal of "integration" reveals itself, and some Negroes have been among the first to realize that futility. For it means that instead of being a slave or an outcaste in the social system the Negro is urged to become a wage earner who sells his labor or a capitalist who buys and sells laborers and who makes money off foreign wars waged aganst colored peoples. He is urged to "improve" himself at institutions of "higher" education and to "integrate" his energies and efforts—with what? With a white, Christian, capitalist system that requires exploitation, racism, and war to keep it going. Under integration the Negro would exchange his old identity of poor-oppressed for comfortable-oppressed. In joining a "people's capitalism" he would become a "white Negro" and an exploitive "free man."

In the past American Negroes have sought various ways in which to integrate themselves into this system. The first was the adoption of its religion, Christianity. But since Christianity was fixed on a white god of its idolatry, offering sanction for a social order governed by whites, this adoption produced inner conflict and a "guilt complex" in Negroes.[60]

Another way was to seek to change color as the leopard his spots, so escaping the black "curse of Cain" by which the white man might identify him and keep him in his appointed place. Up until recently the business of whitening skin and straightening hair was a multi-million dollar business[61]—proving that capitalism will make a profit from Negroes coming or going. Still, technology is limited. And even a light-skinned person born and miseducated in the ghetto or southern

---

[60]Bastide: *Op cit.*, p. 324.

[61]Lincoln, C. Eric: Color and group identity in the United States. *Daedalus*, 96: 532, 1967.

shanty town has difficulty escaping to join the twenty-eight million white persons who have African ancestry.[62]

A third way is what is now called "black capitalism." This is similar to Jewish collaboration with the Nazis. The character of such collaboration is nakedly revealed when Negro soldiers are trained to kill colored soldiers in Vietnam and in other colonial wars. Negroes exploiting other Negroes in industry and business are integrated into a system which disintegrates their colored brothers.

Integration of the Black into the economic and social system as an organization man who functions smoothly as worker or white-collar employee is also futile as a final solution. Negroes must have education and jobs, surely. But must they like whites have these at the expense of other men, races, and societies? To have a job in a capitalist society is to be less than a man; it is but a step toward helping oneself and others transform the society into an association in which each can flourish freely and creatively, without depriving or oppressing anyone on earth.

As a counterstrategy in reaction against integration, some Blacks, e.g., the Black Muslims, seeking to avoid destruction of their identity, have proposed strict separation from white society. This approach falsely identifies white racism as the cause of oppression. Racism is the result, capitalism is the cause. Separation of a community in a highly developed capitalist society means either a greatly restricted way of life, as with the Amish or Hutterites, or eventual reassimilation. But twenty-two million Negroes cannot separate themselves from white society; they are too interwoven into its structure.

In seeking integration or separation, Blacks have tried to recover a sense of personal identity destroyed by capitalism. The slave owner maintained the slave as he would maintain a tool or machine: in order to keep his instrument in working order. But it was equally necessary for him to obliterate the personality of the slave, as it was necessary for the Turks to castrate their Negro administrative functionaries. For the sake of the American plantation system, the Negro had to reproduce his body, but could not use his mind; for Turkish rule, the Negro could not produce a rival family strain, but was required

---

[62]*Ibid.*, p. 540.

to administer. Still, the personality of the American slave was not
entirely destroyed—a fact that is testimony to his courage and tenacity. Nonetheless slavery perpetrated a kind of genocide upon the
Negro people. Upon emancipation of the slaves Congress appropriated
$1,000,000 to pay the slavemasters for their loss in property. But
could the country recompense the more than a million captured Africans[63] for the theft of their humanity? And if such a theft can never
be repaid, how can capitalism ever be justified?

Illiterate, ignorant, and inexperienced in the affairs of modern civilization at the time of emancipation, most American slaves had to
learn how to become farmers, wage earners, and citizens. The marvel
is that in one hundred years, despite their degradation and segregation, they have achieved so much. For we must ask ourselves how it
is possible for a whole people cast into servitude for 350 years to acquire pride and honor. As late as 1946 three out of five Negroes felt
that black is the worst color to be.[64] Shame, guilt, and self-hatred in
the American Blacks are all forms of a self-destructiveness generated
by a racist and warring society. This self-destructiveness is the internalized form of the destructiveness visited upon the Blacks by the
capitalist society for 350 years. A people colonized for so long will
tend to look upon themselves through the eyes of the powerful colonizer as a captive and demeaned people—mere bodies and instruments,
as Aristotle said, fit only for taking orders from a minded, master
class. The Blacks have been the sacrificial lambs of this society—hence
the identification of some of them with the wandering Jews and the
crucified Christ. They have been the waste and garbage of the
industrial system, thrown into that dump of American cities, the
ghetto—hence the identification of some with shiftlessness, delinquency,
crime, and other forms of the "no good" image. They have been
marked in both myth and social fact as "hewers of wood and drawers
of water," and many have accepted that role. To be a man is to
see and be seen, to speak and be spoken to, to work and to be appreciated, to love and to be loved. But the Black became the invisible
man, the inaudible man, the first-to-be-fired and last-to-be-hired man,
the you-Black-stand-back man.

---

[63]Wiedner: *Op. cit.,* p. 67.
[64]Gergen: *Op. cit.,* p. 400.

However, this is only half the story, and in the long run it will be much the lesser half. For in the midst of this massive denial of their identities, the Blacks as a group have risen from the ashes of their nothingness to affirm their humanity. They have never given in to indignity, enslavement, torture, and death. In their own ways they have struggled against their annihilation as individuals and as a race. In such suffering and struggle, they have become strong, and have given to our society courageous, wise, and compassionate people. From Nat Turner to Martin Luther King, Jr., from the slave guerrillas[65] to the best of the Black Panthers, from Frederick Douglass to W. E. B. Du Bois, from Harriet Tubman to the black children who in recent years have braved injury and vile insult to attend integrated schools—millions of Blacks have transformed their imposed weakness into honor and strength, and have wrought out of hurt and disadvantage their own forms of heroism. If it is possible for the Blacks to emerge from *absolute* debasement—being bought and sold as sheer chattels in the marketplace—and still maintain a sense of their humanity and indeed show many whites what it means to struggle for one's humanity—then one can believe that our whole people in America might one day unite to liberate themselves from the bondage of capitalism.

The Judaeo-Christian tradition has taught that the sufferers of history are destined to redeem it. Marx had this insight too. But he saw that the redeemers must be a massive economic class, the industrial workers. Such a proletariat Marx described as "a class with *radical chains*" with "*wrong generally* . . . perpetrated against it . . . which can invoke no *historical* but only its *human* title."[66] Like every oppressed class, the Blacks are called to rectify the wrong-doing of their oppressors. Like the modern proletariat, to whom they overwhelmingly belong, they are called to identify their cause with the cause of *all* oppressed groups. The rise of the protest of Negroes in recent years against their conditions of life—restrictions in the use of public facilities and the ballot, hunger, bad housing, the war, etc.—

[65]Aptheker, Herbert: *To Be Free: Studies in American Negro History*. New York, International, 1948.

[66]Marx, Karl: Contribution to the critique of Hegel's philosophy of right. Introduction, p. 56.

show that the Blacks belong to the more radical section of the population. Because along with other poor workers, they constitute the most oppressed in an oppressive system, they belong to the vanguard of those being forged by the system itself to transform that system. That revolutionary transformation cannot occur except as in emancipating itself the Blacks join with all workers in a struggle for the emancipation of all groups.

The Negro must find his true identity, as all men must, in constructing with his fellow man an order of living that permits no man to own and use another, that places under the power and control of all men the resources of the earth and of human industry. In such an order each man will achieve his unique individual identity as a creator with his fellow creatures. True human identity does not depend on accidental or artificial features—skin color, membership in a class, ethnic and religious affiliation, occupation, income, spending, consumption, education, private property—which are the identifying marks of a person "with class" (status) in the United States. Identity is a function of a man's genuine human powers and achievements. Such identity cannot be created in a dog-eat-dog society where each man is looking out for number one. It is instead the creation of a society in which people create and share their material abundance and in which their day-to-day habits exemplify the rule, "All for each and each for all."[67]

Talcott Parsons has argued that "successful Negro inclusion" in American society "will put the seal on the Marxian error in diagnosing American society," presenting "a true alternative to the Communist pattern on a world-wide basis, one which is not bound to the stereotype of 'capitalism.' "[68] He fails to grasp or even discuss the American economy and its class character, pointing to heavy immigration and upward mobility as preventives of crystallized class divisions. He appeals to the moral and religious factors in the Negro's struggle for citizenship (important but secondary). He interprets legal rights

[67]Lenin, V. I.: *Collected Works.* Moscow, Progress Publishers, 1966. vol. 31, p. 124.

[68]Parsons, Talcott: Full citizenship for the Negro American? A sociological problem. *Daedalus, 94:* 1049, 1965.

as coming closest to the implementation of democratic values.[69] He thus fails to see that the economic structure of monopoly capitalism sets the determining base and motif for all other institutions, roles, and values. If he were a Negro who had suffered, he would not place so much faith in the law, morality, and politics of the system; he would be asking why he lacks money and the opportunities to get it. Talcott Parsons thus harbors the liberal illusion that if capitalism is not examined and not tampered with, "law and order" and "peaceful change" can bring about equality for the Negroes. But the point is that such equality is impossible under capitalism, which puts profit and exploitation before equality. Equality is possible only where its base is eradicated; and that means socialism. But with the timidity and ambivalence of the liberal, Parsons does not want to make a clean break with capitalism. He simply wants to disown its "stereotype." But it is clear that he hates communism more than he hates capitalism. He wants an "alternative" to communism, but he also wants equality for the Negro! Where does that leave him? With capitalism— and without equality.

After he had visited the United States in 1888, Engels several times commented on the bourgeois prejudices and habits of Americans, "a people stubbornly holding on to inherited petty-bourgeois customs."[70] At that time one could attribute this, as Engels did, to a certain immaturity in the failure of an "awkward" people to emancipate itself from a European heritage. Because of the absence of a long self-conscious proletarian tradition, the relatively late development of industrialism, the changing and sometimes relatively faint class lines, and the comparative prosperity of workers, it was easy for many workers to remain under the spell of bourgeois tastes and values. Furthermore, in a society of widespread opportunity, men strove upward. The bourgeois mentality in capitalists or workers is insecure and seeks clues in the behavior of the ruling class as to how to behave.[71] Thus status became associated with one's distance from the

---

[69]*Ibid.*, p. 1019.

[70]Marx, Karl, and Engels, Frederick: *Letters to Americans 1848-1895*, p. 292.

[71]Veblen, Thorstein: *The Theory of the Leisure Class*. New York, Macmillan, 1899.

colored peoples, as these were confronted in the American experience:
the native "redskins," the "niggers" and "chinks" imported as cheap
labor, the "spicks" of Yankee colonial adventure in Latin America,
and the "gooks" encountered in imperialist wars in Korea and Vietnam. The bourgeois backgrounds and dispositions of many Americans
have provided a fertile ground in which a bourgeois ideology might
flourish. And while that ideology was infused with the equalitarian
dream of the Enlightenment, it was also flawed by the philosophy of
capitalism with which it was allied. That was a philosophy that implicitly called for some men to work, some to be exploited, some to
suffer. In this situation racism as a doctrine developed as part of an
ideology to which the ruling groups had continued recourse. And it
was tacitly or openly taken up by those who viewed themselves, in the
present or in the future, as members of the bourgeoisie rather than as
members of the working and oppressed class.

The ultimate task must be to replace the inhumanism of capitalism
with the humanism of socialism. But an important and necessary step
in that direction is to convince many Americans, black and white,
comfortable and poor, that they are members of an oppressed and
working class; that class struggle is the road of their emancipation and
their rule; and that this rule can then become the first stage in a truly
human society. The struggle against racism has been courageously
carried forward by colonized peoples since the beginning of early
capitalist racism in the fifteenth century. In the last two decades the
struggle has produced movements of national liberation throughout
Africa, Asia, and Latin America, as well as the movements for black
liberation in the United States. Such movements are a stage in a
deeper struggle, the struggle against capitalist oppression. They will
come to fulfillment as they are guided by the understanding that
racism along with war is a product of capitalism, and that until
capitalism is abolished no man, black or white or red or brown, can
be free and fulfilled.

XI

PHILOSOPHY AND THE NEW LEFT

In 1844 Marx wrote: "As philosophy finds its *material* weapon in the proletariat, so the proletariat finds its *spiritual* weapon in philosophy." [1] He was describing the conditions necessary for "the emancipation of the *Germans* into *men*," through revolutionary activity.

Marx's statement, in its general form, holds true for us in the United States today. Significant social change comes about when the needs and demands of large numbers of people find their formulation and guidance in ideas and a comprehensive system of ideas or ideology that gives significance to human living. Without the ideas, the demands are blind and disorganized. Without the demands, the ideas are empty. For each to attain its ends, theory and practice must support and advance one another.

In the United States today, however, we have neither the material nor the spiritual conditions requisite for the kind of revolutionary social change Marx had in mind for Germany in 1844. We do not have an industrial proletariat in the nineteenth century European sense. Close to half (44 percent in 1962) of our employed people are white-collar workers—professional and technical workers, managers, officials, proprietors, clerical workers, sales workers. Only 35.8 percent are blue-collar workers,[2] and the percentage every year is declining, hastened by automation. Besides, the value-orientation of a large part of the blue-collar workers is middle-class. However, the exploitation of the workers and the need for social change have not disappeared; they have only changed in character. By contrast, in the 1930's the great mass of industrial workers were either openly exploited in their jobs or

---

[1] Marx, Karl: Contribution to the critique of Hegel's philosophy of right, p. 57.

[2] United States Department of Labor, Bureau of Labor Statistics. Cited in *Britannica Book of the Year 1964. Chicago,* Encyclopedia Britannica, 1964, pp. 343-344.

unemployed. They fought back. The number of strikes in that period far exceeded the number for any other group in any other comparable period. But because of relative affluence, bureaucratic opportunism, and the widespread absence of labor education and of a philosophy of labor, the lure of middle-class ideals and a middle-class philosophy has captured the minds of many blue-collar workers. The "spiritual weapon" of philosophy—a revolutionary philosophy—has yet to be grasped by the workers, be they blue-collar or white-collar.

Being a proletarian, like being a revolutionary, is not only a state of body; it is also a state of mind, wherein one feels with one's whole body his and others' exploitation and follows the lead of certain ideas in order to overcome that exploitation. In the present essay I shall concentrate on the status and influence of ideas—and, in particular, systems of ideas, or philosophies—in American life, not forgetting that they have their basic origins and effects in material conditions where people live and work and where their feelings and dispositions are shaped. Analysis of material conditions, trends, and prospects is necessary; but analysis of philosophical outlooks is also important. And the latter has tended to be overlooked, even by progressives, in our unphilosophical culture.

A man's philosophy consists of his basic beliefs. Such are his beliefs about human nature and its possibilities, about society and history and their nature and significance, about the world of nature and man's relation to it, about values and what man ought to do about them and how, about methods and standards of knowing men, the world, and values. These beliefs are basic in the sense that other beliefs flow from them. If, for example, I believe with some conviction that man is good or can make progress toward good, I will tend to believe that I and American society can be improved. Such beliefs also are basic determinants of action. Believing, for example, in the possibility of human progress, I will tend to act to secure it, in myself and in others. Belief is not merely cortical excitation; it is disposition of the body to act, and a basic belief is a basic disposition, a pervasive and habitual attitude inclined to go over into action. When we understand such habitual attitudes of a person—i.e., his living philosophy—we understand his character, and we can predict what he is likely to do.

What then are the major philosophies of the American people?

It is difficult to answer this question by considering the formal teaching of philosophy in institutions of learning. Unlike the practice in Europe, philosophy is not taught in high schools. A little more than 3 percent of the population (1968) attend colleges and universities full-time and of those approximately half do not finish.[3] For those who do finish, philosophy as a formal course is not in most cases required, and so is not studied. In those rare cases where it is studied, what is taught? Usually a bagatelle of ontology, epistemology, axiology, and various schools of philosophy—analysis, Thomism, existentialism, phenomenology, etc. For most students, such philosophy courses at best titillate; they do not affect and change character. But generally speaking the study of philosophy in higher education has this significance: it is pluralistic, and it is superficial.

The reasons are not far to seek. The dominant interests of the American people are very immediate, practical, private, hedonistic, and materialistic ones, not long-range, theoretical, and spiritual. Repeatedly, on the Allport-Vernon-Lindzey value inventory, college youth, chiefly middle-class, revealed their interests as being mainly economic, social, and political, in the broad senses of these terms. Religious, scientific, and esthetic interests were secondary. While these interests have shifted among many in the past fifteen years, probably a large majority of college youth, chiefly middle-class, still are dominated by values of self-centeredness, conventionality, intolerance of diversity, religion, loyalty to government, and vocationalism.[4] (The "revolution" in the values of youth applies to a minority—though a significant minority—of students.) These youths reflect the values they have unconsciously learned from their parents, peers, and cultural patterns generally. And that is a culture that puts high value on the tangible goods of this life, both durable and nondurable: food, apparel, houses, fuel, furniture, household machines, electricity, radios, television sets, and automobiles are valued not only because they yield certain direct values—bodily comfort, relaxation, stimulating sensations, etc.—but because they carry status value. "The one constant feature of the social

---

[3]Summerskill, John: Dropouts from colleges. In Sanford, Nevitt (Ed.): *The American College*. New York, John Wiley, 1962, p. 627.

[4]Jacob, Philip E.: *Changing Values in College*. New York, Harper, 1957. For a study of recent trends among college youth, see Jencks, Christopher, and Riesman, David: *The Academic Revolution*. Garden City, Doubleday, 1968.

landscape," wrote Harold Laski of the United States, "is the virtually universal passion for physical prosperity." [5] In addition, people value easy social relations. They value power in groups and the manipulation of power. Thus we may confirm with our own unquantified observations the results of careful studies: economic, social, and political (power) value lie at the base of the philosophy of most Americans.

At this point, however, we should make a distinction. We have been talking about the actual values of Americans, the values they live by from day to day. Charles Morris has studied the ideal or "conceived" values of Americans, chiefly college students, and has discovered that the preponderantly preferred way to live, among thirteen choices, is one of dynamic integration of diversity:

> We should at various times and in various ways accept something from all other paths of life, but give no one our exclusive allegiance. At one moment one of them is the more appropriate; at another moment another is the most appropriate. Life should contain enjoyment and action and contemplation in about equal amounts. When either is carried to extremes we lose something important for our life. So we must cultivate flexibility, admit diversity in ourselves, accept the tension which this diversity produces, find a place for detachment in the midst of enjoyment and activity. The goal of life is found in the dynamic integration of enjoyment, action, and contemplation, and so in the dynamic interaction of the various paths of life. One should use all of them in building a life, and no one alone. [6]

It is likely that this idealized way of life masks many differences among individuals. But, in a significant way, it does reflect the diversity of values open to the person of the middle class, while at the same time it points in the direction of a desired unity which is conspicuously absent in our culture at large and in most individuals. This ideal, which contains within it a tension between particular values and the unity of values, in fact amplifies the tension in the real world between existential interests and men's longing for unity of personality and society. It amplifies the excessive pluralism of our culture and its deficient purpose, or, in other words, the real, material interests at work, with their imaginary projection into the future, and the lack of a spiritual,

[5]Laski, Harold: *The American Democracy*. New York, Viking, 1948, p. 13.
[6]Morris, Charles: *Varieties of Human Value,* p. 17.

unifying force that might harmonize them. It expresses the diversity as well as the alienation of our society and the longing to overcome them.

Although many Americans are not so sophisticated as these students, it would be a mistake to say that the average American has no philosophy. He does have a philosophy, which orders things with regard to their relative material value; which pictures others as ambiguously selfish and friendly; which views the world of nature as a commodity, i.e., as something to be used and enjoyed; and which holds to the pragmatic method of knowing, i.e., which holds that things are known insofar as our ideas of them enable us to use them for our purposes.

The average American has a philosophy; he is just not philosophical, i.e., he does not consciously and deliberately philosophize. In short, he does not think about the philosophy he holds, and does not want to do so. So he is likely to dismiss all philosophical claims or demands that he philosophize, as "abstract" and "impractical," as all the while he clings to his unexpressed philosophy of immediate materialism and hedonism. To *examine* one's own philosophy—to analyze it, to evaluate it critically, to try to change and improve it—that would be considered an encroachment on the privacy of the person and a futile exercise. It would be an intellectual activity that is not thought to be needed or valued. The average American is opposed to most forms of intellectual activity, including philosophy, even when the philosophy that is the subject of inquiry is his own.

Anti-intellectualism is not opposition to the use of the intellect, in oneself or others. It is the refusal to use one's intellect, or to allow others to use their intellects, in a consistent, critical, and free way on all basic subjects. It is the rejection of the critical, creative intellect in principle, a rejection of it as a reliable method for dealing with the problems of human life and providing a comprehensive guide. *It is the refusal of radical thought.* It is the habit of resisting consideration of important questions—what to live for, how to relate oneself to others, how to organize society, what reality is, what illusion is, how we come to know and change reality, and so on. In such important questions, the anti-intellectual is fearful of inquiry. He wishes to cling emotionally to traditional habits of thought. He is defensive against those who question such habits. His emotional security and sense of personal well-being and purpose are derived from his identification with such traditional habits. He is threatened by change, conflict, diversity, complexity, ambiguity, tension. He is often an authoritarian personality.

What are the causes of anti-intellectualism in the United States today?

One is the historical habit of pursuing certain values derived from the Protestant-capitalist ethic and way of life. For two hundred years in this country, the good life has been identified with keeping busy and improving the shining hour. An idle mind was the devil's workshop; one's calling in life was not to think but to do. Pragmatism was the explicit, culminating philosophical expression of this view; it identified thinking with doing, meaning with actions, and truth with fulfilled expectations. The fact that the culture has been shifting from orientation to work to orientation toward pleasure has not altered this anti-intellectualism. In some ways it has been reinforced. For, in reaction against the restraints and disciplines and postponed gratifications of past generations, recent generations have tended to seek out their pleasures immediately and uncalculatingly. Consider today the impulsive high school dropout, the early marriage, the free spending, the imprudently chosen career, the paucity of planning in both private and public life.

Another set of causes may be found in the dynamics of ego-identity, in the context of parent-child and man-woman relations, and in the relations of the adult to others and his workaday and social world.

Erik H. Erikson has given us a picture of the type of ego which is commonly produced in our culture and which has now assumed power in many places. He

> remains ready to expect from some enemy, force, or event in the outer world that which, in fact, endangers him from within: from his own angry drives, from his own sense of smallness, and from his own split inner world. Thus he is always irrationally ready to fear invasion by vast and vague forces which are other than himself; strangling encirclements by everything that is not safely clarified as allied; and devastating loss of face before all surrounding mocking audiences.[7]

Many in the administration of the United States government today exemplify such an authoritarian character structure: rigid, stereo-

---

[7]Erikson, Erik H.: *Childhood and Society*, p. 362.

typed, authority-oriented; resistant to new ideas; opposed to controversy, uncertainty, and discussion; ethnocentric; oriented to rule and law; politically and economically conservative; intolerant of ambiguity; blaming others; resistant to introspection and reflection; inclined to view difficulties as extropunitive; and so on. In the United States government today this defensive fearful identity expresses itself with colossal and ruthless power; it is geared into a multibillion dollar military-industrial machine. This institutionalized power begets and requires such power-oriented personalities. And it enjoys the support, or thrives on the indifference, of millions of passive, obedient persons who are alienated from their society and government and from their own basic human dispositions. It grows out of an economic system that requires imperialist expansion and colonial exploitation.

How are these forms of human self-alienation—authoritarianism and passivity—possible on such a wide scale? The fact is that many Americans would be better off materially, and happier and more creative spiritually, if the United States would forsake colonial wars and if class antagonisms were retired from history altogether. But most Americans do not understand this. They are ruled by the ruling ideas of the ruling class—ideas which saturate press, radio, television, schools, and all other major media of communication. And one of these ideas, reinforced by a still lingering McCarthyism and now the administration, is the anti-intellectual notion that it is unpatriotic to dissent. Deeper than this is the fact that a relatively small group holds and exercises the economic and political power, while most are alienated from it—in short, the fact of capitalism. Some minority groups, like the Blacks, are beginning to realize that they do not have such power and are rebelling. Others, mainly those of the white middle stratum, because they live in material comfort, live under the illusion that they have power.

Erikson has described one type of ego-identity common to this group. Although it is not the only middle stratum type, it is common and significant. Such a person is a teen-age boy, Angle-Saxon, Protestant, shy but satisfied with himself, active in sports, sexually dormant, restricted in ego expression. His mother is a typical "Mom"—dominant at home and in the moral life of her family, puritanical in sensual and sexual matters, but not overprotective. As a result many of the boy's feelings are isolated and undeveloped. The bonds that define privileges and obligations at nursery age, according to Erikson, have been greatly weakened; thus autonomy has been impaired. He has learned that functioning like a machine is a virtue. His father is a secondary figure who is not a rival and who later may become a close friend. The main political trait he knows is fairness; his dignity has never been affronted. There is no autocracy (except in Mom) in the family, and a democracy of compromise between the various interests of individuals prevails. He is not an individualist—he has nothing to rebel against and there is no individualist on his horizon by whom to model himself. He is anti-intellectual. Consequently, when he meets real bosses in business and political life, he does not recognize them; "he is too immediately occupied with being efficient and being decent." These mechanized, disguised autocrats of the world expect him to conform and function like a machine, and he does not have the autonomy to resist.[8]

But this account is only a partial one. It should be added that our young man's naivete and illusions about the world (the workers and the Blacks of the United States, Europe, the socialist world, the national liberation movements, colonialism, Asia, Africa, Latin America) are a function of his place in the middle economic stratum, his segregated living conditions, the limited horizons of his high school instruction, and the ideas he gets from press, radio, television, and movies. His mother suffers the result of similar physical and spiritual segregation: cut off from a position of equal functioning alongside men in society, she spends her frustrated energies in an ambivalent neo-Confucian loyalty to her home and family. Captive to the convenience and comfort made possible by the material abundance and gadgets of her household, she also resents her exploitation and subservience, which are too obscure to be more than vaguely felt. So she procures vicarious satisfaction by maintaining some little sovereignty in her own little private domain.[9] The father is the victim of the mass methods and exploitation of business and industry. He is a passive, conforming participant [10] in a large impersonal complex demanding (in Riesman's

---

[8]*Ibid.*, pp. 267-283.

[9]Friedan, Betty: *The Feminine Mystique.* New York, Norton, 1963.

[10]Whyte, William H., Jr.: *The Organization Man.* New York, Simon and Schuster, 1956.

term) "antagonistic cooperation." [11] Thus at home he is inclined to let his wife have a fairly free rein, within certain limits of his otherwise frustrated authority and individuality. For his own son he may, as an older "pal," provide a definite, though intermittent, model of individuality. The son can observe "the old man" performing well in play or in social situations. But if he asks his father what he does for a living, he is apt to receive the stereotyped reply, "I work in an office," or "I am an executive." Such replies suggest a rather ordinary, routine, faceless kind of work; and that is what the work is. There is also the role of the sister in the family, who grows up living out the ambiguities of the young female in a male-dominated society, though such dominant males are far off, invisible, and, for most, never to be identified. Her role and how our young man sees and interprets it also shapes his growing identity and his expectations as to the kind of world that is and will be for him.

There are of course many variations on this middle stratum type of family structure, as well as other types of families with their own distinctive personal identities and their own variations. Negro families differ from white families, and lower stratum families differ from middle stratum ones. But certain problems cut across economic groups.[12] One common and basic feature is the pervasive fact of alienation in our society. Ultimate alienation is alienation from human creative power, i.e., from oneself and others, since creative power is always social in cause and consequence, though it is necessarily *expressed* by individuals. In our society this ultimate alienation takes the form of class ownership and control and class dependence. Although the class owners are not alienated from economic power, they are in fact alienated from real human power. An exploiter of another human being, one who owns another's very existence and his decisions in life, does not have creative human power with others. He has brute physical power over others. In that brute physical relation he is not a human being; he dehumanizes himself and others. To support this kind of exploitive relation which pervades our society and which opposes genuine human creative relations existing in spite of exploitation;

[11] Riesman, David, with Glazer, Nathan, and Denney, Reuel: *The Lonely Crowd.* New York: Doubleday, 1955, p. 103.

[12] Dai, Bingham: Some problems of personality development among Negro children. In Kluckhon, Clyde, and Murray, Henry A. (Eds.): *Personality in Nature, Society, and Culture,* pp. 545-566.

to make such a relation appear to be good and salutary and human—
the ruling groups put a decent face on what they are doing by lies and
myths, and attempt to check and wipe out all critical analysis and
exposure of their lies and myths. Thus capitalism is the basic cause
of anti-intellectualism, which is essential to the continuation of capitalism. The self-deception spread through business, industry, government,
the armed forces, and other institutions enters into the family in various forms. There it becomes transformed into character and is perpetuated in parents and the young.

Those who control monopoly capitalism, who are identified with it
and defend it ideologically, cannot stand outside of it, criticize it, or
accept the criticism of outsiders. The willingness to enter into radical
criticism presupposes the readiness to admit defeat and to change.
Capitalists generally have not exhibited this willingness. A ruling
class will no more willingly give up its ruling ideas than it will give
up its ruling power. Consequently, ruling groups and their spokesmen
in the United States use two strategies. They and their ideological
spokesmen in the United States represent the system of capitalism as
real and good and eternal. And they attack all living criticisms and
challenges to that—especially socialism—as illusory, evil, and tran-
sitory. Thus they use the intellect in defending capitalism and are
anti-intellectual in attacking its critics. But their use of the intellect
in defending capitalism is in fact anti-intellectualism, because it is blind
to facts and logic and makes the worse appear the better cause. Capitalists and their spokesmen are thus naturally opposed to the honesty and
logic of intellectual inquiry because such inquiry reveals the exploita-
tions and evils of capitalism for what they are, and because such revelation incites people to change the system of capitalism. Capitalism is
antisocialism and anticommunism, and anticommunism requires anti-
intellectualism.

Because the rule and ideology of capitalism reach widely and deeply
into the schools, the press, and other information media, its anti-intellectualism is widespread and is unconsciously accepted by many. At
the same time, as revent events show, growing portions of Negroes,
deprived groups, women, students, intellectuals, and workers, faced
with their own conditions of exploitation, alienation, and war, refuse
to be anti-intellectual. They refuse to love capitalism blindly and to

hate socialism blindly. In various degrees they are critical of the system of capitalism that now dominates America. But they are not yet fully and massively and consciously critical. It is the task of progressive intellectuals in the United States to help them become so.

Even so, the people of American culture are diversified in their values and philosophies—though, as we said, most are not consciously critical of their values and basic beliefs. If, as in the columns below, we collate in a rough and common sense way the results of several studies of the values of young Americans, chiefly those of college age, we see that these repeatedly fall into certain clusters or "types." For our purposes here, let us give the types political names: conservative, liberal, progressive, and anarchist. Finer distinctions can of course be made.

Conservative	Liberal	Progressive	Anarchist
Practical, status-oriented group spirit	Scientific, competitive	Humanistic, reflective, sentient, energetic	Rebellious[13]
	Humanistic reflective, sentient, energetic		
Social, Religious	Theoretical, Economic	Economic	Esthetic[14]
Social restraint and self-control, Receptivity and sympathetic concern	Enjoyment and progress in action, with orientation toward self	Enjoyment and progress in action, with orientation toward other than self	Sensuous enjoyment, Withdrawal and self-sufficiency[15]
Apollonian, Christian	Promethean	Mohammedan	Dionysian Buddhist[16]
Conservatism, Supernaturalism	Social Realism, Individual Voluntarism	Social Voluntarism	Anti-Supernaturalism[17]

Each of the terms "conservative," "liberal," "progressive," and "anarchist" has a narrow and a broad meaning. Moreover, some

[13]Pace, C. R.: Five college environments. *College Entrance Examination Board Review,* no. 43, 1960, 24-28.

[14]Allport, Gordon W., Vernon, Philip, E. and Lindzey, Gardner: *A Study of Values.* Boston, Houghton, Mifflin, 1951.

[15]Morris, Charles: *Varieties of Human Value.*

[16]Morris, Charles: *Paths of Life.* New York, Harper, 1942.

[17]Whalley, Elsa: *Individual Life-Philosophies in Relation to Personality and to Systematic Philosophy: An Experimental Study.*

would define certain of these terms favorably and others unfavorably. This difficulty is compounded by the fact that we have above introduced terms which scholars use in their own special senses. There is, however, a core of meaning for each term on which most scholars and laymen would agree, differentiating and relating those meanings or philosophies. The usual way of relating them is to arrange them along a continuum according to the degree or rate of social change which their adherents are prepared to make. Thus the conservative wants to make little social change gradually, while the anarchist, at the other end, wants to make much change rapidly. But there are other relations between these philosophies. A basic cleavage is that between conservatives and progressives, who are oriented to the problems of society and the world and to their solution, and the liberals and anarchists, who are oriented to the self and who take it to be the final source, means, and locus of social change. Thus the conservative and the progressive share an interest in the relations of persons and the conditions of society. But they differ in that the conservative stresses individual understanding and slow social change, while the progressive calls for understanding in action for radical social change. And the reason is that the progressive is convinced of the reality and the value of all men's reason put into collective action, whereas the conservative is inclined to argue that since an elite is gifted with the power of understanding it should guide the society through whatever changes seem to it necessary.

The progressive and liberal are united in the belief that action is enjoyable and produces progress; they thus oppose the calm (cf. the Epicureans) to be found in both the conservative and anarchist camps. But they diverge radically in their estimate of the individual and what his relation is and ought to be relative to society and social change. The liberal viewpoint has developed most fully among the ruling and favored groups of modern class societies, and reached its apogee during recent centuries of western laissez-faire capitalism. Progressivism is the reflex of another movement which is essentially democratic and socialistic. Any alliance between progessives and liberals will unite them in their common opposition to conservatism and oppression; but it will always be strained by the tension between the individualistic and the socialistic viewpoints.

The same may be said of the relation between progressivism and anarchism, except that anarchists ordinarily do not engage in alliances and many of them are not interested in political activity.

The conservatives (with some exceptions) and the liberals have in common a respect for rationality, but divide over the issue of sociality vs. individuality. The term "conservative" to many today connotes extreme individualism in economic, social, and political matters; the philosophies of Herbert Hoover and Barry Goldwater immediately come to mind. Their views of course echo the classical "liberalism" of the eighteenth century, and the fact that this view is now expressed as *The Conscience of a Conservative* is an irony of history. What was then a movement for liberation from mercantilist restraint is now a defensive movement to conserve capitalism. The conservative is thus necessarily interested in the preservation and control of his society, i.e., his control of capital, though he may *speak* in an archaic language. Thus what remains of classical liberalism is its ideological reflex, i.e., the movement for "free" expression of ideas of the individual, a movement which has separated itself from its economic origin and which (as the civil rights activity in America shows) wanders uncertainly between anarchism, progressivism, and conservatism.

The conservative and the anarchist stand at opposite poles, the one fearing disorder, the other hating any order whatsoever. The liberal is naturally allied with the anarchist in his individualism, but his interest in rational action keeps him from going all the way over to anarchism. For if the anarchist engages in action, the action is mainly for the sake of his own individual enjoyment or contemplation.

The rise and development of these philosophies or, more broadly, these personality types, and their relations one to another, is a complex phenomenon conditioned by many factors. We do not have space here to trace these factors, but it is likely that biological, psychological, social, and ecological factors all play a role.

Each type has its better and worse subtypes. The better subtype of conservative is that he values the substantial human values of the past and wishes to conserve them and maintain equilibrium between human values and forces. He stands for rational control, appreciation, moderation, order, and discipline, and on the other side, for obedient adjustment to the demands of the world. The worse subtype displays the tendency to fixity and opposition to human progress. In recent terminology this takes the form of the "authoritarian personality"—addiction to stereotyped thinking, a punitive morality, submission to the powerful, dominance of the weak, conventionality, anti-intellectualism, hostility toward different values, and so on.[18] Such a personality exhibits inflexible domination on the one hand and blind submission on the other. Probably a large proportion of those who voted for Goldwater in 1964 and Nixon in 1968 (in each case, almost a quarter of the total electorate) belonged to this worse type, combining both of its sides. The authoritarian image was expressed and evoked by these men.

The second type, the liberal, has its origins in the eighteenth century bourgeois Enlightenment, with its values of freedom, individualism, diversity, tolerance, gradualism, reason, openness, persuasion, equality, opposition to arbitrary authority, criticism in inquiry, and the like. The liberal is anti-authoritarian, but still believes in the values of society held together by voluntary association rather than by imposed law and rigid conformity. At the same time the liberal has in him that ambiguity and weakness which can open the door to tolerance (if not support) of authoritarianism. We have seen this weakness in the last three Democratic administrations—lack of sustained direction, vacillation, compromise, accomodation, and a growing tendency to give way to adamant and inhuman use of power. In a crisis the liberal's gentlemanly glove sometimes falls away and reveals the iron hand of cruel authority underneath; ideas give way to material interests.

A person with a progressive philosophy identifies himself with the progress, i.e., the creative and social fulfillment, of all persons. "Progress" for him does not mean the conserving and advancing of the wealth and power of the few, as it does for the conservative. Nor does it mean, as it does for the liberal, progress or increase in the freedom of the individual from state control, or variety and tolerance for their own sakes, or even a "welfare" state in which one class dispenses goods to a class from which such goods have already been appropriated. Progress does not mean for him an increase in anarchis-

---

[18]Sanford, Nevitt: Developmental status of the entering freshman. In *The American College*, p. 261.

tic autonomy. The first premise of the progressive philosophy is *human-ism*. This means that man is, or can be, the origin, knower, judge and realizer of value—not a few men, but all men; not a single class over others, but a classless society; not isolated individuals freed from the state, but communicative and cooperative persons composing their own government. The conservative sides with the ruling class; the liberal ambivalently moves between ruling class and ruled class; the anarchist announces himself to be beyond all classes; and the progresive takes the side of the ruled and oppressed class in its struggle for peace, equality, freedom, and brotherhood. The conservative clings to the past; the liberal cannot decide whether to stand on the past or move into the future; and the progressive put his faith in the emerging future in the making. Unlike the liberal, the progressive repudiates capitalism as a basis for the ultimate advancement of mankind, which must be built, he believes, on the radically new basis of democratic socialism. The main force that will usher in a new world, he believes, is comprized by the members of the oppressed groups throughout the world. To be a progressive is to identify one's self and one's values with such groups and to seek to advance their welfare by thought and action. The progressive seeks to conserve the humanistic values of the past and to enrich them with the new freedom of the socialist individual in a socialist society. A progressive viewpoint must reject equally the extremes of authoritarian, elitist oppression, uncontrolled, libertarian freedom which in practice means domination by a leading economic class, and the leaderless society of anarchism. This viewpoint requires democracy in its fullest sense.

Anarchism is a philosophy which opposes all imposition of state authority on the individual and calls for the organization of society along the lines of spontaneous, voluntary association between individuals and groups. Its method of achieving this goal is protest—violent or nonviolent—against existing government. It seeks either pure individualism or voluntary communities independent of existing government. The overt expression of anarchism in American culture is as yet relatively rare, though it has increased in recent years. A few groups have withdrawn from the life of the larger culture to form their own self-sufficient communities. Other forms of protest against government, government policy, or other authority have been diverse—sit in's, boycotts, strikes, occupations of buildings, individual terrorism, etc. Anarchism in America today has no systematic, highly influential spokesman, though writers like Dorothy Day and Paul Goodman have had some influence on the leftist youth.

Anarchism has a long history on our continent. The tradition of political and religious protest provided a primary motivating force for our ancestors' immigration here. They were in flight from the oppression of the political and religious establishments. Thomas Paine wrote: "Government, even in its best state, is but a necessary evil; in its worst state an intolerable one. . . . Government, like dress, is a badge of lost innocence."[19] Paine's voice was a progressive protest against government *over* people and not *out* of them, and many of his fellow Americans shared that view. It is still to be found in mild form among millions today who are in flight to the suburbs away from the city and civic responsibility. In the nineteenth century America provided the open spaces, the land, and the broad tolerance for hundreds of experiments in utopian "stateless" communities, both religious and secular. In the cities, too, anarchism appeared in the International Working Men's Association (1883) and the I. W. W. (1905). Breaking the law in allegiance to a higher loyalty is not a new thing in America. Religious groups like the recusant Quakers, racial groups like the enslaved and insurrectionary Negroes, and industrial groups like the striking workers of the 1930's, have all defied the coercions of state power. The tradition of individual anarchism owes much to men like John Brown, Nat Turner, Thoreau, Emerson, Garrison, and others, though not all were explicit anarchists. If a law be unjust, exhorted Thoreau, "Then I say, break the law. Let your life be a counter friction to stop the machine."[20]

The "New Left" is a mixture of progressive and anarchist philosophies. These may be found side by side in the movements for civil rights, peace, freer education, black liberation, women's liberation, and associated causes. Although they are not entirely unified by common goals, methods, and beliefs, they do have certain things in common, enabling them to unite on certain actions. They are comprized by sections of exploited, alienated groups—Blacks, young workers, stu-

---

[19]Paine, Thomas: *Common Sense,* ch. 1.
[20]Thoreau, Henry David: Civil disobedience.

dents, women, intellectuals, etc.—who have a certain consciousness of their condition; and they are actuated by a profound sense of indignation toward the organization of society and the policies of government. Since the New Left represents a major creative and critical force in the United States today, it is important to develop understanding of its origins, component groups, basic beliefs, and needs, if it is to become a more effective instrument in the progress of the nation.

From a survey for *Fortune,* carried out in October, 1968, among 718 representative young men and women aged eighteen through twenty-four, it was estimated that 750,000 of the nation's 6.7 million full-time college students now identify with the New Left. This group comprizes more than 10 percent of the total. But 40 percent of the college students were not concerned about getting money, jobs, or position. Two-thirds of the latter group believe it appropriate to engage in civil disobedience and to support draft resistance; one-half believe that the United States is a sick society. So the New Left now has a large body of more than one million young people who are cooperative or sympathetic toward it and its goals.[21]

Born during or after the war, these young people do not, for the most part, remember the direct influence of McCarthyism. Unlike many progressives before the Korean War and before the revelations of the twentieth Congress of the CPSU, they are not, for the most part, oriented toward a particular party or program. Many are open to any and all perspectives on the left, and are disinclined to rule out any as irrelevant, except those which appear dogmatic and exclusive. It is a point of scrupulous honor with them not to seem doctrinaire; this fastidiousness is an effort to avoid the sectarian Stalinism of their immediate predecessors, sometimes called the "Old Left," with which they were disillusioned. They are strongly anti-authoritarian, and the pervasive anticommunism of the cold war—of which they are for the most part unaware—has made it easy for them to reject out of hand the Soviet and Chinese models. (The Maoists and the Young Workers Liberation League are exceptions, but they are small.) They follow Herbert Marcuse in denouncing the bureaucrats, technicians, managers, party bosses, and dogmatists of all "totalitarian" systems, capital-

---

[21]*Youth in Turmoil.* New York, Time, 1969, chs. 2, 3.

ist and communist alike. Thus in their search for alternative models
to their own society, they turn to communal utopias, to small socialist countries like Cuba, to charismatic figures like Che Guevara.

The New Left began to take shape in the period of leftist disorienta-
tion in Europe and the United States during the events of 1956 and
following. The writings and activities of C. Wright Mills (*The Power
Elite* appeared in 1956), Camus, Sartre, Paul Goodman, pacifists like
A. J. Muste, Martin Luther King, Jr., Michael Harrington, and
others were influential in articulating the longings of this generation
for a new direction. What they feared most was not McCarthysim,
which to them seemed passé; not communism, which seemed to have
its own problems; not even corporate capitalism, which many came
to decry; but atomic war and universal annihilation. The songs of
Bob Dylan, who has since passed from glory, gave voice to this fear
of the first atomic generation, the A-babies born under the shadow
of the A-bomb and the blind stupidities of a world they never made.
For most, Marxism-Leninism was not a live option. Their minds had
been turned off from that alternative by the ideological oppression of
the cold war. Thus, when they began to become political and thoughtful, they could read Marcuse, who criticized both capitalism and Soviet
communism; but they could not easily read Marx, Engels, and Lenin,
whose chief target of criticism was capitalism.

The first and continuing background of the New Left was the Black
revolt. The relative abundance of jobs and money in the post-war
period did not last long. Negroes, the largest exploited group in the
society, felt the pinch first. The Montgomery (Alabama) bus boy-
cott was waged with solidarity, persistence, and success. On February 1, 1960, eight Negro students sat in at a Woolworth lunch counter
in Greensboro, North Carolina. Not only was the sit-in movement
born; the fires of student power were lit. They flamed immediately
into the organization of the Student Non-Violent Coordinating Committee in the same year. SNCC secured the support of Martin Luther
King, Jr.'s Southern Christian Leadership Conference and took over
its philosophy, emphasizing "conscience," "the moral nature of human existence," and "non-violence."

Kennedy's election in the fall of 1960 heralded the end of the
Eisenhower era, with its placidity, stagnancy, and cautious old age.

The presence of a young man in the White House, with a call for a "new frontier," gave fresh impetus to the New Left. Picketing of Woolworth stores by northern students, in sympathy with southern students, and protests against HUAC and the Chessman execution in California, had already occurred. Then, in 1961, came the CORE Freedom Rides, and the antinuclear tests activity of the Student Peace Union. In 1962 the Northern Students Movement (supporting SNCC), the W. E. B. Du Bois Clubs, the Students for a Democratic Society, were formed. In December of 1964 the Berkeley revolt occurred, and the teach-in's and demonstrations of that year culminated in the antiwar March on Washington of April 17, 1965. A broad coalition, the National Mobilization Committee to End the War in Vietnam (Mobe), subsequently organized enormous peace demonstrations in the east. In the late 1960's Resist supported antidraft actions. But an increasing militancy marked the movement: students occupied universities, a women's liberation movement developed, and the Black Panthers were forced to fight for their lives in ghetto and court.

Although the New Left grew into being spontaneously and pluralistically, without any preconceived pattern, we may describe it and characterize it as a distinctive movement. It consists of Marxists and socialists who are either coalitionists ready to work with other groups (the Panthers, the YWL League, and the Young People's Socialist League, loyal to the Socialist Party) or independent revolutionists. These latter include the Young Socialist Alliance (Trotskyite), the Progressive Labor Party (pro-Chinese), and smaller groups. The nonsocialists comprize the larger of the organized groups in the New Left. During the early 1960's the two most influential ones were SNCC, the oldest of the student New Left, and SDS, which like SNCC was inspired by the sit-in's and, avoiding "ideology," stressed "participatory democracy" and the autonomy of local neighborhood groups. SDS members worked with the poor and deprived of the northern cities and the southern rural regions, concentrating on basic issues like housing, jobs, voting. Their aim was to help build "counter-communities," letting the people themselves decide so that gradually they would be radicalized through the realization of their impotence. The nonsocialists included other groups, like the Northern Students Movement and CORE, which in 1966 abandoned its twenty-three year old policy of nonviolence. In the late 1960's one faction of SDS, the Weathermen, became anarchist and violent, preaching and practicing acts of sabotage, terrorism, smashing of property, arson, and bombing.

What are the basic beliefs, the philosophy, of the New Left? As we have noted, there are both progressive and anarchist elements in it. The anarchism expresses in extreme form the individualism, the anti-intellectualism, the anti-establishmentarianism, the freedom and license that run like hot undercurrents through our mass culture, ready to break forth like geysers from time to time. It is the reverse side of the anarchy and violence of capitalism. Capitalism itself grew out of the individualistic revolt against medieval authoritarianism. It is inherently anarchic. Its "anarchy in social production,"[22] its blind demolition of the natural environment, its colonial wars and imperialist predation, its racism and facism—what are these but anarchism on a massive and "respectable" scale?

At the present moment the anarchists are revolting against the all-seeing eye and all-powerful hand of destructive capitalism—without realizing that their own destructiveness magnifies the very problem they claim to be trying to solve. "You've got to put your body upon the wheels," cried Mario Savio, student leader in the Berkeley revolt, "and the levers and the gears and upon all the apparatus and you have to make it stop." This is in the spirit of an intellectual Luddite or a utopian socialist, who despises mass technology and wants to destroy it so that the individual might be freed from its mechanizing of the individual. There is a romantic flair in the student revolt that that a certain appeal to many Americans: the nostalgic dream of the frontiersman, proud and free, cleanly separated from the corruptions of a massive, industrialized society. The contemporary anarchists invoke their American counterparts of the past: the Wobblies, the Abolitionists, the Underground Railway, the anonymous Negroes of slavery who live on in their spirituals, Thoreau, and the utopian communal experiments.

It is thus natural that a bohemian coterie would congregate on the Left. While the Left is "where the action is," and youth are naturally drawn to action, the action that the bohemian youth wants is anti-

---

[22]Engels, Frederick: *Socialism, Utopian and Scientific*, p. 72.

parental, antischolastic, antimoral, and, if need be, antilegal action. Such action is not often overt street action or political movement. All that is required is that it be an affirmation of individual freedom in the face of the behemoth mob, the leviathan state, and the automated society. This affirmation tends to be solitary or exercised in small and loosely knit groups. It is humanistic and esthetic, inclined to the free and easy idiom of jazz and modern art, cool but experimental and tolerant in human relations. It is "antitotalism" and propluralism, with a breezy Whitmanesque love of the idiosyncratic and arresting. The bohemian would rather be than do, would rather feel than think, would rather "dig" an impromptu tune than lead a crusade, would rather die than change the world. Men have hitherto only understood or used or changed the world; he wishes to enjoy it in delight and detachment. Hence he moves with an unconscious tropism toward the left, not only because of his revulsion for the old order and his passion for revolution, but because of his craving for the new jerusalem of jazz and perhaps the joys of marijuana and heroin.

Bohemianism throughout history has tended to conjoin itself to radical political movements. From the Cynics and antinomian Corinthians to the Anabaptists, from the Owenites to the howling, on-the-road beatniks, some men, conservative as well as radical, have identified revolt against oppressive law with the repudiation of all law. Certain special conditions have predisposed American youth in this direction. Like their counterparts in other technological cultures, who have their own forms of deviancy and delinquency, they are troubled by "ego-diffusion" (Erikson). Their search for personal identity, urgent and intense under the pressure of the physiological changes of adolescence and its expanding sensitivity, is frequently frustrated. And in the case of capitalist cultures, this search is rendered more obscure by capitalism's chaos, aimlessness, and legalized inhumanities. Their revolt carries with it many of the characteristics of that culture; it is emotional, negative, individualistic, anti-intellectual; it is motivated by the dream of private happiness, filled with pleasure and uninterrupted. It is what one psychologist calls "privatism."[23] It is in fact not a *radical* revolt, because it does not deeply and thoroughly desire to

---

[23]Hadden, Jeffrey K.: The private generation. *Psychology Today, 3*: 32-35, 68-69, 1969.

throw off every corrupt vestige of that culture and to eradicate its underlying causes.

Thus the bohemian revolt is manifested in private eccentricities of hair style, dress, exciting locomotion; in the strong beat and loud sounds of rock music; in pushing pot and flaunting sexual oddities; in travel, strenuous and dangerous sports, art, Zen; in the party spirit of political protest (a riot is a party, says Jerry Rubin); and in the epicurean-dionysian be-in's and love-in's such as the Woodstock Music and Art Fair of August 1969—a festival of folk-rock music and communal mingling which attracted 300,000 young people. These bohemian young people want to knock down all the gods of authority—parents, teachers, politicians; and, seeking out their pads and beaches, disport themselves in eternal play. They do not realize, in their youthful dreams, that labor is necessary to life and that labor must be thoughtful if life is to be fulfilled. Thought—radical thought, philosophical thought—is anathema to them. They have examined ideology—conservative, liberal, progressive—and have found it wanting. They are suspicious of ideology, and have fastened themselves to the concrete and the immediate with a religious fanaticism.

The bohemian anarchist point of view and style, although it has no articulate, systematic spokesman (its articulation is mainly subverbal), has had its influence on the progressive movement in the New Left. The nonsocialists have been too involved in specific action projects to be concerned about philosophy. The people on the bottom, they say, do not need leaders; they need participation in making decisions that affect them basically, they need a sense of identity and dignity, they need pure democracy. Once people *know* freedom in practice, they will not need it in theory. Theory and practice seem to exist in inverse ratio: the more democracy experienced, the less philosophy needed. But we may remark that this view confuses authority with authoritarianism, leadership with manipulation, philosophy with dogma, and action with freedom. It is a revival of the old populist notion that philosophy is a plot of the ruling elite and a diversion from the primeval purity of the common man. This view of man and history is of course a whole philosophy in itself, with its hidden assumptions. And the history of the Negro movement on the Left in the United States has already revealed—around the issue of "black power"—a struggle between different philosophies.

The Marxists and socialists, as we have already said, divide into two groups, the coalitionists and revolutionaries. Here again the influence of anarchism may be seen. The latter spend much of their time asserting their support of the Chinese and the third world rather than in correcting the ills of American society. The Du Bois Clubs, the most influential Marxist group, have concentrated on direct action in an effort to secure the coalition of mass movements. So have the Black Panthers. They aim at developing a new and unified base of political power. The "Loyalists" of the Young People's Socialist League concentrate on work within the Democratic Party, aiming at the transformation of the Party and its eventual control by the Blacks and their allies.

Many of the limitations of the members of the New Left stem from the fact that most of them are white and come from middle-class backgrounds. Some of the more realistic ones, through a class analysis of themselves and their movement, realize this. They have tried to correct the limitations by alliances with their black brothers and sisters. By reason of the direct, continuous, and brutal exploitation imposed upon them, most Blacks have radical feelings and respond spontaneously to the intellectual and political leadership of men like Malcolm X, Martin Luther King, Jr., Eldridge Cleaver, and Bobby Seale. It is an index of the maturity of the movement of the New Left that the whites have not produced young leaders of the stature that the Blacks have produced. As the oppression increases against the radical Blacks, such as the Black Panthers, it is important for alliances with white radicals to increase. For there can be no successful radical movement if the blacks and whites are divided. And that is what the government and its agents would like to do—to divide the advanced black militant groups from the whites and in dividing them to continue to rule them.

Some believe that the influence of the dissident youth in American life is small. Talcott Parsons, for example, has said that although American youth is "in a ferment," it gives its *"relative* sanction" to a stable and integrated society.[24] While this estimate was made in 1962, could it have been influenced by Parsons' own cautious political position? Others discount power of the New Left because of its

---

[24]Parsons, Talcott: Youth in the context of American society. *Daedalus, 91*: 122, 1962.

anarchist and disorganized character. Professor Lewis S. Feuer (1969) has criticized the new student movements for not bothering with legal procedures and "the traditional American democratic-liberal approach." He has sought to explain the youth revolt by the unconscious hatred of young people for their fathers.[25] But it is natural and healthy to hate a cruel person, be he one's father or not. Feuer's psychological "explanation" is a way of dodging the objective, human necessity for social revolution. Various other self-appointed guardians of the status quo have rebuked the students for their illegal, immoral, or neurotic behaviour—Daniel Bell, Max Lerner, Nathan Glazer, Sidney Hook, and Seymour Lipset.[26] But it is relevant to point out that a team of psychologists and sociologists from the Center for the Study of Higher Education at the University of California in Berkeley found that the student leaders are not rabble-rousers or beatniks. In a five-year study at eight colleges and universities, they discovered that the student leaders were more committed to the process of learning than most students, and that they "tend to be in unusually serious pursuit of education."[27] Other studies have confirmed this. Eight different studies in the 1960's showed a high degree of convergence in their findings. In summarizing the results of these studies Joseph Katz wrote that student activists

> tend to be more flexible, tolerant and realistic; less dependent upon authority, rules or rituals for managing social relationships. In their values, activists tend to be concerned with self-expression, intellectual orientation, sense of community with and responsiiblity for their fellow men, while the non-activists tend to be more success-oriented, self-denying, conventional, competitive, self-controlled, foresighted and orderly.[28]

Kenneth Keniston corroborated these results in his intensive studies of a few student radicals.[29] While these activists are more intelligent, less prejudiced, and more stable than nonactivists—a finding contradicting the charge that they are neurotic—we must note that the

---

[25]Feuer, Lewis: *The Conflict of Generations.* Basic Books, 1969.

[26]*The New York Times,* March 15, 1965, p. 26.

[27]*The New York Times,* September 7, 1965, p. 33.

[28]Katz, Joseph, in a monograph printed by the United States Office of Education, 1967. Cited in *The New York Times,* June 19, 1967, p. 29.

[29]Keniston, Kenneth: *Young Radicals: Notes on Committed Youth.* New York, Harcourt, 1968.

values of overt action, individual emotional expression, and disorder
do appear in these studies of activists, and that the tendencies toward
anarchy are evident in these young people. Moreover, dissenting social
movements tend to attract unstable and destructive persons to their
causes, and only a few such persons can easily inflame to destructive
action a crowd of people who are not habituated to checking their
emotions and impulses.

The anarchic tendencies evident among the New Left are self-
defeating insofar as they aim at constructive social change. They re-
repeat and compound the chaos of a capitalistic society and give the
ruling groups further warrant for political and military repression.
This does not mean that disruptive tactics have no role to play in
such change. It does mean that self-expressiveness and impulsiveness
as unqualified principles of political action are blind and foolish. The
leaders of socialist revolutions like Lenin and Mao Tse-tung possessed
a remarkable freedom of self-expression. But they were also disciplined, self-denying, self-controlled, foresighted, and orderly. American society will never transform itself from capitalism to socialism
until it begins to transform the self-expressive, anarchic habits of its
past and present through the directive power of self-control, foresight, and order within and between persons. And the young persons
of the New Left cannot play a role of leadership in that transformation until they begin to undergo the same transformation. But to be
self-controlled, foresighted, and orderly means first to think, to develop broad plans, to philosophize about the basic conditions, materials, means, and ends of human living, and to organize one's resources
toward deliberately chosen ends. That means the development and
application of a philosophy of socialism based on the heritage of successful socialism in other countries, but adapted to peculiarly American history and conditions.

Value studies in the United States ordinarily do not seek or find
sharp distinctions between affluent or comfortable groups and deprived or poor groups. One reason for this is that much of the value
research is initiated by university scholars who themselves belong to
middle or upper income groups and who do research on students
belonging to those groups. The "lower class," following W. Lloyd
Warner's terminology, appears to foster "non-conformance" and "re-

bellion" in the face of conflicts. The lower middle class, being a culture of "conformance" and "excessive repressive tendencies," tends to express its conflicts in physical symptom formation. Upper class families display a relatively large incidence of psychosis and psycho-neurosis.[30] Among the nonconforming members of the New Left, it is likely that among both anarchist and progressive groups one would find youth from both lower and middle classes. Both groups are motivated by nonconformance, but the anarchist groups are more concerned with destroying or withdrawing from what they find in society, whereas the latter wish to change and reconstruct society in a *radical* way. Anarchist groups (such as Blacks who want no co-operation with whites) often reflect the hostility and despair that are born of a background of economic and educational poverty, whereas certain bohemian and anarchist groups among the New Left express the emotional and intellectual emptiness of bourgeois upbringing. Young progressives appear to come from both lower and middle in-come groups, but their radical feelings of nonconformance toward society have acquired form and a constructive direction from the ideas to which they have been exposed. In all likelihood, these ideas have emanated from university communities, which are the chief, but not only, sources of ideological dissent and criticism in the United States today. It is possible that an effective radical ideology for America will be shaped by groups like the Blacks (such as the Black Panthers) and the leaders of the industrial workers, whose base is outside the university. But it is not possible for this to be done apart from knowledge of the most effective radical ideology in history, namely, Marxism-Leninism.

In spite of the differences in the New Left, the groups in it have certain common features.

(1) They are opposed to the basic order of society in the United States. They repudiate the basic way of life of that society, with its war and war economy, its racism and discrimination, and its fascist limitation of freedom. They reject the whole system of false, inhuman values, which is connected with this way of life and which dominates most sectors of the society in fact and in ideal: the greedy and anxious

---

[30]Ruesch, Jurgen: Social technique, social status, and social change in illness. In *Personality in Nature, Society, and Culture,* pp. 130-131.

acquisition of material possessions; status-seeking and status symbols; ruthless competitiveness; clever and deceptive manipulation of persons, opportunities, and conditions for personal ends; fear of dissent, and conformity; various forms of dishonesty—lying, hypocrisy, cheating, bribery; and the erosion of personal integrity and trust between persons.

They belive that government, business, the armed forces, and other institutions generate and support individuals and patterns of human relations that are inhuman and unjust. In their criticism of society, however, some stress the political and social defects. SNCC, for example, has organized campaigns of registration and voting in the South, and SDS has initiated community action projects in the ghettoes of northern cities to develop "participatory democracy" around issues like jobs, voting, education, and police brutality. Other groups, like the Du Bois Clubs, now the Young Workers Liberation League, seek economic changes, believing the problems of war, fascism, and racism would in principle be solved if monopolies were abolished and the control of the industries were nationalized and put into the hands of the people. The method of reaching this goal, they believe, is "the united efforts of all democratic elements in our country, composed essentially of the working people allied in the united activity of Negroes and other minorities with whites." Others may agree with them on the goal of socialism, but disagree on what is to be done now. Some of these want to work mainly on problems at the local neighborhood level, others want to work mainly through the Democratic Party.

(2) They are opposed to authoritarianism. In economic terms, this means capitalism; in political terms, fascism; in social terms, class oppression; and in human terms, exploitation. Authoritarianism to many in the New Left means "the power structure " or "power elite" of particular communities, though it is widely recognized that these local structures are united into one single corporate entity dominating the society. Authoritarianism is also associated with a dogmatic state of mind. Many on the New Left are dubious about communism as a theory, though most accept communists as persons—an acceptance which represents a great advance over the attitude of their elders during the Cold War. Communism is an ideology, they believe, and they are skeptical of all ideology. They vehemently disown Stalinism.

Authoriaritanism means for the New Left the repression of the forces of peace, freedom, and equality. Hence the New Left fights it at the point of the draft and the military establishments; at the point of the political repression of certain groups—as the efforts of the House Un-American Activities Committee to intimidate the youth who are aiding the National Liberation Front of South Vietnam, and the effort of the Attorney-General to have the Du Bois Clubs labelled "subversive"; and at the point of the deeply entrenched segregation in the society. But the New Left has not moved in any concerted way in the direction of the source of authoritarianism, namely, the factories, farms, and businesses where the arbitrary authority of monopoly capital is directly imposed.

(3) The groups in the New Left are for democracy. To some, this means democracy in the collective, socialist sense. To perhaps most, however, it means democracy in the traditional bourgeois sense, i.e., individual freedom and participation, obedience to the inner light of conscience, "having the courage of one's conviction," reaching a consensus in Quaker style (followed by SNCC), etc. The full implications of democracy—e.g., proletarian industrial democracy and socialism—are not clear to many in the New Left. Most of them are not proletarians and do not come from proletarian backgrounds. "Democracy" is to them a symbol of the good life. It means essentially freedom from coercive control with the power to conduct one's life as one wishes. "Love" and "brotherhood" are spoken of, but they are still essentially romantic and inchoate notions.

(4) Generally speaking, the New Left is opposed to the established political parties. With the major exception of the Young People's Socialist League, they are convinced that such parties are incorrigibly corrupt. The old SDS and others were fearful that the power structure would "co-opt" the radical independents and thus destroy their power among the masses. They believed that ultimate political power lies with the people, not with the political bosses or leaders or even parties. "Black Power," as Stokely Carmichael, former national chairman of SNCC, said, means the political organization of black people. But it does not mean a party.

(5) The members of the New Left are in general alienated from the Old Left. Some of them say, "We don't trust anyone over thirty."

They are aware that the generation preceding them, from 1945 to 1960, did not fight adequately against the Korean War and Cold War; did not strongly resist McCarthyism; did not stimulate the students of the 1950's to dissent; did not radicalize the labor unions; did not work on the black problems; did not see through Stalinism and the other weaknesses of socialist countries; did not adapt their Marxism to concrete conditions and destroyed themselves with their dogmatism; did not see the dangers of coalition with political parties and ruling groups; and so on. Many of the criticisms of the New Left toward the Old Left are true; at the same time the New Left fails to take account of the achievement of its predecessors or to see the need for unity and continuity. The reaction of the New Left in this respect is peculiarly American; history for it means little, and it works in the naive faith that everything can be accomplished *de novo* in one generation. The accent on youth and youthful values in American culture, and the large numbers of youth, have reinforced this attitude.

(6) The New Left is partially identified in its feelings with the powerless and deprived minority groups in American society. This identification is in part the consequence of an identity crisis through which most adolescents pass in American society. Young people form their values and their self-concept through contact with the real and ideal values around them, as these are evident in their parents, siblings, peers, books, televison programs, etc. American young people thus discover two things: the ideal values presented to them—liberty, equality, brotherhood, justice, peace, honesty—are often contradicted in actual practice; and the society as a whole has no shared, unifying purpose. Not even an anticommunist war unites it. Against this confusing background, how is a young person to develop his own purposes in life, his own sense of identity which unites his private interests and values with those of his countrymen? He has essentially two choices: he can adapt to the society as it is, blindly taking over the confused, contradictory identity of most Americans; or he can rebel.

The members of the New Left are in rebellion. But their rebellion is primarily emotional and, out of a background of diffuse discontent, seeks to move toward and against specific objects. Unlike most people, who have jobs, homes, families, and concrete roles in concrete institutions, the members of the New Left, who are mainly students, cannot direct their frustration against a specific boss or corporation. Even the sources of oppression which they can locate in their own environment—parents, teachers, universities, local police, the selective service system, and the government's Vietnam war—are not sufficient outlet for their rebellious energies. So they feel a natural kinship with similar oppressed and neglected minorities—the Blacks, the industrial workers, the poor farmers, the Puerto Ricans, the urban underprivileged—and have increasingly gravitated to them in common cause. Like them, they are far removed from the sources of power. Like them, they are alternately apathetic and bitter, unresponsive and rebellious toward the established order. Like them, they are drafted to do the work and fight the wars of the elite, privileged, and powerful groups. Like them, they feel they have no future in existing society; and in resisting it, they believe they have nothing to lose but their alienation.

(7) The rebellion of the New Left takes primarily a moral and activist form, and not an intellectual or ideological one. The youth of the New Left are not overtly opposed to the use of the intellect, theoretical or practical. But with typical American perspective they believe that the intellect is instrumental to the fulfillment of specific actions. They are pragmatists at the core; and aside from the socialists among them, they share the faith of pragmatism in reason as exercised by the individual or small group. Moreover, their faith, like pragmatism's, has a strongly moral tone. More than once their moral reactions interfere with their effectiveness; they may vent their moral indignation in demonstrations, or they may become so angry over the conditions they discover in the bureaucracy of a miner's union that they are not prepared to act in an organized way to remedy conditions. They sing songs such as "This Little Light of Mine" and "Do When the Spirit Say Do." And as in the pietistic heritage they are sometimes convinced that sincere feeling and good works can do more to unite people than thought, so they are dubious of ideology or philosophy lest when applied it unite people in the vise of totalitarian dogma.

There is thus a strong undercurrent of anti-intellectualism in the New Left, and it is articulated in various anarchist theories. "Don't read history," says Jerry Rubin. "Get stoned, and look to the future." [31] This emphasis on defiance of discipline and authority, on immediate gratification, on hatred of the past and disregard for the future, on uninhibited expression of impulses, on drug-taking and fantasy, on tantrums and bacchanalias, on individualistically "doing one's thing"—what is this except the spoiled, unhappy, childish behavior which capitalism has induced and which it welcomes as a way of turning aside *real* social change through *critical* and *collective* action? Such self-indulgent behavior is precisely what the dominant monopolists, politicians, and military leaders count on while they do their own dirty work. As long as the population is thus diverted and divided, they do not need to supply bread and circuses, and they can rest comfortably in their role of brute power and exploitation. If the masses of men will willingly dehumanize and brutalize themselves, depriving themselves of thought, foresight, and care for the future of mankind—then their masters will silently applaud, and provide them with access to the media for encouraging others to do the same. And in fact the masters will provide their own money and agents by the thousands to encourage the anarchists to denounce the critical and radical use of the intellect—just as they have denounced and smeared it with their own epithets like "bums," "eggheads," and the like.

What does the New Left in the United States require to attain its maximal effectiveness?

(1) *Coordination in practice.* At the present time, many different groups are working on a variety of issues—registration, voting, jobs, housing, rents, education, peace, etc. But all of these are interrelated. Success or failure in solving one problem depends on and determines success or failure in all the others. A coordinated attack on a set of problems in one community will be more effective than piecemeal, isolated attacks on individual, separated problems in different communities. The coordination of attacks on problems does not mean a monolithic policy for all groups; it simply means cooperation and mutual support. Of special importance is the alliance of the white New Left with the black radicals in the community who are the targets of economic, political, and military repression—and the alliance of the New Left with the radical and militant workers in their plants.

---

[31]Television interview, Channel 13, New York City, March 23, 1970.

(2) *Coordination in theory.* Coordination in practice is most effective when those doing the coordinating are united by a common set of premises and methods. At present, as we have shown, the New Left is marked by a variety of views about man and society and how to improve them. One of the chief obstacles to coordination in theory on the left is a certain negativism regarding authority, leadership, political organization, the Old Left, and the values of history. Unless this skepticism is overcome, the New Left cannot become a very potent force in American society. For human life advances only under the leadership of broad social ideas implemented by broad groups of people with leaders who articulate their ideas and help them to fulfill such ideas. It advances, furthermore, not in a vacuum, but out of specific historical conditions with a specific history. We reach the future from the present—it is what we have to work with; and the present is the living outcome of the past. Thus we are always indirectly remolding the past, whether we think we are or not.

(3) *Connection of progressive leaders with the poor and deprived.* This latter group, comprizing nearly half the population, is presently estranged from political processes. It is, by and large, leaderless. The New Left has recognized its importance and potential, has a feeling for it, and has already made connection with it. But all progressive leaders—most of whom come from the middle or "comfortable" group, and who are intellectuals—must merge their thoughts and skills with this great mass, if philosophy is to find "its *material* weapon in the proletariat."

(4) *Connection of progressive American leaders with the progressive forces outside the United States.* This is particularly important for the peace movement, which is worldwide in scope and derives its strength from its unity. The peace movement in the United States has proceeded in a pluralistic, *ad hoc* way, so that it is not quite true to speak of a single peace movement. This diversity in the American peace movement has been, in part, historically necessitated. Americans are relatively inexperienced in dealing with war and in working for peace; the country is large and diversified; and we have traditionally been isolated from the rest of the world. Democratic contact with peace-workers of other countries would help us to see our tasks more clearly in the context of the world peace movement. Giving us a sense of

the unity of the peace forces around the world, of their common goals but distinctive tactics, it would deepen our demand for a greater unity in our own peace movement and for our own distinctive tactics. It would help to correct errors by enriching us with the experience of others. It would link us to other peace workers, in concrete ways, and would thus lift morale.

The New Left is not the first or the last left in the United States. It grew out of definite historical conditions, and it will in time be transformed into something other than what it is now. But, although small and confined to the youth, it is fresh and invigorating activity which has revived the whole progressive movement. Just as those young people who compose it must, as they grow older, widen and deepen this thought as they acquire jobs and families and move into their own communities, if their progressivism is to grow—so the whole progressive movement must widen and deepen its thought and make itself more effective.

Everyone knows, if he will only reflect on his own everyday practice, that most changes that people effect in human living are made by a certain combination of material force and of a guiding idea. Growing food, building a house, and acquiring an education all require a body acting in a way guided by an idea. As this holds for the individual person, so it does for a group and a society. Lenin recognized this simple truth when he emphasized the union of intellectuals and workers as necessary to revolutionary change in Russia.[32] The young people as well as the other people of the United States are currently in the first stages of effecting social changes of a progressive kind. They are becoming increasingly aware of what the primary social problem is. What remains for them to do is to develop ideas for revolutionary social change that are broad and also specific, philosophical and also relevant to concrete problems, and to unite such ideas with the primary material force of their society, the workers, both blue-collar and white-collar, particularly the workers in the industries vital to the economy. Such a mass-based, philosophical movement calls for its own particular strategies and tactics which must be worked out in the context of American conditions and history. What Marx wrote in 1844 still holds: "As philosophy finds its *material* weapon in the

---

[32]As early as 1902, in *What Is To Be Done?*

proletariat, so the proletariat finds its *spiritual* weapon in philosophy."
We, the people and workers of America who created it and will save
it, must claim it as our own. To do that we must make our philosophy
practical, and we must make our practice philosophical.

XII

THE YOUNG MARX AND
THE YOUNG GENERATION

Aᴍᴇʀɪᴄᴀɴ ʏᴏᴜɴɢ ᴘᴇᴏᴘʟᴇ ᴛᴏᴅᴀʏ more and more speak of "making a revolution." But, as our analysis in the last chapter showed, it is not always clear for them what a successful revolution entails. It may be instructive therefore to look at the development of the young revolutionary Marx—to identify and assess the factors that shaped his personal and philosophical development, and to determine how his development offers lessons for us today.

Young people have ever given to civilization its energy, its zest, its renewal, its revolution. Against the security of their elders, they have put adventure; against certainty, doubt; against tradition, innovation; against conservation, radical change. True, some older men and women have been revolutionaries, while youth has sometimes been conformist and establishmentarian. Nonethelesss, there is an indefeasible dialectic between youth and age.

The Greeks, as usual, had a story for this timeless theme. Father Heaven and Mother Earth, ages ago, created a prehuman race of monsters with power to move mountains and seas. Among them were the Titans who, unlike their brothers, were not only destructive but also beneficent. Dissatisfied with those brothers, Father Heaven imprisoned them in secret places within the earth. But Mother Earth, moved by maternal indignation, appealed to the Titans to rebel. Cronus responded, wounding the old man deeply and assuming lordship of the universe. But this first revolutionary of the world, who ruled for eons, became in his old age reactionary. Fearful of being overthrown he began to devour his children at the moment of birth, that moment of rejuvenation which threatens all older men dedicated to tradition. Thus do all despots: imitating the action of physical time, they aim to destroy all creativity that deviates from their ordered rule, to swallow up all novelty in their omnipotence. It is particularly so in the exradical, enjoying power and privilege. Having repressed his own youthful revolutionary ardor, he is tempted or compelled to suspect it in his offspring and to repress it there.

Now, one of Cronus' sons, Zeus, had inherited those radical genes. Saved from the fate of being crushed by a dominant father, the baby Zeus was hidden away by Mother Earth. So the child grew up to lead a successful revolt against Old Man and his fellow Titans, all establishment men unable to resist the tide of historical change. In this revolt Zeus was aided by Prometheus, a Titanic son of a tired revolutionary. It was this same Prometheus who later fashioned men in upright posture like the gods, stole fire from heaven, and had the courage

> To defy Power, which seems omnipotent;
> To love, and bear; to hope till Hope creates
> From its own wreck the thing it contemplates.[1]

It was this same Prometheus who presided over the birth of Karl Marx and whom Marx took as his hero. It is this same Prometheus who is the rightful god of youth's idolatry. "Prometheus" means "Foresight"; and it is youth who, of all society's generations, is the most visionary and energetic in shaping the future.

Marx had many sides—philosophical, economic, humanistic, socialistic, prophetic. But the core of Karl Marx was his Promethean character—it was Marx the revolutionary. The revolutionary took his start in youth and continued passionately until the day he died. Marx's "idea of happiness" was "to fight"—for the free association of men— till he could fight no more.[2] We must therefore look at Marx's youth to understand the origins and basic character of this revolutionary spirit. And to see its relevance for youth today, we must inquire into its revolutionary spirit and the stages of its development in the life of the young Marx.

The first thing noticeable about Karl's youth is the respectable bourgeois solidity of his background. His grandfather was a rabbi in Trier and was succeeded by the brother of Marx's father in that post. Karl's mother, Dutch-Jewish, came from a century-long line of rabbis. In 1816, two years before Karl's birth, his father, Heinrich Marx,

---

[1]Shelley, Percy Bysshe: Prometheus unbound.
[2]Marx, Karl: Confessions. In *Reminiscences of Marx and Engels,* p. 256.

converted to Christianity, a step upward in the ladder of social emanci-pation. Heinrich Marx was a patriot Prussian, a bourgeois humanist, a successful *Advokat* in Trier. There is evidence that from his father's character, in particular, Karl absorbed the best of the Judaic and Christian traditions, i.e., their human ideals interpreted in the spirit of the German Enlightenment.

Karl has been described as enjoying "a cheerful and care-free youth" in a large family affectionately cared for by his mother and doted on by his father.[3] His parents were happily married, and his sister Sophie, the eldest child, just older than he, seems to have had an important role in bringing up Karl. Apparently his mother, who spoke broken German, did not share in the intellectual life of her husband or son. It is difficult to form a clear idea of Karl's relation to her; but in a letter of 1837 he refers to her as a "great, magnificent woman" (per-haps an adolescent hyperbole), and expresses the hope that his unex-pected arrival home may cheer her.[4] The easy, frank, and affectionate relation of Karl to his father is openly shown in their correspondence while Karl was away at the university.

If we are seeking "the roots of virtue" [5] and of ego strength in Karl Marx, we must look to these years of childhood. Our knowledge is sketchy. The "play age" appears to have provided him with happi-ness, a certain freedom from inhibition, an innovative and humorous bent, a romping confidence (which he displayed later in his relations to his own children), an animal confidence, a trained will. These qualities were nurtured in that basic trust which seems to have been present in relations with his parents and Sophie.

Karl's period in high school was eminently successful. At the *Gym-nasium* he acquired a liberal education of high standards, studying German, the classical languages, Christian doctrine, mathematics, and physics. His leaving certificate remarked on his skill in translating difficult passages in the classics and on his richness of thought and

---

[3]Mehring, Franz: *Karl Marx. The Story of His Life,* trans. by Edward Fitz-gerald. Ann Arbor, University of Michigan, 1962, p. 2.

[4]In Easton, Loyd D., and Guddat, Kurt H. (Eds.): *Writings of the Young Marx on Philosophy and Society,* trans. by Loyd D. Easton and Kurt H. Guddat. Garden City, Doubleday, 1966, p. 49.

[5]Erikson, E. H.: The roots of virtue. In Huxley, Julian (Ed.): *The Humanist Frame.*

deep acquaintance with his subject in his Latin themes.[6] We have also direct evidence of his skill in his essay, "Reflections of a Youth on Choosing an Occupation." [7] Thus Karl's playful confidence had been transformed into definite skills, managerial and pragmatic powers, giving him a link with the adult world. But he was still only a youth of seventeen. His career and all the other tasks of adulthood lay before him.

What resources for the shaping of his adulthood was Karl beginning to acquire? In the first place, his family and school in Trier had what many families and schools in the western world do not have today, a serious axiological orientation. History, as Heinrich and Henrietta Marx looked out on it, had order, meaning, and direction. Heinrich Marx professed to "a pure belief in God," [8] supplemented by a rational conviction in the progress of mankind. At first Jews, then Christians, the parents humanized their religion with the free and reasonable spirit of the eighteenth century Enlightenment. Their adoption of Christianity in 1816 "was an act of civilized progress"; it carried them into the mainstream of European culture and emancipated them from religious and social segregation.[9] Although the father was a nostalgic patriot of the "Old Fritzian" type, he also had mankind in view. Born a subject of the Trier Elector, he became a French subject, then a Prussian one. So he had no overwhelming national feeling. He followed Condorcet's philosophy that man is born good and that his fulfillment requires only the rational removal of social obstacles, chiefly political and religious tyranny. The mature Karl, who never showed excessive feelings of loyalty to any country, was fond of saying, "I am a citizen of the world," and, "Work for humanity." [10] He could easily write, "The workingmen have no country," [11] mistaking his own feelings for those of the proletariat. His involuntary exiles may have contributed to those feelings; but he had adopted his identification with humanity as early as the age of seventeen, and its roots must be found in his family situation.

[6] *Karl Marx. The Story of His Life,* pp. 4-5.

[7] In *Writings of the Young Marx on Philosophy and Society,* pp. 35-39.

[8] *Karl Marx. The Story of His Life,* p. 3.

[9] *Ibid.*

[10] Lafargue, Paul: Reminiscences of Marx. In *Reminiscences of Marx and Engels,* p. 72.

[11] Marx, Karl, and Engels, Friedrich: *Manifesto of the Communist Party,* p. 28.

The society of adults among whom Karl was brought up was not one of harmony. The German landowners and provincial rulers, disorganized by the Napoleonic wars, were determined to ride the returning tide of Bourbon reaction throughout Europe and to roll back all signs of new democratic practice. Under the leadership of Frederick William III, they restored the old feudal system. To them revolutionary ideas were anathema. The landed gentry and aristocracy reinstituted that stagnant and tariff-protected agrarianism which had kept the German states so backward for so many centuries hitherto. Nevertheless, the Revolution and the Napoleonic armies had left behind the irritant of ideas, the gadflies of antithesis, that would not let the old nag of the state rest in peace. Liberal industrialists and traders also wanted to be about their business, but could not. The bourgeoisie and the urban aristocracy, particularly those in the Rhineland which always looked toward France, chafed under these restrictions. Such was the conflict that had helped to produce revolutions in Europe in centuries past. The upshot was the multiplication of police, a large supervisory bureaucracy, censorship, protests by writers and voluntary exiles. The Jews, after Napoleon with his code had liberated them, were forced back into the ghetto or, as in the case of the Marx family, required to join the officially sanctioned Christian Church.[12]

The young Marx must have been aware of these larger conflicts and have taken notice of how they affected his father and others around him. He must have observed the price that his father, sweet-tempered and unmilitant, had paid for his conformity to the state—an assimilated Jew, a liberal bourgeois, who had been locked by the state into an unreasonable decision for himself and his family. Specifically, Karl must have carried in his thought the rebuff his father suffered at the hands of the police when he publicly called for moderate reforms by the King—as well as his father's submissive retraction. We know, moreover, that some of Karl's teachers at the *Gymnasium* were in disfavor with the secret police; it is unlikely that Karl was ignorant of this fact. Do not such experiences sear the memory of a sensitive youth and remain there, vividly waiting for later understanding to reveal their full dimensions of meaning and for the opportunity to cry out publicly against them?

---

[12]Berlin, Isaiah: *Karl Marx. His Life and Environment,* 3rd ed. New York, Oxford, 1963, ch. 2.

In a few years, armed with a university education, the youth would write savage attacks against state censorship and the oppression of the Jews. In his essay on the Jewish question, in 1843, Marx characteristically strove toward a universal viewpoint and universal political emancipation; but he saw that even a liberal political society is dehumanizing, alienating, and contradictory. Was not the young man here settling accounts with those Trier police who had humiliated his father? Was he not avenging the oppression of his "dear Father, best of fathers," by showing the world that he suffered and all Jews and all men suffer because in his work and everyday relations he has not become a "species-being", because he has not "recognized and organized his own . . . social powers"? [13]

Here we have the political Hamlet who has risen up to avenge the spiritual death of his dear father. If his father was rational, then he the heir must be rational and practical. The seeds of Karl's evolution into adulthood thus germinated at home, at school, and in his association at Trier. The quality of his resolve to do something purposeful and significant as an adult took shape early in life. He wrote:

> Never can I calmly realize
> What steadfastly grips my soul,
> Never can I rest in comfort,
> Storms forever through me roll. [14]

A commentator has described the young Marx, probably correctly, as follows:

> . . . with a sharp and lucid intelligence he combined a stubborn and domineering temper, a truculent love of independence, exceptional emotional restraint, and over all a colossal, ungovernable intellectual appetite. [15]

"Is your heart equal to your head?" his father had asked him in a letter to the youth at the University of Bonn. "Has it room for these

---

[13]Marx, Karl: On the Jewish Question. In Marx, Karl: *Early Writings*, trans. and ed. by T. B. Bottomore. New York, McGraw-Hill, 1964, p. 31.

[14]Nimmer kann ich ruhig treiben
Was die Seele stark befasst,
Nimmer still behaglich bleiben
Und ich stürme ohne Rast.

[15]*Karl Marx. His Life and Environment*, p. 28.

tender earthly feelings. . . . ?" [16] Marx had such feelings, as his love for Jenny showed. But he was marching to a distant drum, which his father could not hear and which Karl himself was struggling to make out.

In tracing the formation of this iron-willed character, who was satisfied with no less than finding his final identity in knowing and obeying the iron laws of history, we must mention one other adult influence.

The young Karl lived in an "enriched" environment. Not only did he have the friendship of his father and the instruction of his teachers, but a neighbor and free spirit, Freiherr Ludwig von Westphalen, a high government official and a friend of the family, took a special interest in the youth. This man was a "fervent supporter" of the views of Saint-Simon and one of the first to introduce Karl to them.[17] Steeped in Goethe, Schiller, and Hölderlin,[18] and capable of reciting large parts of Homer and Shakespeare by heart,[19] he cultivated Karl, took walks with him in the woods and along the Moselle Valley, and discussed Dante and Cervantes and the Greek tragedians.[20] Karl retained a deep love for these writers till the end of his days. More important was his warm and devoted relation to Westphalen at a critical period in his life. For the man was more than a tutor; he was, in Karl's words, a "dear fatherly friend," for whom Karl felt "filial love" [21] and to whom he dedicated his doctoral dissertation in glowing terms.

As fate would have it, the eldest son of this gifted, urbane, and kindly man became a careerist and feudalist, while Karl's father desired nothing more for him than a successful bourgeois career. Thus it is that social choice and elective affinities can supply what nature lacks. Westphalen's adoption of Karl and Karl's choice of him gave Karl a spiritual sponsor and confidant, a living model out of the past

---

[16]Quoted in Catlin, George: *The Story of the Political Philosophers.* New York, Tudor, 1939, p. 561.

[17]Kovalevsky, M.: Meetings with Marx. In *Reminiscences of Marx and Engels,* p. 298.

[18]*Karl Marx. His Life and Environment,* p. 32.

[19]Liebknecht, Wilhelm: Reminiscences of Marx. In *Remininscences of Marx and Engels,* p. 130.

[20]*Karl Marx. His Life and Environment,* p. 32.

[21]*Karl Marx. The Story of His Life,* p. 8.

to whom he could link his newly won intellectual freedom, a mature spirit with whom he could identify and whose freedom he could perpetuate and advance. It is in such relations of trust between older and younger generations that the treasures of the past are passed on to the future in a legacy that preserves, builds on, and transforms their value. In such concrete interpersonal relations the older generation knows that what it and its fathers and mothers before it have learned will not be lost but will be extended and improved; and the younger generation in turn knows that what it and its children will learn will not be isolated and alien but will be founded on a solid continuum of human struggle and achievement. Westphalen gave to Karl a sense of the living past, and Karl in turn gave Westphalen a sense of the living future. What more could a son ask of a father, or a father of a son?

When we speak of the influence of the past on Karl, who as a mature man was ever enriching his feeling and thought with the perspectives of the past—we cannot underestimate the influence of the town in which he lived for the first seventeen years of his life. Trier (French Trèves) was the oldest town in Germany, founded about 15 B.C. by the Romans, who imposed their order on the Treveri tribe. Diocletian made Trier the capital of the whole diocese of Gaul, Constantine the Great resided there, and it was the seat of an archbishopric from the ninth to the nineteenth century. Its medieval university (1473-1797) was a great center of monastic learning.[22] The young Karl growing up in such surroundings must have learned much of this long history, not only by word of mouth from his elders, but also from simple physical feelings acquired in confronting recurrently the remains of a long past—the Roman amphitheater, the fortified city gate, the Roman baths and bridge, the brick basilicas, many churches, a Renaissance fountain. Out of such feelings a sense of history is made, as well as a sense of its *weight*. When Marx wrote in *Capital* that "alongside of modern evils a whole series of inherited evils oppress us, arising from the passive survival of antiquated modes of production, with their inevitable train of social and political anachronism" [23]—was he reflecting an unconscious awareness, dating from his boyhood days,

---

[22]Trier. In *Encyclopedia Britannica.* Chicago, Encyclopedia Britannica, 1959, vol. 22, pp. 469-470.

[23]Marx, Karl: *Capital: A Critical Analysis Of Capitalist Production,* vol. I, p. 9.

of how the heavy inheritance of physical structures and mental and emotional habits had confined the free spirits of his father and Westphalen? Was he not always aware of the positive and negative forces present in our material and cultural history?

Finally, as Heinz Monz has pointed out in his 1964 work, *Karl Marx und Trier: Verhältnis, Beziehungen, Einflüsse*, the city of Trier during the period of Karl's youth was racked by social, political, and economic tensions that produced profound unrest. The legal administration of Trier was anti-Prussian and disposed toward freedom, and the city council fought the introduction of Prussian law. The university remained closed, the chief justice resided in Köln, the government dominated the city and occupied the Bishop's Seat (three-fourths of the city were Catholic). Various societies became centers of opposition. Heinrich Marx himself was the main speaker at an occasion honoring Trier representatives in the Provincial Diet. Invitations with a Prussian accent were ignored. Thanks to Karl's headmaster and teacher, Johann Hugo Wyttenbach, a devotee of the French Revolution, the *Gymnasium* that Karl attended had for thirty years turned out critical and independent men. One-fourth of the Trier people lived by alms, and the great majority were sunk in poverty. Trier (population 1825: 12,686) was hemmed in; the old trade routes were blocked and lacked capital. Customs agreements with Bayern and Württemberg displaced the Moselle wine from the Prussian market and brought down the price of wine sharply. Agricultural proceeds were small. Prices continued to rise and unemployment increased. Money and food were scarce, trading inactive, taxes burdensome. Theft developed. State support of debtors increased. In 1830 a bread-fruit warehouse was founded to supply the poor and bring pressure on prices, and Heinrich Marx participated in the association that supported it. No doubt all of these conditions affected Karl, particularly when he was learning from Westphalen the Saint-Simonian doctrine that all this poverty, the consequence of objective conditions more than of human will, might be wiped away by the proper organization of industry through science. Karl remembered the misery of these wretched of the earth: later as editor of the *Rheinische Zeitung* he fought against the class of forest owners and their wood-theft law exploiting the poor; and he heeded the "cries for help" of the Moselle vintagers, cries which echoed from childhood in the conscience of the youth.

The influence of Karl's experiences with the world of nature should not be overlooked. During his youth such a world was easily accessible from the town, and we know that he went with his mentor Westphalen into the countryside for jaunts. During his youthful crisis at the University of Berlin, the young Karl wrote ruefully of having neglected "nature, art, and the world" in favor of his nocturnal studies;[24] and his early philosophy shows a profound appreciation for the qualities and forms of nature and man's necessary sensory and esthetic relation to them.[25] Such appreciation was in all likelihood first awakened in the countryside around Trier and carried in the mature man as he took his own children for Sunday walks in the country.[26]

All of these factors combined to produce a youth self-possessed though somewhat introverted in his driving purpose. He enjoyed considerable social status. His father was well-off, became a *Justizrat* (lawyer of high rank), belonged to a liberal literary society (along with Karl's headmaster), and associated with distinguished government advisors like Ludwig von Westphalen. Karl went to a good school, and was tutored by one of the most cultivated men in the community who embodied the best of the German and classical literary tradition. What this did to him was not to bring him into adjustment with his society, but to take him out of and above it, to give him a perspective of detachment and critical discernment, to lay before him questions which he was to spend a whole lifetime in struggling to answer. He surely must have realized, as every precocious youth does, particularly those attuned to social and political questions, that he stood out from his peers and many of the townspeople. He never afterwards mentioned any of his classmates. But this realization was only inchoate while he remained at Trier. When he went away to Bonn and then Berlin it was quickly focussed and directed, and the Trier youth was on his way to radicalizing himself and his world.

---

[24] Letter to his father, November 10, 1837. In *Writings of the Young Marx on Philosophy and Society*, p. 46.

[25] Marx, Karl: *Economic and Philosophical Manuscripts*, pp. 100, 127, 129, 132-136.

[26] Lafargue, Paul: *Op. cit.*, p. 81.

There is little doubt that Marx contemplated with delight his role in that irony of history by which a class raises up one of its sons in such wise that he will help to overthrow it. This role of the young Marx did not result because he hated his father and wanted to marry his mother, or because he was driven by a will to power, or because he was hard-hearted and economic in his approach to all things. It occurred because the young Marx had the good fortune to enjoy healthy relations in his home life, his school, and his associations with Ludwig and Jenny von Westphalen, and because he took from such relations the ego strength, the human feelings, the emotional drive and commitment, and the interest in large and liberating ideas, that impelled him necessarily to become a revolutionary.

Lenin, in his account of Marx's life, tersely remarks: "The family [of Marx] was well-to-do, cultured, but not revolutionary." [27] But the group to which Karl as a youth belonged was, in part at least, at odds with the ruling, landed promonarchial class—a group liberal and humanistic in outlook, and in trouble with the police. It was also a group which, like Lenin's, gave to some of its youth the education and self-confidence to become, under subsequent favorable conditions, revolutionaries. The adult Marx understood this. We must keep in mind the adolescent Marx—living in the provincial city of Trier and taking in these larger social conflicts—when we read what he wrote at the age of twenty-nine:

> The bourgeoisie finds itself involved in a constant battle. At first with the aristocracy; later on, with those portions of the bourgeoisie itself whose interests have become antagonistic to the progress of industry. . . . The bourgeoisie . . . supplies the proletariat with its own elements of political and general education, in other words, it furnishes the proletariat with weapons for fighting the bourgeoisie.[28]

During the period of his studies in the *Gymnasium* Karl was beginning to face the distinctive crisis of adolescence, namely a decision regarding his life-identity. Erickson defines this as the stage in the evolutionary life-cycle of the individual when fidelity is developed—i.e., "the strength of disciplined devotion."[29] In this period the in-

---

[27]Lenin, V. I.: Karl Marx. In *Reminiscences of Marx and Engels,* p. 28.

[28]*Manifesto of the Communist Party,* pp. 18-19.

[29]Erikson, Erik H.: Youth, fidelity and diversity. *Daedalus, 91*: 23, 1962.

dividual, his associates, and his society together determine what he is and what he shall be, defining him in his present potentiality and his future course, marking him off in his individuality, but also indicating what his relation is and will be to others and to the society as a whole. Both the uniqueness of individuality and the necessity of destiny are defined. The meshing of individual talent and social demand may not be smooth and well regulated; and in that case the adolescent becomes a rebel or a diffuse deviant or a drifter, and the society falls apart. The rebellion may be blind and futile, contributing only to further social disintegration. Or it may lead toward the construction of a new society. But insofar as a society holds together and creatively advances, it makes provision for this integration of individual energy and communal tradition, of the new and the old, of freedom and fate.

Social disintegration expresses itself both in (1) the anomie and estrangement of individuals from the purposes held up by the ruling groups in the society, and in (2) the repression and conformity of the free diversity of individuals by the ruling groups. Somewhere between these two extremes lies the course of a creative society, wherein freedom and necessity are creatively jointed and the older and younger generations create and are created by one another. Revolutionary individuals and movements within societies are efforts to protest against excessive drift and conformity (they develop together) and to create this kind of creative transformation of tradition. If and as such revolutions are successful, they succeed in developing within their own movements this fidelity, i.e., a dialectic identity of individual purposes with social traditions and goals. Creative human diversity is never developed apart from the creative identification of the individual with his familial, social, and human history. The individual is created precisely at that point where he selects, internalizes, and reorganizes the meanings of his society's past. History is thus transformed as it is revived in the individual personality.

This transformation of history goes on continually in every individual personality from birth onward. The organism learns to respond to the signs made by those around him, to make similar signs himself, and to respond to those signs as others respond. Thus he learns the meanings or expectations of others, with their diverse designative, appraisive, prescriptive, and syntactical dimensions. He learns to adopt sets of expectations, or roles, and to take his role within an organization of roles, or institutions. Up until the age of adolescence, this process for the individual person is more or less passive, dominated by adults and the fixities of tradition. With the onset of adolescence, however, radical and qualitative changes occur. There is a spurt of physical growth, so that the body of the child suddenly becomes an adult body. And there is physiological and anatomical transformation —a psychosexual change—which sensitizes the person in all the modes of his being—sexual, emotional, intellectual, active, communicative, aspirational, devotional. The child is in a short period catapulted into the body of an energetic adult. Physically, he cannot go backward to the world of the child; psychically, he is not yet prepared to enter the world of mature adults, though he has suddenly been equipped with the capacities. This is the crisis of adolescence.

The direction of the young Marx's fidelity is revealed in an examination essay, "Reflections of a Youth on Choosing an Occupation,"[30] which he wrote at the age of seventeen shortly before his graduation from the *Gymnasium* and his entrance into the University at Bonn. "To man," he wrote, ". . . the Deity gave a general goal, to improve mankind and himself, but left it up to him to seek the means by which he can attain this goal." Here the young man points out that many factors can deceive us in the choice of a vocation—fantasy, emotion, ambition. In such cases not even reason can be relied on. At this juncture Karl shows how deeply he trusted his parents: "But where shall we look for support when our reason leaves us in the lurch? Our heart calls upon our parents who have walked the path of life, have experienced fate's severity." Let us not mistake this for conservatism, which is nothing more than uncritical obedience to the past. For each man, says Karl, must begin with "deepest conviction," "the innermost voice of the heart," "inspiration." After one's parents are consulted, one must apply one's own analytical powers—testing the inspiration "objectively," perceiving its "burden," knowing its "encumbrances." One must recognize one's existential restrictions: "Our social relations, to some extent, have already begun to form before we are in a position to determine them." Here the young Marx shows an adoles-

---

[30]*Writings of the Young Marx on Philosophy and Society,* pp. 35-39.

cent awareness of self and society, a painful awakening of the idealist imagination to the limits imposed on one's life, a recognition of the rugged and irreversible course of history. There is, in this essay at least, a willingness in the youth to accept the conditions of his life in Trier. But in his sense of dependence on those conditions, the youth also expresses his indebtedness to them and his resolve to assume responsibility for the destiny thrust upon him. That calls us, he says, to be analytical: we must consider "the entire burden and great responsibility to be placed upon us." And in the young Marx this responsibility was to assume a burden no less than that of the destiny of mankind itself.

We can see that, because of the fortunate union of his own capacities with his close personal relations and opportunities for development, the young Marx found, in early adolescence, a happy balance between self and society that would define and sustain his identity throughout life. One must have the physical nature and individual talents, he says, for one's chosen vocation. And, almost over-stern with his stormy nature, he declares that one must cultivate "calmness" in oneself in order to "stand up against life's tempestuous urge." Many a nineteenth century youth had a kindred impulse—to create a personal order of life in the face of a chaotic world. But the young Marx had something greater in mind—ultimate union of personal order with social order through "great and beautiful deeds." This is more than abstract duty. Today the very phrase "identity crisis" suggests a certain bourgeois wistfulness, a loss whose recovery is problematic. The young Marx was bourgeois too, and suffered his own identity crisis. But at seventeen he showed a precocious grasp of the meaning of vocation not only for himself but for *all* men. He was aware of the necessity of "sacrificing our welfare to duty." Thus he displayed a Kantian sense of duty that would have pleased every Prussian bent on practicing the Protestant ethic. But the young Titan was in process of transvaluating merely Prussian and Protestant values.

Now comes the revolutionary part. Once we have tested our inspiration by analysis of the relevant conditions, personal and social, we must apply to it three criteria: it must guarantee us the greatest dignity, it must be based on a truth of which we are "completely convinced," and it must offer "the largest field to work for mankind," approaching "the universal goal for which every position is only a means: perfection."

> Man's nature makes it possible for him to reach his fulfillment only by working for the perfection and welfare of his society. If a person works only for himself he can perhaps be a famous scholar, a great wise man, a distinguished poet, but never a complete, genuinely great man. History calls those the greatest men who ennobled themselves by working for the universal. Experience praises as the most happy the one who made the most people happy. Religion itself teaches us that the ideal for which we are all striving sacrificed itself for humanity, and who would dare to destroy such a statement?

The revolutionary element in this testament of conviction is the repudiation of selfish goals, even those of noble professions, and the identification of youth with "the welfare of humanity." A mere creed of course is not revolutionary—Marx realized that. But a hugely ambitious and world-transforming vision is present here.

This vision assumed in the young Marx a humanistic, Christian form. In a second *Gymnasium* examination essay, he asserted that we are bound to our brothers through the love of Christ, who has sacrificed himself for all.[31] It was a natural form for his idealism. The youth had been baptized into the Evangelical Church of Prussia and had studied Christianity as a required subject in primary and secondary schools; and he had learned of the Christian utopian socialism of Saint-Simon from his father and Westphalen. Karl would soon abandon this form of thinking. In the years following, under the influences of Hegel and then Feuerbach, he came to seek "the Idea in the real itself"[32] and to reject supernaturalistic Christianity. But the vision embracing the welfare of all people living as brothers and sisters is one that he had as early as seventeen, and that he spent his lifetime working out in material, practical ways.

"Reflections of a Youth on Choosing an Occupation" significantly deals not with a specific occupation but with the notion of "vocation" or "calling." Like the Jewish prophets and those who have throughout Christian history dedicated themselves to the service of a supremely significant purpose in a particular office, the young Karl had a sense

---

[31]Cited in *Ibid.*, p. 35.
[32]Letter to his father. In *Ibid.*, p. 46.

of being called to a transcendent task. There is evident in this essay
a feeling of being commanded and compelled by a necessity internal
and external, personal and historical. Later, the young Marx would
write of the necessity of man to produce out of his own need,[33] and
of "the objectification of man's species life" as the aim of his labor.[34]
And the mature Marx would write of "tendencies working with iron
necessity towards inevitable results." [35]   Still later, scholars would
polemicise over the "humanistic" Marx and the "scientific" Marx,
over his "freedom" and his "necessity," not realizing that from the
time of this essay of the seventeen-year old to the end Marx sought
to keep the individual and history in a dialectical unity. In this essay
the young Marx was far from ready to give himself in "disciplined
devotion" to an occupation precipitately and prematurely chosen. But
his life-long commitment, his "farthest goal," was unequivocal. The
young man would settle for nothing less than the highest, the liberation
of all mankind.

Then, as today, many young people and many adults would have
called this approach unrealistic. Choose a specific occupation, they
would say—one that will bring you physical security and personal satisfaction; then your service to society and your philosophy of life can
follow in their own time. The young Marx reasoned (before reading
Hegel) that the real is mankind and nature in their historical development, that the individual person is an agent and servant of this supreme reality and value including, but transcending, its particular
manifestations; that one's first duty is to think through one's ultimate
vocation in life and history and not how one might make a living;
and that once that is done one might easily find one's place and duty
in the whole developing scheme and purpose of things. Who was correct? Today we remember that seventeen-year old who was thinking
first about serving "the welfare of mankind" and who dreamed of
finding his own happiness in helping all others to find happiness. Those
millions who sought first their own happiness have long since been
forgotten. Marx lives on not merely in his thoughts but in those institutions of socialism which have taken their inspiration and guidance

---

[33]Marx, Karl, and Engels, Friedrich: *The German Ideology*, p. 16.

[34]*Economic and Philosophical Manuscripts*, p. 102.

[35]*Capital*, vol. I, pp. 8-9.

from him. The man who dreamed of the "higher" reality which others denounced as merely "ideal" has turned out in the long run to be the most realistic and practical.

There is nothing nihilistic or antinomian about Karl's idealism. Karl's relations with his father were affectionate and open; there is no sign that he had a hang-up in his relations with figures of authority. Here, as throughout his life, Marx puts himself on the side of the best in tradition as he found it. He does not propose a sharp and violent break with the past. Instead, he begins with his heritage as he knows it, locates its humanistic tendencies, and projects these into the future. This was always his way; and the Hegelian method, which was later discovered and developed, and which *conserved* its object while transforming and improving it, was admirably suited to his outlook. Marx became steeped in the culture of the past, but was not drowned by it. One of his friends said of him: "Imagine Rousseau, Voltaire, Holbach, Lessing, Heine and Hegel fused into one person. I say fused, not thrown together in a heap." [36] Throughout his life he was always exploring and integrating into his thinking new domains of life and thought, past and present, through languages, correspondence, and study. He realized that man is a human and hence historical being and that the revolutionizing act begins with the concrete individual's critical and practical transformation of his own situation and tradition.

Normally the preadolescent is protected and proscribed within the limits of a peer group which his society oversees; and his development proceeds without serious complication to himself or his society. But with the emergence of adolescent genitality and energies and the awareness of self, others, and the demands of adulthood, the central human crisis in identity begins. Unlike the other animals, man does not pass with the ease of instinct into tasks and responsibilities of parenthood and adulthood. For he is not only a somatic organism; he is psychosomatic and social, and his rapidly developing psyche is faced with problem of defining its goals and values and of directing itself in relation to the somatic needs from below and the social demands from beyond. Adolescents meet this identity crisis by the different strategies of dependence, domination, and detachment. The pathological extremes of these strategies are passively submitting to others or

---

[36] Moses Hess, cited in Berlin, Isaiah: *Op. cit.,* p. 73.

to a group, aggressively dominating the environment of persons and things, and isolating the self and withdrawing from contact with the world. Perhaps the most common forms of adolescent behavior in the United States today are (1) gangs which combine aggressive and destructive activity against the environment with total loyalty to the rules of the gang, (2) groups which separate themselves from the demands of society, which are relatively passive toward it, and which are motivated by bohemian indulgence, and (3) groups which conform to the expectations of the society and prepare their members for entrance into it. In time, of course, most youths conform to the expectations, roles, and institutions of society; their adolescent search for long-range meanings and commitments in life is channeled into the meanings and commitments of the society. Thus, the essential choices of the adolescent unassimilated to society in most cases are reduced to two: to take refuge in the activity of some kind of group which, with its special name, its insignia and secret words and codes, its initiation and rituals, its solidarity and mutual affirmation, its intimacy, its sense of "we" against "they" and "right" against "wrong," provides a sense of commitment; to defy all forms of social activity, the approved and the disapproved, by the pathway of lonely suffering and piercing criticism.

We have no evidence that the adolescent Marx was either a joiner of an approved or disapproved group, or a lonely sufferer. He does not appear to have run with a gang in the days of the *Gymnasium* or the University, nor does he appear to have been a brooding Kierkegaard or Dostoevsky. He was too skeptical, perceptive, and demanding to be taken in by a spurious commitment to some group with its all-embracing answers. That is the trap into which many young American, in their need for commitment, prematurely fall; hence they remain arrested adolescents for the rest of their lives, practicing a shallow loyalty to groups ranging from the Rotary Club to the nation. Even when the young Marx became a member of the Young Hegelians, he took nothing for granted; in the end he became the leader of men older than himself and outstripped all in his intellectual development. On the other side, the young Marx's social needs and talents were too healthy to drive him into the depths of isolated despair. It is true that he had periods of individual doubt, search, and suffering. But there is evidence that he never let go of the conviction expressed when he was seventeen, that man's nature is social and calls him to work with and for others.[37]

It is quite probable that the young Marx was never seriously tempted to follow the route of joining a passive or active adolescent gang. He lived in a large, bourgeois family which appears to have been strict in its expectations for him both in school and out. Westphalen's influence early oriented him to the cultural world of the adult. His *Gymnasium* essay showed already superior critical powers. And most important, his emotional life and sexual sensitivities were early concentrated on a particular person, to whom be became engaged to be married. This pledge at the age of seventeen seems to have served for Karl the function served for many adolescents by a pledge to a group of their peers: it directed his teeming energies toward another person and lent to them form and duration. In an adolescent world of uncertainty, it was a decision and investment in definiteness. It was the kind of vow which every adolescent needs, i.e., a pledge to commit one's self to someone and to a definite style of life. For Karl it was a test; for he must have known that marriage must wait several if not many years. But it is the kind of test of deprivation and hardship which adolescents seek in order to prove their manhood. Moreover, Karl had an overarching commitment in mind; and he must have intuited that his fiancee would fit into and facilitate that as yet general plan.

A necessary stage in the evolution of the maturing person is love— that intimate sharing of personal concerns with another person, that partnership in search of individual and mutual identity.[38] Love may develop before or after the emergence of a clear-cut vocational goal and well-formed fidelity in life—that is to say, its lightning may strike in early or middle or late adolescence, or in the maturity of adulthood. But in any case, if love functions healthily and contributes to the ongoing maturation of the individual person, it reinforces his decision of fidelity and its released energies help to carry him to the higher levels of adult care and seasoned wisdom. Men and women can ac-

[37]Marx, Karl: Reflections of a Youth on Choosing an Occupation. In *Writings of the Young Marx on Philosophy and Society*, p. 39.

[38]Erikson, E. H.: The roots of virtue. In *The Humanist Frame*, pp. 158-159.

complish a great deal without such love, as the lives of celibate heroes and heroines testify. But they themselves found outlets for that emotional fervor and tenderness toward others which is concentrated with special force in the sentiment and action of romantic love.

As in his relations with his parents, his older sister, his teachers, and his spiritual mentor Westphalen, Karl Marx was lucky in love. It was a love that came to him early and that, like his own purpose in life, lasted until the day he died. Jenny von Westphalen, the daughter of the man who befriended Karl before his adolescence, had been a childhood playmate. Four years his senior, she had no doubt looked down on the younger boy, as older girls tend to do, with a mixture of indulgent humor and motherly affection. Physiologically, she was still older than he, so that when he reached pubescence she was some years beyond him. By this time the carefree play of the children of the neighborhood must have been abandoned, replaced by more sedate games or conversation. No doubt Karl saw the young lady "by chance" many times in the home of her father, to which he had been invited for discussions on the Greek tragedians and the great German poets. Jenny has been described by more than one witness as "healthy, merry and beautiful," the "most beautiful girl in Trèves," [39] with more than the normal complement of intelligence and charm. According to one account, Karl fell in love with her while still at the *Gymnasium,* and before leaving for the University became secretly engaged to her.[40]

The engagement was a bold step, considering not so much the difference in ages as the difference in social levels of the two young people. But in the end the families did not prevent the marriage, which had to wait over seven years—a wait which indicates the durability of the bond and the determination of the two young sweethearts. We can suppose also that this marriage had great significance for Karl. Not only did Jenny possess superlative personal gifts; she was in addition the daughter of his own spiritual father, and to fuse his life with hers would complete the union that he had already formed with her father and that would pass into their children. In being linked with Jenny, Karl would also be linked with the spiritual past which her father

---

[39]Kovalevsky, M. Meetings with Marx. In *Reminiscences of Marx and Engels,* p. 298.
[40]*Ibid.*

embodied. Moreover, in the face of protracted opposition from both sides, for Karl such a marriage would not only be a victory over social class and tradition—Karl would later have his wife sign hotel registers as "Baroness";[41] it would also be a triumph of youth over age, of love over custom, and reason over unreason. And it was such a triumph that the young Titan and the incipient revolutionary needed as a necessary ingredient in his life-plan.

The life-long love affair of Karl and Jenny, initially luck, was in the long run the creation of hard work and fidelity to a purpose which began with their own mutual confirmation and which in time transcended their own private needs and feelings. How keenly do young lovers feel the dead hand of the past upon them! How well do Romeos and Juliets understand that "in bourgeois society [their own society] the past dominates the present"! [42] At the age of twenty-five, just before his marriage, Karl wrote to a friend:

> I can assure you without any romanticism that I am head over heels and in all seriousness in love. We have been engaged now for over seven years and my future wife has had to fight hard struggles on my behalf partly against her pious aristocratic relatives who regard their "Father in Heaven" and the government in Berlin as equal objects of veneration, and partly against my own family in which a number of parsonical individuals and other enemies of mine have got a hold, and these struggles have almost undermined her health. For years, therefore, my future wife and I have been compelled to engage in unnecessary and exhausting conflicts, more so in fact than many people three times our age who are always talking about their "experience of life."[43]

We do not know the nature of these conflicts but can imagine them. According to the daughter Eleanor, the engagement caused "fairly stormy scenes" at home, and her father told her that "at that time he had been a really furious Roland." [44]

Jenny turned out to be as inept in financial matters as Karl;[45] but she was devoted to his work and his cause, shared his intellectual in-

[41]Catlin, George: Op. cit., p. 562.

[42]Manifesto of the Communist Party, p. 24.

[43]Karl Marx. The Story of His Life, pp. 55-56.

[44]Marx-Aveling, Eleanor: Remarks on a letter by the young Marx. In Reminiscences of Marx and Engels, p. 256.

[45]Kugelmann, Franzisca: Small traits of Marx's great character. In Reminiscences of Marx and Engels, p. 279.

terests and his friends, and was the centripetal force in keeping the
family together through years of bitter poverty and the death of four
children. It is impossible to imagine Karl Marx without this emotional
mainstay. She balanced and confirmed his own life-commitment
with her own.

What Jenny supplied to Karl was the security of a warm and stead-
fast love as single-minded in its devotion to her family and husband
as he was in his devotion to his work. Many commentators have remarked on Marx's freedom from sentimentality and have coupled
this with an alleged hardheartedness. But one need only look at his
relations to his Jenny and his children to see that he was a man whose
heart easily and fully ran the gamut of healthy human emotions—joy,
sorrow, indignation, compassion, hope, gall. Liebknecht has observed
that Marx

> was as incapable as a child of wearing a mask or pretending . . . . he
> always spoke his mind completely and without any reserve and his face
> was the mirror of his heart. And when circumstances demanded re-
> straint, he showed a sort of childlike awkwardness that often amused
> his friends.[46]

Marx's stormy nature was evident in his adolescence, but he had
brought it under control and accepted it. In reply to the "Olympian"
notion, the gods of the classics, he said, are eternal passion without
any unrest.[47] In his incapacity for hyprocisy, Marx was like a child.[48]
His wife knew this, and with her, most of all, he was free to express
the full gamut of his feelings. She "often called him 'my big baby' "[49]
and perhaps nothing else tells us more of her affectionate and protective attitude toward him. Probably Liebknecht is correct when he
says that "nobody, not even Engels, knew or understood him better
than she did."[50] Marx's tremendous intellectual achievements and
the relegation of Jenny to the role of housewife have led some to draw
superficial and false conclusions about their relations. "She . . . was,
emotionally and intellectually, entirely dominated by him," writes

---

[46]Liebknecht, Wilhelm: *Op cit.,* p. 106.
[47]Kugelmann, Franzisca: *Op. cit.,* p. 278.
[48]Liebknecht, Wilhelm: *Op cit.,* p. 107.
[49]*Ibid.*
[50]*Ibid.*

Berlin.[51] But let a first-hand observer, their youngest daughter, Eleanor, speak:

> Assuredly two people never enjoyed a joke more than these two . . . .
> To see these two with eyes fixed on anything but one another, for all
> the world two schoolchildren, suffocating with suppressed laughter that
> at last despite all efforts would well forth, is a memory I would not
> barter.[52]

This mutual spirit of playfulness, expressive of a simple trust, was something the two had no doubt developed in their earliest relations in Trier. But Jenny was intelligent and witty in her own right; Heinrich Heine was "full of admiration" for her "penetrating and sensitive mind."[53] Jenny did not write books like Karl; but that was because she was too busy cooking and tending sick children and keeping wolfish creditors from the door and copying out Karl's manuscripts. But her love went into Karl and lives on in those books and in the workers' movement that Karl and Jenny together generated. In 1844, the year after his marriage, the young Marx wrote:

> If you love without evoking love in return, i.e., if you are not able, by
> the *manifestation* of yourself as a loving person, to make yourself a be-
> loved person, then your love is impotent and a misfortune.[54]

It was a lesson he had learned from concrete experience. Twelve years later he wrote to his wife:

> As soon as you are far away, my love for you appears as what it is, as a
> giant in whom all the energy of my spirit and all the disposition of my
> heart compress [zusammendrängt]. I feel myself once more a man, for
> I feel a great passion, and the diversity wherein study and modern educa-
> tion complicate us, and skepticism, with which we necessarily find fault
> with all subjective and objective impressions, are designed utterly to
> make us very small and weak and wrangling and undecided. But love,
> not for Feuerbachian man, not for a Moleschottean digestive process, not
> for the proletariat, but love for a sweetheart [Liebchen], namely, you,
> makes the man once more the man.[55]

---

[51]*Op. cit.*, p. 80.
[52]Marx-Aveling, Eleanor: *Op. cit.*, p. 254.
[53]Lafargue, Paul: *Op. cit.*, p. 82.
[54]*Economic and Philosophical Manuscripts*, p. 168.
[55]My translation.

Do we need further testimony of the intimacy of Karl's relation to Jenny, and the necessity of that relation to his existence and sense of significance?

Karl's year at the University of Bonn in 1835-1836, with its drinking, dueling, and "wild frolics,"[56] must have given the old man pangs of disappointment and apprehension. We know little about this period. But the father complained of "Bills à la Karl," [57] and the bourgeois man, ambitious for his own son to follow in his footsteps in the law, must have had more than once doubts as to whether his son, on whom he had set such high hopes, would succeed. Karl was only seventeen; and even from the meager record of these years it is easy to see that while he loved his father dearly he stubbornly clung to his own dreams, which though not yet specific were quite different from those of his father for him. His father wanted him to study the law; the youth was not yet ready for that, and wisely he did not commit himself to it. For one year he appears simply to have "played around."

Erik H. Erikson has said that some form of "psychological moratorium" between genital maturity and responsible adulthood is built into the development of youth.[58] Adolescence or young adulthood is a period of transition and crisis in which the individual youth struggles to create a new identity out of the elements in his past and present, and to project that identity into the future in the form of a career-plan and philosophy of life (ideology). He knows it is a fateful choice; looking around him, he can see in adults success or failure, happiness or unhappiness, in consequence of their decisions concerning marriage, career, and ideology. Hence he may procrastinate indefinitely or hesitate over-long before making up his mind; he may impulsively grasp the opportunity that is available and immediately promising; or he may gradually settle into a life-style and purpose that suits his nature and the needs of his society. But in all or most cases there seems to be a demand for independent search and exploration. This experimenting of young people is necessarily wasteful, and is done in disregard of the advice of their elders; they make a demand for it.

---

[56]*Karl Marx. The Story of His Life,* p. 5.
[57]*Ibid.*
[58]Erikson, Erik H.: Youth, fidelity and diversity, p. 12.

"Crabbed age and youth cannot live together"—but society tolerates within limits the excesses of youth, and allows some sowing of wild oats. But the pleasures and oddities of youth place a great strain on the care of the parents—which is to say that history goes through strain and travail as every new generation comes to maturity. The later Marx understood this dialectical relation between the settled relations of the past and the insurgent forces of the present, though he expressed it in the general terms of class struggle. More than once he used the figure of a new society maturing "in the womb of the old society."[59] It is a root metaphor of birth, creation, of power, of hope. It is a vision of life that belongs to youth and that throughout Marx's adult life never ceased to glow and to draw him onward.

Most youthful dreams, like most mutations, come to nothing. They are fantasies and fragments, fitfully pursued. They are not organically related to the ongoing process of human life in families, places of work, and other institutions. Young people soon discover that the humdrum business of making a living must be minded. The coercive movements of the society carry them along. The mass of youth, like the mass of men, may dare to dream in moments of leisure or inspiration, but dare not dream too far or too long or with their dreams storm the Bastilles of existing society.

Some, however, persist in dreaming. Such dreamers either withdraw into their own private worlds or, trying to relate their dreams to society, cry to it from afar to come over into their lovely domiciles not built with human hands. Such utopians are in fact in flight from the depressing conditions of present society. At the other extreme conformists decry all imagination, large plans, and bold hopes. They dare not dream, lest their doubts about the present be measured against their hopes and give way to despair. They revert to a short-run, narrow pragmatism. They cringe from criticism and self-criticism. They become the anti-intellectual authoritarians, the defenders of the *status quo,* the deniers of dreams. As early as 1845 the young Marx saw that constructive social change had to combine in dialectical fashion the truth of dreaming with political activity. "Revolutionizing prac-

---

[59]Marx, Karl: *A Contribution to the Critique of Political Economy,* p. 12. See also *Critique of the Gotha Programme, The Civil War in France,* and *Capital.*

tice" is both critical and practical; it moves toward an ideal goal, but it moves through "real, sensuous activity." [60] It was a lesson he had learned from his own experience and reflection. Mere dreaming did not satisfy him; and he refused to be conformed to the world.

The young Marx's psychological moratorium lasted a year. Independent and expensive, the adolescent who appeared to pay no heed to his father's entreaties had his fling at the University, and seems to have gotten the waywardness out of his system. After the year he returned home, no doubt happy to see his dear Jenny again. Their engagement was revealed to their parents, who opposed it but in time became reconciled to it. Although Karl went off in the fall to the University of Berlin and did not hear from his sweetheart for a year, this commitment to Jenny seems to have given his life a balance and a direction that it had hitherto lacked. While with many a young man today an engagement represents an escape from academic work or a premature settling into bourgeois respectability, for the young Karl and Jenny it meant a mutual commitment to a future, unknown but believed in—a partnership of passion and ideas whose flame would sustain man and wife nearly half a century. The young man now had a definite though partial purpose for his life. He might look forward to a marriage at the end of his studies; and such a future permanency with a lovely, devoted friend must have stirred the proud youth to still greater confidence and a resolve now to find his concrete vocation. In the fall of 1836 he filled three exercise books with romantic poems dedicated to Jenny, who according to Marx's sister, received them with "tears of joy and sadness."[61]

In October Karl had transferred to the University of Berlin—a choice not his own.[62] Karl studied hard and accomplished a great many disparate things, as his famous letter of November 10, 1837 shows. Still, his father could not adjust to his son's sublime indifference to money matters—a trait that would remain with the revolutionary dreamer throughout life:

> As if we were made of gold our high and mighty son gets through almost 700 thalers in one year against all our agreements, against all custom, though the very richest do not spend 500. And why? . . . how

---

[60] *Theses on Feuerbach.*
[61] *Karl Marx. The Story of His Life,* p. 10.
[62] *Ibid.,* p. 9.

can a man who invents a new system every week or fortnight and has to tear up what he had previously worked at with so much pains, how can he, I ask, be bothered with trifles? How can he submit to petty regulations? Everyone has his hands in his pocket, and everyone cheats him.[63]

Still later, the father's solicitude and distraction led him to be more direct. He cannot resist saying what many parents are tempted to say to their unresponsive children: "I cannot always drive away the reflection that in your place I should have treated my parents with greater consideration, with more unselfish love."[64]

Karl had not yet graduated altogether from his bohemian stage. While he read voraciously and worked hard at creating "a new system every week or fortnight," neither his thoughts nor his physical surroundings were tidy. Experimentation, though somewhat more orderly and productive than that at Bonn, was still going forward. Let his father speak:

God help us! ! ! Lack of order, a brooding prowling around in all the fields of science, a stuffy brooding under a dismal oil lamp. Going to seed in a scholastic dressing gown with unkempt hair as a change from going to seed with beer glass in hand. Repellent unsociability and the consignment of everything decent, even including consideration for your own father, to a secondary position. The limitation of the social art to a dirty room where in woeful disorder the love letters of a Jenny and the well-meaning exhortations of a father, written with tears, perhaps, are used as pipe-lighters, which, by the way, is better than that they should fall into the hands of third persons as a result of still more irresponsible disorder.[65]

Heinrich Marx, the practical man and the doting father, seeing in his son "splendid natural gifts," feared, as every concerned parent must, and as every youth must, that such talent might be lodged useless in him or frittered away in a planless existence. Next to physical death or incapacitation, it is this spiritual death which is our common fear in a society lacking the requisite habits and institutions for mutual care and for the integration of individual purpose with social goals. Our United States society, in its driving obsession with individual power and status, leaves most individuals stranded and alienated. The

[63]Catlin, George: *Op. cit.,* pp. 561-562.
[64]*Ibid.,* p. 562.
[65]*Karl Marx. The Story of His Life,* p. 13.

young Marx, like every adolescent in class society, knew alienation in this sense. The anxious bourgeois father referred to the "Demon" in his son, wondering whether it would be "heavenly" or "Faustian." [66] Would such a son, so promising, so high-minded and militant, be sufficiently practical and social? "Is your heart equal to your head, to your capacities?"[67] The father could not free himself from the thought that the youth was too egoistic—not knowing that it was his own family that had helped to give Karl the ego strength that would in time turn the world upside down. Those who hold that this most influential of all revolutionaries must have been in rebellion against authority do not perhaps know that Karl carried a picture of his father with him until his death.[68]

Karl's "Demon," however, amidst all the dirt and disarray of his student life, was determined to find its direction. In a letter[69] in which he reviews his year of study, the young man is severely realistic and critical with himself. The serious search for a purpose in life, which showed itself in his *Gymnasium* essay, now appears in more concrete and somewhat desperate form. Nineteen and one-half years old, Karl feels he has come to the end of a period and is ready to search for "a new direction" indicated in the development he has reviewed. He is, in short, on the threshold of young adulthood. In addition, his sense of vocation, in the larger, Fichtean sense of that term, is keen. "We feel compelled," he writes to his father, " to contemplate the past and present with the eagle eye of thought to become aware of our actual position." Here Marx speaks of "world history" which "reflects upon itself." While this is a Hegelian and mystical way of putting the matter, it shows once more the youth's concern to identify his lifework with a comprehensive purpose.

As he himself described it, the young Marx's mood during this period was one of romantic sentiment, withdrawn study, and intense experiments of thought. Whitehead has remarked that the first stage of education is romance. Such was the case with the young Karl and

---

[66]*Ibid.*, p. 4.

[67]Catlin, George: *Op. cit.*, p. 561.

[68]Marx-Aveling, Eleanor: *Op. cit.*, p. 257.

[69]Letter to his father. In *Writings of the Young Marx on Philosophy and Society*, pp. 40-50.

his "storm-tossed feelings." Not only did he burn with a single-minded love for Jenny—"a love that was frenzied with yearning and void of hope"; his whole state of mind was exalted, vague, idealistic, speculative. Faithful to his father's wish that he prepare himself for a practical profession, the young man took up the study of jurisprudence; and in his letter he confides hopefully, like a dutiful son, that he has been advised by an assistant judge as to how he might get ahead in the law: pass the third of the law exams, assume a post as an official in the provincial court of appeal, become an assistant judge, obtain the doctorate, be appointed as professor extraordinary—"provided, of course, that one works hard." It is a touching plan—but vain! For the youth's letter reveals a restless, tempestuous, inquisitive, brooding, independent spirit that would be unhappy for even one day in the confines of a petty or even an important official position. The father's presentiments about the "Demon" were right. The son was not cut out to fit into bourgeois patterns. He confesses that his real interest is not law but philosophy—and so philosophy of law as a compromise. In restrospect he castigates himself for his idealism in this regard; his "metaphysics of law," he says, "was severed from all actual law," while in theory form was separated from content.

But after his more than one year of feverish reading and writing the young Marx showed a mature understanding of the tendency of his work and the lessons of his failures. His poetic period was short-lived. Relegating poetry to the role of "companion," he turned to philosophy of law, writing a work of nearly three hundred pages. "Here," he writes, "I was greatly disturbed by the conflict between what is and what ought to be, a conflict peculiar to idealism." But the pages he wrote did not satisfy him. He tried once more, with the same result. The upshot was a crisis which marks one of the turning points in Marx's life:

> During the first semester I was awake many a night, engaged in these multifarious occupations. I went through many struggles and experienced much stimulation from within and without. Yet, in the end, I found that my mind had not been greatly enriched while I had neglected nature, art, and the world, and had alienated my friends. My body apparently reacted. A physician advised a stay in the country, and so for the first time I traversed the whole spread-out town and went through

the gate to Stralow. I did not anticipate that I, an anemic weakling, should there ripen into a man with a robust and solid frame. A curtain had fallen, my holy of holies had been shattered, and new gods had to be found.

Here we have the first phases of the classical syndrome of personality transformation as found in the acquisition of a sense of religious or secular mission in life. Search for an overruling commitment; withdrawal from society; trial of one or more solutions; frustration; intense inner conflict and doubt; break-down of psychic structure—all are there. Young adults face a number of critical decisions all at once—marriage, education, career, life-goals. Hence for them troubles are apt to come in bunches. Added to the young Marx's "futility" over his "lost labors" were his "grief over Jenny's illness" and his "consuming vexation at having to make an idol of a view I detest," namely, idealism. The young man was resolved to make a fresh start. Having recovered from his illness, he reports, "I burned all my poems, my sketches for novellas, etc."

To whom much is given, much is required; and the young Marx, richly endowed with energy, intelligence, feeling, and devotion, demanded for himself no less than an ultimate commitment which would link his own private thought and life with a universal goal fit for his endowments. After the throes of his crisis—in which his whole psychosomatic organism told him he was on the wrong track—the solution to his problem came in steps. During this period Marx had the renewed insight that "I could not make my way without philosophy." The liberation that he felt in this discovery and in his willing acceptance of his "destiny" is indicated in consequence. In an abstract classification of law—whose study he had followed in obedience to his father's wishes but in contradiction to his own bent—he had produced only "wearisome prolixity." But with his self-discovery born of failure, "I was again able, with good conscience, to throw myself into the arms of philosophy. . . ." The catalyzing factor here was Hegel's philosophy. He writes:

Setting out from idealism . . . I hit upon seeking the Idea in the real itself. If formerly the gods had dwelt above the world, they had now become its center.

> I had read fragments of Hegel's philosophy and had found its grotesque craggy melody unpleasing. I wished to dive into the ocean again but with the definite intention of discovering our mental nature to be just as determined, concrete, and firmly established as our physical— no longer to practice the art of fencing but to bring pure pearls into the sunlight.

He wrote a dialogue toward this end—"a philosophic-dialectical discussion of the godhead manifested as a concept *per se,* as religion, as nature, and as history." But it only produced the vexation already mentioned. Nevertheless, during this period of uncertainty, Marx got to know Hegel "from beginning to end, and most of his disciples as well." He employed Hegel's approach in criticizing the abstractness of his "metaphysics of Law":

> . . . the object itself must be studied in its development; there must be no arbitrary classifications; the rationale of the thing itself must be disclosed in all its contradictoriness and find its unity in itself.

Marx's father died in the following spring (1838) and the young man faced alone the arduous task of carving out his own course in life. He had lost an "adult sponsor" who he knew would stand behind him in spite of his extravagant experiments. In the meantime, however, he had found an intimate group of intellectuals. The *Doktorklub* in Berlin, consisting of university lecturers, teachers, and writers, most of whom were older than Karl, seems to have provided the personal warmth and the intellectual challenge which carried Karl out of his crisis. Although scarcely twenty years old when he first joined the group, Karl became a central figure in it. What he needed was a world of curbs and frictions on which to test his mettle, a way of bringing his restless and rivalrous dispositions into play. He had realized that his own enclosed world had been too abstract and introverted. Now, in the no-holds-barred debates, he began to find himself. He learned that he might stand up and hold his own against men superior to him in age and experience. So, early in life, he was on his way to showing that he was a natural leader in groups engaged in collective social criticism. This early discovery of his *métier* not only saved him from further intellectual futilities; it fortunately pointed him away from an academic career and toward a career of polemics and social action. But the full implications of the vigorous discussion in this group were yet to be realized. For the time being, his activity was a *praxis* of philosophy which is "itself *theoretical*"—a "*criticism* which measures individual existence against essence, particular actuality against the Idea." [70] The young Marx in this period described his own position as "liberal" as contrasted with "positive philosophy" which turns inward instead of outward and hence involves "perversity" and "insanity."[71]

The young Hegelians took as their initial inspiration the work of David Strauss, who in the spirit of the rationalist Hegel stressed the unconscious mystical character of the Gospel story, and who argued that the meaning of Christianity is to be found in history itself and human social needs. Two Young Hegelians had particular influence on Marx: Karl Friedrich Köppen, who placed his hopes in the eighteenth century Enlightenment and in "the spiritual resurrection" of the Prussian king; and Bruno Bauer, who, while also a monarchist, went still farther than Strauss and declared that there was no truth in the Gospel story whatsoever. Bauer exalted "the philosophy of self-consciousness" —that of the Skeptics, Epicureans, and Stoics—which situated the individual with his own independent resources in a decaying world but which, in Christianity, became self-alienated in its postulation of a divine power outside itself. For Bauer, under the spell of Hegel's categories, the solution was for man to achieve consciousness of himself and hence control over his own self-alienation.[72]

These Young Hegelians put themselves against the domesticated Hegelianism of the Junkers and the bureaucrats, a Hegelianism which sanctified the *status quo*. The young rebels, like all youth and all rebels, had to steal their weapons from the entrenched elders; and the main weapons were Hegel's critical rational method and his dialectic. They also had to find a rallying point, a normative point in history, to provide inspiriation and guidance. Following the lead of their master, they found it in the critical philosophies of Greek antiquity—the Skeptics, the antireligious Epicureans, the equalitarian Stoics.

Marx's work on his doctoral dissertation, completed in 1841, car-

---

[70] Notes to the Doctoral Dissertation. In *Writings of the Young Marx on Philosophy and Society*, pp. 61-62.

[71] *Ibid.*, p. 63.

[72] *Karl Marx. The Story of His Life*, pp. 18-25.

ried forward the battle. In his notes for that, Marx uttered one of those several early statements premonitory of the course of his future thought:

> Just as Prometheus, having stolen fire from heaven, begins to build houses and settle on the earth, so philosophy, having extended itself to the world, turns against the apparent world. So now with the Hegelian philosophy.[73]

We can already see the germs of his break with Hegel. The outline of a complete, total philosophy, he says, "is in general conditioned by its development." This provides the basis for its reversal when applied to actuality. As philosophy separates itself from the world, the world is "implicitly split"; it cannot be moving if it is totally complete. Hence the practical application of such a philosophy will be "split and contradictory; its objective universality reverts to subjective forms of individual consciousness in which it lives."[74] In his notes the young Marx saw the sharp antagonism between Hegelian philosophy and society. The crisis of philosophy was evident in its effort to realize itself in the world and thus to liberate itself from the fetters of its own system. The world *resists* such realization. The solution is to *overcome* both the world and philosophy in a mutual transformation of the two. "The world's becoming philosophical is at the same time philosophy's becoming worldly, its realization is at the same time its loss."[75] It was a theme that Marx would take up with greater vigor in 1843 in "Toward the Critique of Hegel's Philosophy of Right." The contradiction and its solution expressed Marx's own personal problem and its projected solution: he foresaw that the only way in which his philosophical career might be made meaningful was to merge it in practical action in the world. It was only a matter of time before he found the outlet for the action. And that outlet, as he predicted, was philosophy's loss but the world's gain.

The young Marx's exploration of Hegel's philosophy was an important transition by which he moved from the religious, liberal humanism of his Gymnasium days to mature philosophy. Hegel—an en-

---

[73]Notes to the Doctoral Dissertation. In *Writings of the Young Marx on Philosophy and Society*, p. 52.

[74]*Ibid.*

[75]*Ibid.*, p. 62.

lightened Christian who had transformed Christian thought into a
secular philosophy of history, but could not carry it all the way toward
a revolutionary program—held up a grand view of man and history.
Every man has a place in this scheme of destiny; every man can contribute to divine-human perfection as it works itself out in the antagonisms and unifications of history. This religious-secular notion
fitted and extended the ideal that the young Marx had been taught.
It gave dialectical motion to that ideal. Marx, Engels, and others
became ardent Hegelians. But Marx and Engels came to realize that
this grand scheme of an Idea on the march through history was not
enough. "To improve mankind and himself," it is not enough for a
man to rely on the Absolute or on pure thought. The question for the
young Marx and Engels, as for the young Lenin, became, "What is
to be done?" They did not abandon Hegel's dynamic method; rather
they absorbed and transformed it into a practical, history-making instrument.

The emphasis on practice was carried forward in the dissertation
itself, completed in March, 1841. What the young Hegelian Marx
found valuable in Epicurus was not his materialism, or his abstract
individualism, but his stress on an "energizing principle" (in contrast
to Democritus) and his Promethean defiance of religious superstition.
Here he arrived at virtually the same position he took *vis à vis* Hegel
and Feuerbach in *Theses on Feuerbach* in 1845, condemning both abstract idealist system and sensuous, atomic materialism. Marx's interest in practice was greatly accelerated by his reading of Feuerbach's
Essence of Christianity, which appeared later in 1841. The effect of
this book on Marx and his fellow Young Hegelians was electric.[76] Late
in January of 1842, in an essay using Luther's feeling for "Nature,"
his "immediate truth," as the touchstone, he declared that Feuerbach's
view of miracles is superior to Strauss.[77] He advised theologians and
philosophers to free themselves from speculation: "There is no other
road for you to *truth* and *freedom* except that leading through the
stream of fire [the *Feuer-bach*]."

---

[76]Engels, Friedrich: *Ludwig Feuerbach and the End of Classical German
Philosophy.*

[77]Marx, Karl: Luther as arbiter between Strauss and Feuerbach. In *Writings
of the Young Marx on Philosophy and Society,* pp. 93-95.

By this time the life of the young Marx had reached a turning point. In the summer of 1841 Bruno Bauer, Karl's best hope of a university position, was himself denied a permanent appointment at Bonn in consequence of his radical religious views. This event closed for Marx forever all academic doors.

The young man must have accepted his fate without complaint, realizing that he did not fit into the world of poseurs, pack rats, opportunists, and hirelings tied to the whims of officious bureaucrats. Without thinking of some solid and durable career, he plunged into controversy. In February of 1842 he completed an acidulous attack on the latest Prussian censorship instruction. In its tartness, it was in the tradition of Voltaire; in its appeal for trust in the people and in the power of truth, it echoed Milton. In April he began to write for the *Rheinische Zeitung*. His first article again attacked censorship. "The first freedom of the press," he said "must be its emancipation from commerce."[78] In the ensuing polemics, he stated with a new clarity his views on philosophy and its relation to the world. In answer to the question of whether philosophy should discuss religious matters in newspaper articles, he asserted:

> Philosophy, above all German philosophy, has a tendency toward solitude, toward systematic seclusion . . . which . . . estranges it from the ready-tongued, alive-to-events newspapers whose only satisfaction is information. . . . It is taken to be a professor of magic whose incantations sound pompous because they are incomprehensible . . . .
> Philosophy does not stand outside the world any more than man's brain is outside him because it is not in his stomach . . . .
> Since every genuine philosophy is the spiritual quintessence of its time, the time must come when philosophy comes into contact and mutual reaction with the actual world. . . . Then philosophy . . . becomes the philosophy of the present world . . . . philosophy is becoming worldly and the world philosophical. . . . Philosophy is introduced into the world by the yelling of its enemies who betray their internal infection by their noisy call for help against the blaze of ideas.[79]

What should be noted here in the young man's thought is a rare thing for his own day or indeed for any day, namely, the effort of a pro-

---

[78]Quoted in *Writings of the Young Marx on Philosophy and Society,* p. 96.

[79]Marx, Karl: The leading article in no. 179 of the *Kölnische Zeitung:* Religion, free press, and philosophy. In *Writings of the Young Marx on Philosophy and Society,* pp. 122-123.

fessionally trained philosopher to bring philosophy out of the university and apply it to politics, and in so doing to transform completely politics—in a word, to integrate the most comprehensive kind of thought with the most comprehensive kind of action.

Marx's practical way of dealing with questions won him the support of the shareholders of the *Rheinische Zeitung,* which had come under the suspicion of the Prussian state. In October, 1842, he was made editor in chief. Earlier, from Bonn, in a number of attacks on the Diet, he had taken up in turn the freedom of the press and the illegal arrest of the Archbishop. Finally he came athwart a material question—a law against the theft of wood in the forests. Now the prophet and crusader for social justice had at last found his cause. He took up the cudgels for "the propertyless masses without political and social rights."[80] His reasoning was Hegelian and historically unsure, but his sense of justice firm and indignant. Because of a reprint of one of Weitling's articles on the Berlin housing question, and a report touching on the socialist question, as well as the new competition it offered, the *Rheinische Zeitung* was accused of flirting with communism by a rival paper. The newly appointed editor was forced to come face to face with an issue that he himself acknowledged as having "European significance."[81] Giving a number of polemical answers, he promised that the paper, "which cannot concede *theoretical reality* to communistic ideas in their present form . . . will submit these ideas to thorough criticism."[82] Marx derided the superficial views of his rival, realizing that it did not believe in socialism, but he knew that "the *theoretical explication* of communistic ideas . . . is the real danger" [83] and called for a serious study of them. In this matter the young man showed practical acumen. He knew the paper was hypocritical, but he would not be drawn into supporting a theoretical or practical cause with which he was acquainted but which he had not fully examined. He also grasped the level of the tactical struggle. From his own experience he knew that the Germans needed first to radicalize their thinking, which meant the radicalizing of the political conditions of

---

[80]*Karl Marx. The Story of His Life,* p. 41.

[81]*Writings of the Young Marx on Philosophy and Society,* p. 132.

[82]*Ibid.,* p. 134.

[83]*Ibid.,* p. 135.

their thinking, and that the current struggle must be waged against state censorship and bourgeois complacency rather than in favor of socialist practice.

At the same time Marx displayed acumen in his dealings with the Young Hegelians in Berlin, who had become a society of "Freemen" engaged in infantile leftist activity. Bruno Bauer argued that the state, private property, and the family must be dissolved as conceptions altogether.[84] They demonstrated in the streets, made scenes in brothels and taverns, and sent to Marx "world-uprooting scribblings, empty of ideas and written in a slovenly style, the whole tinged with a little atheism and communism (which the gentlemen have never bothered to study)."[85] Marx's position as editor of the *Rheinische Zeitung* had helped to give him a realistic political sense which the literary bohemians in Berlin lacked. He was also much the superior in his theoretical development, and he saw, moreover, that the best practice requires the best and most thorough thought.

> I demanded . . . more concreteness, a more detailed treatment of actual conditions and a display of greater practical knowledge of the subjects. . . . I told them that in my opinion it was not right, that it was even immoral, to smuggle communist and socialist dogmas, i.e., an entirely new way of looking at the world, into casual dramatic criticisms, etc., and that if communism were to be discussed at all then it must be done in quite a different fashion and thoroughly. I also asked them to criticize religion by criticizing political conditions rather than the other way about. . . . And finally I told them that if they wanted to deal with philosophy they should flirt less with the ideas of atheism (which is reminiscent of those children who loudly inform anyone who cares to listen that they are not afraid of the bogyman) and do more to acquaint the people with its meaning.[86]

In this counsel we can see the first germ of Marx's attitude toward religion and the necessity for a political and economic treatment of it, as well as the openness of a liberal mind toward socialism and the demand for absolute competence and integrity in one's intellectual commitment.

Inevitably, the *Rheinische Zeitung* was suppressed. The shareholders demanded that the policy of the paper be toned down. Marx refused.

[84] *Karl Marx. The Story of His Life*, p. 45.
[85] *Ibid.*
[86] *Ibid.*, p. 46.

On March 17, 1843, he resigned. "I am tired," he wrote, "of the hypocrisy, the stupidity and the brutality of the authorities and of our submissiveness, pliancy, evasiveness and hairsplitting, and now the government has given me back my freedom. . . . There is nothing more I can do in Germany. One debases oneself here." [87] The young Marx's first job lasted five months. He did not consider it all in vain: "I regard the suppression . . . as an indication of the progress of political consciousness. . . ." [88] He had learned something of the technique and value of sharpening social conflict through ideological struggle, and of advancing the education and political movement of men. Marx's experience as editor gave him a thorough introduction to segments of the community he had never before confronted—the bourgeois shareholders of the paper, the reading public, and the state bureaucracy. Thus he enjoyed an invaluable apprenticeship in the task of "seeking the Idea in the real itself" as he had put it five years earlier, as a young student. [89] The adolescent dream of working for "the welfare of humanity" [90] was beginning to take concrete shape.

Marx's problems and controversies as editor had clarified his own political thinking, and during the period between his resignation in March and his move to Paris in October in the post of a new editorship he set down this new thinking. In a series of letters to Arnold Ruge, the financier of the new journal, the *Deutsche-Französische Jahrbücher,* Marx expressed his feelings about his own nation, Germany. It is plain that for Marx one cannot love and fight for man in the abstract; one's own people suffer and make claims on one, and their concrete problems give meaning and testing to philosophical solutions. Longing to feel pride, he says, one cannot help feeling national shame. But shame is a kind of anger, an incipient revolution. Shame, yes; but never despair. Men may "hope for a long time out of mere stupidity"; then they may realize their hopes "out of sudden insight." [91] Such insight, coming first from the critics, must direct itself to the old world of the Philistines and not flee from them. It must face up to the brute rule of officers and landholders over the brainless mass

---

[87] *Ibid.,* pp. 51-52.
[88] *Ibid.,* p. 51.
[89] *Writings of the Young Marx on Philosophy and Society,* p. 46.
[90] *Ibid.,* p. 39.
[91] *Ibid.,* p. 205.

of men—"a herd of slaves" in a *"political animal kingdom."* In "the
world dehumanized," [92] it must awaken men to freedom and dignity.
Such awakening is possible because "the system of industry and commerce, of property and exploitation of men" leads to a rupture and
its own eventual destruction: "the existence of a suffering mankind
that thinks and of a thinking mankind that is suppressed" must become intolerable to the system.[93] There is a "product to be born,"
says the hopeful Marx, "which the present carries in its womb." [94]

The task of philosophy, therefore, is clear. "We do not anticipate
the world dogmatically, but rather wish to find the new world through
criticism of the old." Philosophy has already been drawn into "the
torment of the struggle." It must engage in *"relentless criticism of all
existing conditions"*—afraid neither of its findings nor of "the conflict
with the powers that be." [95] In its critical analysis of present social
conditions, philosophy will be the midwife of the new order, easing the
process of birth. The philosophical critic "can start with any form of
theoretical and practical consciousness"—Marx believes religion and
politics are "focal points of German's interest—and then develop
the true actuality out of the forms *inherent* in existing actuality as its
ought-to-be and goal." In so doing it will necessarily reveal the contradictions between social ideals and operating assumptions.[96]

> Then we do not face the world in doctrinaire fashion with a new prin-
> ciple, declaring, "Here is truth, kneel here!" We develop new principles
> for the world out of the principles of the world. . . . We merely show
> the world why it actually struggles: and the awareness of this is some-
> thing the world *must* acquire even if it does not want to.[97]

By this time the young Marx fully realized what many reformers never
realize, that the form and direction of liberating social change must
come from men and conditions themselves. They cannot be imposed
from the outside. The process by which philosophy becomes worldly—
Hegel's great goal—is in fact the process by which the world of men
becomes self-critical and active with regard to its own inherent ten-

---

[92] *Ibid.*, p. 206.
[93] *Ibid.*, *pp.* 210-211.
[94] *Ibid.*, p. 211.
[95] *Ibid.*, p. 212.
[96] *Ibid.*, p. 213.
[97] *Ibid.*, p. 214.

dencies of freedom and hope. These letters of Marx's were written from March to September, 1843.[98] At the end of that year, in Paris, this historical materialism, which had been developing step by step in the young Hegelian, suddenly advanced still farther. Marx found that the form and direction of the future lay hidden in that potentially universal class, the proletariat.

In June, 1843, Marx finally consummated his marriage with Jenny Westphalen. That victory after so many years and obstacles no doubt filled him with joy and hope about mankind and the revolution which he sensed coming. His letters to Ruge reflect his confidence and his firm resolve to carry through with all energy his radical vocation in the role of editor of the new journal. Meanwhile he had been working on his "Critique of Hegel's Philosophy of the State," a work which he finished in the summer. In this the influence of Feuerbach's sensuous practice and humanism shows. But Marx's own practical bent and experience had previously made him critical of Hegel. He repeated his earlier criticism of Hegel's monarchy; Marx's radical sentiments drove him to "transform society into a community of men to achieve their highest purposes, a democratic state." [99] He observed that the "identity Hegel has set up between civil society and the state is the identity of *two hostile armies. . . .*" [100] Man's consciousness of the contradiction in bourgeois society was stated still more sharply in "On the Jewish Question" written in the fall of 1843: the state in fact reduces man to an egoistic being with individual "rights," while ideally it looks upon him as a moral person and citizen.[101]

In November of 1843 Marx and his wife moved to Paris, where he took up his new editorial post. The move marked a watershed in his life—a turn from the tradition of Hegelian philosophy to the great fountainhead of the French Revolution. The young Marx had made the most of his home tradition, trying to come to grips with Hegel's thought by exposing its conservative effects (in the apology for monarchy, for example), but also by showing that it had to merge itself with the actual practices of man. Just how this was to be done was

---

[98]*Ibid.*, pp. 203-215.

[99]*Ibid.*, p. 206.

[100]Marx, Karl: Critique of Hegel's Philosophy of the State. In *Writings of the Young Marx on Philosophy and Society,* p. 190.

[101]Marx, Karl: On the Jewish Question, p. 31.

not clear. It really could not be clear to Marx at that time, even with the assistance of the empiricism and humanism of Feuerbach. But it soon became clear in Paris, which was the intellectual capital of the world where the philosophy of materialism was still very much alive and the philosophy of socialism was in process of being born and developed. Marx "plunged into this rejuvenating flood."[102] He discovered the literature on the working class; he associated with socialist workers and their secret societies; he met French democrats and socialists and the leaders of the German secret society, the League of the Just; he took up the study of political economy; he contributed to *Vorwärts* and helped to edit it; he met Engels and began with him to write *The Holy Family*—all within the space of one year. No other single year was so productive or formative for the young Marx. In fact, before the end of 1843, when Marx had been in Paris two months, the direction of his new thought had become clear in his article, "Contribution to the Critique of Hegel's Philosophy of Right. Introduction." Knowing Marx's own intensely personal struggles to bring about the liberation of his own people from oppression, we can see how this article in its fervor reflects that existential involvement and an ecstasy with the newly found solution.

> Where, then, is the *positive* possibility of a German emancipation?
> *Answer:* In the formation of a class with radical chains . . . a sphere which has a universal character by its universal suffering and claims no *particular right* because no *particular wrong* but *wrong generally* is perpetrated against it . . . a sphere, finally, which cannot emancipate itself without emancipating all other spheres of society, which, in a word, is the *complete loss* of man and hence can win itself only through the *complete re-winning of man*. This dissolution of society as a particular estate is the *proletariat*.[103]

The finest fruit of the Paris period was the *Economic and Philosophical Manuscripts*, written in the late summer of 1844. In its analysis of alienated labor, capital, private property, and communism, the young Marx brought his youthful intellectual struggles to a brilliant culmination. Turning Hegel's dialectical method to an analysis of man's most concrete problem, his alienation from himself and others

---

[102] *Karl Marx. The Story of His Life*, p. 74.

[103] Marx, Karl: Contribution to the Critique of Hegel's Philosophy of Right. Introduction, pp. 56-57.

and his own labor, Marx showed how one might be Hegelian and
Feuerbachian, dialectical and materialistic, philosophical and humanistic in his criticism. While thus settling accounts with his philosophical
fathers—rising above all by assimilating and integrating the best of
each—Marx also pointed in the direction of his necessary future
work. If the fundamental condition of man's dehumanization and
alienation lies in the system of capital, then man must understand and
change that system at its roots. Here we have the sign and command
of what man as thinker and actor must do. Here we have the sign
that the young Marx had found his revolutionary vocation in concrete
form, a vocation which he would spend the rest of his days fulfilling.

Unlike most of the humanists of his day, the young Marx discerned
that all humanism, however noble in theory, remains abstract and
futile unless it can inform, guide, and advance the activity of a real
political movement of people. Marx had begun to learn about socialism before he went to Paris. In 1842 he and Engels had met
Moses Hess, who introduced the Young Hegelians to philosophical
communism. In his "Critique of Hegel's Philosophy of the State,"
finished in the summer of 1843, Marx spoke of "socialized man" for
the first time, as in the article, "Toward the Critique of Hegel's Philosophy of Law: Introduction," written later that year, he mentioned
for the first time the proletariat. All the while, however, the young
man remained the independent, hardheaded realist, criticizing in a
letter to Ruge in September, 1943, the communist utopias with which
he was familiar as dogmatic, abstract, and far out from the real world.
In Paris the rich mix of the young Marx's observations and reflections
all shot together in a magnificent synthesis. Idea and historical action,
theory and practice, philosophy and the proletariat—all fell into place
as necessary parts of a dialectical and material movement of men
creating their own world and their own liberation and fulfillment.
The center and motive power of this movement was the workers; the
guide was philosophy. In Paris Marx met these workers and their leaders from many European countries, and he got a feeling for their
movement and cause. Whereas influential thinkers like the great Hegel
had spoken of the power of the "Idea," and the radical young Hegelians had been dissuaded from that philosophically by Feuerbach's
materialism, Marx now saw with his own eyes that the profoundest

power in history is concrete working men banded together by common oppression and inspired by a common vision to build a brotherhood. He saw that if a social system of exploitation could be raised upon their toiling, bending backs, then that same system might be overturned if they rose up in revolutionary protest and demanded a more humane order. The young Marx involved himself in political struggle on many fronts, organizing associations and parties, chief among them the Communist League of 1847, and engaging in revolutionary activity in Germany, France, Belgium, and England. Thus at an early age the young Titan had found his mission in life—commitment to the cause of the revolutionary workers' movement. Marx was the first philosopher to put himself in an effective, creative way on the side of the industrial workers. That is why his thought has had more influence than any other on the fulfillment of the industrial workers, and that is why, as Engels correctly declared, "his name will endure through the ages, and so also will his work!"

The works that Marx wrote after the summer of 1844—culminating with the *Manifesto* published in February, 1848—represent primarily the consolidation and development of his first creative year's labor in Paris. *The Holy Family,* written with Engels in late 1844, and *The German Ideology,* composed by the two in 1845-1846, were both backward glances over travelled roads, as well as prophecies of future struggles. They sought to settle accounts with German idealism—to show that intellectual criticism is insufficient to change the old social order, and that it is only the workers who create and change things. The revolutionary political work of the young Titans had given élan and power to their writing. The first efforts to develop historical materialism in *The German Ideology* found a concrete polemical victim in Proudhon. Marx's *The Poverty of Philosophy,* written in 1847, exposed the petit-bourgeois utopianism and "verbal anarchism" of Proudhon and stressed the importance of the class struggle as the prime historical fact from which all political action must begin. The *Manifesto of the Communist Party* was a permanent milestone in the history of communism, but also a succinct epitome and synthesis of the tendencies that had been coming to a peak in the young Marx's feeling and thought. It was a powerful fusion of passion and ideas, of commitment and science, of history and philosophy and polemics, of theoretical comprehension and a practical program of a political party. "Neutral" historians may wonder how such a document could have such an influence throughout the world. The only way to understand that is to feel and understand how the young Marx and Engels put themselves in the shoes of the workers and employed their intellectual powers to grasp realistically how the workers were exploited and how they might be freed.

In the two years that followed, Marx and Engels were in the thick of the revolutionary struggle. Political agitation, articles, leaflets, arrests, expulsions from nations, trials (and Engels' own participation in military clashes) marked their activity during this period of upheaval throughout Europe. The two young revolutionaries rushed—or were pushed—from one country to another to support the workers' risings and to build their Communist League. They learned the concrete meaning of class struggle at a time when workers had little knowledge of how to organize and direct their revolting energies. They learned the limitations and the possibilities of the workers' movement for emancipation.

When Marx, an exile from Paris, arrived in London with his family in August 1849, at the age of thirty-one, he was still a young man. But in his Promethean struggles in philosophy and in revolutionary action he had already stolen fire from the heavens. He had already given that fire to the workers—the fire that lights the path to freedom. It was this fire that enabled one-third of the workers of the world in the next century to fulfill the promise of the young editors of *Neue Rheinische Zeitung*: "emancipation of the working class!"

The life of the young Marx was revolutionary not merely in the sense that he sought ways of making radical changes in society, but in the deeper sense that he sought a revolutionizing way of life. Marx's own Faustian development shows that he was dissatisfied with every specific form of fulfillment as the end-point of man's life. No particular perspective, role, institution, or society, he realized, could contain and exhaust the capacities of man for freedom and creativity. Hence he was the eternal protester, crying out against the enslavement and alienation produced by the modes of production and social organization of class societies which have defined human history. The young Marx himself refused to confine himself to the role of a fragment and appendage in an industrial and social system. He refused to be de-humanized. He insisted on his own integrity to change and develop in his own way, to be many-sided, to think and act and associate freely, "to doubt everything." [104] He believed that man had a species-need to become a universal being; that in his process of fulfilling all sides of his nature he had to remain open toward past and future; and that in the creative moments of his present he had to transform the past in the direction of a transcendent future.

A true revolutionary not only smashes the evil idols of his fathers; he helps to create a way of life that will free his children for a more abundant and joyful existence. Such "revolutionizing practice" [105] defines true human history.[106] But the young Marx understood that the emergence of man into the free light of his own human history does not occur spontaneously in a vacuum; it is the consequence of certain trends in the prehistoric stage, namely, our present conditions. Hence he sought to find a collective and political path to that goal. He never doubted that history—that is to say, men collectively—bears in itself the unborn child of its own glorious future. Man has only to deliver that future through the courage and fidelity of his action. But in the process, Marx never lost sight of the goal and he never attached himself idolatrously to any means—a set of ideas, an ideology, a party, an organization. Marx embodied in his own commitment a revolu-tionizing style of life which he discerned as the generic character and goal of man and man's history as a species. That is a dialectic process wherein man interacts with other men and with nature, creating and being created in the direction of fulfilling all of his powers in a con-structive way. Marx saw this process as occurring more or less un-consciously throughout human history; and he saw the principal ob-struction hitherto as class society, which inhibits the process by which man frees himself from the limits of his ignorance, apathy, inertness, uncommunicativeness, selfishness, and lack of commitment to large and universal human goals. When one is committed to such a creative process and lives by it, then one lives in a revolutionizing way; he can-not rest until the whole of human society is liberated through and

---

[104]Marx, Karl: Confessions. In *Reminiscences of Marx and Engels,* p. 266.
[105]Marx, Karl: *Theses on Feuerbach.*
[106]Marx, Karl: *A Contribution to the Critique of Political Economy,* p. 13.

for it. To be revolutionary in this way is to be truly human. The inhuman way is the way of one who will not change, who will not learn, who will not grow—who, in a word, will not interact creatively with others and the world. The young Marx strove to be truly human: he wanted to be a free, fulfilled human being and he wanted all others to be free, fulfilled human beings too.

What can the younger generation today (particularly that in the United States) learn from the life and thought of the young Marx?

Whatever can be learned as ways of behaving or as beliefs cannot be specific, for what is specific arises from specific circumstances and circumstances change. Insofar as circumstances today differ from those of the young Marx's day, we must look to the *general,* the *generic,* the essential, the human features of his life and thought which apply, *mutatis mutandis,* to every set of circumstances and hence to our own. For his work to become of value to us, we must extract the universal from the particular set of circumstances in which it was developed and apply it to our own.

(1) *Adult sponsors.* Young people cannot choose the parents who will raise them, though, as they reach adolescence and young adulthood, they can begin to discriminate between the better and worse features in their parental cultural heritage and choose between the two. Understanding one's parents in this way, i.e., dialectically, is difficult. But one's parents constitute the first and most immediate and concrete portion of human history that one encounters. How one deals with this portion of one's past is apt to be a measure of how one will appropriate the whole of human history. Will one rebel blindly and totally against them? Submit to them? Withdraw from them? In such responses we can see writ small the larger responses of men in history: anarchism, conformism, utopianism. If one wishes to make creative changes in society, one must distinguish the best from the worst in one's past, eradicate the worst, carry along the best, and add to it one's own contribution. Moreover, young adults are in process of becoming either parents themselves or else adults who will exercise an influence on children and young people. If they expect to change history, here is their great chance. Are they prepared to make the most of the opportunity? Are they clear about the general goals for mankind? Do they understand the conditions of the society in which they must live and work, and the practical means to those goals?

The young Marx was conscious of a "generation gap" in his own life, but he did not go on from there to justify cutting himself off from the older generation or to neglect past and present conditions. In his association with older persons, whether bourgeois or proletarian, Marx sought what was useful to human life and welfare. "Nothing human is alien to me," [107] he was fond of quoting.

(2) *Education.* Until the late teens, most young people have little freedom to determine the conditions of their education. Up to this period they are the products of the necessities of the decisions and habits of their parents and the particular conditions of the nature and society in which they have grown up. But society recognizes that at some point in their adolescence or young adulthood they are ready to be initiated into the opportunities and responsibilities of the adult world. Physical maturation and genital maturity are the obvious signs of this readiness. But the youth also displays what is associated with this physical development, a heightened capacity to feel, to think, and to act. He can reflect about the world and about himself. He experiences an intensified and often painful awareness of his feelings, his body, himself, others, the perspectives of others in art and literature, and nature.

Adolescents respond to this upsurge of awareness in various ways. Some give way to uninhibited physical expression of indiscriminate feeling—in speedy automobiles, in frenetic dancing, in sports, in gregarious racing around the town. Some pour their feelings into some specialized object or mode of activity—into another person, or into sex, or into occupation preparation. Some check and inhibit their feelings and thoughts, and become squares. Some adapt their awareness to the forms and demands of their society—they become precociously overadjusted. Some carry their new awareness into themselves, brooding over who they are and what they might or might not be. Some employ their reflective powers to plan, for themselves or society; others abandon planning, and give way to the impulses of the moment.

The young Marx in the Trier *Gymnasium* had already engaged in the painful process of examining himself and his world. We can see in his essay, "Reflections of a Youth on Choosing an Occupation," a serious struggle with the question. It is true that he was fulfilling a stock academic assignment. But it is clear also that he had thought

---

[107]Confessions: In *Reminiscences of Marx and Engels,* p. 266.

seriously about the question, and that he had arrived at the conclusion that a man must merge his own individual plan in life with a plan for the whole of humanity. Far from being a conformist to Trier or German or European society, he was also equally far from being a rank individualist who rejected all social values. He was following the intuition that man knows himself most fully when he knows the generically human in himself and others, and that he fulfills himself when he helps to fulfill others. No one should say that Marx's adjustment was easy. He had feelings as diverse and intense and "storm-tossed" as any adolescent [108]—in fact, more intense, because his rich life of ideas enhanced and complicated those feelings. But he in time became able to handle and direct them creatively because he found a goal adequate to his passions.

(3) *Commitment.* The constant theme running throughout the life of the young and the old Marx is his commitment to "the welfare of humanity." If we look at the content of this commitment, we see humanism. If we look at its goals, we see idealism. If we look at its movement and style, we see fidelity. Human commitment—trust in ourselves and others, conviction in our individual and collective human worth, willingness to persist and take risks in behalf of people—is our basic virtue. It is something which, in our mammalian natures, we are born with; but we also have it thrust upon us, through the trust that others show us; and it is something we achieve by conscious choice.

Early in adolescence the young Marx displayed a singleness of purpose, a passionate and comprehensive idealism—so much so that his father later was prompted to ask the young zealot if his heart had room for "tender, earthly feelings" which bring "consolation" to men.[109] Marx had a purity of devotion and an obliviousness to his own personal welfare that reminds one of Shelley. Ruge wrote in 1844 of how, in his passion to assimilate the newfound wealth of the world of Paris, Marx had not been to bed for three or four nights and had worked himself sick.[110] It was not the first time or the last time he would sacrifice his health to his overruling commitment.

---

[108]Letter to his father. In *Writings of the Young Marx on Philosophy and Society,* p. 49.

[109]Catlin, George: *Op. cit.,* p. 561.

[110]*Karl Marx. The Story of His Life,* p. 74.

There is no question that the young Marx got this driving idealism from the religion of his childhood; and in his adolescent essay on choosing an occupation his idealism is expressed in religious form: "To man, too, Deity gave a general goal, to improve mankind and himself. . . . Religion itself teaches us that the ideal for which we are all striving sacrificed itself for humanity. . . ."[111] Marx soon dropped this specific language and belief. His essay, in fact, is essentially humanistic, so that the dropping of the husk for the kernel was merely a matter of time. But the generic aspiration toward the highest and the "divine" continued and grew from strength to strength. It is no accident or simple metaphor that led the young Marx in the early period to speak of "the gods" and his relations to them. "My holy of holies had been shattered, and new gods had to be found."[112] "I set out [to discuss] the godhead manifested as a concept per se, as religion, as nature, and as history." [113] We must "acknowledge the consciousness of man as the supreme divinity." [114] The "gods" represent for him the highest, the most significant, the ultimate directive for human life and history. And Marx's early development shows that he gradually assimilated them to himself and human history, until that directive became the power immanent in men to create and fulfill themselves. The fact that man is discovered to possess his own hidden divinity, that he has within himself the power of perfectibility, does not diminish his commitment. On the contrary, if man has the possibility to fulfill himself and his history, then he is charged with final responsibility over it.

When we turn to the commitment of the younger generation—to *any* kind of commitment—we encounter a problem. For many, brought up in a Jewish or Christian tradition, God is dead; the traditional notion of the divine is an empty notion, lacking empirical and rational confirmation or the power to evoke commitment. For many others, uninfluenced by any living religious tradition, God is not dead—he has never been born. The secular correlate of this is that ideology is dead,

---

[111]Marx, Karl: Reflections of a Youth on Choosing an Occupation. In *Writings of the Young Marx on Philosophy and Society,* pp. 35, 39.

[112]Letter to his father. In *Ibid.,* p. 46.

[113]*Ibid.,* p. 47.

[114]Marx, Karl: Contribution to the critique of Hegel's philosophy of right. Introduction. In *Op. cit.,* p. 51.

for ideology does for secular commitment what theology has done for religious commitment. Both ideology and theology symbolize, structure, and direct the feeling and action of commitment. Walter Rostow, a chief architect of President Johnson's foreign policy, concluded from the premise of dead ideology that revolution in the world is dead too. That is because he is looking at his own dead thoughts and arrogantly supposing that his own emptiness and cynicism prevail for the Vietnamese guerrillas and the black Americans.

Is commitment—man's commitment to "the welfare of humanity" in a radical way that transforms human lives and history—resurrectable? We must look for the material and ideational sources of commitment. First, there must be a felt sense of deprivation, a sense that is felt in the whole human being toward the whole human being. Mere physical deprivation is not enough; one must *feel* a lack, an injury, in one's *human* essence, in one's freedom and dignity and creativity *as a man*. That one need not experience actual poverty to experience this dehumanization is evidenced by the many committed leaders of men —from Marx, Engels, and Lenin to W. E. B. Du Bois and Martin Luther King, Jr.—who were in their youth not themselves poor. Second, there must be association with other persons who share some form of common commitment to humanity and who live it out in common activity. Such commitment may be learned from one's parents, teachers, peers, or persons organized into a group committed to a significant cause. Third, there must be a formulation of one's commitment, so that it enlightens one's action and one's action in turn is given concrete meaning and correction.

Young people until they are economically independent are not free to choose the material conditions of their lives. But man does have a remarkable power of resilience, a capacity to take from his environment what he needs once he has become sensitized to that need and environment. Thus the need—the one great need—that we all have is for an overarching commitment to man and his fulfillment. And whether poor or not, we can find around us today and among the remembered armies of the mighty dead many a hero and model for our own commitment. Young people can choose their teachers, within limits; their schools; their courses of study; their conditions of dwelling; their friends and loved ones; those groups and movements of persons with whom they choose to work for particular causes; and their philosophies.

Finally, young people are free to think about and formulate their commitment. Such freedom does not exist abstractly, apart from concrete conditions which stimulate them to think (persons with whom they are intimately associated, events that affect them, decisions and problems they face) and resources for thinking (books, articles, lectures, discussions). There is a fatalistic feeling among some young people that one's commitment is something over which one has no control. This is a partial truth transformed into an alleged whole truth. We absorb and appropriate our commitments unconsciously; the values we believe in and live out and sacrifice for are learned in the first instance quite apart from conscious analysis and decision. If a person keeps going in life he possesses in some measure a commitment to himself and to others. What thought can do is to focus attention on such commitment and to ask such kind of questions of it as will conduce to strengthening and advancing that commitment. What is it that I believe in? What goals ought I to work for? What kind of life do I envisage for myself and others? What can I distinctively and specifically contribute to the progress of humanity toward those goals? What must be my relations to others in this process?

Marx was a materialist, in reaction against those who believed that history might be changed simply in consequence of the thoughts buzzing in their heads. But some have forgotten the role of man's decision and self-forged commitment in shaping events. Here the power of critical thought, of self-understanding, of philosophy, is critical. One's philosophy is one's symbolized style of life, one's way of selecting and organizing and planning events; it is the *general form* that one's commitment is ready to take. Hence philosophy is essential to commitment. Without philosophy, commitment remains ordinary and sunk in the habits and pitfalls of unconscious behavior. Without commitment philosophy becomes an abstract indulgence in piddling trivialities.

(4). *Love.* What has been said applying to commitment also applies to love. We love and are loved in part because of unconscious sensitivities and selectivities that we have learned from others. At the same time we can enhance or inhibit the power of love and direct it by our own conscious thought. We fall prey to the illusions of our own class society if we suppose love to be like a commodity that can be given or taken at will, that can be won or lost by our shrewdness at investment. Love aimed at and demanded is not real love; it is a compensation for a falsified need, an obsession. Love is a yearning for union in difference, and the greatest love is a yearning for union with the whole of humanity and creation itself. But to yearn in that way one must already in a sense be filled with the power of outgoing and of sacrifice.

There is in some youthful love the needfulness of the child; and the "flower children" with "flower power" quite frankly wish to remain children in their approach to the problems of society. But in such cases who will assume adult responsibility for those problems? Strong love, love that moves toward others in the form of commitment and caring, becomes responsible and hence thoughtful. Having already passed beyond egocentricity, it wishes to transform pity or compassion by asking what must be done to improve the human condition and by then undertaking to do it. If one lives in that way, he will have all the love from others, and more, that anyone could ever wish for.

(5) *Historical tasks.* In striving to understand himself and others, as well as the forces of history, the young Marx developed a sense of realism which enabled him to work with timely effectiveness. We may protest that the European society of his time was more fluid, more polarized, more disposed to social change and revolution than our own United States society. This is true. But we forget that numbers of intelligent men looked at society then and, because of distorting subjective factors, estimated it incorrectly. Hegel was overoptimistic; Bauer was liberal and opportunistic; Ruge was pessimistic; Proudhon and Bakunin were anarchistic; the utopians were sectarian. Marx was one of the few who could assess the situation step by step, who could detect the propitious tactics. He had a strong ego, to be sure, but he was not egocentric and was in consequence able to see and assess both long-range processes and contemporary changing conditions. He thus avoided sectarianism and opportunism, determinism and voluntarism, skipping stages and tailism. Besides his endownments and traits of character, Marx enjoyed one advantage that we do not: he was not burdened with the system of Marxism and the complications and deviations that have grown up within it. Rather, he was in the process of creating his own system of thinking and acting in responses to changing conditions. He was, in short, formulating hypotheses for working which were undergoing scientific elaboration and revision in interaction with new conditions. Marx was ever probing for those growing

points of human history where thinkers and leaders of men might work most effectively—ever trying to put his finger on the current of events and to lead the rising tide of revolutionizing men on to victory. He realized that to lead men, one must help them to get what they most deeply demand. To do this, the thinker and critic must, as he said, "show the world why it actually struggles." [115] And the thinker must discover the particular struggles that engage men most fully, identify himself with men in these struggles, and articulate the causes, forms, and directions of such struggles. Such activity represents the union of head and heart, of thinker and worker, of thought and practice, which is the driving force of history.

(6) *Unity of thought and practice.* The great impulse of Marx's life was to unify thought through practice, and practice through thought, in a totalizing way. From Hegel he had learned a passion for totalizing thought. How might man make such a profound philosophical yearning worldly? Even before he had studied philosophy systematically and had gotten deeply into Hegel, the young Marx had displayed a restless desire to find out how mind operates as a material force in the world. He had, he reports in his summary of his academic year 1836-1837, "the definite intention of discovering our mental nature to be just as determined, concrete, and firmly established as our physical. . . ."[116] His reading of Feuerbach and his own reflections on experience taught him that the sources for the world's unity lie in the world itself, i.e., in concrete men with their concrete relations and conditions. Hence this totalizing dream had to be actualized through the totalizing and dialectical movement of men both thinking and acting with absolute commitment. The young Marx's evolution toward this orientation moved from religion through philosophy to politics. Religion supplied the general humanistic dream and ideal; philosophy, the critical and dialectical method; and politics, the material and historical application. In Marx's mature development, all these phases were carried along together and integrated. In Marx's creative and Promethean career, religion, philosophy, and politics in their tradi-

---

[115]Letter of Marx to Ruge, September, 1843. In *Writings of the Young Marx on Philosophy and Society*, p. 214.

[116]Marx, Karl: Letter to his father. In *Writings of the Young Marx on Philosophy and Society*, p. 46.

tional senses had all been absorbed, but transformed in a new synthesis that discarded their alienated character and anticipated a fully human mankind and history.

Neither young people, nor a society, nor men can choose and determine all the factors that go into their evolution. Contemporary American young people cannot imitate Marx's development. For example, even if they come out of religious backgrounds, young people today do not have the religious background that the young Marx had. His youthful religion was clear, humanistic, optimistic; theirs is apt to be supernaturalistic or existential. Moreover, Hegelianism is no longer potent; and in the United States youth is inclined to be non-philosophical or even antiphilosophical. The indifference and antagonism of United States young people toward philosophy derives from the conditions of their own society and its history. Geographical isolation; cultural alienation from a fixed European tradition and intellectual life of a leisure class; anti-élitism; the pressures to produce immediate and pragmatic solutions in industry, in agriculture, in government, and on the frontier; the preoccupation with material goods and security; the mobility and opportunism of American life—all have conspired to turn mid-North Americans away from theory to practice. But is there any question that in consequence the practice has been blind, individualistic, competitive, acquisitive, fragmented, chaotic, wasteful, antihuman, and destructive? Many young people are burning with a desire to be "activists" and to be "where the action is." But that desire is only a variant of the pattern that dominates their society, and in their resistance to the large ideas of philosophy and ideology and in their demand for immediate results of action, they only repeat the anti-intellectualism of their culture.

This demand among the youth for quick and tangible results of action is also a reflection of the increasing aggravation of society's problems and the coresponding desperation which people feel. This demand ranges from anarchistic destructiveness ("Burn, baby, burn"), to an ultimate faith in the politics of the electoral system. In these cases one can see a flight from thorough, comprehensive, and long-range solutions. So complex and enormous do the problems of society seem, so late seems the hour for redeeming man, so promising but so threatening is the situation, that many alternate between rashness and resignation, between hope and despair. These extremities, this ambivalence, signify that society itself has not yet polarized itself into consciously antagonistic factions. For more than two centuries the United States has been a class society whose modes of material and spiritual exploitation have been themselves differentiated and diffused so as to make it difficult for many to identify them. The slavery of the black man was obvious; so was the suffering of the day laborer during the rise of the industrial system in the late nineteenth and early twentieth century. But America is large and diversified; and the expansion of the white-collar world has served to blur these sharp antagonisms.[117]

In addition, America has been a melting pot, not only of economic and ethnic groups, but also of values and value-systems, both actual and idealized. As a consequence, no other society has been so highly pluralized, so mixed. In addition, all Americans have shared the democratic dream of free and equal progress for all members of society, though the dream was denied in practice. Hence, because of the diffusion of exploitation, the pluralization, and the democratic dream, most Americans have not consciously focused on the struggle between the oppressors and the oppressed. In recent times the closest that Americans have come to revolutionary movements have been the struggles of industrial workers of the 1930's and of the Blacks of the 1960's. Members of both groups, by reason of their common oppression and common places of work and dwelling, could easily articulate their felt antagonism against the ruling order. But that articulation did not usually take philosophical form. In the case of Martin Luther King, Jr., an ideologist of the Negro movement, one could discern a growing radicalization of his thought as the movement itself acquired increasing numbers and feelings and self-consciousness.

Like the young Marx, young people are not required to wait until masses are on the march before they begin to think about basic issues. People are already engaged in action—in living, in making a living, in suffering, in struggling against deprivations and oppressions, in hoping. The unity of thought and practice at that point means helping people to find and to understand the unitary tendency already present in their activities. This requires that one be honest and courageous in facing one's situation and that of all the oppressed in

<hr>

[117]Mills, C. Wright: *White Collar*. New York, Oxford, 1956.

one's society. One must not only feel one's own personal oppression and hope; one must feel it so deeply that one feels it as a *human* being, as a *species-being* who suffers and hopes for and with all oppressed humanity. But such *universal* feeling in one's particular being requires *thought*, i.e., conscious outreach and identification with the genus, the general, which thought alone makes possible. Thus the unity of thought and practice means by definition the merging of the activity of the particular individual with the activity of general human society.

Such action of passionate thought, of thoughtful passion, requires courage. It requires courage to face one's own feelings of despair and hope—which are the respective internalizations of the destructive and progressive forces in one's society—and to struggle with them. It requires courage to choose in favor of the progressive and reject the destructive; to discern the tendency of the progressive in oneself and one's fellow human beings; to clarify in thought the form and direction of that tendency. "We must make the actual pressure of oppression more pressing," said the young Marx of the German people, "by adding to it the consciousness of pressure and make the shame more shameful by publicizing it."[118] If young people expect to lead and transform a dehumanized people, they must face up to and understand that dehumanization in themselves and others; they must give passionate voice to it; they must point the way by which the people are already in process of liberating themselves and in that very process are becoming unified and human.

The courage to think about the good and evil of oneself and one's society and about the ultimate values of human life is evidence of a larger, existential courage, the courage to be and to become one's human self in a human society. Man in his depths yearns for a unity within himself and with others, for a unity of human history with itself and with the world of nature. But in his fragmentations and alienation, he dares not to allow himself to yearn in that direction, lest he be unable to cope with the contradiction in his life between the reality and the dream. Readiness and willingness to think about the basic philosophical questions—what man and his world are, what values in that world he ought to seek and create, what methods of thought and

---

[118]Marx, Karl: Toward the critique of Hegel's philosophy of law: introduction. In *Writings of the Young Marx on Philosophy and Society,* p. 253.

action he ought to use toward those ends—are indications of a struggle toward that larger and unified ideal which defines the farther side of man in his essential striving. For a philosophy is a great plan—a plan of thought made for a plan of action, a comprehensive and universal plan, a human plan. It is the conscious formulation and projection of man's deepest yearning. To philosophize about what man is and what he might be in practice is to move beyond the confinement of the immediate; to conquer the fears which bind us to that; to transcend the half-way expediencies of action; to put aside the small thoughts and compromises which diminish the full stature of man. To philosophize is to free one's thought toward the universal and the fully human. It is to take a courageous step in the affirmation and fulfillment of man.

(7) *Linkage of present thought with past thought*. History is all of one piece. Where there are advances or retrogressions, the break is only apparent. Underlying qualitative leaps there is a quantitative continuity. Hence it is foolish to suppose that we can shake off the influences from our past. The decision we are continuously faced with is to select, emphasize, and organize the factors which we inherit. American young people, like Americans generally, tend to want to forget history. This tendency itself is an inheritance of their own history wherein the sons of immigrants wanted to forget their ties to European society. The other side of this forgetfulness is the *ad hoc* pragmatism of Americans. But there can be no effective guidance of human action without taking into account the tendencies and habits of action. Such tendencies and habits, extending over generations, is what history is. And insofar as history has had conscious human direction, it has included the exercise of thought and the formulation of ideologies that have had positive and negative effects on the progress of men in history. Hence there can be no effective guidance of human action in the present without thorough and critical consideration of the great ideological systems of the past. "Experience," which is the shibboleth of Americans and is apt to be the idol of young Americans in rebellion against their parents, is a dear teacher, and only a fool will refuse to learn from the thought of the past. Perhaps one of the reasons why young people will not take the thought of Marx seriously is that he is now over thirty, and it is believed that no one over thirty

can be trusted. A simple act of historical imagination would put them in shoes of a young thoughtful radical who had far more influence on history than all their claims for their radicalism. And the young Marx had that influence precisely because he had enriched his own resources for present action by a careful and critical study of his past, i.e., mankind's past.

(8) *Independence*. We have spoken of the young Marx's revolutionizing way of life and of his commitment to it as the humanizing way. Independence of thought and action for him were not negative and selfish. He wished to be critical toward every claim for truth and value not merely to satisfy himself and to be freed from crippling restrictions. He wished also to liberate himself and all men into an affirmative dialectic with one another and with the world in which they would discover and develop their powers and construct their own history. Independence for him meant freedom from blind necessity and freedom in and through those necessities of our natures without which we would be little or nothing. Such necessities are the primary needs of our psychosomatic makeup—the needs for survival, for physical safety, for supportive relations with other persons, for explorative activity, for sensory and emotional and cognitive satisfaction, for autonomy and creativity. We do not wish to become free from these needs in the sense that we wish to be separated from them. Rather, we become free insofar as we and others recognize them and as we take steps to fulfill these needs.

The truly independent man thus faces toward both past and future. He possesses the courage to acknowledge and criticize all forms of thought, customs, and institutions which retard or injure the free development of men. He is also committed to discovering and providing the conditions necessary for that individual and social life which fulfills and thus frees man. Such freedom in its very nature cannot be confined by a specific and fixed form of thought or action. It is a revolutionizing way of life in which all that man feels and thinks and plans and aspires to must be tested, corrected, and improved in an ongoing action with other men and the world. It requires man's commitment to a creative process determining created values. Man's freedom finds its ultimate meaning in such a life and such a commitment.

Creation occurs at that point where envisaged novel possibilities for the future are merged with conditions and processes inherited from the past. Possibilities, however vividly envisaged, remain remote and abstract if they cannot be made relevant to such conditions and processes. On the other hand, mere repetition of the past without consideration of the future is equally uncreative. Romanticism, individualism, anarchism, and utopianism tend to ignore the compulsions that the past lays upon man. Conservatism clutches the contents and forms of the past and resists imagination, adventure, and novelty. Between such extremes we can locate the work of Marx and all creative and revolutionary figures in history who labored with a conscious and unconscious dependence on the past and an undaunted independence of it in order to solve new problems in new ways. Men's "social existence determines their consciousness,"[119] the older Marx said. He also said, "I am not a Marxist,"[120] and "I presuppose a reader who is willing . . . to think for himself."[121]

In the novelty of its genetic complex—i.e., its possibilities for thought and feeling and action—and in the novelty of the conditions of its existence, youth is given its opportunities for changing history. But how it will respond to them is conditioned by the kind of past it inherits and its relation to that past. Its past does not exercise a final compulsion over it; but it sets the limits within which present action takes place. In the present the individual person has the power to select, emphasize, organize, and direct the influences at work on him. His creative action is *in* events and not *above* them. Youth's inherited past, moreover, directly and unconsciously shapes the actions and values of youth for close to two decades. If youth inherits an authoritarian and violent past, it will tend to respond to that in an aggressive-submissive way. If it inherits a liberal and indulgent past, it will tend to respond in a similar way. Both somatically and psychically, youth reproduces the qualities of its preceding generation. And whether its outward attitude is one of conformity or rebellion, it tends to recapitulate the personal characteristics of its parents and peers and teachers. The danger in achieving the identity of young adulthood is either (1)

---

[119]Marx, Karl: *A Contribution to the Critique of Political Economy*, pp. 11-12.
[120]Engels to C. Schmidt, August 5, 1890. In Marx, Karl, and Engels, Frederick: *Selected Correspondence*, p. 496.
[121]Marx, Karl: *Capital*, vol. I, p. 8.

deficient assimilation of the heritage of the past or (2) assimilation of such kind that it overwhelms the freedom of the individual person and turns him into a conformist and organization man, or else that it produces a resentment and open rebellion which alienates him from the inheritance of the past in both society and himself. In the first case, creativity is inhibited; in the second, it is rendered irrelevant.

To be creative, youth must be independent in direct relation to the creative tendencies of its social tradition. It must assimilate its past, i.e., learn its history both in and through the older generations; but it must discover the best of that tradition, the most human and the most durable, and seek to extend it. In the United States this means, I think, the tradition of humanism (in both religious and secular forms), of democracy, of liberation movements of the oppressed (Blacks, laborers, women, minorities), of socialism, of diversity.

Today, more than one hundred and fifty years after his birth, we are still talking about the young Marx—not because of blind veneration, but because of our realization that the makers of the human future are the young people of every generation and because we can see in the young Marx a worthy model. That does not mean that he was perfect and cannot and should not be transcended. It simply means that he shows every generation that the link that holds the long chain of the human species together through history is the young person who, being entrusted with the heritage of his race, carries it forward with courage, fidelity, love, and commitment.

INDEX